Electronic Document Preparation and Management

for *CSEC*®

First Edition

Authors' acknowledgements

We, the authors, wish to express our appreciation to supporters and contributors who helped us brave the challenge of writing a textbook, Electronic Document Preparation and Management (EDPM) for the many diverse students. EDPM is a complex subject as it combines the technical knowledge and skills needed in today's highly computerised working environment as well as the standard rules, protocols and keyboarding skills required for formal document preparation.

We are grateful for the expert input of our computer science and information technologists, Christopher Adams and Shivani Ramlal as well as colleagues who shared expertise in teaching diverse students and their experience in marking for the Caribbean Examinations Council (CXC).

Next, our children and grandchildren deserve our gratitude for doing without our loving attention over the past several months as we laboured over this text to make it the best in the market.

Finally, we thank God for His grace and favour that kept us moving and jumping hurdles in a positive manner.

Although every effort has been made to ensure that website addresses are correct at the time of going to press, Hachette Learning cannot be held responsible for the content of any website mentioned in this book. It is sometimes possible to find a relocated web page by typing in the address of the home page for a website in the URL window of your browser.

Hachette UK's policy is to use papers that are natural, renewable and recyclable products, and made from wood grown in well-managed forests and other controlled sources. The logging and manufacturing processes are expected to conform to the environmental regulations of the country of origin.

To order, please visit www.HachetteLearning.com or contact Customer Service at education@hachette.co.uk/+44 (0)1235 827827.

ISBN: 978 1 0360 1513 8

© Gaynelle Holdip and Pat Holdip-Julien 2026

This edition published in 2026 by Hachette Learning (a trading division of Hodder & Stoughton Limited)

An Hachette UK Company

Carmelite House

50 Victoria Embankment

London EC4Y 0DZ

www.HachetteLearning.com

The authorised representative in the EEA is Hachette Ireland, 8 Castlecourt Centre, Dublin 15, D15 XTP3, Ireland (email: info@hbgi.ie)

Impression number   10 9 8 7 6 5 4 3 2 1

Year   2030 2029 2028 2027 2026

All rights reserved. Apart from any use permitted under UK copyright law, no part of this publication may be reproduced or transmitted in any form or by any means, electronic or mechanical, including photocopying and recording, or held within any information storage and retrieval system, without permission in writing from the publisher or under licence from the Copyright Licensing Agency Limited. Further details of such licences (for reprographic reproduction) may be obtained from the Copyright Licensing Agency Limited, www.cla.co.uk

Cover illustration © Atstock Productions/Shutterstock.com

Illustrations by Stéphan Theron and Vian Oelofsen

Typeset in Bliss light by IO Publishing

Printed in the UK by Bell & Bain Ltd, Glasgow

A catalogue record for this title is available from the British Library.

Contents

Introduction iv
About the authors iv
How to use this book iv

Section 1

CHAPTER 1 Introduction to the computer 2
CHAPTER 2 Input devices or peripherals 15
CHAPTER 3 Output devices or peripherals 25
CHAPTER 4 Computer storage, security and care 34

Section 2

CHAPTER 5 Basics of keyboard mastery 44
CHAPTER 6 Mastering the keys 55
CHAPTER 7 Mastering the upper and lower keys 66

Section 3

CHAPTER 8 Formatting and editing basics 82
CHAPTER 9 Advanced formatting, editing and proofreading 96
CHAPTER 10 Business documents 112
CHAPTER 11 Simple and advanced displays 143
CHAPTER 12 Specialised documents 164
CHAPTER 13 Basic spreadsheet techniques 186
CHAPTER 14 Advanced spreadsheet techniques 204
CHAPTER 15 Database applications 223
CHAPTER 16 Presentation and graphic applications 237

Section 4

CHAPTER 17 Electronic communication 252
CHAPTER 18 Document management 264

Section 5

CHAPTER 19 Work standards and ethics in the business environment 278
CHAPTER 20 School-based assessment 287

Glossary 294
Index 304
Acknowledgements 308

Introduction

This first edition of *Electronic Document Preparation and Management for CSEC*® comprehensively covers the newest CSEC® Electronic Document Preparation and Management (EDPM) Syllabus. As a first edition, it offers a fresh, up-to-date approach with core knowledge and skills expanded to include the use of digital technology in the Caribbean classroom for examination success and after this, in the world of work. Features include a full-colour design, in-chapter activities, helpful hints, did you know, key terms, practice, research and exam-style questions, School-based assessment (SBA) guidance and a glossary. An enhanced eBook version as well as online digital support are also available.

About the authors

Dr. Gaynelle Holdip is a former acting Director, and retired Curriculum Coordinator at the Ministry of Education, Trinidad and Tobago. She is also a published author. Her career achievements include contributing to and managing the development of curriculum for both the secondary and primary school systems with a special focus on supporting the diverse classroom environment including technical-vocational students. She has lectured at The University of the West Indies and worked in curriculum development for the Southern Caribbean and the National Training Agency. She has worked as a Chief Examiner with the Caribbean Examinations Council.

Pat Holdip-Julien is a former teacher of Electronic Document Preparation and Management (EDPM) and Office Administration for over fifteen years at the Five Rivers Secondary School, Trinidad and Tobago. She has extensive previous workplace experience as an Office Administrator and Executive Assistant/Secretary with several large companies.

How to use this book

This book is aligned to the CSEC® Electronic Document Preparation and Management (EDPM) Syllabus effective for examination from 2026. It is divided into five sections, each subdivided into chapters, which cover essential foundational knowledge and offer practical-based activities and skills support for mixed-ability classrooms.

The **objectives** found at the start of each chapter state the syllabus objectives that are covered within the chapter.

> **Objectives**
> By the end of this chapter, you will be able to:
> - describe computers
> - discuss the evolution of computers
> - describe the basic components of a computer
> - distinguish between operating systems and applications
> - describe computer processes and the computerised environment
> - compare different types of computers
> - discuss the advantages and disadvantages of computer use.

In-chapter **Activities** help students to check their understanding of key content and develop their skills in constructing answers to exam-style questions.

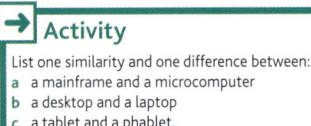

> **Activity**
> List one similarity and one difference between:
> a a mainframe and a microcomputer
> b a desktop and a laptop
> c a tablet and a phablet.

Key terms within each chapter help students to focus, learn and revise important words and phrases, expanding their vocabulary specific to this subject.

> **Key terms**
> **antivirus application** Software that monitors and filters incoming and outgoing data and prevents unwelcome data from entering and corrupting a computer system
> **Blu-ray Disc** A portable item that companies and individuals use to store large files such as videos and movies
> **byte** The smallest unit of measurement for assessing storage capacity; the amount of storage required for a single character of text
> **cache memory** Extremely high-speed volatile memory used for faster manipulation of data
> **cloud-based storage (CS)** The facility provided by an extremely large storage capacity of connected data centres

Helpful hints provide useful tips on key content and skills practice to help students build their competence.

> **Helpful hint**
> It's a good idea to set your line spacing before preparing your document. Students often prepare their documents in single line spacing and forget to change to double or 1.5, as instructed.

Did you know? are interesting or fun bits of knowledge for enjoyment.

> **Did you know?**
> Firewalls got their names from the use of structures such as brick walls and metal sheets that are used to keep actual fire from leaping from one place to another.

Practice, **research** and **exam-style questions** offer students multiple-choice and short-answer questions at the end of each chapter to support exam-focused practice and SBA research.

> **Practice, research and exam-style questions**
>
> **Multiple-choice questions**
>
> 1 Which of the options is the **least** active function of computers?
>   A Inputting
>   B Storing
>   C Outputting
>   D Processing
>
> 2 The capacity of a stored file is usually measured in …
>   A bits.
>   B bytes.
>   C gigabytes.
>   D pixels.
>
> 8 Which description is a major challenge of cloud storage?
>   A Dependence on stable internet connectivity
>   B Limited scalability
>   C High degree of agility
>   D Slow read/write speeds
>
> 9 Fossy Bank wants to scale up its storage capacity but still maintain strong data protection. Which actions will be most cost effective?
>   A Distributing storage to cloud-based systems
>   B Building more on-premises local storage
>   C Avoiding use of data-compression software
>   D Buying a large amount of external drive devices

Section 1

Chapter 1 Introduction to the computer
Chapter 2 Input peripherals
Chapter 3 Output peripherals
Chapter 4 Computer storage, security and care

Introduction to the computer

> **Objectives**
>
> By the end of this chapter, you will be able to:
>
> - describe computers
> - discuss the evolution of computers
> - describe the basic components of a computer
> - distinguish between operating systems and applications
> - describe computer processes and the computerised environment
> - compare different types of computers
> - discuss the advantages and disadvantages of computer use.

Introduction

A computer *computes*, or calculates, mathematical sums to solve problems. One of the first known computer *devices* was the **abacus**, which is a rectangular frame with beads strung on parallel rods. You may have used an abacus in your early school years.

Many years later, **analog computers** were invented. Analog computers use physical properties such as sound, light, weight, temperature and movement, called analog **data**, that we can measure on a continually changing scale. Mechanical, gas or hydraulic components are stimulated by these quantities and render output as a reading on a scale or a dial. Analog computers include those that measure distance (odometer), speed (speedometer), segments of time (wall clock), body temperature (thermometer), earthquake tremors (seismometer) and combinations of measurements (flight simulators). They continue to help solve personal, professional and scientific problems.

Between 1830 and 1850, Charles Babbage (who is thought to be the inventor of the first computer) wrote about the possibility of **digital computers**, and another man called George Boole invented the kind of logical mathematics that would make it work (now commonly known as Boolean logic).

However, the first working electronic computer was invented only in the 1940s, nearly 100 years later. Since then, new technology has been developed continually and more efficient ways to compute, display pictures and make sounds have been invented.

Computer engineers manipulate electronic circuits on boards using **codes** to trigger actions. This modern **type of computer** is called a *digital computer*. It produces **digital media** in the form of text, numbers, images, sounds/audio or a combination of these, such as videos. The items or documents created by these devices need to be prepared and managed properly by using standard rules or **protocols**.

Computers have evolved at a very fast rate, and scientists and engineers continue to develop new models and types. Today, we have many forms of *electronic devices* that we call *computers* or *computerised devices*, which we use in all aspects of our lives at home, school and work. Figures 1.1 and 1.2 show examples of computerised devices used to perform specialised tasks, such as measuring vehicle speed and distance travelled, and training pilots through simulation. This chapter will introduce you to a range of such computers.

Did you know?
Computers speak a special language consisting of only 1s and 0s.

1 Introduction to the computer

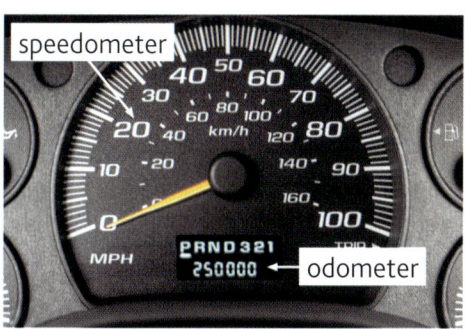

Figure 1.1 A speedometer and odometer

Figure 1.2 A flight simulator

> **Did you know?**
> In the 1960s, the people doing the complex calculations to send humans into space were called computers.

What is a computer?

Most modern computers are electronic, meaning that they are made up of **hardware** and **software** components. Together, hardware and software make up the system that performs the functions users need.

Components of the computer system

The components of a **computer system** consist of both physical, or *tangible*, parts called the *hardware* (Figure 1.3) and the instructions, or *commands*, that make the system operational, called the *software*.

Hardware

> 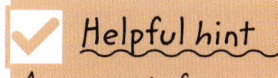 **Helpful hint**
> A mnemonic for components: Mother in the tower controls the power, processor, drive, and peripherals.

The main item of hardware is the **motherboard**, which is encased in a metal or plastic box called the *cabinet* or *tower*. The motherboard holds all the major components of a general-purpose computer, such as the **central processing unit (CPU)**, the power supply and a storage area for its memory called the **hard drive**. The motherboard allows connectivity between these components and between several input and output devices called **peripherals**, but the key component is the CPU. CPUs vary in size, from a tiny microprocessor to a huge standalone device called a **mainframe**. As it works, the temperature of the CPU increases and there is usually an internal fan to keep it cool.

Figure 1.3 The hardware components of a PC

Software

Computer software is a set of instructions, or *commands*, that tells the computer what to do, such as how to change raw data into useful information and how to store data or information. There are currently two major types of software: **operating systems (OS)** and **application software (apps)**. Apps are also called *programs*.

Operating systems are software that manages a computer system. An operating system like Microsoft Windows or macOS ensures that the computer can start (*boot up*) and close (*shut down*) safely. Users can use the keyboard, monitor, memory drive and all the other hardware devices because the OS is coordinating the running of application software. The OS usually comes pre-installed on computers (often as part of an OEM license). While it appears to be included, the cost is typically built into the price of the hardware. When this is damaged, the computer is said to have *crashed*.

Application software is a general term for four types of programs:

- The first type is a general set of high-level instructions for the computer, with **Office 365** (also known as **Microsoft Office 365**) being the most popular with users.
- The second type of program is part of the general app and is for tasks that most users need. In **Office 365**, there is a word-processing app (**Microsoft Word**) for creating documents. There is another app (**Microsoft Excel**) that can capture, rearrange and process data on pages called *spreadsheets*. If there is a lot of data to be processed, a database app (**Microsoft Access**) can help manage it. Also in **Office 365**, there is an app for presenting information in a series of brief points, images and graphics in the form of slides (**Microsoft PowerPoint**).
- The third type of application software is for special purposes or situations. It is used by industries (such as hotel management), businesses (for example accounting and management) and individuals (including *web browsers*, *graphics software*, educational software and *antivirus software*) to meet their particular needs.
- The fourth type of software provides document-collaboration tools for use over networks of computers. One popular example is Google Docs™ a web-based word-processing program, which is free and available to users with a Google account. These programs are for teams or groups who need to create, add to and edit documents saved in a shared space called a *drive*. Later in this chapter, the importance of the network, or *web*, for accessibility to these applications will become clear.

You will learn about word-processing, spreadsheet, database-management, presentation and graphic software in later chapters.

Processes of the computer system

The modern computer system does more than compute or calculate; it is created to communicate. The four actions undertaken by the communication system are inputting, processing, outputting and storage (Figure 1.5).

Inputting

The computer user decides what digital media to enter. The user also decides what input device to use for their desired outcome, for example the keyboard is generally used to input text, numbers and special characters, and the microphone is used for sounds and speech.

Slots on the side of the computer, called **ports**, are connected to the motherboard and act as points of connection (**interfaces**) between the computer and external peripheral devices. Computer ports are therefore also called *communication ports* (Figure 1.4).

1 Introduction to the computer

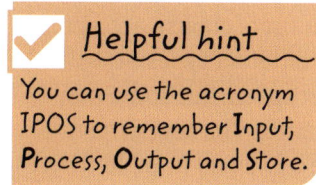

Helpful hint

You can use the acronym IPOS to remember Input, Process, Output and Store.

Processing

The computer receives data from peripherals and other computers, and manipulates it as the user gives instructions via the appropriate software. Computer processing includes:

- measuring data against a standard
- organising data into groups or categories
- combining different kinds of data into new formats, for example videos and recordings
- producing reports, articles and essays
- creating graphics and images, such as photographs and charts.

Figure 1.4 Wired ports for connecting the CPU with peripherals via the motherboard

Computer processing makes data understandable, manageable and useful. The user can share the information with others, and is able to solve problems and make decisions more easily.

Outputting

The computer communicates with the user by providing or transmitting the processed data as information to an output device. The user can see the information on a monitor; use a projector to send it to another screen; hear the information from a speaker; and/or read the information from a printed document.

Storage

Computers are able to save digital media for later use on internal (inside the computer) storage devices such as the hard drive, and external storage devices (detachable from the computer) such as *flash drives* and external hard drives. There are also storage devices that do not need to be in the computer, but collect the digital media remotely using the internet.

The processes of the computer will be discussed in greater detail in later chapters.

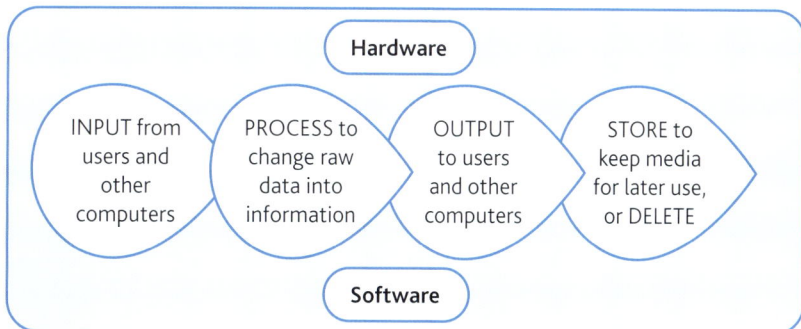

Figure 1.5 The computer's processes

The computerised environment

Today, computers are not operated in isolation. Instead, they operate in communication with other computers to access and share information as needed in a system called a network. The most popular global network is called the Internet and is a platform for the major source of information called the **World Wide Web (www)**.

SECTION 1

Types of computers

Computers come in various sizes and processing speeds, which users choose according to the specific purpose they require. Although there are many different types of computers, they all operate in a similar fashion and at a similar speed, but some may be lighter or slimmer than others and are called by different names. The seven main types of computers and the features that distinguish them are explained in Table 1.1. The pictures will also help you to tell one from the other.

Table 1.1 The seven main types of computers

Type of computer	Description	Image
Supercomputer	<ul><li>Extremely powerful</li><li>Can perform millions of calculations quickly</li><li>Often used for scientific and engineering functions</li></ul>	
Mainframe/ server computer	<ul><li>Large and powerful computer arranged in a system with a high volume of memory</li><li>Very useful where there are many users in one organisation or many organisations of different kinds that need to input lots of data that requires a great deal of processing and storage facilities</li></ul>	
Minicomputer	<ul><li>Also called a *mid-range* computer</li><li>Smaller in size than a mainframe but has similar features, such as a high capacity for storing data and information</li></ul>	
Microcomputer/ desktop computer	<ul><li>A standalone and compact computer that consists of a metal or plastic cabinet containing its own data-processing unit, a memory unit and a single printed circuit board</li><li>Usually, the tower is linked by cables to separate input and output units, such as the mouse, keyboard, monitor and printer/scanner</li></ul>	Desktop computer

> **Did you know?**
> Microcomputers are often called *personal computers (PCs)* or *desktop computers* because they are stationary and are hardly ever moved.

1 Introduction to the computer

Workstation	• Usually more powerful than an ordinary PC because of its greater speeds and memory • Found most often in offices and business places • Often connected to large-scale office equipment available for use by other employees, such as printers and copiers	
Notebook/ netbook/ laptop/tablet	• Versions of portable computers that are smaller and lighter than PCs, with a lower processing power • Input and output devices, such as the mouse, keyboard and monitor, are built into a single unit • In upgraded versions, the methods of inputting data are included as a software application, e.g. a built-in keyboard, while others have features such as touchscreens, cameras and microphones • Over time, they have become slimmer and lighter and can be taken anywhere for work or entertainment	 Tablet
Smartphone/ smartwatch/ phablet	• Highly computerised forms of personal possessions, such as a cellphone or a watch • Highly portable versions of the personal computer, which work with many of the same applications as PCs • Allow users to load data via a touchscreen and a special pen called a *stylus*; communicate via voice, images and text; source and stream information; and store and process data • Can be loaded with personalised applications such as those that monitor and manage heart rates, sleep patterns and daily routines using alarms, messages, reminders and timers • The phablet is a combination of a phone and a tablet; is larger than a smartphone but smaller than a tablet	Cellphone Smartwatch Phablet 

SECTION 1

In this section, you will learn about the advantages of computer use, and then how innovations in computer use have evolved.

> ✓ **Helpful hint**
> You can use the graphics in this section to help you to understand the text.

Advantages and disadvantages of computer use

Enduring advantages of computer use

Workers today work with computers or computerised machinery. The functionalities and capabilities of computer hardware and software are constantly improved by rival developers. However, there are certain benefits to using computers that have remained constant since they were first invented, while additional benefits have evolved over time (Figures 1.6 and 1.7). Enduring advantages of computer use include:

- **Storage and easy retrieval of data/information:**
Businesses and individuals have always needed a system for keeping records, whether these are customer information or the family's budget. Gradually, these records increase in size and become tedious to maintain. Computers take up small physical spaces but simplify the storage of millions of records in files, folders and directories, eliminating the need for paper and bulky file cabinets. They can even store multiple versions of documents on internal or external devices. In this way, changes can be tracked and even reversed.

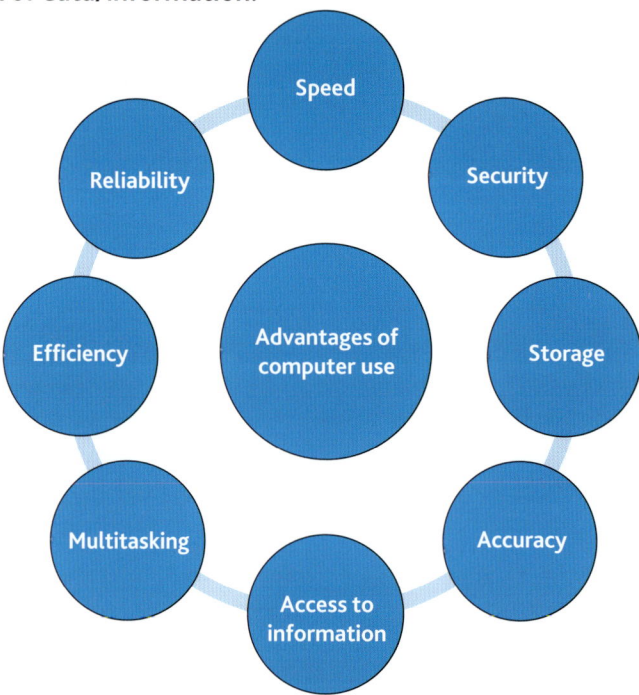

Figure 1.6 The ever-present advantages of using computers

- **Speed and efficiency:**
Computers have improved productivity by programming tasks so that they take a fraction of the time they would take humans to complete. Complex mathematical operations using scientific and engineering formulae can be performed in seconds. Accounting software expedites financial calculations. Documents such as letters and reports can be typed up using standard rules (formats and templates); checked for language, grammar and spelling; translated into another language; printed, signed, scanned and emailed; and stored for later use, all in a short time.

- **Accuracy and reliability:**
Computers are accurate when they perform calculations, but only if the data and instructions are correct. In other words, if garbage is input then garbage will be output! It is important to input data and information accurately. When computers are used properly, the information produced can be relied upon for problem-solving and decision-making.

- **Accessibility:**
  Using the internet, information is easily available in a short time. Many topics, especially current events, can be found easily via libraries, databases and platforms. Synchronisation across multiple devices means users can access digital media from anywhere that computer networking facilities are found. Students can access resources from places other than traditional sources such as textbooks. Online courses and e-learning platforms offer individual experiences, including simulations and step-by-step instructions for practical work.
- **Security:**
  Businesses need to lock away files that contain confidential information. However, physical files are still subject to theft and fire and water damage. Users can ensure that information is secure from threats using cybersecurity measures. Employees are required to comply with company rules, such as using strong passwords; using office computers for business tasks only; limiting access to office workstations; and using and securing backup storage as needed. These measures can:
  - protect information such as customer information and property
  - protect against infection of malware *viruses* from unauthorised users
  - remove or deny unwanted programs or respond quickly to cyberthreats
  - prevent fraud; identity theft; and theft of intellectual property, trade secrets and manufacturing processes.

Evolving advantages of computer use

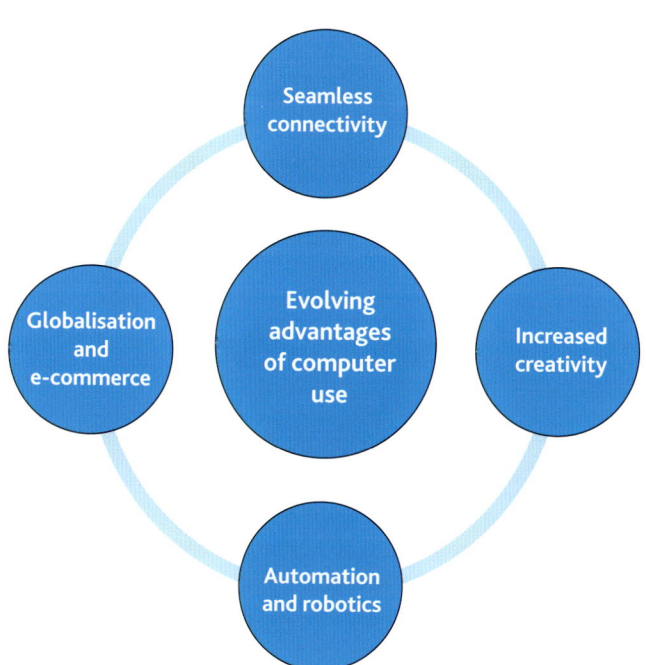

Figure 1.7 The continually improving advantages of using computers

- **Seamless connectivity:**
  Computers facilitate seamless communication through emails, videoconferences and social media platforms, connecting people globally in real time. People can collaborate efficiently and effectively, as geography, culture and even language are no longer barriers.
- **Improved creativity:**
  Graphic design, self-publishing, video-editing and music-production software have been developed to provide tools for creative expression. The products can be displayed, and shared with private and public groups.
- **Automation and robotics:**
  Although automated production lines have been used for a long time, innovative computerisation has introduced robots. Robotics has significantly increased precision and efficiency in manufacturing processes and service industries. The costs of production have been lowered; this includes the reduction of errors, which also helps lower costs.
- **Globalisation and e-commerce:**
  Computers are necessary for e-commerce and the globalisation of trade. They enable businesses to procure (obtain) resources and reach customers anywhere in the world. Consumers have enormous choices, from the retail trades of food, shelter and clothing to services such as banking, investment, insurance, entertainment and recreation, including gaming, streaming and virtual-reality experiences while connecting with other players globally.

SECTION 1

Disadvantages of computer use

Although there are many advantages to using computers, there are also many disadvantages (Figure 1.8). These disadvantages can be classified into four categories: business-related issues, health risks, environmental impacts and social impacts.

- **Business-related issues:**
These issues include job displacement, initial costs, privacy concerns and cybercrimes. Automation and robotics have eliminated the need for humans to carry out certain dangerous and repetitive jobs, but they have also increased unemployment and underemployment. The costs of setting up suitable systems and procuring software need consideration. Software quickly becomes outdated, requiring frequent upgrades and replacements, leading to additional expense.

  Cybersecurity threats are another disadvantage as computers are vulnerable to malware, viruses and cyberattacks, with the possible theft of information such as trade secrets, personnel records and databases via hacking. These data breaches can lead to financial and reputational losses.

- **Health risks:**
One of the reasons for developing and adopting computers for use in businesses was to increase worker productivity. Computers were also seen as a means of communication, and sources of engagement and entertainment. However, computers have brought on physical and mental-health risks. Prolonged and/or improper use of computers leads to injuries such as repetitive strain injuries, including wrist and eye strain; back and neck pain; sedentary living; poor eating habits; and lifestyle-related medical conditions. Gaming and streaming platforms and onscreen entertainment cause employees to procrastinate (delay doing tasks) and neglect personal and work relationships, and their responsibilities.

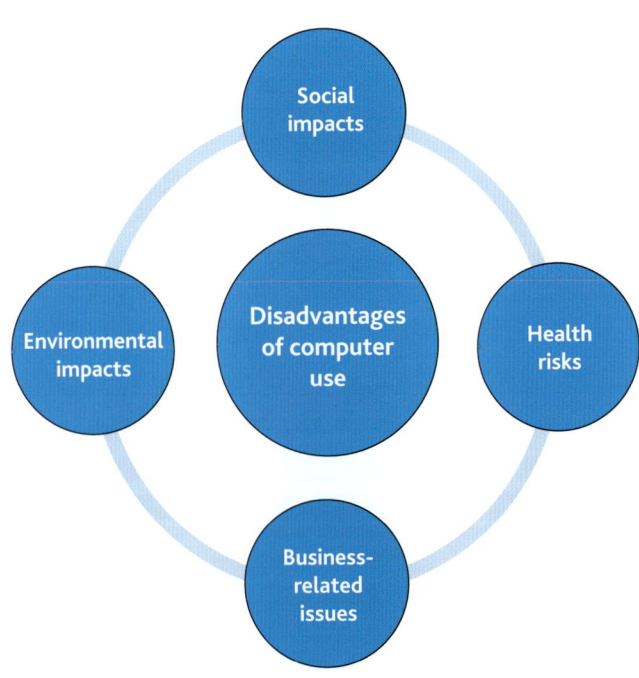

Figure 1.8 Disadvantages of computer use

- **Environmental impacts:**
The improper disposal of computers, computerised appliances and equipment and mobile phones releases up to 1 000 different chemical substances into the environment. These hazardous chemicals leach into soil and water, posing risks to ecosystems and human health.

  Operating computers and supporting computer networks use a huge amount of electrical energy, which comes from non-renewable sources. The enormous resources used in the production of electricity contribute to pollution, loss of different animal species, global warming and climate change.

Social impacts:

Individuals can be negatively affected by the prevalence of computers in their lives. There is a high dependence on computers for accessing information, goods and services. The disadvantage arises when people receive misinformation or are encouraged to overspend, fall into credit card debt or buy unnecessary items. Many adults and even children suffer from distraction or addiction-like symptoms as they spend time interacting with games and social media, yet are socially isolated. The misuse of social media platforms has also led to painful and even deadly experiences such as cyberbullying and exploitation.

Activity
Describe two or three instances where negative aspects of computer use could impact individuals.

Career corner
A specialist in document preparation and management used to be called a *secretary*. Today, the basic qualification for this career is an Associate Degree or another vocational qualification in secretarial skills.

Activity
List one similarity and one difference between:
a   a mainframe and a microcomputer
b   a desktop and a laptop
c   a tablet and a phablet.

Key terms

abacus A very early device for computing, i.e. processing numbers

analog computer Computer that uses physical properties to carry out computer operations

application software (app) A set of instructions for the computer that uses specially-written code to execute input, processing, storage and data exchange tasks

central processing unit (CPU) The main compilation of electronic circuitry that understands coded instruction for processing digital data

code The language used by programmers to 'speak' to computers – to tell them what to do and in what order – in the form of different combinations of the digits 0 and 1

computer system A set of physical and non-physical components that work together to carry out computational, data-processing and communication tasks automatically and efficiently

data Material that can be converted to a digital form and processed by a computer; *information* is processed data, but is treated as raw data when it is to be subjected to further processing

desktop computer A standalone and compact computer

digital computer A computer with electronic circuits on boards that use codes to trigger actions

digital media Data that has been processed, which takes the form of text, numbers, images, sounds/audio or a combination of these, such as videos; also called *output* and *information*

SECTION 1

electronic circuit A network of different physical parts through which electricity flows in ways that enable processing and conversion of signals

hard drive A storage area for a computer's memory

hardware The physical and tangible parts of a computer

interface Boundaries or points on devices that allow the exchange of information for computer operations to occur between the computer and users as well as between computer parts

laptop Portable computer that is smaller and lighter than a PC and has lower processing power

mainframe A huge standalone computer with the capability to process a huge amount of data in a short time

microcomputer A stationary computer that is hardly ever moved; often called a personal computer (PC) or desktop computer

minicomputer Smaller in size than a mainframe but with similar features, such as a high capacity for storing data and information

motherboard The main board or compilation of electronic circuitry into which other units or boards such as the CPU, power supply, fan and peripherals are connected and controlled

net/network A series of computers, connected with or without physical wires, designed to communicate, or *inter-operate*, with one **extranet** – the most widely used is the **internet**

netbook/notebook Portable computer that is smaller and lighter than a PC and with lower processing power

operating system (OS) Major application or program that acts as a platform for other applications to work efficiently and smoothly for users

output peripheral Hardware for displaying data, which includes display screens or monitors, printers, speakers and projectors

peripherals Devices created to utilise the capabilities of the computer by employing its input, output, processing, and storage mechanisms

phablet A combination of a phone and a tablet; larger than a smartphone but smaller than a tablet

port Slot on the side of a computer that acts as a point of connection for peripherals to the motherboard

protocol The standard rules that govern how data is formatted, transmitted and received by other computers

server computer A large and powerful computer arranged in a system with a high volume of memory

smartphone A highly computerised cellphone

smartwatch A highly computerised watch

software The instructions or commands that make a computer's system operational

supercomputer An extremely powerful computer that can perform millions of calculations quickly; often used for scientific and engineering functions

tablet A portable, lightweight computer with a touchscreen and built-in keyboard, camera and microphone

types of computers Two main types of computers are analog computers and digital computers

workstation A computer more powerful than an ordinary PC because of its greater speeds and memory

World Wide Web (www) Huge amounts of information located on independent computers across the world, which is freely available via links and keywords

🏠 Summary

In this chapter, you have learned about:

- the evolution of the computer over time
- components of a computer
- processes of computer use and their environment
- types of computers we use today
- advantages and disadvantages of using computers.

Practice, research and exam-style questions

Multiple-choice questions

1. Which term is the general name for a computer?
   - A Electronic device
   - B Display device
   - C Robotic device
   - D Bionic device

2. Which of these does *not* use a central processing unit?
   - A Workstation
   - B Notebook
   - C Workbook
   - D Laptop

3. Which of these devices is a combination of *two* types of computer devices?
   - A Phablet
   - B Tablet
   - C Smartphone
   - D Smartwatch

4. Complete this sentence with the correct phrase: While operating, analog computers use
   - A arithmetical operations.
   - B physical stimuli.
   - C automated electricity.
   - D error-free data.

5. All these terms are examples of computer hardware *except* the:
   - A monitor
   - B microchip
   - C program
   - D transistor

6. *Software* is another name for:
   - A instructions to the computer
   - B specific purposes of the user
   - C well-padded computer chairs
   - D awareness of possible computer uses

7. The internet is the name for worldwide access to other:
   - A computers
   - B databases
   - C organisations
   - D media

8. Which of these actions allows computer users to be more efficient?
   - A Searches for information
   - B Automation of tasks
   - C Fixes for software glitches
   - D Replication of program output

9. Which of these actions is the most *likely* source of computer errors?
   - A Inputting
   - B Storing
   - C Outputting
   - D Processing

10. One disadvantage of the digitalisation of business operations is:
    - A increased computer use by employees.
    - B reduction in the number of employees.
    - C computerisation of manual operations.
    - D increased incidents of misplaced records.

SECTION 1

Short-answer questions

1. Items **a–j** are descriptions of devices used in a computerised environment. Items **i–x** are the names of some devices. Match the description with the appropriate device.

	Descriptions: This device …		Names
a	… is for internal data storage.	i	Computer
b	… needs a constant supply of power.	ii	Phablet
c	… works with touchscreen technology to replace fingers.	iii	Digital pen
d	… allows the user to enter data in text form.	iv	Hard drive
e	… can convert a document to a digital format.	v	Supercomputer
f	… can write directly on a computer screen.	vi	Stylus
g	… allows the user to enter data using speech.	vii	Keyboard
h	… can display text or pictures on a screen.	viii	Scanner
i	… is a combined computer and telephone.	ix	Microphone
j	… performs millions of calculations in seconds.	x	Projector

2. The slide rule is a type of analog computer. Research what it does and how it works.

3. Draw your own diagram that combines information on the components of a computer system with notes about the basic activity each component carries out.

4. Describe three advantages a business gains from using computers.

5. Copy and complete this table, using examples *not* named in this chapter.

	Example
Word-processing	
Spreadsheet	
Database management	
Presentation	
Industry-wide use	
Business-level use	
Web-browser software	
Graphics software	
Educational software	
Antivirus software	

2 Input devices or peripherals

> 🏠 **Objectives**
>
> By the end of this chapter, you will be able to:
>
> - define the term *input device*
> - list and describe seven kinds of input peripherals
> - explain what input peripherals look like and how they work.

Introduction

In Chapter 1, you learned about the inputting process. This is the stage when the computer user decides what output is to be produced and what **input device** they will use to communicate with the computer to achieve the goal. This device is the **user interface (UI)**.

This chapter describes the devices used in this first stage of communication between the computer and the user. These are called *input devices*. Input devices are pieces of computer hardware that allow users to enter the data that software applications will manipulate to produce the desired output. The data may be raw data that must be *input*, or entered, by the user, or it may be processed data that was stored in the user's computer or another computer.

In Chapter 1, you learned that software applications are commands that enable digital content, such as text, images and audio, to be readable and processable by the computer.

Some input devices are embedded in the computer case and connected by internal wires. Input devices, located outside the case, are called **input peripherals**, and they can be connected to the computer through an external cable or wire placed in the appropriate port.

Some input devices have been *adapted* to meet the special needs of certain users, such as disabled people and gamers. Names of input devices and descriptions of what they look like and how they work are set out in the remainder of this chapter.

Input devices

The main kinds of input devices are:

- keyboards
- mice/mouses
- variations of the keyboard and mouse
- microphones
- optical input devices
- magnet-based input readers
- **adapted input devices**.

SECTION 1

> **Did you know?**
> QWERTY keyboards are arranged to space out the letters most often used in English. They help to prevent our fingers from crossing one another when typing.

Input devices: what they look like and how they work

Keyboards

The **keyboard** is the most familiar input device, with a history that is older than the oldest computer. It is still made up of knobs, called *keys*, for letters, numbers and special shapes called **characters** (Figure 2.1). The **QWERTY keyboard** is widely used for those writing in English. It was invented in 1870, and is named after the first six letters that appear on the left-hand side of the keyboard.

The keyboard is usually connected to the CPU by internal or external cables. However, computers with modern technology, such as mobile computers including smartphones or tablets, may link with keyboards wirelessly or may have software that shows the keyboard as characters on the screen. An onscreen keyboard is called a **virtual keyboard**.

While the keyboard layout of most computers follows the QWERTY system for producing documents, they also include special keys that have various functions. For example, there are keys to manipulate the audio volume, keys to adjust the brightness of the monitor and numeric keys for calculating sums quickly.

> *Special function keys and shortcut keys on the computer keyboard and their uses will be explored in detail in Chapters 5 to 7.*

Figure 2.1 A computer version of a QWERTY keyboard, including its special function keys, placed around the letters and numbers

> **Did you know?**
> The first computer mouse looked a bit like a toy. It was invented in 1964 and was made of a wooden body on two wheels.

Mice/mouses

The **mouse** deciphers the movements that the user performs (clicking or rolling) into specific instructions for the computer (Figure 2.2). It is considered an input pointing device because it is used to move a companion image called a **cursor** (or *runner*) horizontally or vertically across the monitor or screen. The cursor points to various areas so that the user can apply actions to applications, icons, folders or files, such as selecting, dragging and dropping, opening, adding text or images and closing. Some mice, such as joysticks (Figure 2.3) and trackballs, are adaptations of the basic pointing input device for people who play computer games (Figure 2.4). Other devices are adapted for people with disabilities.

Figure 2.2 A clicking mouse

Figure 2.3 A joystick

Figure 2.4 A gaming mouse

2 Input devices or peripherals

> → **Activity**
>
> A mouse must point directly at an item on a computer screen for it to be selected: true or false?

Variations of the keyboard and mouse

As more and more people use computers, the **usability** features of devices and applications become important. Currently, users of computerised devices such as laptops and smartphones expect enhanced efficiency and ease of use, especially for those with few computer skills.

- Usability was first developed to test the operation of computers using windows, icons, text fields, canvases, menus and pointers. However, users were mostly still tied to external input resources such as keyboards and mice.
- Wireless and Bluetooth®-enabled mice are conveniently portable and offer freedom from any cord tethering the mouse to the computer. However, they do rely on signals to communicate with the computer and, where the signal is weak or interrupted, the mouse will be disconnected from the computer. Wireless mice require batteries, which must be charged or replaced regularly to avoid interruptions in use.
- The development of graphical user interface (GUI) software (touchscreen technology) has introduced input devices such as the touchpad, touchscreen, light pen and digital pen.
    - The *touchpad*, which is found mainly on laptops, allows the user to control the movement of the cursor on the screen by using their fingers to glide, swipe or even click across its surface (Figure 2.5).
    - The *touchscreen* allows users to perform commands similar to those used on touchpads, with their fingers or stylus pens interacting directly with the screen. On small devices such as tablets, phablets, smartphones and smartwatches, the GUI allows for zooming in and out and rotating images on screens with fingers.
    - A *stylus* is shaped like a pen and is built to interface directly with a touchscreen (Figure 2.6). Some styluses are passive, containing no internal electrical components and hence do not require charging. Active styluses work with batteries and can relay more information to a touchscreen device, including through writing by hand on its surface.
    - A *light pen* works by throwing light onto a screen that bounces the light back to its tip. It is often used for selecting a place on a screen with great precision, especially when making presentations at meetings and conferences.
    - A *digital pen* inputs data into a graphic tablet, and is used by artists and designers for drawing and sketching purposes.

Figure 2.5 Using fingers on a trackpad to control the cursor

Figure 2.6 Using a stylus to input data

> **→ Activity**
>
> An electronic or digital pen is a tool for creating e-signatures: true or false?

Microphones

A **microphone** captures sound waves, which are in analog format. Specialised software converts the sound waves into electrical signals, which can be entered in digital formats into computers. The verbal messages, music or other sounds – that is, data in audio form – can be encoded, reproduced, edited, combined, transmitted or recorded for later use.

Some microphones collect data from one or two directions only: unidirectional and bidirectional. These are best for voice-messaging or recording interviews. Omnidirectional microphones can cover a wide area of sound waves and are best for meetings and conferences but may also collect background noise. Figure 2.7 shows unidirectional and omnidirectional microphones.

Unidirectional microphone   Omnidirectional microphone

Figure 2.7 Unidirectional and omnidirectional microphones

> **→ Activity**
>
> Name one difference between unidirectional and omnidirectional microphones.

Optical input devices

Common devices

Common **optical input devices** include digital cameras, webcams and scanners.

- A *digital camera* is an input device that captures images using a system of lenses and photosensitive components (Figure 2.8). It uses a sensor to convert light into electronic signals, which are then processed into a digital image. The image is stored on a memory card, where it can be viewed, edited and shared. This device runs on batteries, and usually has a slot for a memory card for saving pictures and videos. Smartphones also have a camera, and photographs can be saved and shared via the internet to other applications, such as WhatsApp and email accounts.

2 Input devices or peripherals

- A *webcam* is a digital camera built into a laptop or attached to a PC (Figure 2.8). It transmits data in real time over the internet, and is commonly used for videoconferencing, live-streaming, online meetings and recording videos.
- A *scanner* is an input device that uses optical character recognition (OCR) software to recognise and take a picture of characters, words, sentences, lines, images and other shapes (Figure 2.8). The OCR converts the information from the original document into a digital format called *scans* and *screenshots*. When saved in the computer's memory, they can be displayed and edited using special software.

Webcam

Other **character recognition methods** include optics, magnets, acoustics, graphics and vibrations

Digital camera

Scanner

Figure 2.8 A digital camera, webcam and scanner

Specialised devices

Optical mark recognition software is used in several input devices that have been developed for users' particular needs. They include optical mark recognition readers and barcode readers.

- An **optical mark recognition (OMR)** reader is a special scanner that processes forms that are collected in large amounts (Figure 2.9). These forms include test answer sheets, surveys, reply forms, attendance sheets, checklists and other plain-paper forms printed by a laser printer. Data in the form of darkened circles, ticks in rectangles or filled-in boxes are scanned very quickly, and the information is input into the computer for processing.

Figure 2.9 An OMR reader and the kinds of data it reads

SECTION 1

- A **barcode reader**, also called a *price scanner* or *point-of-sale (PoS) scanner*, reads barcodes, which appear as lines of various thicknesses and contain basic details about products (Figure 2.10). The reader inputs the details about the product being sold into an inventory database. A business can keep track of increases or decreases in the stock of the product. A *QR code* can be in black and white or colour and is a more sophisticated version of a barcode, containing more information (Figure 2.11).

Figure 2.10 A barcode and barcode reader

Figure 2.11 A QR code

> **Did you know?**
> Currency validators use both optical and magnetic readers to detect security features embedded in bank notes.

Magnet-based input devices

Most people have at least one small plastic card in their possession that has a magnetic strip on one side. These strips allow access to personal and financial information. The **magnetic input devices** that take information from magnetic strips include magnetic strip readers and magnetic ink character readers.

- A **magnetic strip reader (MSR)** decodes information contained under the piece of dark tape found on the back of the plastic rectangles used for credit, debit and store loyalty cards. These cards are read by tapping, swiping or inserting them into the reader, which then detects the magnetic field generated by the strip.
- A **magnetic ink character recognition (MICR) reader** collects data from documents such as cheques, which were printed using magnetic ink and special characters (Figure 2.12). The MICR, equipped with magnetic sensors, can interpret encoded information and enable automated data extraction and processing. This process verifies the legitimacy of cheques and makes them easier to cash. Although today few banks encourage the use of personal cheques, they continue to issue manager's cheques to make large payments.

Figure 2.12 Cards issued by banks and stores encourage cashless sales

> **Activity**
> Name three ways that a magnetic strip reader collects information from a credit or debit card.

Adapted input devices

Some of the input devices already covered have been redesigned to meet the needs of physically disabled users. Many blind and partially sighted people can learn to type using a keyboard with raised shapes on the keys that users can feel (Figure 2.13). Blind people who know how to read and write Braille can also use a Braille note taker or embosser to input characters on special paper.

Input devices adapted for people who are deaf or hard of hearing respond to facial expressions and sign language, and also lip-read.

People who are paralysed or have reduced mobility can use **eye-tracking cameras** that perform actions or move a mouse pointer. The same tracking and controlling of mouse actions can be performed by *gesture-recognition devices*, which respond to pedals that users move with their feet, hands and other body parts. Other pointing devices mounted on hats or bands, joystick mice and **virtual-reality controllers (VRCs)** can be operated using turns of the head, arm, chin, foot, lip or even tongue. Voice recognition software can be used to operate **speech-to-text generators** that type or turn sounds into text for entry into a computer system.

> **Did you know?**
> Braille is a special code that uses a combination of six-dot cells that identify letters, numbers, punctuation and even entire words of a language. Different languages may have their own unique Braille code. People use their fingers to read Braille.

Figure 2.13 A partially sighted person using a Braille keyboard

> **Activity**
> Name two groups of people who are helped by adapted input devices.

SECTION 1

Key terms

adapted input devices Devices redesigned to meet the needs of users with disabilities or specialised interests such as gaming, for example, joysticks, trackballs, eye-tracking cameras, gesture-recognition devices and speech-to-text generators

barcode reader A device that reads barcodes, which are lines of various thicknesses that contain basic details about products

characters Shapes (letters/numbers), marks (punctuation), pieces of code, sounds or symbols (icons) that devices and software convert into computer-readable language

cursor/runner A shape that moves horizontally or vertically across a monitor or screen in response to a user's manipulation

eye-tracking camera A camera that performs actions or moves a mouse pointer by following a user's eye movements

gesture-recognition device A device that can track and control mouse actions by responding to pedals moved by users' feet, hands and other body parts

input device/peripheral An internal or external device, connected to a computer via a cable or wire through the appropriate port or wirelessly using Wi-Fi® or Bluetooth®, that deciphers users' movements into instructions for the computer

keyboard The holder of an arrangement of letters, numbers and special characters on physical or virtual buttons called *keys*

magnetic ink character recognition (MICR) reader A device that reads characters printed in magnetic ink, commonly used by banks to process cheques quickly and accurately

magnetic input device A magnetic ink character reader or magnetic strip reader, which use sensors to detect magnetic fields or magnetic inks

magnetic strip reader A device that uses sensors to detect and decode information

microphone An input device that collects sound waves or vibrations from speech, music or other sources for conversion to electrical and then digital formats by specialised software

mouse An input device that is clicked or rolled to move a companion image called a *cursor* to access any feature available on a computer ribbon or active page

optical input device Use a combination of photosensitive cells to convert real objects and documents into images and pictures that are machine-readable

optical mark recognition (OMR) reader A special scanner that processes large numbers of forms

speech-to-text generator An input device that types or turns sounds into text for entry into a computer system

touchscreen technology Technology used to input data based on the ability of physical forces to respond to the electric currents produced by the body, especially at the fingertips

usability A method of rating computer peripherals and features in terms of their efficiency and ease of use

user interface (UI) The point at which information is exchanged between users and computers; between computer components; or between computers and peripherals

virtual keyboard Software that shows a keyboard as characters on a screen

virtual-reality controller An input device operated by turns of the head, arm, chin, foot, lip or even tongue

 ### Summary

In this chapter, you have learned:

- a definition of the term *input device*
- about seven kinds of input devices
- how these input devices and peripherals work.

Practice, research and exam-style questions

Multiple-choice questions

1. Which input device is commonly used for typing documents?
   A Scanner
   B Keyboard
   C Microphone
   D Digitiser

2. A virtual keyboard displayed on a touchscreen …
   A is permanent and unchangeable.
   B can be changed to the user's choice of layout.
   C requires a physical connection.
   D appears only on desktop computers.

3. In what direction can a mouse make a cursor travel?
   A 360-degree circular movement
   B To any point on the window
   C Straight up and down
   D Only straight across the page

4. On a touchscreen device, which type of input is detected?
   A Pressure
   B Heat
   C Sound
   D Light

5. Sound waves captured by a microphone are *never*…
   A stored as raw data.
   B converted into digital form.
   C filtered by noise-reduction software.
   D amplified and output.

6. Digital cameras capture …
   A scanned documents.
   B barcode labels.
   C images.
   D audio files.

7. A scanner is primarily used for what purpose?
   A Printing documents
   B Displaying images
   C Converting items to digital format
   D Listening to audio

8. One important element of the credit card system is the …
   A optical-card recogniser.
   B magnetic-strip reader.
   C tracking ball and socket.
   D eye-movement tracker.

9. Which device would be most suitable for a person who is deaf or hard of hearing?
   A A speech-to-text generator
   B A microphone
   C A voice-to-text generator
   D A virtual-reality controller

10. A partially sighted person can use a facial-recognition system for security because it uses a …
    A barcode scanner and monitor.
    B camera and specialised software.
    C microphone and stylus.
    D trackball and joystick.

Short-answer questions

1. Research *three* things that Wi-Fi® and Bluetooth® have in common.

2. Which of the three Caribbean Examinations Council (CXC)® examination papers, do you think, is marked using OMRR technology: Paper 1, 2 or 3?

3. List two disadvantages of using a wireless mouse.

SECTION 1

4 Complete the crossword.

Clues across

2 Pen for interfacing directly with a computer
4 Laptop or PC camera commonly used for videoconferencing
7 For collecting sounds for computer processing
8 Device that allows direct interfacing with a computer using fingers
9 The first six letters on the left-hand side of a standard keyboard
10 General term for computer drawing or sketching or a picture

Clues down

1 The most commonly used cursor controller
3 Converts a document in hard copy to a soft copy
5 The general term for features on a keyboard
6 Lines on a sticker that contain basic details about a product

3 Output devices or peripherals

> ### 🏠 Objectives
> By the end of this chapter, you will be able to:
> - define the term *output device*
> - list and describe seven kinds of output devices and peripherals
> - explain what output devices and peripherals look like and how they work.

Introduction

In Chapter 1, you learned that the outputting stage is the computer communicating with the user by providing or transmitting information to an **output device/peripheral**. An *output device* is a piece of hardware that serves primarily to communicate the results of software processing to the user.

In this chapter, you will name these devices and examine what they look like and how they work. Some output devices may be *adapted* to meet the needs of different users and look different, although they perform similar functions. In addition, certain output devices act to receive and process data and are also able to display their messages to the user. This capacity makes them **input** *and* **output (I/O) devices**. Whether it is an output peripheral or an I/O device, messages are presented in the form of text, sounds, images, charts, graphics, special shapes or combinations of these forms. The user decides on the form of the display and chooses the appropriate set of devices for the purpose.

Output devices

The main kinds of output and I/O devices are:

- monitors
- printers
- sound cards
- speakers and headphones
- video cards
- projectors
- specialised output devices
- locators.

Output devices: what they look like and how they work

Monitors

A **monitor** is also called a *video display unit (VDU)*, a *video display terminal (VDT)*, a *visual interface* or a *screen*. It produces a visual display of text, images, video and graphics generated by the CPU and a graphics card. With it, a user can add and subtract content, correct errors in documents, play games and browse the web.

SECTION 1

Monitors range in size, but many people use monitors that are about 60–70 centimetres (24–27 inches). Gaming monitors may be much bigger. Monitors are made up of two sheets of a flexible clear material. Between the two sheets of material is a layer of liquid crystal **diodes** (LCD) or an arrangement of light emitting diodes (LED).

The LCD-type screen uses a small fluorescent light at the back (a backlight) that glows when an electric voltage is applied, while the diodes of an LED-type screen glow on their own. Most monitors are LCDs. They use less energy than LEDs but produce less colourful pictures.

The monitor is usually connected to a microphone, a camera and speakers. One powerful connection that enables the transmission of high-quality audio and video streams between the computer and the monitor is called a *High-Definition Multimedia Interface (HDMI®)*. Monitors that incorporate touch-sensitive glass (touchscreen technology) can be described as an I/O device (Figure 3.1).

Figure 3.1 Using a touchscreen monitor

> ### ➡ Activity
> Name two differences between an LCD monitor and an LED monitor.

Printers

A **printer** is a device that places text, images, graphics, special characters or combinations of these on paper or other materials of different compositions and sizes. Most print jobs are done on paper, but printing on vinyl and fabric are part of commercial printing businesses (Figures 3.2 and 3.3).

Figure 3.2 Use of vinyl printing

Figure 3.3 Use of fabric printing

3 Output devices or peripherals

There are several types of printers, which use different methods, including stamping, spraying, pressing, heating and cutting. Computer-aided printing is also used by engineers, architects, advertisers, manufacturers and designers who need large-format and wide-format, full-sized technical drawings, billboards and blueprints.

Printers and their different methods are illustrated in Table 3.1.

Table 3.1 Printers and methods

Method and printer example	How it works	Image
Stamping: **impact printer**	Printheads (metal pins engraved with letters and special characters) strike an inked ribbon. The ribbon transfers the engraved words onto paper. Several copies of a document can be made by placing carbon paper between sheets of paper. It is still used when very formal, individual documents such as university degree certificates are to be printed on special parchment paper.	
Spraying: **inkjet printer**	Droplets of black, red, blue, yellow and cyan ink are sprayed from cartridges onto materials at great speed, while the material to be printed moves through a series of rollers.	
Pressing: **laser printer**	An electrical charge is used to press coloured inky material, called *toner particles*, onto paper. Pressure and heat are then applied to fuse the ink onto the paper permanently.	
Heating: **direct-thermal printer**	Pressure and heat are applied to printheads that strike special heat-sensitive paper. Many black dots form the letters or the images. Alternatively, the **thermal-transfer printer** melts wax or resin of a single colour onto the thermal paper.	

SECTION 1

Computer-aided **plotter printer**	A computer program is instructed to draw continuous lines to produce large-format text, many different coloured images or graphics on large sheets of paper, vinyl, cardboard, fabric, plastic, plywood or aluminium. Some plotters use special cutting or stamping tools to repeat the same pattern on fabric, plastic or vinyl, ensuring there is no change in size, shape or colour.	

Inkjet printers are smaller and quieter. They are most useful for printing limited amounts of short documents, such as newsletters and manuals for homes and small offices. Larger and more expensive *laser printers* are best for bigger offices, where a number of users carry out printing jobs of different kinds and sizes. *Thermal printers* are quiet and efficient, producing items that require fine detail, such as barcodes, shipping labels, prepaid phone receipts and bank card receipts. *Plotter printers* tend to be used by technical and professional people who need large-format or highly detailed prints.

 **Activity**

Which type or types of printer would most likely be found in homes and small offices?

Sound cards, speakers and headphones

A **sound card**, also called an **audio card**, *audio adaptor* or *sound adaptor* is an I/O device. It receives signals from a computer, converts recorded or generated digital data into a vibrational pattern and then transmits the pattern to other output devices such as **speakers** or **headphones**. Both speakers and headphones come in different shapes and sizes, including tiny ear pods that are almost invisible but still produce excellent sound quality.

Both speakers and earphones produce audio messages that can be heard by the listener as they converse with others over the internet; listen to the radio, music or an audiobook; watch television; or play games. Both speakers and headphones typically connect to a single device through either a wired or wireless connection.

Figure 3.4 A speaker presenting to a general audience while some people wear headphones to hear the simultaneous translation

However, whereas speakers cast sounds broadly (broadcasting) according to the volume, headphones allow one user to listen to audio directly in their ears. Headphones can cancel out noises and are helpful for simultaneous translation (Figure 3.4), taking notes for a report or listening to a personal playlist.

Video cards

A **video card**, also called a **graphics card** or **video adaptor**, is an I/O device that contains a graphics processing unit (GPU). Most computers have a video card installed, but some may have more processing power than others. The GPU works with the CPU to send graphical information to a video display device such as a monitor, a television or a projector. The communication between the GPU and the CPU takes place through internal (integrated or embedded GPU) wires or external (discrete GPU) cables connected to one or more ports on the side of the video card. Additional video cards can be connected for use in advanced tasks such as video-editing and gaming.

Projectors

A **projector** is a device that shines a beam of light through different lenses, shaped as prisms, to project an image or video onto a surface. The output is generated by a computer's video card or from data saved on an external drive. The projector can be connected to the computer either with a cable or wirelessly. The surface can be a wall or a large screen, sheet of paper or piece of fabric. The most common use of projectors is for presentations to large audiences, such as a class or a meeting.

Specialised output devices

Some output devices have been modified, adapted or invented to meet the special needs of users, including businesses, digital artists and differently abled people. Many output devices, including Braille readers, text-to-speech generators, graphic tablets and biometric systems, perform both input and output functions. Other inventions are connected to popular technological devices such as smartphones, or provide important information for business operations such as weather forecasts.

- A *Braille embosser* (see Chapter 2) is an output device. It is a type of impact printer that converts text on a computer screen into raised dots on special paper. A **Braille terminal** or **reader** is similar but, in this case, blind and deafblind people who have learned the Braille alphabet can feel and read computer text immediately as it is being shown on the monitor. The text is converted into the Braille code, line by line, by the reader, which has been programmed to push round-tipped pins through holes in the flat surface of the terminal.
- A **text-to-speech generator** converts computer text into sound so that partially sighted people can hear it instead of reading it. Software such as the voice-assistant feature read aloud information found online. Other speech-generating devices track eye movement on a screen and read the corresponding words loudly enough for people who are hard of hearing.
- A **graphic tablet** (Figure 3.5) is an I/O device that displays drawings and sketches input by artists, engineers and architects, who use a stylus pen to draw manually and directly on the graphic tablet.

Figure 3.5 Artist using a graphic tablet

SECTION 1

Fingerprint recognition

Iris recognition

Figure 3.6 Identification via fingerprint and iris recognition

> **Did you know?**
> Everyone has a different pattern of veins in their palm, which makes a palmprint an excellent biometric security feature.

- A **biometric reader** is an I/O device as it uses software that can take in information about distinctive physiological features, such as fingerprints, faces, irises (of the eyes as shown in Figure 3.6)) and voices, and use them to identify or authenticate individuals' identification cards. The authentication information output is very useful where computer use is high and access to stored information is limited to approved people only.

> **➡ Activity**
> Name **two** output devices that are designed to help people who are partially sighted.

Locators

A device with **locator technology** allows computers in satellites to determine the specific location on the Earth's surface of a receiving device, such as a smartphone or computer. The **Global Positioning System (GPS)** uses satellites that orbit the Earth in synchronous motion more than 16 000 kilometres above it. GPS can output the smartphone holder's exact location by using accurate timings from four satellites as they pass overhead.

Software on the GPS system or the computer interprets the position or location data and uses it to provide services to the user or others. One such service is location history, which tells the user where they have travelled during a particular period. This is useful when employees make claims for travelling expenses; when individuals and businesses want to locate suppliers of goods and services that are nearest to their sites; or for sending location information to customers who are purchasing goods and/or services.

> **Key terms**
>
> **adapted output device** A device that is modified or redesigned to meet the special needs of users; includes Braille readers and speech generators
>
> **audio card** Also called a *sound card*, *audio adaptor* or *sound adaptor*; an I/O device that receives signals from a computer, converts recorded or generated digital data into a vibrational pattern and transmits the pattern to other output devices, such as speakers or headphones

biometric reader An I/O device that collects biological information, such as face and retinal scans and fingerprints, to ensure that access to a business's computers is limited

Braille embosser A type of impact printer that converts text on a computer screen into the raised dots on special paper

Braille reader A device that allows users to feel and read computer text in Braille as it appears on a monitor; it is programmed to push round-tipped pins through holes in the flat surface of the Braille terminal as the text is converted into Braille line by line

diode Semiconductor that allows electricity to flow in one direction only, which makes it suitable for visual displays

direct-thermal printer A printer that applies pressure and heat to printheads, which strike special heat-sensitive paper causing many black dots to form the letters or images

Global Positioning System (GPS) Technology that shows the location of a device by using satellites that orbit the Earth

graphics card See *video card*

graphic tablet An I/O device that allows the creation and display of drawings and sketches

headphones Device that allows one user to listen to audio generated by a computer

impact printer A printer whose printheads (metal pins engraved with letters and special characters) strike an inked ribbon; the ribbon transfers the engraved words onto paper

inkjet printer A printer that sprays droplets of black, red, blue, yellow and cyan ink from cartridges onto materials at great speed, while the material moves through a series of rollers

input/output (I/O) device A device that takes in raw data and displays processed data almost simultaneously

laser printer A printer that uses an electrical charge to press coloured inky material, called *toner particles*, onto paper and then applies pressure and heat to fuse the ink onto the paper permanently

locator technology A program that allows a network of computers connected to satellites to determine the specific location on the Earth's surface of a receiving device, such as a smartphone or another computer; the Global Positioning System (GPS) is the best-known locator system

monitor A device that provides visual displays of information using either liquid crystal or light-emitting diodes

output devices/peripherals Devices that display information to the user in their desired form, including text, audio and video

plotter printer A printer whose computer program instructs it to draw continuous lines to produce large-format text, images of many different colours and graphics on large sheets of paper, vinyl, cardboard, fabric, plastic, plywood or aluminium

printer A device that places text, images, graphics, special characters or combinations of these on paper or other materials by different means, including thermal (direct/transfer), impact, inkjet, laser and plotter

projector A device that shines a beam of light through different lenses shaped as prisms to project an image or video onto a surface

sound card See *audio card*

speaker A device that reproduces sounds generated by a computer

text-to-speech generator A device that converts computer text into sound so that partially sighted people can hear the information they want to read

thermal-transfer printer A printer that melts wax or resin of a single colour onto thermal paper

upload and download The actions of **saving** and **retrieving** digital media to or from web addresses or to personal electronic storage places

video adaptor See *video card*

video card Also called a *graphics card* or *video adaptor*; an I/O device that contains a graphics processing unit (GPU) for instructing a computer to assemble thousands of picture elements (*pixels*) into an image or video via a monitor

SECTION 1

> **Summary**
>
> In this chapter, you have learned:
> - a definition of the term *input device*
> - about several types of input devices and peripherals
> - how these input devices and peripherals work.

Practice, research and exam-style questions

Multiple-choice questions

1. A computer monitor is also known as a …
   - A screen.
   - B motherboard.
   - C supervisor.
   - D multimedia.

2. A video card presents processed information …
   - A in print only.
   - B on screen and in print.
   - C in print and sound only.
   - D on screen and in sound.

3. Complete this sentence with the correct phrase: A printer is […] device.
   - A an output
   - B a processing
   - C an input
   - D a storage

4. Which of these options is *not* an input/output device?
   - A A touchscreen monitor
   - B An iris scanner
   - C A video card
   - D A cursor

5. Speakers perform a similar function to …
   - A headphones.
   - B cartridges.
   - C sound cards.
   - D projectors.

6. A thermal printer needs …
   - A bond paper.
   - B plasticised paper.
   - C heat-sensitive paper.
   - D stiffened paper.

7. GPS stands for …
   - A Global Printing System.
   - B Global Positioning System.
   - C Geo-optical Plotting System.
   - D Geographical Placement System.

8. All these options provide information to biometric devices *except*:
   - A A thumbprint
   - B A personal stylus
   - C Nose shape
   - D Voice depth

9. Video presentations to audiences of two or more people would be most useful via …
   - A a monitor.
   - B a video card.
   - C a projector.
   - D an audio card.

10. Which of these pairs are useful output tools for law enforcement?
    - A Locator and biometric devices
    - B Video and audio cards
    - C Touchscreens and monitors
    - D Graphic tablets and plotters

Short-answer questions

1. Research how a video card helps a user watch YouTube videos.

2. Items **i–vi** are types of printing devices. Items **a–f** are descriptions of how they work. Match the description with the type of printer.

	This printer …		Names
a	… uses metal pins to strike an inked ribbon; suitable for formal documents.	i	Inkjet printer
b	… sprays droplets of ink onto various materials for high-speed printing.	ii	Laser printer
c	… uses electrical charges to transfer toner onto paper, fusing it with heat for permanent prints.	iii	Plotter printer
d	… uses heat on special paper to create images or text with black dots.	iv	Thermal-transfer printer
e	… melts wax or resin onto special paper for printing.	v	Impact printer
f	… produces large-format drawings and graphics; often used in technical fields such as engineering and design.	vi	Direct thermal printer

3. In a group, choose *one* of these output devices and explain how it contributes to productivity in an office.
   - Video cards
   - Printers
   - Speakers
   - Locators

   Take turns and share your answers with other groups.

4 Computer storage, security and care

> **Objectives**
>
> By the end of this chapter, you will be able to:
>
> - explain the importance of computer storage, care and security in the computing environment
> - define the term *storage device*
> - classify storage devices in three ways
> - list and describe three classes of storage devices
> - explain what some storage devices look like and how they work
> - discuss the benefits and challenges of different storage devices
> - practise health and safety in the computerised environment.

Introduction

While users can save both raw data and information for later use, it is just as important to be able to retrieve stored data rapidly and easily. Several mechanisms have been developed to achieve and increase the storage and retrieval functions of computers, including internal memory devices, external memory devices and access to the internet and the Cloud. These developments have brought with them physical dangers and threats that may be avoided by consistent and proper care of the computer and peripherals. In addition, solutions must be found to prevent cyberattacks that threaten the computer storage environment.

Computer storage devices

A computer storage device consists of a container with very large or very small **plates** or **platters** that are coated with magnetic material. These plates are also called *disks* or **drives**. The information to be stored is converted by electrical impulses to electrons that can 'reside' on the plates. Every item or character of text takes up a tiny space on the plate. Some storage devices are internal or built into a computer's motherboard, while others are external and plugged into the motherboard through ports or sent wirelessly to the networks of various kinds.

Storage devices vary greatly in terms of:

- storage capacity
- how they are categorised
- their main purpose
- how data is stored on them.

Measuring storage capacity

A **byte** is the basic unit of measurement for assessing storage capacity. It is the amount of space required to store a single character of text. Most small space devices, such as *memory cards* or *jump drives*, provide 1–5 **gigabytes** of storage capacity, which is roughly equivalent to between 1 billion and 5 billion bytes of text. Desktop computers and laptops provide **terabytes** of storage. One terabyte is equivalent to 1 024 gigabytes.

However, even several terabytes may not be enough to hold all the documents, songs, photographs, images and videos a user owns.

>  **Activity**
>
> Calculate how many bytes there are in 1 terabyte.

Categorising storage devices

Several differences between various storage devices can be used to classify or categorise them.

- Storage devices may be *internal* (located inside the computer) or *external* (located outside the computer).
    - Internal storage is also described as **primary**; that is, it is essential to the functioning of a computer.
    - External storage devices are described as **secondary** as they are not necessary for the computer's operation, but are helpful to users.
- Storage devices may be **portable** and able to be carried around in pockets and bags. Memory sticks, jump drives and credit and debit cards are all small and easily carried. Other devices are *not* portable. External storage devices, such as a mainframe or server computer, can be as large as buildings.
  Big local businesses such as banks, and global companies such as Google and YouTube, who must collect, save and share huge amounts of information, use internal *and* external networks (including the internet), which are attached to huge banks of servers.
- Storage devices may be **volatile**; that is, they need a constant supply of electricity. The data stored on them is not accessible to users or is only stored temporarily.

Other devices are **non-volatile**. They retain data for some time without electricity. Each of these types of devices has different ways of performing the storage function.

How storage devices work

Internal and primary storage drives

The (CPU) must access stored data to be able to follow a user's instructions. It makes use of **read-only memory (ROM)**, **random-access memory (RAM)**, **cache memory** and **internal hard disk drives (IHDD)** when it has access to electricity.

- **ROM** is the non-volatile memory chip that stores data and instructions so that the computer can start up.
- **RAM** (or *main memory*) is the volatile source of files and programs stored on a chip. The data is stored in bits and pieces, or *fragments*. When a user tries to retrieve files, RAM sends a stream of electrons, in an unsystematic or random pattern, to the CPU as instructed by the operating system. The CPU reassembles the bytes into the original pattern for use. Computers with more RAM capacity can hold larger files and programs for processing, thus enhancing performance.

SECTION 1

> **Did you know?**
> The first IHDD weighed a tonne but you could not store even one song on it!

- *Cache memory*, although volatile, pulls copies of frequently accessed data and programs from the RAM into itself, at a high speed, when the computer is restarted. This allows the CPU to access this data incredibly quickly. RAM is limited in storage capacity compared to cache memory. However, cache memory, though smaller in size, can store more data and works faster.
- *Internal hard disk drives (IHDDs)* are the most tangible and non-volatile of storage devices, embedded in the motherboard so that the chance of loss of files is reduced (Figure 4.1). They store all the digital media (files and folders filled with documents, images, audio clips and videos) collected over years of use in a permanent form.

IHDDs are electro-mechanical in operation. They consist of one or more rigid plates coated with magnetic material that spin rapidly as the data is converted to electrical impulses that are 'written' on the plates and stored in random blocks. When a user needs to retrieve data, the IHDD collects it from the random places where the different parts of the media were stored.

Figure 4.1 An internal hard disk drive

> ➜ **Activity**
> Why are RAM, cache memory and IHDDs described as *primary* storage devices?

Secondary storage drives

Secondary drives have the same purpose as the IHDD but may differ in: how they access the computer and their power supply; their capacity for storage; and how they operate to write and read the data to be stored (Figure 4.2). There are four types of secondary storage drives; all of them are non-volatile, but not all of them are portable.

Figure 4.2 A large drive (platter) coated with magnetic material

External hard disk drives (EHDDs)

EHDDs are the most popular form of secondary storage. These drives (or *platters*) may be as large as a desktop computer or as small as a pack of cards (Figure 4.3). They are attached to a computer for power using a USB cable plugged into a port. If the EHDD is large, it may not be very portable. EHDDs generally add between 1 and 10 terabytes of storage capacity to a computer.

Figure 4.3 A small drive (platter) coated with magnetic material

4 Computer storage, security and care

> **Did you know?**
> Some SSD devices are smaller than a fingernail.

Solid state drives (SSDs)

SSDs are smaller, more portable drives than EHDDs. They include memory cards, flash drives, jump drives and **pen drives** (Figure 4.4). They use a different mechanism than EHDDs to store data of between 20 and 64 gigabytes. They are called **solid state drives** as, instead of spinning plates and motors, they employ **flash memory** that sends rapid messages to microchips. SSDs are faster in executing storage tasks and are smaller and lighter, while holding much more data than HDDs. These drives are usually plugged directly into ports as and when needed.

Optical drives

Compact discs (CDs), Blu-ray Discs™ and **digital video discs (DVDs)** are portable items that are still used by companies and individuals to store large files such as videos and movies (Figure 4.4). Lasers are used to 'write' data onto magnetic tapes to create these **optical drives**. Special lasers in CD or DVD devices are used to 'read' the data for users.

Flash drive   Memory card   CDs and DVDs

Figure 4.4 A flash drive, memory card and CDs/DVDs

Network-attached storage (NAS)

Intranet and extranet storage

Many government departments, international businesses and big national companies, such as banks and insurance companies, which accumulate a lot of data, have their own IT infrastructure. These are large and powerful mainframe computers or servers, housed in separate buildings. These buildings are called **data centres** (Figure 4.5). The high volume of memory of the computer servers in data centres can store files containing information such as customer data, employee manuals used for training, company policies and procedures, company and industry news, and other information accessible through the company's **intranet** or **extranet**.

Figure 4.5 A data centre

SECTION 1

Cloud-based (CS) storage

The most popular form of large-scale storage for individuals and companies that need **Network-attached storage** are the ones that make use of the extremely large storage capacity of connected data centres known as the **Cloud**. Users can pay to upload or store their data to the cloud and be able to access their data from any internet-connected device. Some organisations can afford to have their own cloud-based accounts.

Some businesses pay independent companies who own data centres located anywhere in the world. Some companies that possess data centres may allow members of the public to use their storage capacity as part of their offering. For example, Google stores files automatically for individuals (Google Drive™ online storage service) and businesses (Google Workspace™ productivity and collaboration tools) who have Gmail™ email service accounts. Microsoft OneDrive provides a similar service to users with Outlook accounts.

Benefits of using NAS include lower costs than a company building their own storage infrastructure, quick and secure access for authorised users, and easy recovery from the loss of hard drives, including from poor care practices.

One issue with the use of NAS is the enormous amount of electric power that is used for operations.

Health and safety practices in the computerised environment

Presently, most businesses work with computers in some form. They depend on stored data about their assets, including stock levels, employees, customers and suppliers to a great extent. It is important that they insist on health and safety practices, both for the computers and peripherals and the users themselves.

Cyber-care practices for computers and peripherals

Cyber-based attacks require both proactive and reactive actions from businesses. Cyberattacks are computer security issues that need to be taken seriously, by creating and enforcing policies. The most serious threats come from internal and external sources which: hack into stored data; disrupt services by preventing access to data; or release private data into the public space. Most companies with viruses that prevent use a range of **data-protection** security measures to prevent these occurrences.

Solutions to combatting internal threats include:

- reducing accessibility by placing data such as personal identification numbers and passcodes under strong password protection
- installing machines called *readers* that require either one (*unimodal*) biometric measure, for example a fingerprint, or more (*multimodal*) measures, for example a palmprint and a voice print, for access to computer spaces including rooms and buildings
- banning the use of ports by unauthorised external devices
- installing onsite electricity generators to reduce the threat of loss of electricity for long periods of time.

Solutions to combatting external threats include:

- installing hardware to put up **firewalls** and software such as **antivirus applications** that monitor and filter incoming and outgoing data and prevent unwelcome data from entering and corrupting a computer system

> **Did you know?**
> Smartphones power down to protect themselves if they're left in a hot place for too long.

Did you know?
Firewalls got their names from the use of structures such as brick walls and metal sheets that are used to keep actual fire from leaping from one place to another.

- constantly updating software and using patches when weaknesses in security are identified
- minimising dependence on the internet, which may be subject to frequent disruptions, by providing or paying for automatic or timed backup storage facilities
- employing security and anti-hacker personnel to examine security measures and recommend how to make them stronger.

Activity
Copy and complete the table by giving *one* advantage and *one* disadvantage of using an external hard drive and a network-based storage facility.

	An external hard drive	A network-based storage facility
Advantage		
Disadvantage		

Care practices for users

A company should use preventative measures and policies to avoid health problems for their employees connected to the use of computers. *Ergonomics* is the study of the work environment and providing the most suitable workspaces. The goal of ergonomics is to lessen strain, fatigue and risk of injury to employees. Companies should consider:

- the supply of appropriate workstations, including ergonomically correct desks, and chairs to support proper posture; chairs should be adjustable for different body sizes, and foot rests should be available on request
- the correct type of computer (PCs or laptops) for the business's purposes, including standard or ergonomic keyboards
- how workstations are positioned to ensure stability and avoid obstruction: the correct placement of the computer monitor and peripherals can avoid strain injuries and other threats to user health. Power cords to electrical outlets should be positioned in safe places, such as alongside the edge of walls or covered by recommended safety materials
- proper lighting, comfortable temperatures, dampened noise and adequate ventilation
- policies that include instructions about taking health breaks and helping to meet injury care or expenses.

Activity
Give *three* reasons why correct ergonomic equipment increases productivity.

SECTION 1

Key terms

antivirus application Software that monitors and filters incoming and outgoing data and prevents unwelcome data from entering and corrupting a computer system

Blu-ray Disc™ A portable item that companies and individuals use to store large files such as videos and movies

byte The smallest unit of measurement for assessing storage capacity; the amount of storage required for a single character of text

cache memory Extremely high-speed volatile memory used for faster manipulation of data

cloud-based storage (CS) The facility provided by an extremely large storage capacity of connected data centres

compact disc (CD) A portable item that companies and individuals use to store large files such as videos and movies

data centre A building that hosts large and powerful mainframe computers or servers for storage

data protection Methods including firewalls, antivirus programs and backup storage for preventing loss, corruption and unintended access to data

digital video disc (DVD) A portable item that companies and individuals use to store large files such as videos and movies

drives Long-term, non-volatile, internal and external storage devices, such as hard disk drives, solid state drives, jump drives, pen drives, memory cards, and flash drives

external hard disk drive (EHDD) The most popular form of secondary storage, attached to a computer for power using a USB cable plugged into a port; if it is large it may not be very portable

extranet A series of computers, connected with or without physical wires for communicating with one another; open to public access

firewall Software that monitors and filters incoming and outgoing data and prevents unwelcome data from entering and corrupting a computer system

flash memory Memory that sends rapid messages to microchips

gigabyte 1 billion bytes

internal hard disk drive (IHDD) The tangible, non-volatile storage device that is embedded in the motherboard and stores all digital media in a permanent form

intranet A series of computers, connected with or without physical wires for communicating with one another; limited to a particular organisation

network-attached storage (NAS) A data storage location placed on either a company's intranet or on an extranet and stored on large and powerful mainframe computers or servers housed in buildings separate from the companies using them

non-volatile Memory tool that does not lose data even after the electrical supply is disconnected

optical drive Portable items such as CDs, Blu-ray Discs™, which have had lasers store information on their magnetic tapes

plates/platters Circular disks in hard disk drives coated in magnetic material; information to be stored is converted by electrical impulses to electrons that can 'reside' on the plates

port A physical or digital point of entry or access between a computer and peripherals

portable storage device Self-contained storage devices that can be easily transported between locations and connected to a computer using a physical port, such as memory sticks, jump drives

primary storage Internal storage, essential to computer functioning

random-access memory (RAM) Short-term, volatile, internal storage space for files and programs that are in current use or recently used

read-only memory (ROM) Non-volatile memory that stores data and instructions that allow the computer to start up

4 Computer storage, security and care

secondary storage device External storage, not necessary for the computer's operation but helpful to users
solid state drive (SSD) A small, portable drive, such as a memory card, flash drive, jump drive, and pen drive
terabyte 1024 gigabytes
volatile Memory that loses data when the electrical supply is lost

 Summary

In this chapter, you have learned:

- the importance of data storage and retrieval
- how data is stored and retrieved from external and internal storage devices
- different types of storage systems have different capacities and functions
- proper care and maintenance of a computer involves following proper practices, programs, protocols and robust security policies
- that following good ergonomics and health practices related to computer use are essential for that user health, productivity and safety.

Practice, research and exam-style questions

Multiple-choice questions

1. Which of the options is the *least* active function of computers?
   A Inputting
   B Storing
   C Outputting
   D Processing

2. The capacity of a stored file is usually measured in …
   A bits.
   B bytes.
   C gigabytes.
   D pixels.

3. Which of these is a *not* a secondary storage device?
   A Hard disk drive (HDD)
   B RAM
   C Flash drive
   D Blu-ray Disc™

4. Which of these storage devices uses lasers to store data?
   A SSD
   B CD-ROM
   C HDD
   D Flash drive

5. Which of these storage terms is an example of volatile storage?
   A SSD
   B HDD
   C RAM
   D USB

6. The ability of cloud storage to allow access from multiple devices and locations is an example of which kind of advantage?
   A Cost efficiency
   B Production efficiency
   C Security management
   D Data management

7. Which action is necessary for good functionality when storing data in the cloud?
   A Remaining offline until all data is stored
   B Using high-cost service providers
   C Building one's own infrastructure
   D Ensuring data is properly secured with firewalls

8. Which description is a major challenge of cloud storage?
   A Dependence on stable internet connectivity
   B Limited scalability
   C High degree of agility
   D Slow read/write speeds

41

SECTION 1

9 Fossy Bank wants to scale up its storage capacity but still maintain strong data protection. Which actions will be most cost effective?
   A Distributing storage to cloud-based systems
   B Building more on-premises local storage
   C Avoiding use of data-compression software
   D Buying a large amount of external drive devices

10 Data duplication often results from …
   A attempts to back up data.
   B compressing data into zipped files.
   C poor file-naming practices.
   D attempts to remove data to save space.

Short-answer questions

1 Research and describe a storage device that is both portable and non-volatile.

2 Explain the difference between how data is saved on a flash drive and on a CD.

3 The sellers of cloud storage services compete with one another in terms of their *agility* and their *scalability*. Research the meaning of each term.

4 Research the 20:20:20 rule of computer use for health and its importance.

5 List *two* advantages and *two* disadvantages of:
   a an external hard drive
   b a network-based storage facility.

6 a Research two popular antivirus applications.
   b Explain why these are popular with (i) students (ii) in businesses.

Section 2

CHAPTER 5   Basics of keyboard mastery
CHAPTER 6   Mastering the keys
CHAPTER 7   Mastering the upper and lower keys

5 Basics of keyboard mastery

 Objectives

By the end of this chapter, you will be able to:

- identify the basic knowledge and skills needed to work as a keyboard operator in a computerised environment
- list six keyboarding tasks carried out in a computerised environment
- demonstrate correct positioning for body and equipment
- reduce negative effects of keyboarding actions
- operate the start and shut down features of a computer
- explain the function of the taskbar and ribbon in a word-processing software display
- describe the purpose of four major tabs shown on the ribbon (file, home, layout, insert).

Introduction

This chapter reviews and introduces some key information you need if you are preparing and managing **documents** in a **computerised environment**. It covers three key areas of knowledge and skill: caring for your computer and workspace, mastering the keyboard, and operating the computer. In addition, remember that there are two kinds of software: operating system (OS) software and application software (apps), both of which allow the user to perform a range of tasks.

Caring for your computer and workspace

Working in a comfortable and well-organised workspace enhances user productivity. Proper maintenance of your workspace is essential for the optimal performance and longevity of your computer. Consider the following best practices:

- Cleaning the workspace: Regularly dust your computer, and wipe down monitors, peripherals, and surrounding areas before starting your machine.
- Maintaining suitable temperatures: Ensure that your work environment is kept at an appropriate temperature to support the optimum operation of the machinery.
- Following software update schedules: Keep to company policies or approved notifications for updating of files, software, and data protection measures.

Mastering the keyboard

Mastering the keyboard – that is, quick and accurate typing – is the main or key skill in **electronic document preparation and management (EDPM)**. However, **keyboarding** in a computerised environment is a little different from traditional typing. You will be working with the OS and apps, and it is important that you become familiar with the language of computerised keyboarding. When using a personal computer (PC), you will be able to:

- create **content**, including documents, setting out their information in different ways (called layout and format), for example letters, poems and financial statements look different from each other because they are set out differently from each other

5 Basics of keyboard mastery

- present and process data into forms that not only provide information differently but also allow for better understanding and further processing, including presentations, spreadsheets and database tables
- save your creations for later use in files and folders; note that computers have preset folders called *directories* where you can search for your saved, **uploaded** or **downloaded** content
- apply the rules and the specifications (formats) that are required for the work you are doing, for example you can:
  - change the appearance of the text (font type and size, **bolding**, *italicising*, underlining)
  - space your typed lines, before or after typing (*spacing*)
  - place your page numbers in different positions (*pagination*)
  - set all lines of text on one side of the page or the other (**alignment**)
  - input text that will appear on every page (*headers* or *footers*)
  - correct errors.
- insert text that was typed earlier and saved (*file data*); templates, **tables**, pictures, images, videos and even audio information can be placed (cut, copied and pasted) into electronically prepared documents
- collaborate with others to create more detailed, accurate and informative documents
- share documents with others using electronic communication (**e-communication**) methods or other means.

You will now learn to master the computer as well as the keyboard.

> **Did you know?**
> Most fully charged batteries in laptops that are used constantly last for several hours before needing an external supply. However, you will not know if it is fully charged until you turn it on.

Correct posture and peripheral placement

The first action you will take is to ensure that your computer is ready to work. Computers at workstations need a power supply from a power supply unit. It is even better if there is a surge protector (or power bar) between the computer and the wall socket to prevent damage from electricity surges.

You should sit at your workstation in an ergonomically suitable chair for computer users. These chairs are designed so that the keyboard operator is comfortable and safe from strain injuries that may be caused by sitting at computer desks for long periods of time.

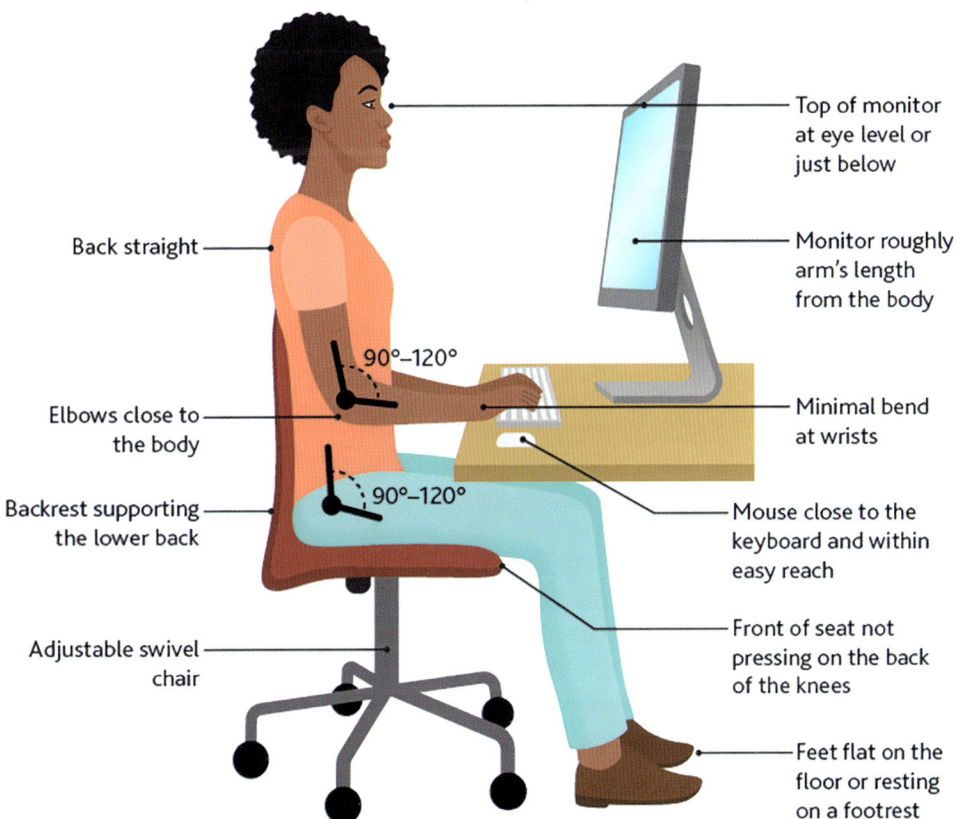

Figure 5.1 Correct posture and placement of monitor, keyboard and mouse

Finally, when preparing documents using a computer keyboard and peripherals, you should assume the correct posture. Figure 5.1 shows some characteristics of a keyboard operator who is demonstrating correct posture, as well as correct monitor placement.

- Their back is straight and their feet are flat on the floor or resting on a foot rest.
- Their elbows are bent at a comfortable angle, kept close to the body, with shoulders relaxed and wrists bent only minimally when resting on the desk.
- The ergonomically suitable chair ensures that the lower back is properly supported and the seat does not press on the back of the knees. The chair can swivel so that the keyboard operator can reach any additional tools they need.
- The top of the monitor or computer screen is set at (or just below) eye level, and the monitor itself is at arms' length from the keyboard operator. The mouse is near the keyboard and can be reached without stretching.

Attaining correct posture, and proper placement of the monitor and the mouse are important as they help in achieving speed and accuracy. Even more important, they prevent **negative effects** on the human body.

Negative effects of keyboarding

Sitting improperly for any length of time can result in strain-type injuries to your back, neck and shoulders. Seats that are unsuitable are also hazardous to health and safety. If monitors are placed incorrectly, or the lighting is bad, this may result in physical discomfort such as eyestrain and headaches, leading to loss of productivity. You can reduce these negative effects and increase your focus and concentration by taking the following actions. You should ensure that:

- the correct type of chair is supplied; furthermore, some businesses provide standing ergonomic desks or sitting/**standing desks** to encourage some physical activity and reduce the occurrence of strain injuries (Figure 5.2)
- the screen monitor is well lit, both overhead and at the internal light source called the *backlight*; keyboarders may also make use of special spectacles that reduce the glare from computer screens
- you take frequent breaks to walk around, stretch and manipulate your hands and wrists to improve blood circulation
- you rest your eyes from the screen every 20–30 minutes, even if there is no scheduled break.

> **Did you know?**
> Encouraging a worker to move away from the workstation occasionally may result in increased productivity!

Figure 5.2 Standing desks and proper fixtures and fittings can reduce injuries.

→ Activity
List two benefits of maintaining correct posture at the computer.

Starting the computer

Now that you are sitting (or standing), using the correct positions for your body and the equipment, you can start up the computer using the following steps.

1 Look for the power button on the computer case or tower or the top or bottom row of buttons on a laptop. The *start up* or *power* button has this symbol on it: ⏻. Note that the same button can be used to *shut down* the computer quickly.
2 Press the power button, and the computer's cache memory (see Chapter 4) will provide the instructions to the computer to open its functionalities.
3 The monitor should turn on automatically, or it may have a separate power button. After a few seconds, an image called *wallpaper* should appear. Wallpapers may be preset by the manufacturer but can be changed or customised by the user, either from factory-installed pictures or images you have saved in your personal library on the computer.
4 On some computers, the operating system's sign-in (log-in) screen will appear first. Logging in may be allowed automatically; however, for security reasons, some computers or some companies require a username and/or a password to gain access to a computer's features. If prompted, enter the security details and the final opening screen will appear. This is your *desktop directory* (or simply *desktop*).
5 The desktop directory is one of the preinstalled places for important operating system folders, such as settings and the recycle bin. Every such folder is labelled with both a small picture or symbol (an *icon*) and a text description (file or folder name). You could place apps that you use often on the desktop for easy access. Make the desktop directory look different by adjusting the icon size; rearranging icons by putting more space between them; and changing the background.

> **Did you know?**
> Signing in or logging in is similar to signing an attendance book with your name and initial.

Using the mouse

Using the mouse, you can open apps, files or folders quickly or make changes to what you see on the screen. Applying key *mouse techniques* is part of the computer keyboard operator's skillset. In Chapter 2, the mouse was described as an input device that moves a shape on the screen (the cursor) horizontally or vertically. The cursor or pointer responds to the movement of the fingers or other parts of the user, who **clicks** or rolls, pulls or pushes a moveable part of the device. The moveable parts of the traditional mouse are called *buttons*, with one on the right and one on the left of a rolling ball or wheel. Mice may be adapted for people who have a dominant left hand, or a dominant right hand or who have a disability.

Tips for using the mouse

1 Place the front of the mouse near the heel of your palm, with your thumb placed down one side and your fourth and little fingers down the other the side.
2 If you are using a mouse adapted for right-handedness, the index finger will be positioned on the left mouse button and the middle finger will be positioned on the right button. The wheel is generally manipulated by the index finger.
3 A mouse is often connected to a computer by a cord, although wireless and Bluetooth® mice are also available. It is best to keep the mouse facing in a way that keeps the cord at the top, away from entangling your fingers or other peripherals on the workstation.

> **Did you know?**
> The double-click button is generally on the left (*left-click*) while the right-click button is generally on the right, but left-handed mice are also available.

4 The mouse should be operated on a mousepad: a piece of material that allows the mouse to move smoothly and precisely, while preventing a scratched desk and dust build-up on the mouse.
5 Keep looking at your monitor, not the mouse. To move the cursor to the position you want it to be on the screen, move the mouse up/down, left/right or diagonally across the mousepad. The cursor will move in the direction you instruct it. When you get where you wish to be, press the button under your index finger (left-click) and a tiny blinking vertical line will appear. This is called the **insertion point**. The key you touch will appear on the screen at the insertion point.
6 The double-click motion is used to open directories, files and folders. Practise double-clicking until you can do so smoothly while keeping the mouse stationary and the cursor on the folder or file icon, and not the name of the item.

Due to the development of graphical user interface (GUI) systems and touchscreen technology, there are several other devices that can control a cursor. Learning how to use the mouse and/or these other devices should be part of your keyboarding skillset.

Useful tools and capabilities in Microsoft apps

The **taskbar** and **ribbon** are two features that help to make computerised keyboarding productive, efficient and creative.

The taskbar

The taskbar is an element of the computer's OS that allows the user to see and work with important applications simultaneously and efficiently. In the Windows OS, users can:

- access the major directory that holds all the other folders, and have them available for use
- see the icons and open the apps that are used in document preparation
- click on the icon for the browser that takes the user to the internet
- pin any other frequently used programs on the taskbar, such as the apps controlling the printer or media player
- receive information about, among other subjects, current weather conditions, the current date and time, battery life and the Wi-Fi® connection to the internet.

Two very important buttons on the taskbar are the **start button** and the **search button**. A click on the start button gives access to apps that ensure the smooth operation of the computer, such as task manager, disk manager and device manager. It also can be used to shut down, put the computer to **sleep**, *restart* and sign out of the computer.

The search button can be used to find devices and applications easily. Clicking on the magnifying glass icon or typing a keyword into the white space will help you find, for example, the printer or scanner applications, or your saved games and the settings icon where you can make changes. In other operating systems, the taskbar is called the **menu bar**, and it may use different icons for their display.

The ribbon or menu bar

Each application in the Microsoft Office 365 suite of applications, mentioned in Chapter 1, displays a row of terms and icons that allow you to find and use tools to complete tasks. It is called the *ribbon* or *menu bar* and it can be found at the top of the screen. In the Microsoft Word application, there are as many as eleven ribbon tabs or groups of commands, each with its own set of **subtabs**. Some subtabs have sets of commands within them.

The file, home, layout and insert **tabs** are the most used ribbon tabs when keyboarders are preparing documents:

- The **file tab** has at least four major subtabs: open, save, print and close, which the user will find in a dropdown ribbon on the left side of the screen when the *file* button is left-clicked. Remembering to save your work before closing a file is important.
- The **home tab** has five major subtabs or menus: clipboard, font, paragraph, styles and editing. Each menu has its own submenus of commands. The home ribbon displays some of the most used of these sub-submenus. For example, the paragraph submenu shows commands for line spacing, numbering and sorting a list of words alphabetically.
- The **layout tab** includes the submenus page setup, paragraph and arrange. These commands, and their subcommands, help with the orderly and effective presentation of information on a Word page according to specifications for different types of documents. In page setup, for example, the user can change the size of the paper from a small size for a party invitation to a larger one for a legal document.
- The **insert tab** is a menu with eight submenus, including commands for inserting tables, pictures, page numbers and other items used frequently when creating Word documents.

> ➡ **Activity**
>
> Which submenu would you use to sort a list of terms into alphabetical order?

Opening and closing application pages

Each application in Office 365 (Figure 5.3) has a different ribbon, as the set of tools or functionalities vary across apps. (see Figure 5.4 for Word, Figure 5.5 for Excel, Figure 5.6 for Access and Figure 5.7 for PowerPoint). Use the mouse to left-click on the appropriate icon on the taskbar to view the ribbon and layout of the opening page.

If the application is not on the taskbar, use the 'search' white space to find it. Note that each application's opening page is different, as the function of each application varies.

Figure 5.3 Icons for Microsoft Word, Excel, Access and PowerPoint

SECTION 2

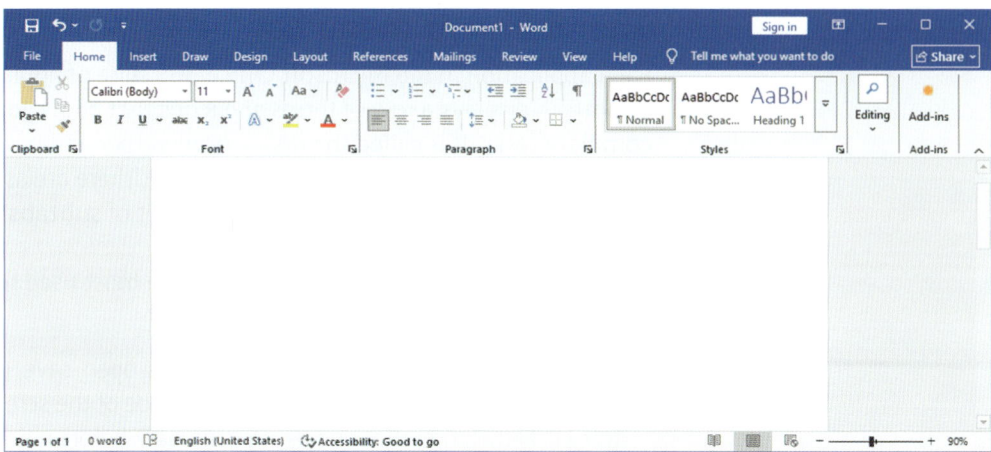

Figure 5.4 Opening a blank page in Word

In later chapters, you will learn other skills, such as navigating up, down and across pages, documents, spreadsheets and database tables using scrollbars located at the right side and bottom of the window.

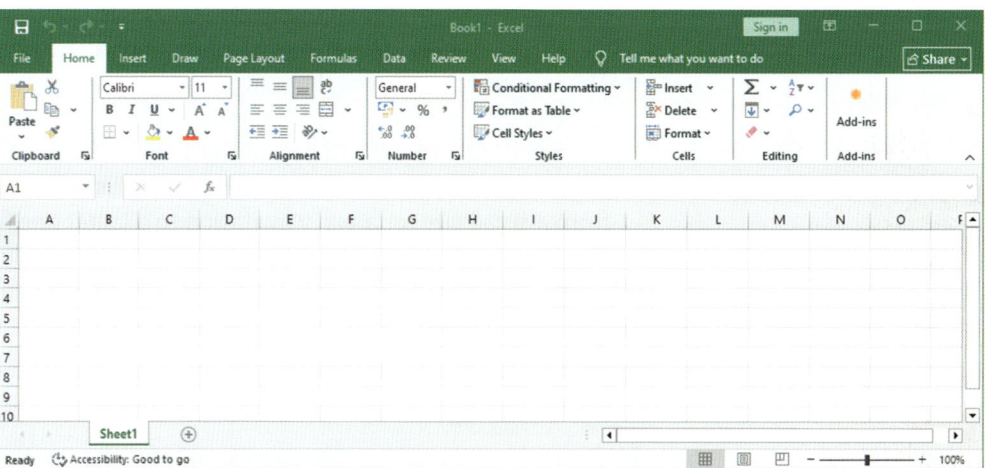

Figure 5.5 Opening a blank page in Excel

Chapters 7–15 will provide more explanations and practice on how the ribbons with their buttons are used to create, save, share and manage digital media in the modern office.

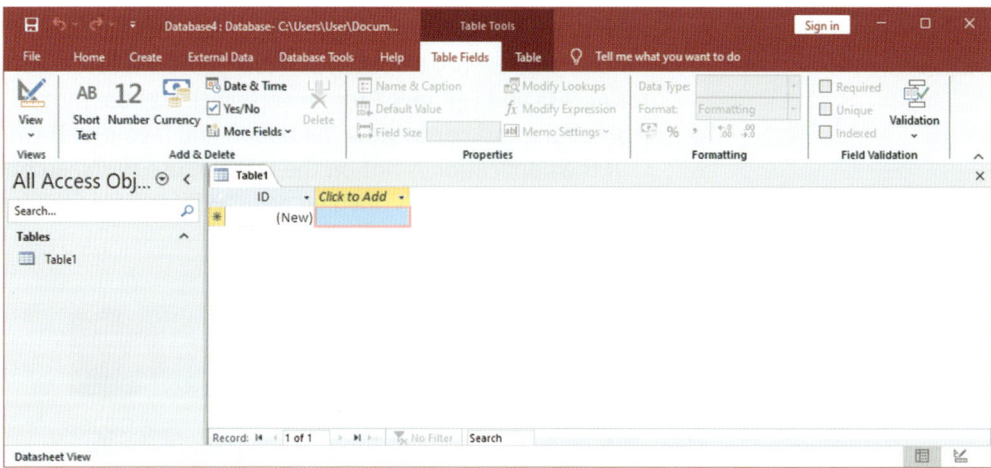

Figure 5.6 Opening a blank page in Access

5   Basics of keyboard mastery

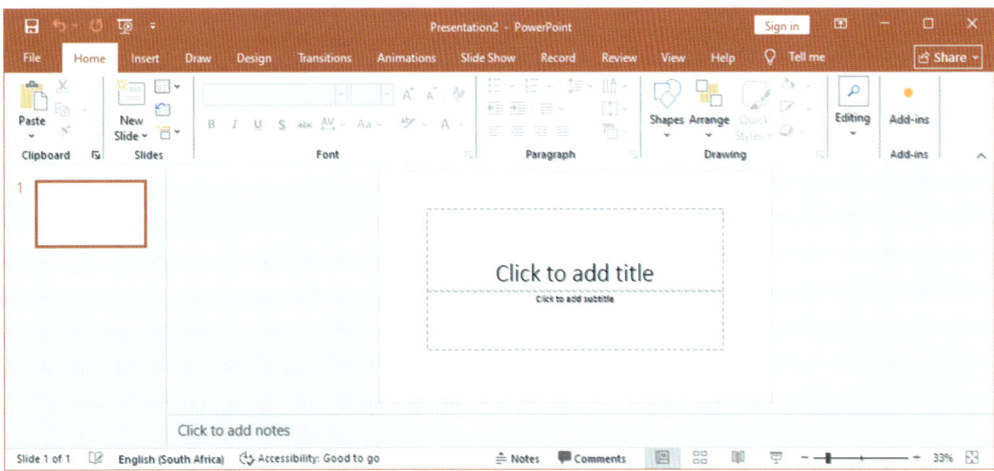

Figure 5.7 Opening blank page in PowerPoint

Close a page by clicking on the × at the extreme right on the ribbon.

The capabilities of the different applications in Office 365 are represented by words and icons on their individual menu bars.

For now, the computer must be shut down quickly and safely using the following steps.

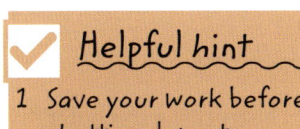

Helpful hint

1 Save your work before shutting down to prevent any loss of unsaved work.
2 Shut down regularly and use that time to get automatic updates for applications.
3 Putting the computer to sleep allows for quick wake-ups.

Closing the computer

1 Using the mouse, right-click on the start button on the left of the taskbar.
2 Move the cursor to the 'shut down or sign out' line (second line from the bottom).
3 Left-click on the shutdown line, and the monitor should go black.
4 Alternatively, use a shortcut. On the keyboard, press the key labelled F4 at the same time as the key labelled Alt (Alt + F4). This will also bring up the shutdown command, and you can left-click OK.
5 In emergencies, pressing the power button will shut down the computer immediately.

If you have files or programs still open or in use, the computer will remind you to save before closing the files and/or apps.

Key terms

click Push down on the moveable parts (*buttons*) of a traditional mouse; there is one on the right and one on the left of a rolling ball or wheel

computerised environment The modern office space, comprising workstations furnished with electronic devices, mainly computers and wired and wireless peripherals

content Forms of digital media that include documents, pictures, images, videos and even audio information that can be prepared through access to applications via keyboarding

document A type of digital media that is the main product of keyboarding in applications; while some are printed, others remain in electronic format for saving, manipulating and/or retrieving

e-communication Sharing digital media with others using the capabilities of computers and computer networks

SECTION 2

electronic document preparation and management (EDPM) The art and science of performing clerical and administrative document preparation and management tasks knowledgeably, skilfully and competently in the computerised environment

ergonomic A description for an office space and its furniture that has been designed for human efficiency, safety and comfort

file tab Tab on the left side of a window that has at least four major subtabs: open, save, print and close

format and edit Manipulate different types of digital media by applying rules or specifications and making changes as required

home tab Tab on the left side of a window that has five major subtabs or menus: clipboard, font, paragraph, styles and editing; each menu has its own submenu of commands

insert tab A menu with eight submenus, including commands for inserting tables, pictures, page numbers and other items used frequently when creating Word documents

insertion point A tiny blinking vertical line indicating the active point for inputting data on a page

keyboarding The set of knowledge and skills demonstrated through mastering the many features of computers and a range of applications

layout tab A menu that includes the submenus 'page setup', 'paragraph' and 'arrange', which help with the orderly and effective presentation of information on a Microsoft Word page, according to specifications for different types of documents

menu bar A row of terms and icons in an app that allows the user to find and use tools to complete tasks

mouse techniques A description of the manipulation of a mouse to instruct the computer by clicking, rolling, dragging, selecting and dropping

negative effects The disadvantages to people and business relationships from overusing computers in office environments; these include poor physical and psychological states, as well as lowered productivity and costly fixes

ribbon A row of terms and icons that show the range of capabilities provided for EDPM by individual applications

saving and retrieving Storing documents in files, folders and directories, and reopening stored documents

search button Feature for finding devices and applications easily

sleep A mode that allows a computer to conserve energy

standing desk A heightened desk that allows a user to stand while using a computer

start button A virtual button that gives access to apps that ensure the smooth operation of the computer, such as task manager, disk manager and device manager

subtabs Access to the several capabilities of tabs – some contribute to one main task, while others provide a number of options or menus for EDPM; common subtabs include 'clipboard' and 'font'

tabs Major features on ribbons of all applications that provide key capabilities for creating, formatting and editing digital media; common tabs include file, home, layout and insert, and each tab contains subtabs and menus

taskbar An element of a computer's OS that allows the user to see and work with important applications simultaneously and efficiently

 Summary

In this chapter, you have learned how to:

- start and close a computer
- operate within a computerised environment to reduce negative health effects
- operate a mouse efficiently
- access useful tools and capabilities of apps.

Practice, research and exam-style questions

Multiple-choice questions

1. Which of the options is a negative effect of constant computer use?
   A Repetitive joint strain
   B Cost of purchasing ergonomic chairs and keyboards
   C Constant screen-saver changes
   D Failure to upkeep maintenance schedules

2. Which of these conditions may be the result of excessive screen time?
   A 20:20:20 vision
   B Disrupted sleep
   C Repetitive compression
   D Overactive imagination

3. Cramps in the wrists and hands can be the result of …
   A squeezing the nerves in the wrists.
   B sitting too long at a computer.
   C not lifting the wrists high enough.
   D poor posture of the neck and back.

4. A keyboard operator in a computerised environment does *not* need to practise …
   A changing typewriter ribbon.
   B mouse-handling techniques.
   C touchscreen typing.
   D using shortcut key combinations.

5. Which statement represents a correct position when using a traditional mouse?
   A Turn the mouse so that the cord is below your wrist
   B Turn the mouse so that the cord is facing outward
   C Place the mouse so that the moveable parts are unobstructed
   D Place the mouse so that it is at arms' length of the keyboard operator

6. In Microsoft Word, the home tab holds the …
   A styles subtab.
   B save subtab.
   C tables subtab.
   D page setup subtab.

7. Which keyboard button can be used to start and close the computer?
   A Power button
   B Taskbar
   C Scroll button
   D Alt button

8. What remains the same when using Office 365 Word, Excel, Access or PowerPoint?
   A Taskbar
   B Scroll bars
   C Ribbon
   D Opening page

9. Which instruction is the most important when shutting down the computer?
   A Always save your work
   B Always place your wireless mouse in its case
   C Always shut down, restart and shut down again
   D Always put a dust cover on the tower

10. Which icon does *not* represent an application in Office 365?
    A

    B

    C

    D

SECTION 2

Short-answer questions

1. Identify *two* of the latest trends in office design that seek to increase worker comfort and safety needs.

2. Here are *ten* words and phrases on the topic of using a mouse. Replace the letters in the paragraph with the appropriate option from those provided.

damage	arm's length	techniques
wired	computerised	wireless
mousepad	left-handed	mouse
ports		

Mouse-navigation **a** are an important skillset of a keyboard operator in a **b** environment. The **c** should be positioned at **d** from the user and placed on a **e** to prevent **f** to the workstation furniture. **g** mice use power from the computer through cables that are connected to USB **h**. Although the mouse is well protected, a **i** mouse may fall off a desk very easily. Adapted mice are available so that **j** people can use them.

6 Mastering the keys

> **Objectives**
>
> By the end of this chapter, you will be able to:
> - identify the different types of keys on the QWERTY keyboard
> - perform keyboard exercises using the 'home row' keys
> - perform keyboard exercises using special keys.

Introduction

Although the *QWERTY keyboard* was invented as long ago as the late 1800s, some of the rules for using the computer *keyboard* safely and efficiently remain. For example, practice and more practice of traditional finger placement and finger movements on the keys is necessary. In this chapter, you will begin to develop your skills and master the keys using the letters, numbers and special *characters* on the keyboard.

Learning the keyboard

The keyboard used in the computerised environment has many more keys than the original QWERTY keyboard. The modern user is expected to be aware of the appearance and purpose of all keys, starting with the basic *alphanumeric keys*. Figure 6.1 details the various groups of keys, and is followed by their descriptions in Table 6.1. Note that not all keyboards are exactly the same. Some keyboards may have certain key groups positioned in different places. The name given to the group may also be different.

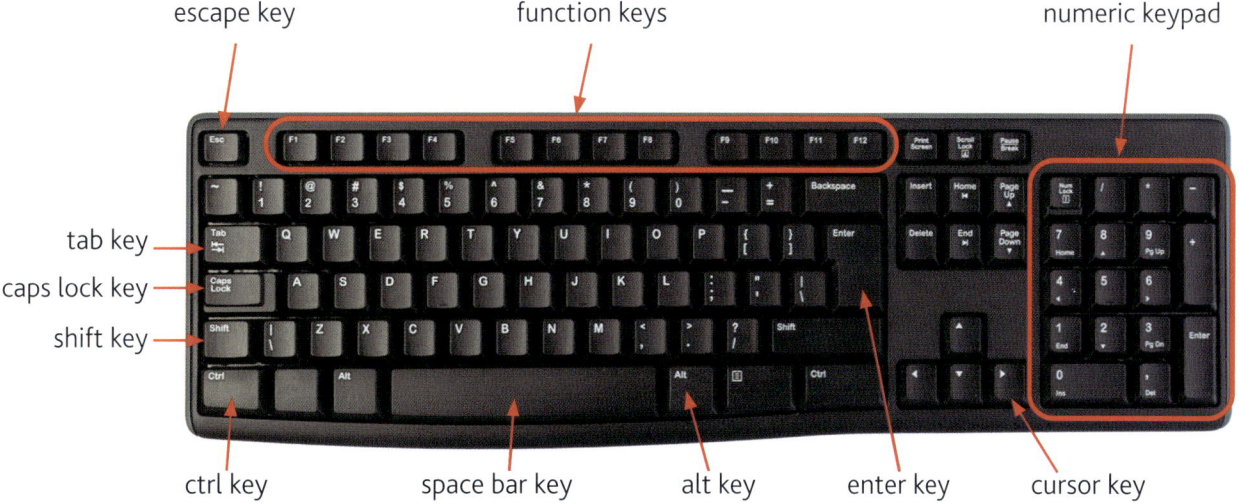

Figure 6.1 A computer keyboard

Table 6.1 Key descriptions

Keys and key groups	Description
Esc/escape key	Pushing this key stops applications from performing their functions, to save time and enhance efficiency, e.g. when the wrong file is opening or there is a need to move quickly to another application.
Function keys	These keys, labelled F1–F12, are usually found at the top of the keyboard. Their tasks are predetermined by the OS. For example, F1 is used as help or user support to answer troubleshooting questions. On laptops, these keys are often paired with another function (*double-function key*) to save space, e.g. F1 is also a 'mute volume' key. To access the top-level function key, you need to use one of the control keys.
Modifier keys	These keys affect the action of another key when they are pressed in the same motion. They are labelled *ctrl* or *command*, **fn**, *alt* or *shift*. Often there are two of them, on the right and the left side of the keyboard, for quick access. They also perform **shortcuts**. *Shortcuts* are quick ways to do frequently needed actions when these keys are combined with alphabet keys, e.g. pressing the ctrl key and C at the same time allows you to copy a selected passage.
Navigation keys	These enable you to move the insertion point quickly to the start or end of a page, to a line you have typed, to a single word or even to remove a single character (a space between words is considered a character). Keys labelled **backspace**, *home*, **end**, **page up** or **page down** or showing directional arrows help to do this. The *tab* key is used to set or preset an amount of white or blank space before or after a typed line in a document. This is called the *indent level*. The **enter** key moves text or images down to a new line, and the **delete** key removes text or images entirely, including errors in your document. *Backspace* can also delete material if it is selected using the mouse.
Toggle keys	Toggle keys lock off the functioning of other keys, as needed. The **caps lock key** ensures that every letter typed appears in uppercase form only. Pressing a shift key and a letter has the same effect, but does not remain locked. The **num lock key** gives access to the digits on the number pad, and must be pressed a second time to disable 'num lock'.
Numeric keys	Keys labelled 0–9 form a number pad on the right side of the keyboard. Together with symbols for arithmetical operations (+, -, * and /), they are used to calculate sums quickly. Alternatively, some keyboards provide access to an onscreen calculator via its own group of keys above the number pad.
Alphanumeric keys	These are located at the central part of the keyboard and contain: • letters A–Z • special characters, including punctuation marks, square brackets, curly brackets, 'less than' and 'more than' signs and back and forward slashes • a top row of keys is labelled 0–9, but also show other special characters, including the @, $, %, & and parentheses (brackets) • the **space bar**, which places one space (e.g. between words and sentences) each time it is pressed.

Introduction to word processing

In the Caribbean, Microsoft Word has become the standard application for creating text-based documents such as letters, memoranda, reports, manuscripts and more. There are several steps to follow to create a document, beginning with opening a blank page in the application. Knowing how to save your document as a file and closing it is also important.

Steps to create, save and close a Word document

Create

To create a new Word document, left-click your mouse on the 'start' key on the taskbar, as you were shown in Chapter 5. Look for the Word icon and left-click again. A new blank page may appear immediately, or you may see a few preset documents for various purposes, for example invitations, menus and calendar pages. Click on the **blank document template**. Note that, if you already have a document open, the 'file' tab on the ribbon can be used to get to the 'blank document' template.

Save

To save your document (although it is still blank), left-click on the 'file' tab on the ribbon and left-click on 'save as'. A panel will open that gives you three choices. (See Figure 6.2.)

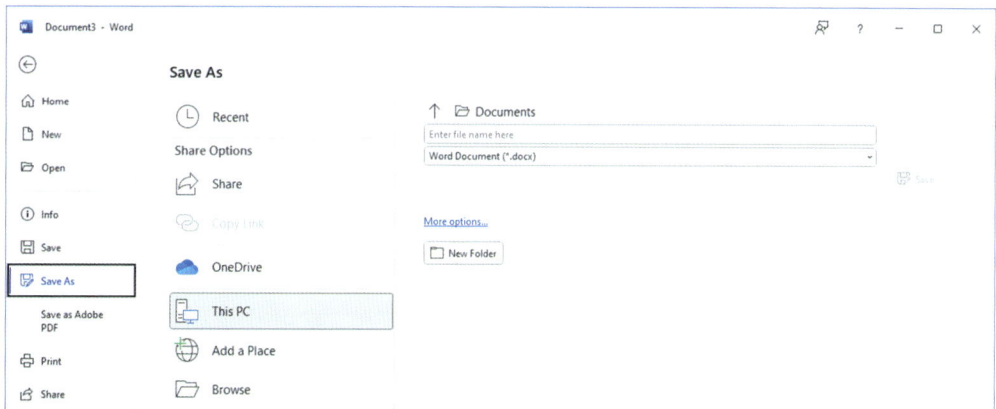

Figure 6.2 A 'save as' panel

1. The first choice is where to save the document. For your first save, it would be best to save it in the directory or major folder called 'documents'. Most files and folders will be saved there. Another location for saved documents, as you learned in Chapter 5, is the desktop. However, you can create your own named folders for different types of documents as you manage your electronic documents over time.

2. The second is what name to use to save it. Word will suggest a name based on the first words in your document. It is best to create a name that will help you to retrieve it easily. A good choice for the name of a document may be 'Report on …' or 'Minutes of …' or the name of the person to whom a letter is addressed. If the document is a new version and both are to be kept in the folder, the name should indicate this by either a number or a date.

SECTION 2

3 The third choice is what type of saving extension to use. At this stage, there are two options: as a Word document (.docx), or in a Portable Document Format (.pdf). A pdf document retains all the features you have set in it, for example the tab spacing (see above) or the size of the letters (font size). The receiver cannot change these easily without special permissions.

Close

To close a document is very easy. You can go to the top right-hand corner of the screen and left-click the mouse on the ×. You can go into the 'file' tab on the ribbon and left-click the 'close' subtab or you can press the ctrl and W keys on the keyboard. Note that, if you have made any changes to your document and not saved those changes, there will be a prompt for you to do so before the screen goes black and the document disappears from view. The document has now become a *file*.

>  **Activity**
>
> Name *two* other places to save files other than in the computer's main or secondary folders. (Look back at Chapter 4.)

Mastering the alphanumeric keys

You will now begin to learn and take the opportunity to practice finger positioning and finger and hand movements on the alphanumeric keys. The aim is to visualise where keys are in relation to others and be able to choose the right keys without looking at the keyboard (**touch typing**). The accompanying visuals will help you.

The 'home' keys

In this section, you will learn which keys are the **home keys** and how to identify them using the fingers on your left and right hands, as well as using special marks on certain keys. Remember that each letter, punctuation mark, special mark and space between words is called a *character*.

Here are the first six steps for keying mastery.

Step 1: Finding the 'home' keys

a The 'home' keys are identified on the middle row of the keyboard with the letters in line: **A, S, D, F, G, H, J, K, L** and the *semicolon* **(;)**. This row is called the *home row* and it holds the 'home' keys. It is from this row that all other alphanumeric rows are accessed.

b Look carefully and you will find that two keys – **F** and **J** – have horizontal lines under them. This helps you to feel the 'home row' when you close your eyes or look away from the keyboard. Try to feel for the horizontal lines without looking. Compare how they feel to the **G** and the **H**, which are next to the **F** and the **J**.

c Using the correct posture you learned about in Chapter 5, raise your wrists slightly and place your fingers (except the thumbs) as in Figure 6.3. The lineup of the letters **A, S, D** and **F** will be touched by the fingers of the left hand. The lineup of **;, L, K** and **J** will be touched by the fingers of the right hand. The thumbs will be used to press the space bar.

6 Mastering the keys

Figure 6.3 Fingers touching the 'home' keys

Step 2: Left-hand keying practice

a Confirm the placement of your left-hand fingers by following Table 6.2.

Table 6.2 Position of the left hand on the home keys

Finger placement	Character/letter
little finger	A
ring finger	S
middle finger	D
index finger	F
thumb	space bar

b Close your eyes and repeat the order of letters under your left hand – **A**, **S**, **D**, **F**; **A**, **S**, **D**, **F** – without moving your fingers.

c Keeping your eyes closed, begin by pressing key **A**, then the *space bar* with your thumb, key **S** and again the *space bar*, key **D** and the *space bar* and finally key **F** and the *space bar*.

d Feel the keys and repeat the characters (letters) to yourself as you type. Remember to feel for the horizontal bar under the **F**. Move very slowly at first as you make a memory with your fingers. Keep your right hand in place on the other home keys all the time.

e Repeat the **A**, *space*, **S**, *space*, **D**, *space*, **F**, *space* attempt at least three more times before opening your eyes.

Before starting the next exercise:

- don't look at your fingers
- keep your right-hand fingers still
- use your thumb to place a space after each letter/character or combination of characters
- say the name of every character (letters and space) silently as you type.

SECTION 2

> **Did you know?**
> Use only a light touch of the keys, otherwise the typed character will show up several times, rather than once. Train your brain and your fingers will follow.

Two-letter combinations

Now try two-letter combinations. Follow the instructions slowly and carefully. Your speed will improve as you stretch your fingers and create muscle and brain memories. When your eyes are open, look at your monitor and check for accuracy. This will improve the more you practise.

1 Type each combination of these twelve items of two characters followed by a space a total of ten times:
as ad af sa sd sf da df ds fa fd fs
2 Practise each line three times before moving to the next combination.

Three-letter combinations

1 Type each combination of these six items of three characters followed by a space a total of ten times:
add ads sad saf dad fad
2 Practice each line three times before moving to the next combination.

Four-letter combinations

1 Type each combination of these three items of three characters followed by a space a total of ten times:
adds dads fads
2 Practise each line three times before moving to the next combination.

Step 3: Right-hand keying practice

a Place your fingers on the home row.
b Confirm the placement of your right-hand fingers according to Table 6.3.

Table 6.3 Right-hand keying

Finger placement	Character/letter
little finger	;
ring finger	L
middle finger	K
index finger	J
thumb	space bar

> **Did you know?**
> Pressing the key in a rhythm helps. Close your eyes and sing the characters in your head as you type.

c Close your eyes and repeat the order of letters under your right hand, starting with the little finger and without moving your fingers: ;, L, K, J.
d Keeping your eyes closed, begin by pressing key ;, then the *space bar* with your thumb, key **L** and again the *space bar*, key **K** and the *space bar* and finally **J** and *space bar*.
e Feel the keys and repeat the characters (letters and semicolon) to yourself as you type. Remember to feel for the horizontal bar under the **J**. Move very slowly at first as you make a memory with your fingers. Keep your left hand in place on the other home keys all the time.
f Repeat the **;**, *space*, **L**, *space*, **K**, *space*, **J**, *space* attempt at least three more times before opening your eyes.

6 Mastering the keys

> **→ Activity**
>
> 1 What are the *four* characters on the home row under the left fingers?
> 2 What are the *four* characters on the home row under the right fingers?

Before starting the next exercise, remember:

- don't look at your fingers
- keep your left-hand fingers still
- use your thumb to place a space after each letter/character
- say the name of every character (letters, punctuation and space) silently as you type.

The exercises that follow are similar to those you have already done for your left hand.

Two-character exercises for the right hand

Repeat the following two-character combinations ten times with spaces:
;k lk kl

Three-character exercises for the right hand

Repeat the following three-character combinations ten times with spaces:
jkl ;jk kl;

Four-character exercises for the right hand

Repeat the following four-character combinations ten times with spaces:
kl;j ;lkj klj;

Step 4: Switching hands keying practice

This step will test your brain as you concentrate on using the correct finger and correct hand. In trying the exercises, it will help if you:

- keep your eyes closed
- visualise the home row keys
- repeat the exercise pattern of characters silently
- go slowly at first.

1 Type each combination of these 3/4/5 characters followed by a space, a total of ten times:
  lad fak as; lass, lajs asks
2 Practise each line three times before moving to the next combination.
  More complex practice exercises will require you to go more slowly as you keep your eyes on the text changes:

  - sak sak ask sak sak asks sak sak ask s;k
  - falls falds falls falds falls fall; fall; falk fal;s fak;s

Now try a series of words using the home row keys **A**, **S**, **D**, **F**, **;**, **L**, **K**, **J** only. Remember the space between each word:

- all lass flask falls alaska
- sass a lad, jalk; ask dad

Practise each line three times before moving to the next combination.

Step 5: Mastering the G and H keys

Figure 6.4 G and H keys in the middle of the home row

The **G** and **H** keys (Figure 6.4), positioned in the middle of the home row must be pressed by the nearest index finger. The left index finger is used for the **G** key, and the right index finger for the **H** key. The technique requires that you practise moving the respective index finger from **F** to **G** and **J** to **H** *without* moving the other fingers from their positions on the home keys.

Table 6.4 provides some exercises for this new step in mastering the keys.

Table 6.4 Using the G and using the H

G: using the left index finger	fg fg fg fg fg fg fg fg fg fg
	dg dg dg dg dg dg dg dg dg
	sg sg sg sg sg sg sg sg sg
	ag ag ag ag ag ag ag ag ag ag
	fag sags gas fag sag gas dag gag sad fad
	flag glad gall ga;k gaff gags lags ;ags slag glass
H: using the right index finger	jh jh jh jh jh jh jh jh jh jh
	kh kh kh kh kh kh kh kh
	lh lh lh lh lh lh lh lh lh lh
	h; h; h; h; h; h; h; h; h; h;
	jhg jad jhs jah hjg jak jhh
	jalk jha; jafd jahs jag; jffd jhad; jsah

Step 6: Switching letter cases

You may have noticed that, although the alphabet keys are shown as uppercase letters on the keyboard, when you type, they are shown as lowercase letters on the document. Either the modifier key *shift* or the toggle key *caps lock* can be used to switch from typing in lowercase to typing in uppercase letters (Figure 6.5). Since whole words or sentences in uppercase are rarely necessary, the shift key is more likely to be used.

6 Mastering the keys

Did you know?
Printers in the 1700s used to keep the small, more frequently used ('common') letters in a case that was closer (or lower) to their typesetting desks and the larger, less frequently used ('capital') letters in an (upper) case further away.

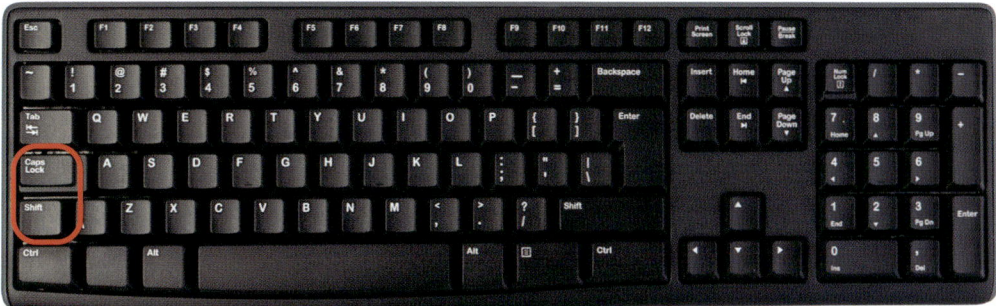

Figure 6.5 Caps lock and shift keys on the left of the keyboard

How to switch letter cases:

- Note that there are *two* shift keys, located on the right and left sides of the lower keys. The little finger on either hand is used to press the shift keys.
- To type any uppercase letter on the left side of the keyboard, use the right shift key and the right little finger.
- To type any uppercase letter on the right side of the keyboard, use the left shift key and the left little finger.
- If a whole word is to be typed in uppercase letters, use the caps lock key.
- Note that neither the shift key nor the caps lock key makes any change to the semi-colon on the right side.

Table 6.5 provides some practice exercises for switching between uppercase and lowercase letters. Remember your space bar. Concentrate on stretching:

- the little fingers to the shift key
- the thumbs to the space bar
- the index fingers to the G and H keys.

Table 6.5 Switching between uppercase and lowercase letters

Using right shift and left home keys	Adds Dads Fads GdfS Adfg DsAa GffS DGfs
Using left shift and right home keys	Jlkj Hjk; ;hfD lhsL HKg; JLfD JhHd Lsalh
Switching between left and right home keys	Alss sDFk Gags lags ;ags slFK
Using caps lock	FLAGS GLASS HALL

Key terms

backspace The key that removes a single character
blank document The first page of a new Word file available for keying in characters
caps lock key The key that allows every letter typed to appear in uppercase form
delete The key that removes text or images entirely
end A navigational key that takes the insertion point to the end of a line
enter The key that moves text or images down to a new line
fn A key that affects the action of another key when they are pressed in the same motion

SECTION 2

> **function keys** Operating system keys, labelled F1–F12, located at the top of a keyboard and used for predetermined tasks, such as controlling the speaker volume
> **home keys** The central row of keys on a standard keyboard (**A, S, D, F, G, H, J, K, L, ;**) where fingers are positioned before beginning to type
> **num lock key** Key that enables access to the digits on the number pad
> **numeric keys** Keys labelled 0–9 that form a number pad on the right side of the keyboard
> **page down** A navigational key for moving the insertion point to the bottom of the page
> **page up** A navigational key for moving the insertion point to the start of the page
> **shortcut** A way to bypass the mouse by combining the modifier/control keys with alphabet keys, enabling the quick performance of frequent tasks, such as copy and paste
> **space bar** Key that places one space between words and sentences each time it is pressed
> **template** A page that has fixed formatting features, such as places to hold predetermined information in specific ways, such as dates
> **touch typing** The placement and movement in a particular order and direction of fingers to assigned keys

 ## Summary

In this chapter, you have learned about:

- the steps to open, save and close a Word document
- features such as the function keys, modifier keys, alphanumeric keys and navigation keys
- the keys on the home row (**A, S, D, F, G, H, J, K, L, ;**)
- the correct placement of fingers on the home row keys, and practised two-, three-, four- and five-letter combinations, with space bar thumb presses
- how all keys are shown in lowercase letter form (**a, s, d, f, g, h, j, k, l, ;**) when typed without modification
- the role of the modifying *shift* key for a temporary change, and the *caps lock* toggle for longer-term change, to achieve uppercase letter forms
- how to achieve fast and accurate keyboarding skills.

Practice, research and exam-style questions

Multiple-choice questions

1 Which of these keys closes down functions abruptly?
   A Caps lock
   B Num lock
   C F2
   D Esc

2 Word-processing apps manipulate mainly …
   A text.
   B images.
   C cells.
   D sheets.

3 Navigation keys …
   A move cursors and pointers.
   B move insertion points.
   C control upper-level functions.
   D print screenshots.

4 Which of these items is *not* used as a blank document?
   A A page available for typing in a word-processing app
   B A page using a Portable Document Format (pdf)
   C A template containing several placeholders
   D A spreadsheet auto-filled with standard data

5 Which consideration is *not* relevant when saving a document in a word-processing app?
   A Where to save the document
   B What type of 'saving extension' to use
   C Why to save the document
   D What name to use to save it

6 On a QWERTY keyboard, the letters A, S, D, F, J, K, L are called the
   A top row keys.
   B home row keys.
   C function row keys.
   D toggle keys.

7 When beginning a word-processing exercise, the correct position would be with:
   A little fingers on A and ;
   B fingers just above the keyboard.
   C all fingers on the space bar.
   D index fingers on G and H.

8 Which pair of keys have identifiers for the home row?
   A A and ;
   B G and H
   C F and J
   D S and K

9 The insertion point is a:
   A vertical line indicating where the next character typed will be placed on the page.
   B horizontal line indicating a selected number of words to be deleted.
   C a diagonal line that separates parts of an arithmetical calculation.
   D a vertical line that separates alphanumerical and numerical buttons.

10 Which key allows you to type in uppercase letters only?
    A Home lock
    B Num lock
    C Scroll lock
    D Cap lock

Short answer questions can be found in online support material.

7 Mastering the upper and lower keys

> **Objectives**
>
> By the end of this chapter, you will be able to:
>
> - demonstrate mastery of the home, upper, lower and special keys
> - perform keyboard exercises using the alphanumeric keys
> - type words and complete sentences using the alphanumeric keys
> - demonstrate speed and accuracy at the keyboard.

Introduction

In this chapter, you will continue to master the keyboard by focusing on the upper and lower keys. Beginning with finger positioning on the home keys, you will need to stretch your fingers to reach those keys above and below the home row. The aim is to remember where keys are in relation to others. With practice, you will learn to choose the right keys to type words and sentences accurately, and with acceptable speed, without looking at the keyboard. However, sentences usually include *punctuation* marks so, in this chapter, you will practise exercises that include the finger and hand movements to type these marks. This chapter also includes the technique to type **number** and **symbol keys** and to use the number pad efficiently. You will now practise some warm-up exercises to help you do this.

Warm-up exercise: home keys

This warm-up exercise focuses on the skills you practised at the end of Chapter 6. It requires you to type combinations of lowercase and uppercase home keys using the shift key and the space bar.

Try to complete the following exercise in two minutes:

1. Use your mouse to open a blank document in a word-processing application.
2. Begin with correct placement of your fingers on the home keys.
3. Type these combinations of characters:
    adds   hall   sadK   FaGs;   sDjk   JLfD   hlFK   flAsG;   GasH   Jlk;
    Dash   LasH   FlAsK
4. Continue typing and stop at the end of two minutes.
5. Compare your effort with the correct combinations from step 3 to assess whether you achieved a minimum of 50% correct.

Mastering the upper-row keys

The upper keys are those on the top row of the keyboard, which appear in the order: **Q, W, E, R, T, Y, U, I, O, P** (Figure 7.1).

Take note that the four fingers of the left hand need to master five letters (**Q, W, E, R, T**) and the four fingers of the right hand need to command five letters (**Y, U, I, O, P**). This means that each index finger has to stretch to reach two keys on the **upper row**. Recall that these same index fingers also need to reach the **G** and **H** on the home row keys.

7 Mastering the upper and lower keys

> **Did you know?**
>
> The little finger moves diagonally to reach the shift key; the ring and middle fingers move vertically to their partners on the upper row; and the thumb still controls the space bar. The strong index finger has a lot of work to do stretching to several keys on the keyboard.

Figure 7.1 Upper-row keys

Steps to master the upper-row keys

Left-hand upper-row practice

Starting from the placement of fingers on the home row, note the movement of each finger of the left hand to an upper-row key (see Table 7.1 and Figure 7.2).

Table 7.1 Position of the left hand for the upper row

Finger placement	Placement on home-row key	Placement on upper-row character/letter
little finger	A	Q
ring finger	S	W
middle finger	D	E
index finger	F	R/T
thumb	space bar	space bar

Figure 7.2 Upper-row keys for the left hand

SECTION 2

The combinations that follow will help you to make the link between the home-row keys and the partnering upper-row keys for the left hand. Practise line, slowly at first, three times each. Try not to look at the keyboard, but visualise the direction in which your fingers need to move. Feel the keys and repeat the characters in your mind as you type.

These new practice exercises incorporate other letters on the home row.

1. Focus on the movement of the *middle finger* of the left hand.
   de de de de de fe fe fe fe fe
   ae ae ae se se sea sea sea sell self
   ded ded dead dead deal deal deaf deaf
   led led led lead lead lead leaf leaf
   seed seed seed sled sled shed shed
   fed fed feed feed feel head head heal

2. Practise using the *index finger* of the left hand.
   fr fr fr fr fr dr dr dr dr dr
   ar ar ar ar ar sr sr sr sr sr
   gr gr gr gr jr jr kr kr ;r ;r
   jar jar are are are far far far fare fare
   gear gear gear hare hare hare rake rake
   hear hear sear sear seer seer jeer jeer jeer

3. Practise with *left index finger* from **F** to **T** first, and then to both **R** and **T**.
   gt gt gt gt gt ft ft ft ft ft ft ft dt dt dt dt dt dt
   at at at at at ate ate ate sat sat sat set set
   fat fat fat fat rat rat rat rat hat hat hat
   jerk jerk jest hate hate hart hart late late state state
   rate rate rate rest rest rest stare stare
   fate fate fare fare fare tear tear taste

4. Reintroduce the shift key and the *little finger* and type capital letters on the left side of the keyboard. Press the right shift key with the *right little finger*.
   Art Art Jet Jet Hat Hat Hart Hart
   Hear Hear Hear Dear Dear Dear
   Data Data Data Date Date Date
   Fret Fret Fret Lest Lest Lest

5. Move to the **W** key from the **S** key using the *ring finger* of the left hand.
   we we we we we we wa wa wa wa wa wa
   ws ws ws ws ws ws wd wd wd wd wd wd
   wet wet wet wet wet wag wag wag wag wag
   war war war war war wad wad wad wad wad
   ware ware ware wade wade wade were were wear wear
   walk walk walk wall wall wall well well west west waste

6. Practise using the *little finger* of the left hand for the **Q** key.
   Qa qa qa qa qa qa qa qa qa qa qa qa qa
   Qf qf qf qf qf qf qf qf qf qf qf qf qf qf qf qf
   Qa qd qd qd qd qd qd qd qd qd qd qd qd
   Qad qad qad qad qaw qaw qaw qaw
   Qare qare qare qare qare qare qare

7. Practise these 5-and 6-letter words using the *left hand* on the home-row keys and upper-row keys and the *right hand* on the home-row keys only.
   Healer hearth dealer safer Leader jaded Sledder street shade Father flare fatter Heart wader thread Later

7 Mastering the upper and lower keys

Right-hand upper-row practice

Starting from the placement of fingers on the home row, note the movement of each finger of the right hand to an upper-row key (see Table 7.2 and Figure 7.3).

Table 7.2 Position of the right hand for the upper row

Finger placement	Placement on home-row key	Placement on upper-row character/letter
little finger	; (semicolon)	P
ring finger	L	O
middle finger	K	I
index finger	J	U/Y
thumb	space bar	space bar

Figure 7.3 Upper-row keys for the right hand

The combinations that follow will help you to make the link between the home-row keys and the partnering upper-row keys for the right hand. Practise each combination's line three times each. These practise exercises incorporate other letters on the home row.

1 Focus initially on the movement of the *little finger* of the right hand from ; to **P**, to become accustomed to that upward movement and the return to the home row. However, no words start with ;. So, with practice, you will move to letter combinations.
;p ;p ;p ;p ;p ;p ;p; p ;p ;p
pj pj pj pj pj pk pk pk pk pk
pl pl pl pl pl ph ph ps ps pd pd
pat pat pat pat pat pet pet pet pet pet
pew pew pew paw paw paw pas pas pas pas
peg peg pal pal pal pale pale pare pare
pear pear past past past paste pest pest

SECTION 2

2. Practise using the *ring finger* of your right hand to reach the **O** key from **L**.
   or or or or or or or or or or
   do do do do ok ok ok oj oj oh oh
   ort ort ort lol lol lol lol top top top
   opt opt opt opt owe owe owe owe
   pot pot pot ore ore ore ode ode old old old old
   gold gold glop glop sold sold golf golf golf gloat
3. Practise using the *middle finger* of your right hand to reach the **I** key from **K**.
   ki ki ki ki ki ki ik ik ik
   il il il il li li ip ip ip ij ij
   oil oil oil tie tie tie tie tip tip tip
   lie lie lie sit sit sit sir sir air air air stair
   quit quit quit quite quite quote quote site site
   kite kite kite kite mite mite mite mite mote mote
4. Practise using the *index finger* of your right hand to move from **J** to **U** and **J** to **Y** or across from **U** to **Y**.
   uj uj uj uj uj ju ju ju ju ju
   uk uk uk uk uk ku ku ku ku ku
   uh uh uh ug ug ug ugly ugly glue glue
   hut hut hut put put put gut gut out out
   our our our que que que quay quay quay
   pour pour pour pout pouty gout gout
   four four four hour hour hour sort sort loud loudly
5. Finally, practise these 5-, 6- and 7-letter words using the *right hand* and *left hand* on the home-row keys and upper-row keys only.
   Appear lopped toast Guest plotted roped Slope slotted quest peered flared fathered

Proofreading skills will be discussed in Chapter 9.

Correction of errors

Practising the previous exercises will help you see an increase in your speed and confidence. Timing yourself and aiming to complete the last line in less than a minute will also help.

However, increasing your speed also increases the chance of making mistakes. Accuracy takes time and practice. It is important that the final document is free from errors, both in terms of spelling and grammar, and is considered **mailable**.

If you or someone else examines your work, you will be engaging in the process of **proofreading**. You must become familiar with the signs that indicate different types of errors and be able to proofread your work and the work of others.

7 Mastering the upper and lower keys

Mastering the lower-row keys

Steps to master the lower-row keys

Left-hand lower-row practice

Starting from the placement of fingers on the home row, note the movement of each finger of the left hand to a lower-row key (see Table 7.3 and Figure 7.4).

Table 7.3 Position of the left hand for the lower row

Finger placement	Placement on home-row key	Placement on upper-row character/letter
little finger	A	Z
ring finger	S	X
middle finger	D	C
index finger	F	V/B
thumb	space bar	space bar

Figure 7.4 Lower-row keys for the left hand

The combinations that follow will help you to make the link between the home-row keys and the partnering **lower row** keys for the left hand. Practise each combination's line three times each. These practice exercises incorporate not only other letters on the home row, but also letters on the upper row for both hands.

1 The **B** on the lower row is typed by the *index finger* of the left hand moving from **F**.
   bg bg bg bg bg bg bg bg bg bg
   bk bk bk bk bk bd bd bd bd bd
   bad bad bad bad bat bat bat bat bag bag
   bet bet bet bed bed but but buy buy big big

SECTION 2

2. The **V** on the lower row is typed by the *index finger* of the left hand moving from **F**.
   vf vf vf vf vf vf vf vf vf vf
   va va va va va vi vi vi vi vi
   via via via via vip vip vip vip vis vis vis
   vet vet vet vow vow vow vay vay vay
   vest vest vest very very vile vile vise vise
   vote vote vote above quave vast wave save

3. The **C** on the lower row is typed by the *middle finger* of the left hand moving from **D**.
   cd cd cd cd cd cd cd cd cd cd
   dc dc dc dc ce ce ce cv cv cb cd cd cf
   cat cat cat car car car cab cab cab cap cap
   caw caw caw cod cod cod caf caf cas cas
   cha cha cha cal cal cer cer cer cut cut
   chip chip chip call call cold cold cold cave cave
   case case cape cape cape cope cope cord cord

4. The **X** on the lower row is typed by the *ring finger* of the left hand moving from **S** on the home row.
   xs xs xs xs xs xs xs xs xs xs
   xd xd xd xd xw xw xw xr xr xr
   ext ext ext exc exc exe exe exr exr exa exa
   six six six sex sex sex sex set set set
   fix fix fix lax lax lax wax wax fox fox
   taxi taxi taxi flax flax flax flax flex flex
   exit exit exit crux crux crix crix crax

5. The **Z** on the lower row is typed by the *little finger* of the left hand moving from **A** or the shift key.
   za za za za za za za za za za
   zu zu zu zu zu zo zo zo zo zo
   zoo zoo zoo zap zap zap zoe zoe zip zip
   zero zero zero lazy lazy lazy zeal zeal zeal
   haze haze haze hazel hazel hazy hazy jazz jazz

Right-hand lower-row practice

Starting from the placement of fingers on the home row, note the movement of each finger of the right hand to a lower-row key (see Table 7.4 and Figure 7.5).

Table 7.4 Position of the right hand for the lower row

Finger placement	Placement on home-row key	Placement on upper-row character/letter
little finger	; (semicolon)	/ (common or forward slash)
ring finger	L	. (full stop/period)
middle finger	K	, (comma)
index finger	J	M/N
thumb	space bar	space bar

7 Mastering the upper and lower keys

Figure 7.5 Lower-row keys for the right hand

The combinations that follow will help you to make the link between the home-row keys and the partnering lower-row keys for the right hand. Practise each combination's line three times each. These practice exercises incorporate other letters on the keyboard.

1 Start with the **M** key and then practise the **N** key, as both are typed by the *index finger* of the right hand moving from the **J** key on the home row.
me me me me me me me me me me
ma ma ma ma mi mi mi mi mu mu mu
mom mom mom man man man met met mit mit
mop mop mud mud mud med med med
milk milk melt melt meld meld mold mold mace mace
mate mate mast mast mute mute mule mule
nh nh nh nh nh nh nh nh nh
no no no ni ni ni nw nw nw jn jn in in
new new now now net net nit nit nil nil
nab nab nap nap nip nip nav nav nic nic can can
nice nice navy navy knit knit pine pine pore pore

2 Demonstrating mastery of the keyboard by typing some longer words that you are likely to use in your workplace is good practice. You should also practise incorporating the shift key with the appropriate *little finger*. Here are some words for you to try that include uppercase and lowercase letters.

absolute	*justification*	*streamline*
frugality	*Keeping*	*tenacity*
correspondence	*lively*	*Uncomfortable*
definitely	*movingly*	*Verity*
Expenditure	*notorious*	*wasteful*
friendly	*opportune*	*excessive*
grateful	*Postponement*	*zestful*
Healthy	*querulous*	
ignorance	*reference*	

3 The *middle finger* of the right hand is responsible for typing the comma (,). This punctuation mark is often used in sentences to indicate a short pause. This is especially useful when typing long sentences and speeches. Like all punctuation marks, commas are placed immediately after the last character or letter, followed by one space. There is no space between a word and the punctuation mark.

4 Practise moving the *middle finger* of the right hand from the **K** on the home row to add a comma after a word or group of words.
a, a, a, ag, at, as, an, se, dr, fr, ca, un,
que, wet, eve, red, ted, yet, met, let, vet, set, net
lit, pit, zip, mit, lit, sit, bit, nit, zit, hit, fit, lip, kit,
pill, mill, melt, help, mold, fold, wire, mire, sire,
mace, race, help, pelt, wail, fail, mail, bail, hail,
trace, exist, quiet, fight, pilot, right, fight, might,
farce, waste, height, alight, wafer, quest, blaze,
what a waste, please help, so be it, he said that,

5 Practise moving the *ring finger* of your right hand from the **L** on the home row to add a full stop after a word or group of words. In line with the latest edition of the recommended APA Style Guide, insert one space only after a full stop or other punctuation at the end of a sentence.
A full stop is used:
- at the end of a sentence
- after abbreviations, such as Co. (Company) and Ltd. (Limited)
- after first-name initials and before surnames, such as V. Adams, S. John, L. Hinds
- after titles, such as Dr. St. Mr. Mrs.

6 The punctuation mark on the lower row that is typed by the *little finger* of the right hand is the common or forward slash (/). This symbol is used to:
- separate words in a sentence
- denote division, separation or alternative options
- write dates, fractions, abbreviations and URLs
- navigate between pages in a document
- indicate division in mathematical expressions.

The best way to practise moving to the punctuation marks on the lower row from the home row is through typing sentences. Here are some for you to try. Practise each at least three times:
James asked Celia whether to invite all/some of her friends to the party.
The menu consisted of a choice of meat/fish.
If/when Karla ever shows up, we can all head out to the party together.
I looked up into an angry face, began to tremble/sob, waiting for my punishment.

Mastering the numbers and symbols row

In the same way that the alpha keys on the keyboard are used by specific fingers, the same applies to the number and symbol keys located above the upper row. However, your fingers will not be asked to stretch, but to hover over their assigned number or symbol (see Figures 7.6 and 7.7).

7 Mastering the upper and lower keys

Figure 7.6 Number keys for the left hand

Figure 7.7 Number keys for the right hand

Steps to master the number-row keys

Left-hand number-row practice

Note the number keys assigned to the fingers of the left hand in Table 7.5 and then practise the combinations of letters and numbers below it.

SECTION 2

Table 7.5 Position of the left hand for the number row

Finger placement	Character/letter
little finger	1
ring finger	2
middle finger	3
index finger	4/5
thumb	space bar

1qa 1qa 1qa 1qa 1qa 1qa, 1qa, 1qa, 1qa, 1qa, 1qa
2ws, 2ws, 2ws, 2ws, 2ws, 2ws, 2ws, 2ws, 2ws, 2ws, 2ws
3ed, 3ed, 3ed, 3ed, 3ed, 3ed, 3ed, 3ed, 3ed, 3ed, 3ed, 3ed
4rf, 4rf, 4rf, 4rf, 4rf, 4rf, 4rf, 4rf, 4rf, 4rf, 4rf, 4rf, 4rf, 4rf, 4rf, 4rf
5tg, 5tg, 5tg, 5tg, 5tg, 5tg, 5tg, 5tg, 5tg, 5tg, 5tg, 5tg, 5tg, 5tg, 5tg

Right-hand number-row practice

Now do the same for the fingers of the right hand, following Table 7.6, and then practise the combinations of letters and numbers below it.

Table 7.6 Position of the right hand for the number row

Finger placement	Character/letter
little finger	0
ring finger	9
middle finger	8
index finger	6/7
thumb	space bar

0p; 0p; 0p; 0p; 0p; 0p; 0p; 0p; 0p; 0p; 0p; 0p; 0p;
9ol 9ol 9ol 9ol 9ol 9ol 9ol 9ol 9ol 9ol 9ol 9ol
8ik 8ik 8ik 8ik 8ik 8ik 8ik 8ik 8ik 8ik 8ik 8ik
7uj 7uj 7uj 7uj 7uj 7uj 7uj 7uj 7uj 7uj 7uj 7uj
6yh 6yh 6yh 6yh 6yh 6yh 6yh 6yh 6yh 6yh 6yh

> **Did you know?**
> Left keys: right shift key
> Right keys: left shift key

Steps to master the symbol-row keys

You learned in Chapter 6 that symbols are placed on the same keys as numbers. They are made functional by holding down a shift key before pressing the desired symbol. Note that the same fingers are used for the corresponding number keys. However, remember that, when using the left hand for typing, the little finger on the right hand operates the shift key on the right side. The opposite occurs when using the right hand for typing its assigned symbols.

Left-hand symbol-row practice

Note the symbol keys assigned to the fingers of the left hand in Table 7.7.

7 Mastering the upper and lower keys

Table 7.7 Position of the left hand for the symbol keys

Finger placement	Character/letter
little finger	!
ring finger	@
middle finger	#
index finger	$/%
thumb	space bar

Hold and release the right shift key to type the symbols shown in Table 7.7.
aq! aq! aq! aq! aq! aq! aq! aq! aq! aq!
sw@ sw@ sw@ sw@ sw@ sw@
de# de# de# de# de# de# de# de# de#
fr$ fr$ fr$ fr$ fr$ fr$ fr$ fr$ fr$ fr$ fr$
gt% gt% gt% gt% gt% gt% gt% gt%

Right-hand symbol-row practice

Note the symbol keys assigned to the fingers of the right hand in Table 7.8.

Table 7.8 Position of the right hand for the symbol keys

Finger placement	Character/letter
little finger	)
ring finger	(
middle finger	*
index finger	&/^
thumb	space bar

Hold and release the left shift key to type the symbols shown in Table 7.8.
)p;)p;)p;)p;)p;;)p;)p;)p;)p;
(ol (ol (ol (ol (ol (ol (ol (ol (0l
*ik *ik *ik *ik *ik *ik *ik *ik *ik*
&uj &uj &uj &uj &uj &uj &uj &uj
^yh ^yh ^yh ^yh ^yh ^yh ^yh ^yh ^

Here are some combinations of letters, numbers and symbols to practise your reaches to all parts of the alphanumeric keyboard. Look carefully for the punctuation marks before spaces.
zaq1 zaq1 zaq1 zaq1 zaq1 xsw2 xsw2 xsw2
@cde3 @cde3 #cde3 #cde3)vfr4)vfr4 ;vfr4 ;vfr4
bg,t5 bg,t5 bg,t5 bg,t5 nh*y6 nh*y6 nh*y6 nh%y6 nh%y6
mju7 mju7 mju7, ki8 ,ki8 ,ki8 ,ki8 ,ki8
.lo9 .lo9 .lo9 .lo9 . /;p0 /;p0 /;p0 /;p0 /;p0

Special mention

A number of symbols, both those often used and some rarely used, are located above other symbols but on the same key. Where more than one symbol is located on a key, press the shift key (right or left) and the desired key (at the same time) to access the symbol located at the top.

SECTION 2

Special symbols

There are a number of symbols that appear on the same key on the alphanumeric keyboard as other symbols (Table 7.9). While most of them are rarely used, some appear in certain documents on a regular basis. Below is a list of these symbols and their names.

Table 7.9 Symbols that appear on the same keys as other symbols on an alphanumeric keyboard

Symbol	Name
~	tilde or swung dash
`	accent or grave
_	low dash
-	hyphen/en dash/em dash
+	plus sign
=	equal sign
{ }	open and close brace/curly brackets
[ ]	open and close square brackets
|	vertical pipe
\	back slash (goes from left to right)
:	colon
"	double quotation
'	single quotation
<	less than (points left)
>	greater than (points right)
?	question mark

You will learn about different types of documents, called displays, in Chapters 10–16.

Mastering the numeric keypad

The **numeric keypad** is located on the right-hand side of the alphanumeric keyboard (Figure 7.8). A numeric keypad can also be a separate device attached to a computer. It allows the user to complete calculations faster than using the alphanumeric keyboard. Using the toggle key 'num lock' allows the keyboard operator to type out large numbers more quickly.

Figure 7.8 The numeric keypad

7 Mastering the upper and lower keys

There are also other uses for the numeric keypad, as shown in Table 7.10.

Table 7.10 Uses for the numeric keypad, other than calculations and typing long numbers

Key	Use
num lock	When this key is pressed, only the *numbers* on the number part of keypad can be used (not the other uses detailed below)
/ (forward slash)	In calculations, this symbol is used for division
* (asterisk)	In calculations, this symbol is used for multiplication
- (hyphen)	In calculations, this symbol is used for subtraction
+ (plus)	In calculations, this symbol is used for addition
numeric 7	Can be used as the 'home' key
numeric 8	Can be used as the 'up arrow' key
numeric 9	Can be used as the 'page up' key
numeric 4	Can be used as the 'left arrow' key
numeric 5	The base for the home keys (it has a bump, like letters **F** and **J**)
numeric 6	Can be used as the 'right arrow' key
numeric 1	Can be used as the 'end key'
numeric 2	Can be used as the 'down arrow' key
numeric 3	Can be used as the 'page down' key
numeric 0	Can be used as the 'insert' key
period (.)	Can be used as the 'delete' key
enter	Used to return or move to another line.

Key terms

lower row The keys below the home row, consisting of the letters and punctuation marks Z, X, C, V, B, N, M, ,, ., /

mailable document The final version of a document that conforms to specifications free from spelling and grammatical errors, following the process of proofreading

number keys The keys 0–9

numeric keypad The keys labelled 0–9 and symbols for arithmetic operations (**+**, **-**, ***** and **/**) that form a keypad on the right side of a keyboard

proofreading Checking a document for quality and clarity, including freedom from spelling and grammatical errors; repetition; and typographical and punctuation errors

punctuation keys The keys for typing punctuation characters, which are part of the writing system that separates written language into units to simplify and clarify what is being expressed

symbol keys The keys for typing special characters; mainly located above the number keys and include @, #, $, %, &, (,)

upper row The keys above the home row, consisting of the letters **Q, W, E, R, T, Y, U, I, O, P**, tab and some punctuation marks

SECTION 2

> **Summary**
>
> In this chapter, you learned:
>
> - to master the keyboard by using the techniques for accessing the keys on the upper and lower rows
> - to stretch and reach for the keys that lie above and below the home row
> - to type punctuation marks, numbers and symbols
> - to use the numeric keypad
> - where keys are in relation to others
> - to type with accuracy and increasing speed.

Practice, research and exam-style questions

Multiple-choice questions

1 Which of these words can be typed using the left hand only?
   A paste
   B poised
   C faced
   D deport

2 Which of these words can be typed using the right hand only?
   A paste
   B polyp
   C faced
   D deport

3 Which of these terms describes a document free from errors?
   A Proofread
   B Manuscript
   C Mailable
   D Practised

4 Which of these symbols is used when writing dates, fractions or abbreviations?
   A /
   B \
   C +
   D *

5 Which of these symbols does *not* appear on the numeric keypad?
   A /
   B \
   C +
   D *

Short-answer questions

1 Type the paragraph below. Type this paragraph within five minutes, then repeat the same paragraph with a time of three minutes, then one minute. Should you finish the paragraph before time is called, start again at the beginning of the paragraph until the time is expired. This is to assess your speed and accuracy.

> All interviews were held in places and on dates agreed upon by informants and researcher, and there were general expressions of happiness in participating once again in the effort at telling the story. Indeed, it would appear that informants were more prepared to reflect on that period in their lives than on the first occasion. Interview times varied from twenty-two minutes for Coriander, who had spoken at length in 2025, to fifty-two minutes for Oregano, who continued to share just as generously as the first time.

2 Type the paragraph below, following the same instructions as for question **1**. Use all caps to name the passage 'vacation time'.

> Vacation time is indeed an exciting time, when we can all relax and enjoy our time/days in any manner we like. Some may travel to visit friends and family. Those who travel overseas usually visit places never before seen or return to some place that they found favourable for shopping or sight-seeing. Many bus tours are available for this, and these tours can be accessed by going on the National Transportation website. Some may even venture to the beaches and explore parts of their country. Going to the beach is always an exciting adventure, especially for those who love the sea and sand; in some parts of the world this is taken for granted, while in many other parts it is considered a privilege to visit such a place. Whichever way time is used for vacation, make sure it is a memorable one.

Section 3

CHAPTER 8 Formatting and editing basics
CHAPTER 9 Advanced formatting, editing and proofreading
CHAPTER 10 Business documents
CHAPTER 11 Simple and advanced displays
CHAPTER 12 Specialised documents
CHAPTER 13 Basic spreadsheet techniques
CHAPTER 14 Advanced spreadsheet techniques
CHAPTER 15 Database applications
CHAPTER 16 Presentation and graphic applications

8 Formatting and editing basics

In this chapter, basic formatting options available under the 'home' and 'layout' menus on the ribbon of Microsoft Word will be applied to the examples of simple and advanced displays and specialised documents, which you will see set out in Chapters 10, 11 and 12.

In Chapter 4, the importance of storing data was discussed. In Chapter 5, two key features of the 'file' menu on the ribbon — save and save as — were shown. In Chapter 6, the question of what name to use to save a file was asked.

🏠 Objectives

By the end of this chapter, you will be able to:

- use standard naming conventions when saving files
- apply basic formatting tools to common business documents
- apply headings to documents
- apply basic editing tools to common business documents.

Introduction

Congratulations on achieving a degree of mastery in your keyboard skills! You will now display these skills by creating business documents enhanced with several formatting features.

First, you will need to save your documents as named files and then to place similar files into named folders. These files will demonstrate not only your keyboarding skills, but your decisions on how you would like your work to appear. This is called **formatting**. Basic and advanced options are available on the ribbons of applications.

Naming files, folders and directories

It is important to be able to retrieve files and folders, and standard ways to name files (**naming conventions**) have been created to do this. Business offices should ensure that all staff involved with creating, retrieving, amending and saving files are aware of the conventions to be applied consistently across the organisation. Table 8.1 describes four qualities of a useful naming convention, with examples.

Table 8.1 Naming conventions

Quality	Considerations	Examples
Descriptive	Include a short but descriptive name for a file and a folder	Mins of BOD Mtg 2023-2024 Fin Sts - Yr 2023-2024 Priority Custs. A-G
Standard character use	Use only letters, numbers, underscores (_) and hyphens (-)	Folder: Employees Statutory_deductions Files in folder above: Employees L-Z_NIS pyts Employees L-Z PAYE deductions
Production dating	Use a standard format consistently Use numbers only, rather than a mix of words and numbers	dd-mm-yy OR yyyy-mm-dd, i.e. 27-01-24 OR 2024-01-27 27 Jan 2024
Versioning	Apply version numbers or dates if the evolution of a document is important; this also helps to trace a document	Chapter 6 v3 Investigation Rep-Tom Brown v3

> **→ Activity**
>
> What are the meanings of these abbreviations:
> - Mins
> - Chap
> - V3
> - Ltr
> - Memo?

Formatting

Formatting is a process during which the layout and appearance of characters, parts of a document (sentences and paragraphs) or the whole of a document are changed to meet the needs of the creator. Formatting can be used to:

- maintain the standards of formality and presentation required in an industry
- add emphasis to words and paragraphs
- increase attractiveness for readers.

There are different ways of looking at formatting, including character, page and paragraph formatting. In this chapter, we will categorise formatting tools into those that are useful for *page set-up* and those tools accessed as **insertions** of formatting features. The categories are outlined in Table 8.2.

Table 8.2 Categories of formatting features

Page set-up	Insertions
• Orientation	• Pre-keyed text
• Page/paper types and sizes	• Page numbers
• Margins and alignment	• Headers and footers, footnotes and endnotes
• Line spacing	
• Font styles: weight, size, colour, bold, italics, underline	• Symbols, tables, graphics, text boxes and objects
• Highlighting and text special effects	• Backgrounds and watermarks
• Numbering, **bulleting** and sorting	• Breaks
• Borders and shading	• Links
	• Auto text (e.g. signature line, date/time stamps)

Did you know?
Many page set-up features are only functional when there is some text on the page.

These features are accessible through manipulation of your mouse on the application ribbon (see Chapter 5) or through shortcuts involving the keyboard function keys and other tools. In this chapter, the *page set-up* features and their application to common business documents will be discussed.

Orientation

When a blank document is opened, a rectangular page is presented as if you are holding a sheet of paper in front of you. The normal (or *default*) view is that the shorter side of the page runs horizontally and the slightly longer side runs vertically. This way of presenting the document is called *portrait orientation*. It accommodates text, tables and graphics within a boundary or *margin* (discussed in the following section).

SECTION 3

However, occasionally a table must accommodate a lot of data, or a graphic needs more space at the side than at the top. In this case, **landscape orientation** is more useful. Landscape orientation may also be used for documents such as invitations, menus, flyers and brochures. The change from portrait orientation to landscape orientation may also be necessary within a document.

To change the orientation of a whole document:

1 Click on any part of the document.
2 Click on 'layout' on the ribbon. To the left, you will see the subtab 'orientation'.
3 Click on orientation and then on landscape. The whole document will be reoriented from portrait view to landscape view.

Margins and alignment

Margins

Margins are the empty or clear spaces around the text and graphics in a document. Margins are set to maintain control over the length of lines of text and prevent run-off text at either edge of the page. If margins are not set, then document information will be lost. Many institutions require specific margins for presenting assignments. Margins are useful for entering comments or notes. If a document is printed for binding, inadequate margins at the left or at the top mean that the binding will obscure information in the text.

In word-processing applications such as Microsoft Word, margins can be preset to meet various reading layouts (Figure 8.1); however, they can be customised to meet the needs of the creator. The steps to place margins in a blank document are:

1 Use the mouse to left-click on the layout tab on the ribbon.
2 Click on the down arrow of the margins menu, and the margin settings will appear.
3 Note the *default* (preset/normal/usual) setting puts a 2.54 cm (1 inch) margin on all four sides of the page. Other preset margins are shown in Figure 8.1.
4 Select the margin (if it is not preset) to meet the standard required for the document. For example, if the document is to be bound, the left margin may be customised with an increase. Click on the 'custom margin' option and make changes as required to any edge of your document.

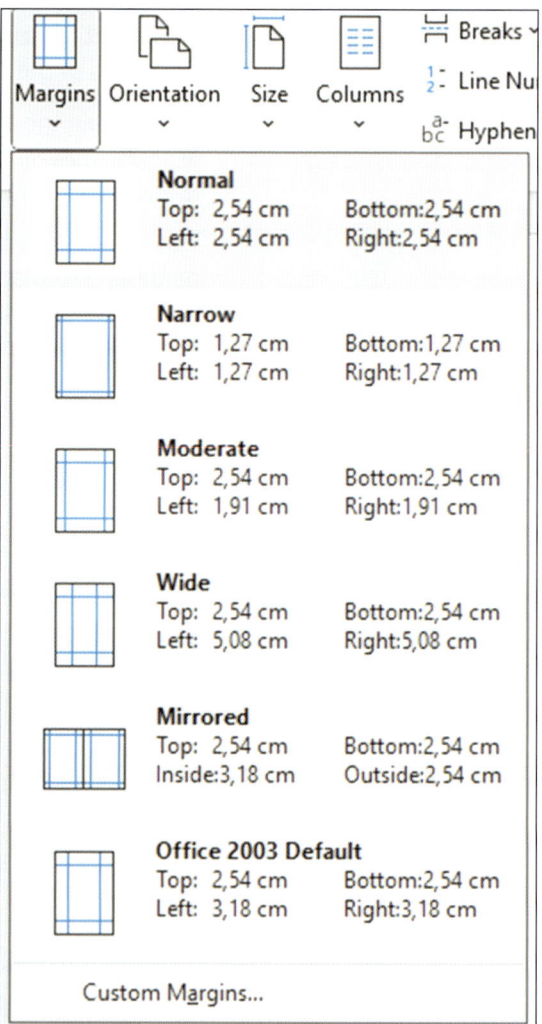

Figure 8.1 Preset margin settings

8 Formatting and editing basics

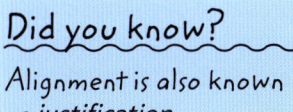

Did you know?
Alignment is also known as justification.

Alignment

The process of aligning text is closely linked to margin placement. *Alignment* identifies where and how texts are placed in relation to the edges of documents.

In Microsoft Word, texts are automatically placed, or aligned, to the left margin. If your customised left margin is 5.08 cm (2 inches), your first text entry will be placed there.

When aligned or not aligned to a particular margin, the edges of text will be displayed in different ways. Table 8.3 includes descriptions of what it means for text to be *aligned* in different ways. Note carefully the position of the text in the cells.

Table 8.3 Alignment

Left-aligned	Text starts at the left margin and moves to the right, showing an uneven right margin.
Right-aligned	Text starts at the left margin and moves to the right; however, the right margin remains even but the left margin is ragged.
Centre-aligned	Text is centred on the page but not at equal distances for every line. This may result in ragged lines at the left and right of the paragraph.
Fully justified	Text is spaced so that it goes completely across from left to right and aligns neatly and evenly within both left and right margins.

The steps to align text are straightforward:

1 On the ribbon of the home tab, look for the 'paragraph' subtab.
2 To the bottom right, observe four sets of four horizontal lines. Through its shape, each icon portrays the type of alignment available (Figure 8.2).

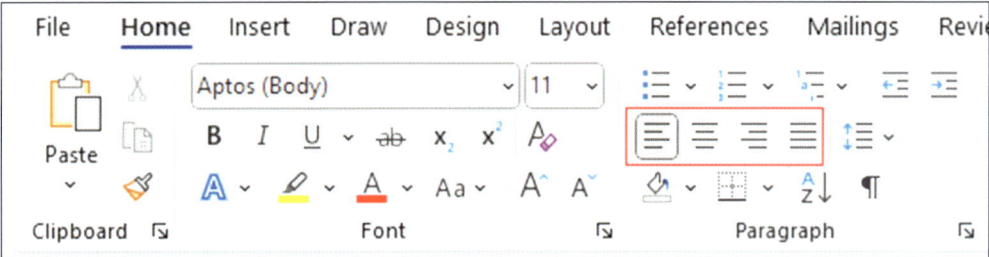

Figure 8.2 Preset alignment options

3 Select the paragraphs you wish to align differently and left-click your mouse.

Line spacing

When lines of text are too close, readability/legibility, the number of characters that can fit on a page and the document's overall appearance are affected.

The paragraph subtab on the home ribbon provides access to the line-spacing tool. When opened, you will find six preset spacing options, ranging from the close 1.0 (single line spacing) to the wide 3.0 (triple line spacing). There are also customisable options available for spacing values in between.

SECTION 3

Did you know?
A manuscript is so called because it was originally a handwritten document. Manu comes from the Latin word *manus*, meaning 'hand'.

✓ Helpful hint
It's a good idea to set your line spacing before preparing your document. Students often prepare their documents in single line spacing and forget to change to double or 1.5, as instructed.

Spacing, indent and block styles are layout options that are used with different types of documents. They will be explained further in Chapter 10.

Line-spacing standards vary with the type of document being prepared. A **manuscript** document, such as a report or essay, may require 1.5 or double line spacing. A **form** may require triple line spacing in some of its sections. As the keyboardist, follow the instructions given in the source document.

There are two ways to adjust line spacing:

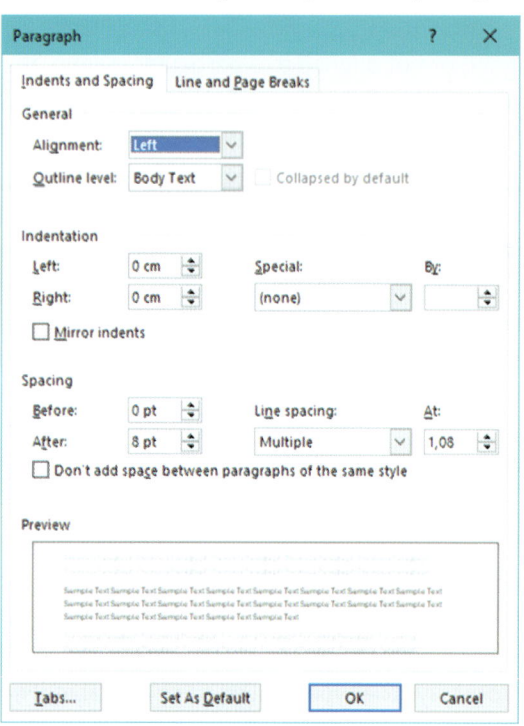

Figure 8.3 Paragraph dropdown box

1 Select the paragraph or page for line-spacing adjustment.
   Go to the home tab on the ribbon and locate the 'paragraph' section (Figure 8.3). Click the icon with the blue double-headed arrow and select your desired line spacing. The selected passage will display the new line spacing.
   Or:
2 Click on the arrow in the right corner of the 'paragraph' subtab and enter information in the 'line spacing' window of the dropdown box.
This second option gives you more precise control of your line spacing in the selected passage.

 **Activity**
1 Under which tab can you find margin options?
2 Under which subtab can you find alignment and line-spacing options?

Font styles

Documents are typed using letter shapes (fonts) of different:

- basic geometrical forms (rounded or squared, with or without tails and flourishes)
- weights (light, regular, bold or extra bold)
- sizes (number of points/pt, usually ranging from 8 pt to 96 pt)
- colours (for visual and emotional impact)
- relations to the vertical (upright or slanted).

Considerations for font style choices

The right choice of font style may need to meet industry standards, enhance the readability of a text, influence how the business is perceived and help with effective communication. Changing the font, the font weight, font size and font colour can be quick and easy, using the mouse and the numerous options on the 'font' subtab on the home tab (Figure 8.4).

> **Did you know?**
> Font psychologists study how individuals react emotionally to the font they see.

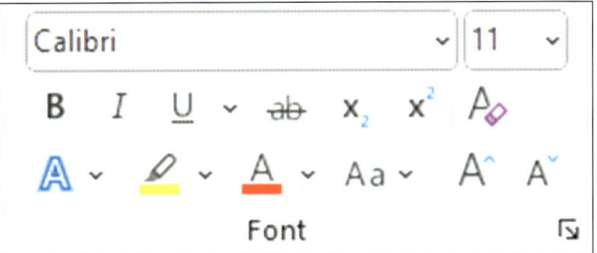

Figure 8.4 Font subtab on home tab

Varying the font

The combination of the five font styles listed above results in a particular font or family of fonts. *Font styles* refers to the choice of a particular font, font family or mix of fonts presented in a document. The names of some fonts that are used regularly in keyboarding assignments are:

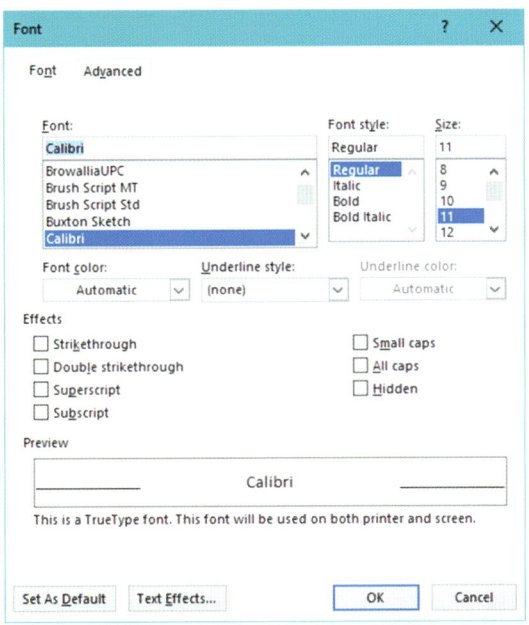

- Calibri – suitable for a wide range of documents
- Times New Roman – used in academic and professional documents
- Garamond – suitable for books, articles and formal documents
- Georgia – works well in both print and digital formats
- Arial – used for digital documents and website design.

Figure 8.5 Font options

> **→ Activity**
>
> What might be the difference in appeal of more rounded letter shapes than those with rigid vertical lines?

To change fonts, follow these steps:

1 Select the words, sentences, paragraphs or pages to change.
2 Go to the home tab on the ribbon and locate the font subtab, where there is a window at the top. This window shows the font in use on the selection. It is often the default option, set beforehand (Figure 8.5).
3 Left-click the arrow and make your choice of font.
4 A right-click anywhere on the document will also allow you access to the font subtab.

SECTION 3

Varying font weight

- Choosing whether to use a lightweight or a heavyweight version of a font depends on the need for emphasis of one or more parts of the message. For example, **headings**, addresses, subject lines and names in a document may be distinguished by heavier font weights. Quotations and numbers might be made more obvious using light font weights.
- Do not use the weighty version of the font (characters in bold) if the amount of space taken up on the page is a consideration.
- Different font weights convey different emotional messages, from the authoritative and formal tone of legal documents to the creative and inviting tone of menus and advertisements.
- **Bold**, *italics* and underline are used for showing differences in emphasis in documents.
    - **Bold** provides a stronger emphasis than *italics*, and may be used in a passage or presentation to emphasise key words, technical terms or actions that someone needs to carry out.
    - *Particular content is often set off from paragraphs by using italicised words;* italicisation is also used to draw attention to a significant word within a sentence or to introduce a section of quoted content.
    - Occasionally, **bold** and *italics* are used together.
    - Underline/underscore is often used for making subject lines and paragraph headings distinct.

There are two methods for varying font weight. The first is connected to the choice of fonts, as many of them have versions with different weights. For example, Arial has the heavyweight Arial Black form and the Arial Narrow version. The second method is to:

1. select the words, sentences, paragraphs or pages that will be changed
2. go to the home tab on the ribbon and locate the tabs labelled **B** and *I*
3. choose the one that provides the desired weight.
4. note that, in addition, you are able to underline key words and phrases.

Varying font size

- Choosing the right font size depends on the document's purpose, design, reader, medium and content. For text within the body of a document, most fonts can be read easily at 10–12 point size, while for headings it may need to be bigger (14–24 points).
- Placement within the typing space also affects size choice. Covering a graphic with large-size fonts might reduce its usefulness and visual appeal.
- A larger font size is needed for notices intended to be placed on notice boards and for visually impaired readers, while small fonts can be read up close on smartphones and tablets. However, some fonts, for example script fonts, are difficult to read at smaller sizes but are useful for certain jobs, such as inserting e-signatures.

> **Did you know?**
>
> It is worth remembering that 'less is more' when it comes to formatting. For example, you don't need bold, italic, capitalisation AND underline to make your point!

> **Did you know?**
>
> A font size chart displays the various sizes of fonts in relation to each other. It also helps to determine the best font size for the intended purpose and readers.

 **Activity**

What are e-signatures?

Varying font colour

Choosing the right colour combinations is an important skill. Colour can be used to organise and spotlight a message; convey, or evoke, positive or negative emotions; increase interest and appeal; or distract from the intended message.

Changing the font colour can be quick and easy, using these steps:

1 Select the words, sentences, paragraphs or pages that will be changed.
2 Go to the home tab on the ribbon and locate the 'font' subtab.
3 Click the icon with the uppercase A and a bar of colour below it.
4 Select your desired text colour.

Varying all aspects of font styles at once

It is possible to make several changes on the same selected passage via one menu: Click on the arrow in the right corner of the font subtab and enter information in the differently labelled windows of the dropdown box. This menu gives you access to all the individual options for font weight, size and other text effects.

Highlighting and text effects

There are several more features available in the font subtab, for example placing a colour over selected text to highlight it in a passage. If you wish to remove or change the highlight colour, select the text and click again.

There are also ways to place special effects on the text to change its appearance. The outlined blue A to the left of the highlight button provides access to shadow, reflective or glow effects that make work stand out on special documents such as invitations, posters and flyers. Take some time to explore what is available.

Numbering, bulleting and sorting

Many business documents contain items that are best displayed as a list (Figure 8.6). For example, when describing a process to be followed, the steps should be set out so that people can identify the order to follow. It is advisable to use numbers.

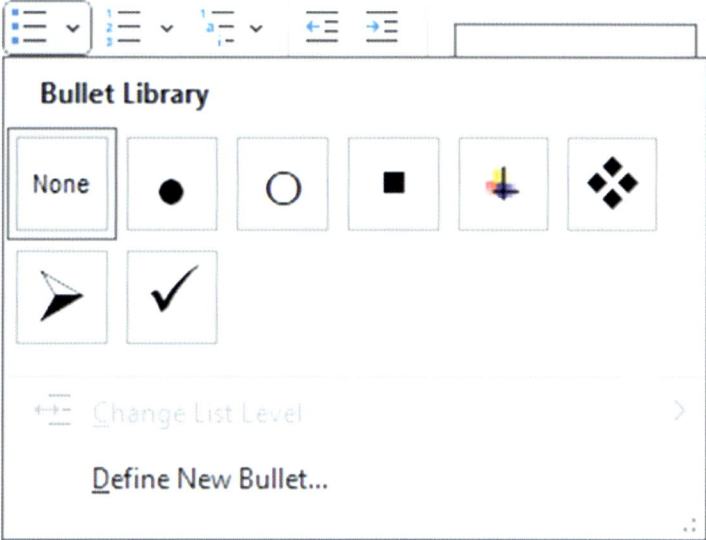

Figure 8.6 Bullets and numbering dialog boxes

However, if the order does not matter, then bullets can be substituted. For example, if the features of a new model smartphone are listed, it would be advisable to use bullets.

Numbering

To use a numbering format, select the items to be listed and click on the icon showing tiny numbers on the top line of the paragraph subtab on the home tab, then choose any one of the options available in the numbering library. If the list requires that some numbered data is expanded to include an additional list (*nested list*), select the subordinate data and click on the 'document numbering' format using a different style than the main number format. Have a look at this example:

1 Mix the dry ingredients together.
2 Mix the wet ingredients together.
3 Add the wet ingredients to the dry ingredients slowly while stirring.
   a Do not add the dry ingredients to the wet ingredients.
   b Make sure that you are stirring constantly.
4 Place the mixture in a greased container.
5 Refrigerate for two hours.

Note that more complex numbering formats are available in the icon on the right of the simple numbering system (Figure 8.7). These formats are useful for legal documents and reports that have to display a great deal of main texts and subtexts.

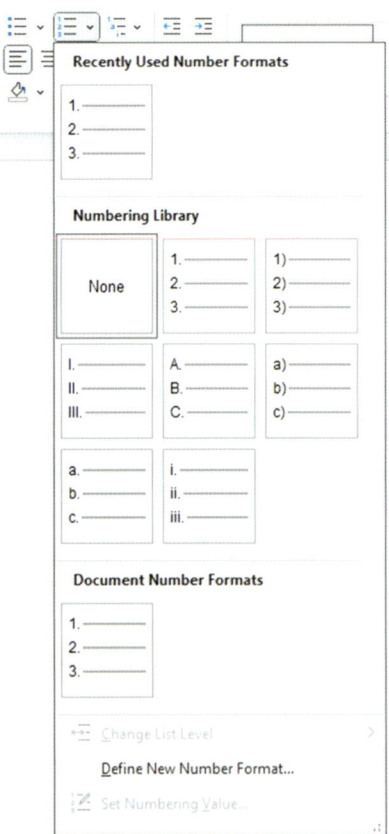

Figure 8.7 Extended numbering options

→ Activity

Other than Arabic numbers (1, 2, 3 …), name *two* other numeral systems.

Bulleting

The process of using bullets is very similar to the process of using numbers, except that the icon on the same top line of the paragraph subtab shows tiny black circles. When opened, the bullets dialog box shows circles as the default and most popular bullet shape. There is a limited choice of bullets, including the familiar tick. However, you can create your own bullet shape by using the 'define new bullet' option.

Explore the options available, including being able to bullet or number within the main body of text by selecting and choosing your bullet or number style (Figure 8.8).

Sorting

When a list is long, it might be a good idea to have it arranged in some order. The default 'sort' command is in descending alphabetical order (A–Z) but the data could also be sorted in ascending order (Z–A). This facility can be found at the top right of the paragraph subtab.

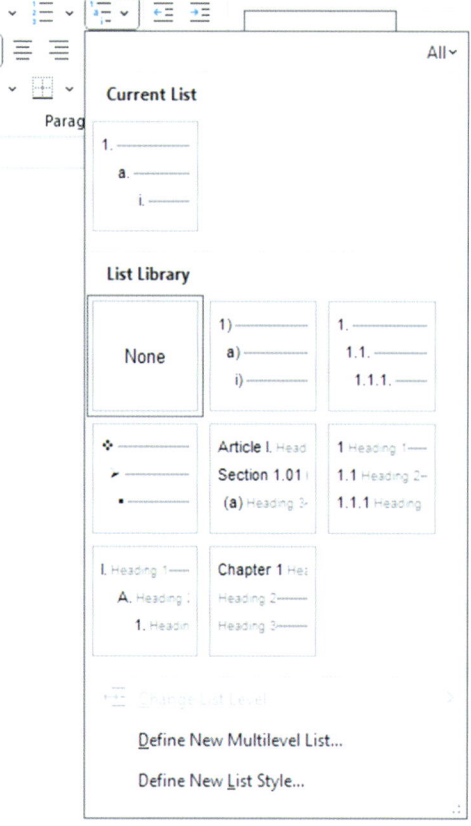

Figure 8.8 Custom-made bullets

Headings

Headings indicate to the reader the main subject matter of a passage of text. They are located at the start of the passage to which they refer, but differ in font size, in the use of capitalisation and in alignment (Table 8.4). There are standard heading arrangements set out by academic institutions, but organisations may have their own customised styles.

Table 8.4 Types of heading

Heading	Description	Example
Main	<ul><li>Provides the main idea of the whole document in a few words</li><li>Located at the start of the document in the centre or left margin</li><li>May be in a larger font size than the rest of the document, bolded to show emphasis, and may be spaced (separated letters)</li></ul>	**OFFICE ORIENTATION** (centre-aligned) or **OFFICE ORIENTATION** (**left-aligned** and spaced)

SECTION 3

Sub	<ul><li>Provides a more specific idea about the subject of the document</li><li>Located below the main heading, may use a smaller font size, and initial letters only in uppercase (the first letter of each word is a capital letter)</li><li>May be left- or centre-aligned</li></ul>	**OFFICE ADMINISTRATION**
		(main: **left-aligned**)
		    TYPES OF OFFICE LAYOUT
		    (sub: **centre-aligned**)

Shoulder	<ul><li>Provides an idea of the topic discussed in a section of the document</li><li>Located above the paragraph text, left-aligned but set two spaces in from the section start</li><li>May be set out in uppercase letters or initial capitals and underscored</li></ul>	2 spaces in **Open Plan Office Layout** With no separators between workstations, only furniture might provide some privacy and define your particular space.
Paragraph	<ul><li>Provides an idea of the topic discussed in a section/paragraph of the document</li><li>Located in line with the text but separated by a full stop or colon</li><li>Set out with initial capitals</li></ul>	Open Plan Office Layout: With no separators between workstations, only furniture might provide some privacy and define your particular space.
Marginal or side	<ul><li>Aligned at the left margin, but the paragraph is kept within a section to the right side of the page</li><li>Set out with initial capitals</li><li>Used in the preparation of programmes, plays, minutes of meetings, itineraries and similar documents</li></ul>	Open Plan Office Layout With no separators between workstations, only furniture might provide some privacy and define your particular space.
Column and row	<ul><li>Used in tables</li><li>Identifies titles or labels that categorise all the entries in a particular column</li><li>Usually centred in the top cell of the column and emboldened</li><li>May be overseen by a compound heading in merged cells</li></ul>	column <table><tr><td colspan="3">**BASIC NEEDS**</td></tr><tr><td></td><td>**Col 1**</td><td>**Col 2**</td></tr><tr><td>**Foods**</td><td>Meats</td><td>Vegetables</td></tr><tr><td>**Clothing**</td><td>Outer</td><td>Under</td></tr><tr><td>**Shelter**</td><td>Permanent</td><td>Temporary</td></tr></table>row

Borders and shading

Text borders, page borders and shading

Inserting **borders** around areas containing special text within a page or across a whole page is a useful way of emphasising parts of the content. Shading also adds colour and depth to text, and is even more attractive than highlighting. Documents for public use, such as flyers and newsletters, and for employment purposes such as certificates and resumes, are enhanced with the use of borders of different thicknesses and patterns. However, choose carefully from the wide variety of colours that can be used for shading.

Helpful hint

The options for font choices, borders and shading are also available in the 'design' tab on the Word ribbon.

Too much colour may not be regarded as professional for business documents. The process of adding borders or shading is:

1 Select the text around which the border or shading will be placed.
2 Select the paragraph subtab and look on the bottom row for the relevant icon.
3 The border icon dropdown box provides the range of possible border placement, for example left only, right only, inside only or all borders (on every side and inside).
4 The shading icon dropdown box provides options for many colours and shades for your consideration.

To remove borders or shading is just as easy as applying them. Select the text or page with the unwanted border or shading and choose the 'no border' or 'no shading option' from the dropdown box.

Key terms

alignment Where and how texts are placed in relation to the edges of a page

bold A stronger emphasis than *italics*; may be used to emphasise key words, technical terms or action items in a passage or presentation

borders Lines of different thicknesses and patterns placed around selected text to add visual appeal or to indicate importance

bulleting A tool to manage lists of items, points or other content using a non-sequential method

centre-aligned Text centred on a page, but not at equal distances for every line, which may result in ragged lines at the left and right of the paragraph

font A form of writing of different geometrical shapes, sizes, weights and slants from the vertical

formatting The use of tools to organise the layout and appearance of characters, sentences, paragraphs or the whole of a document

fully justified Text spaced so that it goes completely across from left to right of a document and aligns neatly and evenly within both left and right margins

heading Indicates the main subject matter of a passage, located at the start of the text it refers to; differs in font size, use of capitalisation, and alignment from the page margin

highlighting Emphasising parts of content by adding a colour, shadow, reflection or glow to selected words or phrases

insertion Formatting feature that includes pre-keyed text, page numbers, headers and footers, breaks and links

italics Emphasis used to draw attention to a significant word within a sentence or to introduce a section of quoted content

landscape orientation When the longer side of the page runs horizontally and the slightly shorter side runs vertically

left-aligned Text starts at the left margin and moves to the right, resulting in an uneven right margin

line spacing The function that separates lines of text for reading purposes, preset to range from single line spacing to triple line spacing

manuscript A text-filled document, which used to be written by hand

margins The clear spaces around the text and graphics in a document; they control the length of lines of text and prevent run-off text at either edge of the page

naming convention The process, used consistently, to name a file or folder before first save, using a brief descriptive word or phrase, date of creation or modification based on a standard format and version numbers where relevant

numbering A way of ordering a list when the order of things in the list should be followed, for example, instructions

SECTION 3

> **page set-up** A category of functions and tools, such as page size and orientation, line spacing, margin alignment, font styles, which are provided as defaults and options for document formatting
> **portrait orientation** When the shorter side of the page runs horizontally and the slightly longer side runs vertically
> **right-aligned** Text starts at the left margin and moves to the right; the right margin remains even but the left margin is ragged
> **shading** Emphasising parts of content by adding a colour, shadow, reflection or glow to selected words or phrases in a more attractive way than simply highlighting
> **sorting** Arranging a list in order according to particular criteria, such as alphabetically
> **special effect** A way to change a text's appearance, such as shadow, reflective or glow effects
> **underline** Emphasis, often used for making subject lines and paragraph headings distinct; also called *underscore*

🏠 Summary

In this chapter, you have learned how to:

- make formatting decisions about the appearance of a document before and after keying in its content
- choose margins, line spacing and font style in your initial page set-up decisions
- consider enhancements, such as highlighting and text effects, numbering, bulleting, sorting, borders and shading
- name and save your file as early as possible for later retrieval and further adjustments.

Practice, research and exam-style questions

Multiple-choice questions

1. Which of these terms is *not* a commonly used font?
   - A Calibri
   - B Stencil
   - C Arial
   - D Times New Roman

2. Which alignment type results in *no* ragged edges?
   - A Centre-aligned
   - B Fully justified
   - C Left-aligned
   - D Right-aligned

3. Which of these statements is *true*?
   - A Using the bold icon adds weight to a font
   - B Mixing font sizes refers to words with uppercase and lowercase letters
   - C Colourful fonts are not allowed in any business document
   - D No word should be both underlined and emboldened

4. Which of these instructions is *not* doable?
   - A Heading – Arial Black
   - B Text body – align right
   - C Passage – from 12 pt to 14 pt
   - D Word list – scramble

5. Which of these documents is *most* likely to use a 3.0 line spacing?
   - A Dissertation
   - B Survey form
   - C Formal letter
   - D Cash register receipt

6. A good reason to use minimum line spacing is the …
   - A page count.
   - B legibility.
   - C font style.
   - D clarity.

7   Numbers would be preferred to bullets when it is important to …
    A use a variety of font sizes.
    B display customisation skills.
    C insist on confidentiality.
    D encourage a step-by-step approach.

8   Complete this sentence with the correct phrase: A word-processing application does not allow the use of […] in a file name.
    A a forward slash
    B capital letters
    C an underscore
    D a hyphen

9   Which of these options is *not* a type of header?
    A Paragraph
    B Shoulder
    C Roman
    D Margin

10 Which of these actions is *not* a formatting activity?
    A Putting in borders
    B Finding word repetitions
    C Changing paper orientation
    D Making font style choices

Short-answer questions

1   Complete the sentences by selecting the appropriate word from the 'Key terms' list for this chapter.
    a *Portrait* and *landscape* are the two page […] options.
    b […] is used when there are process steps to follow for best results.
    c A page with […] […] alignment looks more professional as there are no ragged edges to the text.
    d Firms should establish and promote a proper […] […] for saving files.
    e A […] is more likely to need varying line spaces.

2   You have received the source document below with these instructions:
    a Retype the letter using a 5.08 cm (2 inch) margin on the left edge of the page and a 2.54 cm (1 inch) margin on all other edges.
    i   Right-align the name and address of the potential customer.
    ii   Left-align the date, the greeting and the body of the letter.
    iii Centre-align the closing 'Yours sincerely', put the name in uppercase letters and use a script font on an e-signature.
    b Change the font from the (default) font on the screen to Garamond 14 pt.
    c Use double line spacing in the body of the letter.
    d Use a colour on the words 'premium package'.
    e Bold the name and address of the resort.
    f Put a double underline under the cost of the reservation.
    g Reduce the font size of the sentence below the signature to 10 pt.
    h Name the file 'Premium Package 2', save and close.

Frella Dobbs
LP #3 Torarica Road
San Cruz
Suriname
14 September 2026
Dear Mrs Dobbs

Thank you for your interest in the premium package offer from La Fancy Resorts, Paramaribo. The total cost for your family of five is US$2200 for 4 days and 5 nights and includes breakfast and dinner. (This cost does not include expenses associated with your choice of activity.) Please find at www.funinsun.com a list of 13 activities that are suitable for families. We await your confirmation of a reservation with a deposit of 50% of the amount quoted.

Yours sincerely

Judith Frurell

Customer representative

La Fancy Resorts reserve the right to refuse acceptance of requests for booking without the payment of 50% of the amount quoted at least 7 days before guest arrival.

9 Advanced formatting, editing and proofreading

> **Objectives**
>
> By the end of this chapter, you will be able to:
>
> - identify advanced formatting tools
> - apply advanced formatting tools to common business documents
> - apply proofreading techniques to create a mailable document
> - apply advanced editing tools to common business documents and manuscripts.

Introduction

In this chapter, you will use advanced formatting tools. These tools focus on inserting into documents additional information such as **page numbering**, **headers** and **footers**, **footnotes** and **endnotes**, **symbols**, **text boxes**, objects and pre-keyed material. Also included are security elements such as **background** and **watermarks**, and **breaks** and **links**. However, the more elements that are added to a document, the greater the need for *proofreading* and *editing*. This is especially important when applied to correcting manuscripts. In addition, familiarity with standard abbreviations is essential for transforming drafts into mailable versions.

Page numbering

Page numbers help to locate a particular page in a document easily. They are printed on most of the pages, providing an order or sequence that can be used as a reference. Often, page numbers are placed at the bottom centre of the page, but they can be located at the top, right, left or side of the page. It all depends on the style chosen by the author. Page numbers may be inserted using the common Arabic form (1, 2, 3, 4) or Roman numerals (i, ii, iii, iv). There is also the option to add simple design features to add interest to the page.

To enter page numbers in a Microsoft Word document:

1. Click the insert tab on the ribbon.
2. Go to the header & footer subtab.
3. Click the down arrow next to 'page number' (Figure 9.1).
4. Select where you wish to place your page number.

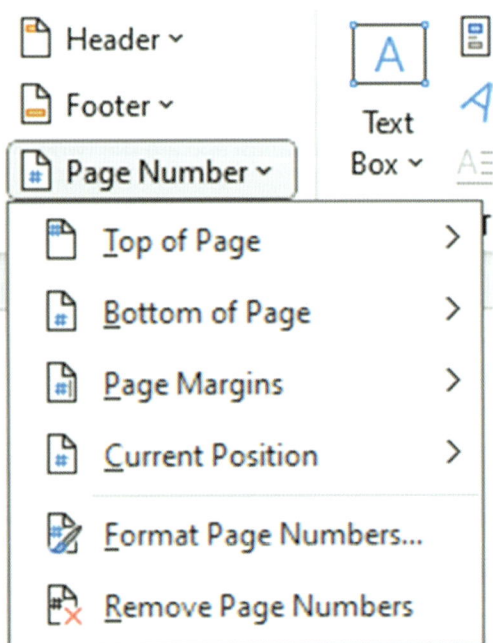

Figure 9.1 Preset page numbering positions and design

9 Advanced formatting, editing and proofreading

If you wish, you can vary the amount of information to be included, such as the word 'Page' or 'Chapter'. You may click on 'remove page numbers' in the same menu, as needed.

Headers and footers

Headers are not the same as headings. Headers are created to include information such as the title, name and page numbers on every page of a document except (in most cases) on the cover page and the front and back covers of a book or report. When a header is created, whatever is to be included is generally repeated in the same location throughout the document.

Letterheads may also be created using the header tool. In this case, it may include the company's logo as well as useful information such as the company's name, address and contact information.

Footers utilise the same process and are found in the same subtab on the insert menu.

These are the steps to create a header or footer:

1 Click the down arrow next to either 'header' or 'footer', depending on what you want to include (Figure 9.2).
2 Click on the down arrow to select the type of header or footer to use.
3 Fill in the information for the header or footer.
4 Close the header and footer when you are finished.

You will learn more about letterheads in Chapter 10.

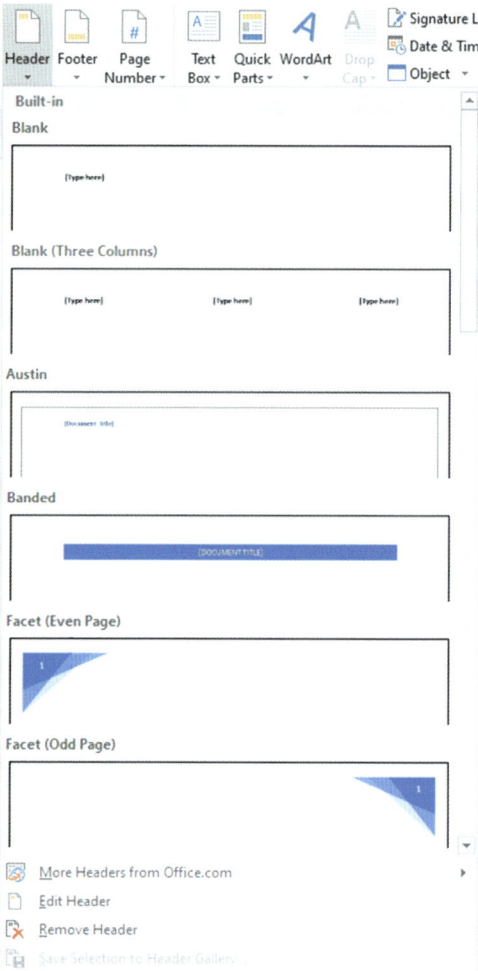
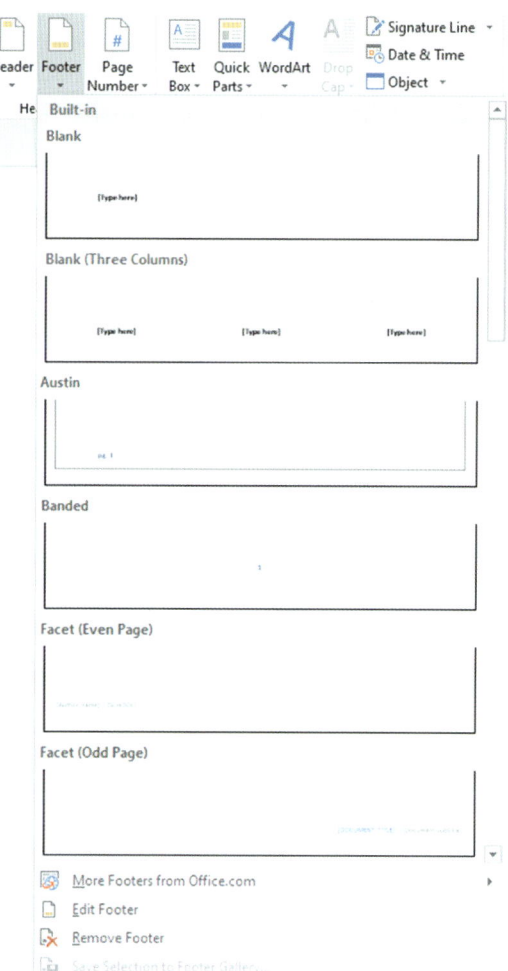

Figure 9.2 Header and footer options

The text of the header or footer will appear on the page and all subsequent pages. If you wish to amend the header or footer, double-click in the header or footer space and proceed as above.

Footnotes and endnotes

Footnotes are more detailed footers. They consist of one or more short notes placed at the bottom of pages in academic papers, journals and technical reports. These notes provide additional information, explanations, comments and citations related to specific points in the main text. The reader is alerted to the relevant and specific information by the placement of a number within the text, with its corresponding number in the footnote.

Endnotes are like footnotes but, rather than appearing at the foot of the page, they are placed at the end of a section, chapter, article, research paper, report or book, on a separate page. Both footnotes and endnotes are linked to the relevant additional text by numbers in superscript. Organisations usually have a style guide on the use of footnotes and endnotes.

The steps to insert a footnote or endnote are as follows:

1. Position your cursor where you want the footnote reference number or endnote reference number to appear in the main text.
2. Click on the references tab on the Word ribbon.
3. Click 'insert footnote' or 'insert endnote': Word will automatically insert a superscript number and create a footnote section at the bottom of the page where you can type your note, *or* create an endnote in the empty space at the end of your text.
4. To create a subsequent footnote, use the 'next footnote' dropdown arrow and proceed. (The default formatting style for Word does not cater for endnotes.)
5. To edit a footnote, simply click on the footnote and make the changes.
6. To remove a footnote, right-click the 'footnote reference number' in the main text and select 'remove footnote'. Both the number and the text will disappear.

> **Activity**
>
> Can a writer include both footnotes and endnotes in a document?

> **Activity**
>
> Name **two** writing style guides used for academic papers.

> **Did you know?**
>
> When a character is shown in a very small font size and placed above the script or line of the main text, it is called a *superscript*, for example . This effect is one of the options available in the font subtab dropdown box.

Symbols, text boxes and objects

The insert tab has subtabs to enable you to insert tables, illustrations, media, links and symbols. Many of the menu items in the subtabs have their own dropdown boxes that provide additional options. All of these are accessible with the mouse. In this chapter, you will learn how to insert pre-keyed text, symbols and text boxes. Spend some time exploring the many other menu options.

Symbols

There are many special symbols that exist other than the commonly used ones that appear on the keyboard. Those can be accessed using the shift keys, as shown in Chapter 8. The 'symbol' menu provides numerous other symbols that are useful for specialised documents, such as articles in a mathematics journal.

Insertions of graphics is discussed in more detail in Chapter 16.

The steps to insert a symbol are as follows:

1. Place your insertion point where you wish to insert your symbol.
2. To access the symbol dialog box, click on 'insert' on the ribbon.
3. Move all the way to the right of the ribbon, and you will see the symbol menu.
4. Select 'symbol' or choose 'more symbols' (Figure 9.3).
5. Click on your desired symbol.
6. Close the symbol subtab.

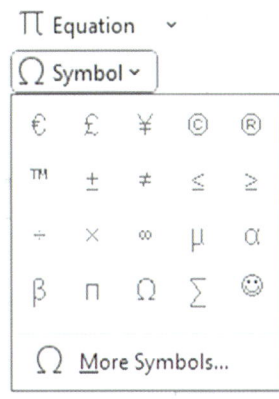

Figure 9.3 Symbol dialog box

Text boxes and other objects

You may occasionally need to insert or embed text, a graphic, or image within the main text. Placing it within a *text box* will make it more prominent. Although there are six types of default text boxes available, the 'simple text box' is the easiest to use. The steps to enter a text box into your documents are as follows:

1. Place your insertion point where the text box should appear.
2. Click on the insert tab and go to the text subtab.
3. Click on 'text box' and choose the most appropriate one. A rectangle will appear on your page, with control buttons for making it bigger or smaller.
4. Type or paste your text or image into the text box.

You can also draw a text box to the size you want. This also allows you greater control when there is limited space in the main text.

Note that if the insertion point is in the middle of text, or close to it, the text box will separate the main text and wrap it around itself, so press 'enter' at least once before or after the main text that will remain outside the text box.

> **Helpful hint**
>
> If you want to remove the text box, make sure the cursor is on one of the sides before deleting or cutting. If the cursor is inside the box, only the text will be removed.

> **Helpful hint**
>
> If you wish to place an object such as a picture or graph, a one row by one column table is better.

Backgrounds and watermarks

Backgrounds and watermarks are images or texts that appear behind the text of a document. *Backgrounds* help to add visual appeal, and emphasise the theme of the document. *Watermarks* act as identifying marks, so some companies use their logos as a watermark, while others use their company name. Watermarks also provide some security to work by adding 'Confidential' or 'Urgent' or another phrase behind the main text. They also go some way towards protecting documents from being copied without permission or acknowledgement.

Backgrounds

Backgrounds allow you to be creative, as you can use different colours, fonts, effects and even a picture to make your documents distinctive. Once you have developed a combination that you like, you can add it to 'styles' as a custom background. You can even make it the default background for all subsequent documents. Note that inserting a background affects your whole document; not just the current page. Ensure that your choice of colours (subtle rather than bright), font weights, font sizes, pictures and text effects for your background do not detract from your main text or reduce its legibility.

SECTION 3

The steps to insert a background are as follows:

1 Open your Word document.
2 Click on the 'design' tab and go to the 'page background' subtab.
3 Click on 'page colour' and apply your preferred colour.
4 Select 'fill effects' to choose gradient, texture, pattern or picture from the dialog box.
5 Save your document.

Watermarks

While watermarks are less obtrusive than backgrounds, they are more limited in terms of choice but are a better option for professional work. Watermarks can be embedded in a document as text or images, such as a logo, pictures and other symbols. Watermarks are often placed on currency notes, long legal documents and reports as they are effective in preventing counterfeiting.

The steps to create a *text watermark* are a slight variation from creating a *picture watermark*, but they both start with steps 1–3:

1 Open your Word document.
2 Click on the design tab.
3 Under the 'page background' menu, go to 'watermark'.

For text watermarks:

4 Use the side bar along the watermark dialog box to choose from several common terms and phrases, such as DRAFT or DO NOT COPY.
5 Click on 'custom watermark' to create your own design.
6 Select 'printed watermark' and choose your language, words, font, font size and font colour. The 'layout' option allows you to place your watermark in either a horizontal or diagonal position on the page.

For picture watermarks:

4 Click on 'custom watermark' and choose 'picture watermark'.
5 Find a picture from your personal picture directory, your Microsoft OneDrive cloud storage or search for an image online.
6 Choose the picture you want and select 'insert'.

> **Did you know?**
> Watermarks can be removed from original/source documents, therefore typing over watermarked documents is unethical.

Activity

Should backgrounds and watermarks be visually appealing? Justify your answer.

Breaks

Use the 'breaks' menu on the layout tab and page set-up subtab when working with text, tables, columns, images and objects within one document with multiple pages. You may need to control the flow of text from one page to another as your default line spacing may interrupt a smooth flow. If you simply keep using the enter button, the problem will only be fixed temporarily. Once new material is added or deleted below, the problem reoccurs or even worsens. Word offers options such as page breaks, column breaks, wrap text breaks and section breaks to remove or prevent these issues. Table 9.1 shows some examples of situations where inserting breaks is useful.

9 Advanced formatting, editing and proofreading

Table 9.1 Inserting breaks

Text layout issue	Solution
The title of an image or the first line of a paragraph is cut off	*Page break* to put complementary text together
One term in a list of terms must be placed in the next column over	*Column break* above the term to be moved
The text surrounding an image or object has different purposes and formats from the image	*Text wrapping break* to enable recognition of the differences
A paragraph is shown as part of a column of terms, and formatting needs to be different	*Page break* to move the paragraph and enable editing tools *Section break* where passages are long
A table, text box or object needs more space to hold data than is available in portrait view	*Section break* before and after to enable landscape orientation and return to portrait view as necessary

This is an example of steps to follow to access break functions:

1 Place the insertion point to the left of the beginning of the second paragraph.
2 Click on the layout tab, and the breaks menu at the top right of the page set-up subtab.
3 Click on either 'next page' or 'continuous page' under the section break, either to move all text to the next page or to place a break between two paragraphs.
4 Go to the end of the table, object or passage and create another section break to enable a return to a previously formatted document.

These steps will be discussed again when you create business and special documents in the coming chapters.

 Activity

What are the results if you choose 'even page' or 'odd page' under 'section break' when separating passages of text?

Links

You may not be able to fit all the information on a topic into one document. Linking a word or phrase to another source of information is an efficient way of expanding the knowledge base. Several software applications offer ways to link complementary material using hyperlinks if the additional information is in another file, application, website or email contact list. If the material is in another part of the same document, use the insert tab (with its links subtab) to place a link within your current document.

Proofreading

Proofreading is a process that attempts to achieve the production of mailable documents that are free from spelling, grammar, punctuation and formatting errors. This process is carried out by reviewing each line of the document, looking for errors and ensuring corrections are made *before* sending out the final document.

A document that has been proofread (so there are no errors) gives an impression of high standards and professionalism. Note that formatting choices are treated as errors when they do not follow standard rules. When errors are discovered, the text must be edited. Word provides several ways, including shortcuts, to accomplish this task.

The editing tools for correcting spelling, grammar and repetition errors are explained below.

Spelling and grammar check

Spelling

Microsoft Word has a built-in English language dictionary based on US spellings. The spell **check** function automatically checks your spelling against the dictionary while you type. A broken red line appears under any word spelled incorrectly according to the dictionary. Names that Word does not recognise are also red-lined. If you right-click on the red-lined word, the following options are presented:

- **Ignore:** If you wish to ignore a spell-checked word, click this button and Word will remove the red line for that particular word where it is placed, but it will be red-lined again if it appears in another part of the document.
- **Ignore all:** This option removes the red line wherever the 'misspelled' word appears.
- **Add to dictionary:** This option allows you to add a red-lined word to the Microsoft dictionary. The added word will no longer be red-lined as a misspelled word.
- **Change:** The Microsoft dictionary usually suggests a correct version, and changes the misspelled word if this option is chosen.
- **Change all:** This option changes all instances of the same misspelled word; not just the first one.
- **AutoCorrect:** If you choose one of the suggestions, Word adds an entry to AutoCorrect that will automatically fix this spelling mistake in the future.

> **Did you know?**
> There are ways to amend your spell check, as some ways to spell words in United Kingdom (UK) English are different from United States (US) English.

Grammar

Grammatical errors include poor subject–verb agreement, double negatives and poorly constructed sentences. A green line appears under words or sentences as an alert to the writer.

A double blue line appears under the areas thought to be questionable, for example where words are spelled accurately but incorrectly used; where there is inappropriate capitalisation; or where there is unnecessary spacing between words. You must decide whether to ignore the alert or make a change.

> **Did you know?**
> Word will place red lines under words used in your country's dialect, abbreviations and slang words.

Synonym and thesaurus

You can enhance a piece of writing by using a varied vocabulary. Try to avoid repetition, that is, using identical words every time for the same idea. Right-click on the repeated word and find 'synonym' as an option in the menu. The synonym menu presents several suggestions as alternative words for use. Note that not all the suggestions are suitable for the purpose; your knowledge of vocabulary will help you to make a good choice.

If the synonym button has no suggestions or the suggestions are unacceptable, access the 'thesaurus' feature. A thesaurus is a special dictionary that categorises words similar in meaning. In some cases, a thesaurus suggests antonyms (words opposite in meaning). Note that the Thesaurus button is available in the Synonym dropdown box.

9 Advanced formatting, editing and proofreading

>  **Activity**
>
> Find **5** words suggested as synonyms by the thesaurus for the term 'unacceptable'.

Proofreading marks

When a text is proofread, there are special symbols that act as a shortcut to explain the changes that are required. You may be presented with a marked-up manuscript for you to take in the corrections to the electronic version, or you may be required to proofread and mark up a document yourself. Table 9.2 explains the marks to use.

Table 9.2 Manuscript correction signs

Name of sign	Meaning	Example	Correction
Stet: 'let it stand' ✓	A previous correction to be ignored and the original words should be retained	Refreshments were ~~going~~ to be served at noon. stet	Refreshments were going to be served at noon
	The sentence has a wrong or unnecessary word; retain others	He was overdone and overbearing	He was overbearing
Run on:	Continue the new sentence in the same paragraph	Phillip felt a hatred towards Raine. He was overbearing.	Phillip felt a hatred towards Raine. He was overbearing.
Lowercase: l.c. underline	The underlined or stroked word should not be capitalised; show in lowercase only	The Word should be lc Capitalised. lc	The word should not be capitalised
Uppercase: u.c. underline	The underlined word should be capitalised/shown in uppercase	The word should be UC capitalised	The Word should be capitalised
New paragraph: NP, * or // or ⌐	Start a new paragraph from that point in the text	Phillip felt a hatred towards Raine. *Raine's overbearing ways meant that he could not do as he wanted with his own money	Phillip felt a hatred towards Raine. Raine's overbearing ways meant that he could not do as he wanted with his own money
Indent ⌐ Or **move to the left** ←	Request to indent line to the right or move line to the left	⌐Phillip felt a hatred towards Raine. ← Phillip felt a hatred towards Raine.	Phillip felt a hatred towards Raine. Phillip felt a hatred towards Raine.

SECTION 3

Mark	Meaning	Example	Result

Line up (align):
• Horizontally: line above and below
    very
• Vertically: place one on top of the other
    Happy birthday
	Handwritten words to be lined up next to each other or placed on top of each other, as required	The day is _____ and calm
		    cool
		
		Happy birthday
			The day is cool and calm
			
			Happy
			birthday

Start text lower on the page: **Move text up:**	Place the next set of text at a lower point than its current place Place the next set of text at a higher point than its current place	My poor results should show my lower place on the class roster. I am due to move up on the class roster.	My poor results should show my lower place on the class roster. I am due to move up on the class roster.
Insert: followed by characters, words or punctuation	Insert missing words, punctuation or special characters	The position of some students on the class roster, for Aaliyah and Samara gives a poor representation of their abilities keep trying everyone!	The position of some students on the class roster, for example Aaliyah and Samara, gives a poor representation of their abilities; keep trying everyone!
Delete:	Delete text that has a stroke through it	Say it again again!	Say it again!

Transpose:
horizontally 'trs 1–2'
or
vertically 'trs1–2'
	Shift words or numbers to a new position in the line or listing	That bottom and top go together nicely.
		
		    Able
		    Damus
		    Beta
		    Coro
			That top and bottom go together nicely.
			
			    Able
			    Beta
			    Coro
			    Damus

Initial caps: ini caps	Capitalise first letter of each word in text	Do not litter	Do Not Litter
Closed caps: cl. caps/closed caps	Remove spaces between letters in capitalised words	cl caps WEST FIELD COMPLEX will be on the letterhead.	WESTFIELD COMPLEX will be on the letterhead.
Spaced caps: sp. caps/ spaced caps	Leave a space between each letter in the underlined words and put each letter in uppercase and leave three spaces between words	sp caps Westfield Complex will be on the letterhead.	W E S T F I E L D C O M P L E X will be on the letterhead.
Close up: close	Remove the space at the point indicated	The girl was crying with tiredness.	The girl was crying with tiredness.

Insert space: here #	Insert a space at the point underlined	The girl was crying with#tiredness.	The girl was crying with tiredness.
Move the section in the balloon to the position indicated: (who entered)	Indicates the correct placement of an omitted or misplaced phrase	(, who entered,) The girl was crying with tiredness.	The girl, who entered, was crying with tiredness.

Editing techniques

Editing text means both manipulating text and making corrections in a manner that would lead to a desired end result. This process may include inserting additional material; deleting words and images; and cutting, copying, pasting, moving, finding and replacing text in a document. Microsoft Word provides more than one way of carrying out these actions, including the use of the function keys and a modifier key (see Chapter 6). The steps and shortcuts to use these editing techniques are described in the next few sections.

Add and delete

Adding/insert

There are times when you may need to add text to an already processed document. One step-by-step process for adding text requires that you:

1. Click on the folder icon on the taskbar at the bottom of the monitor.
2. Find the directory that holds the document to be amended.
3. Open the appropriate Word document (using the name under which it was saved).
4. Click where you want to insert text.
5. Start typing; text to the right of the cursor will move as the document is edited.

Deleting/overtyping

Deleting text may be required to correct work or to remove material from a previously typed document. The steps vary in accordance with the extent of characters that are to be deleted.

Minimal characters:

1. Place the cursor to the left of the few characters or words you wish to delete.
2. Press the delete key, close to the top right of the keyboard. Any character, letter or symbol will be removed.

Paragraphs:

1. Highlight the paragraph by left-clicking with the mouse and dragging until you have covered the information you wish to delete.
2. Click the delete key.

SECTION 3

Large collections of paragraphs or whole documents:

1 For deleting a complete document, use the 'select' button on the home tab; note the options.
2 Choose the appropriate option, for example 'select all', to highlight the entire document.
3 Click the delete key.

Overtyping

Alternatively, you can use **overtype** mode to delete/erase words to the right of the cursor while typing the new words. There are two ways to access the overtype mode. After placing your insertion point to the left of the words to be erased, press the *insert* key on the keyboard (located to the right of the top row of keys) and begin to type. Be sure you know when to stop, and press the insert key again.

The second way to access the overtype mode:

1 Select the file tab on the ribbon.
2 Select the options subtab (located at the bottom), and the 'Word options' dialog box will appear.
3 Click on 'advanced' and, under 'editing options', do *one* of the following:
   ■ Select the 'use the Insert key to control overtype mode' check box
   or
   ■ Select the 'use overtype mode' check box to use the overtype mode continuously.

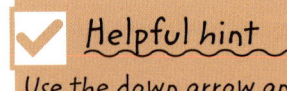

Helpful hint

Use the down arrow and open the clipboard while editing. If it is not kept open, only the last item cut or copied will be available for pasting.

Cut, copy and paste

Cutting, *copying* and *pasting* actions work in similar and complementary ways to make changes to your document. The *clipboard*, which is the first subtab on the home tab, is very helpful for holding material that is cut or copied. Note that images, tables and objects when cut or copied may not show up on the clipboard; instead, the words 'preview not available' may appear. The items are usually still available for pasting.

Generally, the cut or copied material remains available for pasting from the clipboard until it is cleared from the clipboard or the file is saved and/or closed.

Cut

Cutting pre-keyed items from a document either for permanent deletion or for use elsewhere is one of the editing tools available in Microsoft applications. This may take the form of cutting out a word, line, sentence, paragraph, table, graphic or object from a document page. Cutting the item generally places it on the clipboard, and it becomes available for pasting either in the same document or another document. The steps to cut and paste text are:

1 Highlight the text to be cut. Go to the home tab and click on the cut icon.
2 The material is placed on the clipboard, but disappears from the page.
3 Press delete (for permanent deletion)
   or

If the text is being cut to place elsewhere in the document or in another document, place the insertion point where you want to paste the material and left-click on the paste icon, or use ctrl + X (for cut) and ctrl + V (to paste) to accomplish the same actions.

Copy

Copying text follows a similar process to cutting text, but the material remains in the source document. The steps to copy and paste text are:

9 Advanced formatting, editing and proofreading

1. Highlight the text to be copied. Go to the home tab and click on the copy icon.
2. The material is placed on the clipboard.
3. Locate the place you wish to put the text and click on the paste icon, or use ctrl C (for copy) and use ctrl V (to paste) to accomplish the same actions.

 Activity

State **one** major difference between 'cut and paste' and 'copy and paste'.

Paste

The *paste* option works hand in hand with cut and copy as, in both cases, placing the cut or copied text requires the paste option for placement. Here are some tips for using the paste options efficiently:

- Make sure you position your cursor in the correct place before placing your text.
- Use the appropriate paste option after clicking on paste in the clipboard subtab. One will keep the format from the source document, while a different option will change the format to match the new document. Note that cutting, copying and pasting can also be accessed by right highlighting the word, sentence or passage and right-clicking. A dropdown box will appear that includes these options.

Move (drag and drop)

Moving your texts (**text movement**) can take various forms. You can use cut, copy and paste, or you can use the drag-and-drop method. This method varies, depending on whether the item is a small amount of text or a whole document.

To move a small amount of text:

1. Use the mouse to highlight the text you wish to move.
2. Keeping the left button of the mouse button depressed, drag the highlighted text in a smooth motion. (If you lift the mouse from the mousepad, the selection will remain in its original position.)

To move whole files/folders:

1. Identify the directory or the folder into which you want to drop the file.
2. Left-click on the file in the directory/folder that it is in currently, and do not release it.
3. Drag the selected file smoothly, close to the directory or folder and take careful note of the destination folder before releasing it.
4. The folder is no longer in its previous location.

> **Did you know?**
> 'Lost' files or folders are often files or folders placed in the wrong destination folder.

Find and replace

It may be necessary to locate all the places a key word was used to amend or adjust some information. The 'find' tool, located on the home tab, becomes very useful. When reviewing your essay or large document, you may realise that a more suitable word or phrase can be used instead of what was used in the source document.

 Activity

When proofreading a document, you find the word 'competition' repeated several times. What menu might you use to solve the problem of repetition?

SECTION 3

> **Did you know?**
> It is fairly useless to look for short letter combinations, for example 'the', as there will be hundreds of instances.

>  **Helpful hint**
> Be careful with 'replace all'. It will change the letter combination that is located in the middle of another word. Therefore, save your document before making too many changes, in case you need to go back to the original document.

In that case, the 'replace' tool decreases the time it takes to locate and then change each word individually.

Here is the process to find text:

1 Go to the home tab on the ribbon.
2 Select the find icon in the editing subtab.
3 Click on the down arrow.
4 A window called the 'navigation pane' will appear on the left before the clipboard.
5 Type in the box the word or phrase you wish to find. All instances of the word, as well as combinations of the same letters as the word, will be highlighted.

Here is the process to find and replace text:

1 Click 'replace' in the editing subtab.
2 A 'find and replace' dialog box will open.
3 Type the word or phrase you wish to replace in the 'find what' window. Choose from the options either to replace one instance (replace), replace all instances (replace all) or review and replace the word one at a time (find next).

The shortcut ctrl H also opens the 'find and replace' dialog box for you to execute the steps above.

The 'undo' feature, or the shortcut ctrl Z, is very helpful if you made any unplanned changes.

Punctuation

Punctuation marks sometimes appear to be missing from draft documents. When you proofread documents, you must be familiar with the organisation's policy on whether to use *open punctuation* or *closed punctuation*. An organisation may insist on closed punctuation (the inclusion of full stops) in abbreviations in formal letters to external parties, but may be less strict in memoranda to internal parties. The word-processing application may use a red, green and blue tool to alert keyboardists to potential errors, but these can be overridden. When the organisation's policy is clear, errors may not in fact be errors after all.

Table 9.3 provides examples of the differences between open and closed punctuation.

Table 9.3 Open and closed punctuation

Open punctuation	Closed punctuation
eg	e.g.
etc	etc.
ie	i.e.
Messrs	Messrs.
Mr	Mr.
Mrs	Mrs.
Ms	Ms (full stop not necessary)
am	a.m.
pm	p.m.

Abbreviations

Many draft manuscripts contain abbreviations. You are expected to be familiar with and substitute the full term where these abbreviations appear. Table 9.4 provides some common ones seen in business documents.

Table 9.4 Abbreviations

Abbreviation	Full term	Abbreviation	Full term	Abbreviation	Full term
accom	accommodation	dept	department	sin/sinc	sincerely
advert	advertisement	ffly	faithfully	th	that
a/c	account	fr	from	w	with
approx	approximately	hv	have	wl	will
appt	appointment	necy	necessary	yr	year/your
bn	been	ref	reference	yrs	yours
co	company	sh	shall	Days of the week: Mon, Tue, Wed, Thurs, Fri, Sat, Sun	Monday, Tuesday, Wednesday, Thursday, Friday, Saturday, Sunday
dr	dear	shd	should	Months of the year: Jan, Feb, Mar, Apr, May, Jun, Jul, Aug, Sept, Oct, Nov, Dec	January, February, March, April, May, June, July, August, September, October, November, December

---

Key terms

background An image that appears behind a document's text for visual appeal

break A way to manipulate whole pages, such as keeping text separate through page breaks or changing orientations through section breaks

check Function that automatically assesses spelling, grammar and use of language against built-in resources, such as dictionary, thesaurus and grammar rules

endnotes Short notes placed at the end of chapters in academic and technical books, papers, journals and reports to provide additional information, explanations, comments and citations

footers Ways of communicating standard information about an organisation by repeating text or marks at the bottom of each page in a document

footnotes Short notes placed at the bottom of pages in academic and technical books, papers, journals and reports to provide additional information, explanations, comments and citations

headers Ways of communicating standard information about an organisation by repeating text or marks at the top of each page in a document

link A method of providing additional information on a topic by inserting a highlight on a word or phrase that sends the reader to that other source of information

overtyping A tool that allows the erasure of words to the right of the cursor while keying in new words

page numbering A tool that places sequential numbers on designated pages, providing an order that can be used as a reference or to find information in a manuscript easily

symbol A common or uncommon mark or shape for interpretation by the reader

SECTION 3

> **text box** A facility that allows the placement of text anywhere on a page by overriding line spacing and margin defaults
> **text movement** A way of manipulating text, images and objects, including tools to cut, copy, paste, drag and drop, delete, insert, find and replace; items are selected using either the left-click and drag method or the select button
> **watermark** An image that appears behind a document's text as an identifier, security measure or copyright protection

Summary

In this chapter, you have learned how to:

- utilise advanced formatting tools, such as cut and paste, and insertions, such as page numbering and headers and footers
- employ repositories of information, such as the synonym list and the thesaurus
- embed informational and security elements that enhance document functionality and professional appearance, such as backgrounds and watermarks
- apply proofreading and editing signs and symbols, and recognise and replace abbreviations with their full terms
- appreciate the actions that transform draft documents into clear, polished, mailable versions.

Practice, research and exam-style questions

Multiple-choice questions

1. Which of these is an editing technique?
   - A Putting in borders
   - B Finding repetitions
   - C Landscaping orientation
   - D Font style choice

2. Supplementary information, citations or explanations are best placed in …
   - A footnotes.
   - B footers.
   - C headers.
   - D headings.

3. Superscript numbers are used to identify …
   - A sequential endnotes.
   - B random endnotes.
   - C ending footers.
   - D sequential headers.

4. A nested list is a …
   - A main list within the main text.
   - B subordinate list in a main list.
   - C list carrying a customised bullet.
   - D list of the labels for an image or object.

5. Which of these purposes is *not* a justification for the use of both backgrounds and watermarks?
   - A Copyright protection
   - B Security
   - C Branding
   - D Readability

6. What does this proofreader's mark mean: ?
   - A Close up
   - B Delete
   - C Insert a number
   - D No error here

7. A draft manuscript includes this sentence:

   > All persons on the compound after work hours, including *upperlevel managers*, must be registered with the security desk before the close of the day.

   On enquiry, you discover that the writer wants you to emphasise the words underlined. Which of the following proofreading terms should have been added on the manuscript to indicate this?

   - A Trs
   - B ini caps
   - C Stet
   - D N.P.

8 The options for a multiple-choice question were laid out like this:
   A fair   B clear   C dear   D sear
   The author prefers that the options be set out in alphabetical order. Which of the following terms should be used to indicate that preference?
   A Trs
   B Stet
   C Run on
   D Flush

9 The full-term substitute for the abbreviation 'w' is …
   A will
   B withhold
   C without
   D with

10 Which of these collections of terms is *not* usually abbreviated in drafts to be proofread?
   A Days
   B Months
   C Styles
   D Titles

True or false?

1 Pages are always numbered using Arabic numerals.
2 Numbers have value; numerals are designs.
3 The shortcut keys for cut and paste are ctrl C and ctrl V.
4 Overtyping is a rapid method for deleting unwanted text.
5 A thesaurus is another kind of dictionary.

Short-answer questions

The passage below contains several abbreviations, spelling and other errors. Rewrite the passage while correcting all errors. Circle all the corrections that you make.

Dr; Madam/Sir

This is to advice that 5 blender-processor purchased from your store, on 15

Dec 2026, are detective. The blades of three are dull and show sign of wear. Two of the items work only on the blender settings.

Our Purchasing officer has made three visits to your store no solution was offered. The decision has been made to sease payment of the agreed monthly in-stallment of 550 until we come to a satisfactory good solution.

Yours in trade

Phyllis Goodsen

Production Manager

10 Business documents

> ## Objectives
> By the end of this chapter, you will be able to:
> - identify sizes and orientation of stationery
> - choose appropriate stationery for specific purposes
> - identify, format and edit envelopes and labels
> - prepare properly formatted and edited business documents for internal and external recipients
> - create and use letterheads and special notations
> - prepare properly formatted and edited business documents from key information points provided via written or audio skeleton notes
> - insert simple graphics into a document.

Introduction

This chapter provides guidance about the rules and expectations when preparing business *correspondence*. In the first part of this chapter, the focus is on the stationery used for manual correspondence. Stationery options include different paper types and sizes, as well as **envelope** types and sizes. There is also information on the use of labels and *special notations*. Then you will learn about the rules for preparing different documents. These documents have been categorised as:

1. correspondence with mainly internal parties
2. correspondence with mainly external stakeholders.

Examples of each category place an emphasis on the rules of line spacing and the usefulness of tables in keeping text properly aligned.

In the final section of this chapter, you will learn about using Word's **mail-merge** feature to dispatch similar **letters** (with some differences in content) to many people at the same time.

At the end of each major section is an activity for practising preparation of properly formatted and edited correspondence, given skeleton information and instructions.

Stationery

Business documents are written or printed on stationery and enclosed in envelopes to be hand-delivered or mailed. Although currently most business communication is conducted electronically, the use of appropriate stationery remains a significant aspect of document preparation. There are rules governing the type and size of paper to use for various forms of business documents. These options influence the different types and sizes of envelopes to use.

Tables 10.1–10.3 set out:

1. **types of paper**
2. **paper sizes** and **uses**
3. envelopes and the paper sizes that match them.

10 Business documents

Types of paper

Paper types range from thin and light flimsy paper to sturdy parchment paper. Other papers are specially coated to respond to heat, to absorb ink, to provide a glossy look or to enable rapid duplication.

Table 10.1 Types of paper

Paper	Description and use
Bond paper	High-quality paper, frequently used for documents such as letters, forms and contracts
Cardstock	Suitable for projects requiring sturdiness, e.g. business cards, postcards and greetings cards
Coated paper	Used for high-quality printing, e.g. magazines, brochures and product packaging
Copy paper	The most commonly used paper, as businesses use it for printing many types of documents; it is cheaper and thinner than printer paper and suitable for most business documents
Flimsy paper	Thin and light; can be used in multiple draft projects where copies are not to be stored
Glossy paper	Used for printing photos and promotional materials, e.g. marketing flyers, brochures and magazines; can make text and colours appear livelier
Inkjet paper	Designed to absorb ink rapidly and evenly; available in various types of finishes, e.g. satin glossy and matte, and often used to print documents that require high-resolution images for better colour and clarity
No carbon required (NCR)	A set of 3–5 different sheets of paper chemically treated so that duplicates can be printed
Parchment	High quality, heavy and useful for special projects, e.g. certificates decorated with artistic handwritten (*calligraphic*) information
Thermal paper	Specially coated in a material designed to change colour when exposed to heat; often comes in roll form and is used in adding machines, cash registers, thermal printers and credit/debit card machines to print receipts – many original fax machines also used it

Paper sizes and uses

Paper is manufactured in various sizes using standard measurements set by the International Organization for Standardization. The A series is the most used worldwide. The A4 size and the letter size (which is slightly shorter and wider) are the two most commonly used sizes for documents.

Table 10.2 Paper sizes and uses

ISO name	Measurement (centimetres)	Measurement (inches)	Purposes
A0	84.1 cm × 118.9 cm	33.1 inches × 46.8 inches	Posters, large presentations, technical drawings, wall maps
A1	59.4 cm × 84.1 cm	23.4 inches × 33.1 inches	Advertising posters, flip charts, wall maps
A2	42.0 cm × 59.4 cm	16.5 inches × 23.4 inches	Diagrams, artwork, maps, timetables, calendars, travel schedules

A3	29.7 cm × 42.0 cm	11.7 inches × 16.5 inches	Spreadsheets, legal documents, travel schedules, maps, sketch pads, financial statements
A4 Letter size	21.0 cm × 29.7 cm 21.6 cm × 27.9 cm	8.3 inches × 11.7 inches 8.5 inches × 11.0 inches	Business letters, reports, minutes, chairperson's agenda, specifications, long memoranda, invoices, legal documents, advertisements, forms, itineraries, manuscripts, display work
A5	14.8 cm × 21.0 cm	5.8 inches × 8.3 inches	Short memoranda, short letters, notices, agendas, debit/credit notes, invitations, vouchers, circulation slips
A6	10.5 cm × 14.8 cm	4.1 inches × 5.8 inches	Postcards, debit/credit notes, invitations, message pads, receipts, index cards, petty-cash vouchers
A7	7.4 cm × 10.5 cm	2.9 inches × 4.1 inches	Complimentary slips, address labels, index cards, dockets
A8	5.2 cm × 7.4 cm	2 inches × 2.9 inches	Business cards, address labels
A9	3.7 cm × 5.2 cm	1.5 inches × 2 inches	Document labels, price tags
A10	2.6 cm × 3.7 cm	1 inches × 1.5 inches	Postage stamps

Envelope types, sizes and uses

Envelopes are packaging materials for documents, made of a specific type of paper. They are designed to protect the documents enclosed, and display recipients' addresses.

Choice of envelopes

An organisation's choice of envelope is influenced by the:

- content (which determines the size of paper and therefore envelope)
- number of pages of the content
- quality of material (stiffness of material; need for padding; the thin transparent film that works as a window)
- size and position of the closure flaps.

Table 10.3 illustrates some of the envelope types available, with the ISO standard sizes of paper recommended to match.

Table 10.3 Envelope sizes and paper-size match

Name of envelope	Measurement (centimetres)	Measurement (inches)	Paper-size match
C3	32.4 cm × 45.8 cm	$12\frac{3}{4}$ inches × 18 inches	A3 sheet flat; A2 sheet folded once
C4	22.9 cm × 32.4 cm	9 inches × $12\frac{3}{4}$ inches	A4 sheet flat; A3 sheet folded once
C5	16.2 cm × 12.9 cm	$6\frac{3}{8}$ inches × 9 inches	A5 sheet flat; A4 sheet folded once
C6	11.4 cm × 16.2 cm	$4\frac{1}{2}$ inches × $6\frac{3}{8}$ inches	A5 sheet folded once; A4 sheet folded in quarters
$C\frac{5}{6}$	11.4 cm × 22.9 cm	$4\frac{1}{2}$ inches × 9 inches	A4 sheet folded in thirds
$C\frac{7}{6}$	8.1 cm × 16.2 cm	$3\frac{1}{4}$ inches × $6\frac{3}{8}$ inches	A5 sheet folded in thirds

C7	8.1 cm × 11.4 cm	$3\frac{1}{4}$ inches × $4\frac{1}{2}$ inches	A5 sheet folded in quarters
B4	25.0 cm × 35.3 cm	$9\frac{7}{8}$ inches × $13\frac{7}{8}$ inches	C4 envelope; A4 sheet flat
B5	17.6 cm × 25.0 cm	7 inches × $9\frac{7}{8}$ inches	C5 envelope, A5 sheet flat
B6	12.5 cm × 17.6 cm	5 inches × 7 inches	A4 folded in quarters
DL	11.0 cm × 25.0 cm	$4\frac{1}{4}$ inches × $8\frac{3}{4}$ inches	A4 sheet folded in thirds; A5 sheet folded in half lengthways (similar size to the C5/6 envelope)

Labels on envelopes

A label is a small piece of paper coated with an adhesive that is stuck on an envelope to display the recipient's name and address. Another label may display the sender's name and address, but organisations often use envelopes preprinted with that information.

Special notations on envelopes

Envelopes are often stamped with special notations that instruct the mail room, delivery service or post office how to process the contents. These notations, such as *confidential*, *special delivery*, *private*, *classified*, *by hand* or *certified mail*, are often placed above the recipient's address.

Standard document features

There are several features that are common to most documents, and these are listed and described in Table 10.4. Additional features that are found in letters appear in a later subsection.

Table 10.4 Standard document features

Standard document feature	Description
Letterhead	Usually includes the name of the business, its address, telephone and fax numbers, email address and its social media handles, including its website; the heading may or may not include the company's logo
Reference	A combination of letters and numbers that allows both the sender and the recipient to identify, respond to, retrieve and verify a communication
Date/date as postmark	The day, month and year on which the document was typed, or the date on which it was sent for delivery
Subject heading	Topic addressed in the document
Body of letter	Text and objects conveying the message or the matter being discussed
Signature	Area left for the signature of the person authorised to sign the letter
Signatory	Name of the person signing the letter, e.g. Anthony Jones
Designation	Position of person signing the letter, e.g. Marketing Manager

Selecting stationery and styles for an assignment

EDPM specialists must be prepared to respond to requests for the preparation of different assignments. Possible assignments include the preparation of:

- business letters of various styles, including circulars, forms and templates
- letterheads for the first page of letters
- memos and other documents (notices, agendas and minutes)
- envelopes and labels.

When selecting stationery and styles for an assignment, choices will include the:

- paper type and size, envelope, label and colours
- page setup and insertions
- letterhead (company logo and information) or no header
- specific document style
- branding and security features to incorporate.

Mail merge

The Microsoft Word feature called *mail merge* is a very useful tool designed to save time when sending documents to small or large numbers of recipients. It is found in the 'mailings' tab on the Word ribbon. This feature gives organisations the opportunity to customise each person's information while retaining some standard data or format within a document. For example, the tool would allow Atlas Communications to send out individually addressed letters to its many customers informing them of the changes in prices.

In summary, mail merge can be used to customise the following communication forms for distribution:

- Form letters or circulars
- Statements of account (bills) to customers
- Emails
- Catalogues
- Brochures
- Newsletters
- Labels
- Envelopes
- Directories.

To use mail merge, the organisation creates the *primary source*, such as the letter, notice or bill statement. The primary source is named and saved to a file for easy retrieval. This file can be prepared before or after the creation of a database of customers, employees or other stakeholders, which is called the *secondary source*. The mail-merge feature works with the business's database or an extract from it. Therefore, creating accurate tables (databases) is important, and should contain such information as:

- titles (Mr./Mrs./Ms./Dr./Sr.)
- first and last (also middle) names
- full or partial addresses
- relationship with the business (customer/employee/stakeholder/supplier)
- information that is particular to the organisation (for example a school might have an identifier for all students required to complete an SBA, or an agricultural supply store might make the distinction between farmers of vegetables from ground provision farmers).

The database can be manipulated (that is, sorted and filtered) for the particular purpose each time there is a need to communicate on a large scale. For example, a school might wish to send information about subject choices to the parents/guardians of Form Three students only. This small database would be extracted from the records of all current parents/guardians across the entire school, and a mail merge created to send the circular letter.

Creating a mail merge

The simplest way to create a mail merge is by using the mail-merge wizard, which provides a step-by-step approach to creating a mail merge. Table 10.5 sets out the steps that Atlas Communications would follow.

Table 10.5 also provides information on the reasons for the actions and/or alternatives that another organisation might use to carry out a mail merge.

Table 10.5 Using the mail-merge wizard

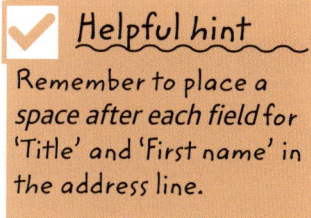

Helpful hint
Remember to place a space after each field for 'Title' and 'First name' in the address line.

Steps	Actions	Observations/comments
1	• Click on the mailings tab on the Word ribbon. • Click on the subtab 'select recipients'. • Choose 'use an existing list'.	A new list is prepared if there is no existing list of recipients.
2	The data source window asks for the file name; enter 'Stationery Credit Customers (Large)'.	The database appears in a table with your current column headings.
3	• Select 'customise columns' and add, remove and amend the information if necessary, or rename a column (field). • Insert any new information in the fields, using the tab key to move from one entry to the next. • After completing each row change, click on 'new entry' to go to the next row. • Save and name the data list: 'Current Stationery Credit Customers (Large)', after all the changes.	This allows you to: • create your personalised approach to recipients • add any recent customer for large purchases • remove or amend obsolete data, e.g. change of address.
4	Check that the main circular document 'New Stationery Prices' is available for selection.	It might be best to prepare this beforehand so that necessary proofreading, amendments and approvals take place.
5	• Go to the mailings tab on the ribbon and select 'start mail merge'. • Click on 'letters', select 'recipients' and 'use existing list'. • Click on open for a list of all saved databases. • Choose 'Current Stationery Credit Customers (Large)'.	

SECTION 3

6	• Choose 'insert merge fields' to select and place recipients' addresses in the inside address space and the greeting line. • Preview the letter again and remove the comma from the salutation, as it is a fully blocked letter (open punctuation).	• You can also choose 'address block' and 'greeting line' from your 'insert merge fields' group. • The greeting line gives the salutation, e.g. 'Dear Mr. XX'/'Dear Sir/Madam'/'Dear Parent'. • A properly edited and proofread document meets professional standards.
7	• Move to 'preview results group' and click on the forward arrows to review recipients' information, including address. • Click 'finish' and 'merge' on the menu bar.	• Letters are available for printing and delivery. • There are paper-folding, envelope-stuffing and labelling computerised devices that can be programmed for these actions.

> **✓ Helpful hint**
>
> Documents contain formatting features that are obvious to the trained eye. For example, an expert can tell whether the clear line of space between items is too large or too small.

Standard document preparation terms

Certain terms that describe style and formatting options appear regularly when preparing documents. The choices are affected by:

- the type of document
- the relationship with the receiver
- the sender's document presentation rules.

These options are listed and defined in Table 10.7. Margins according to paper size are shown in Table 10.6.

Table 10.6 Margins according to paper size

Paper size	
A4	A5
Top	
2.54 cm/ 1 inch or 3.18 cm/ 1.5 inches	2.54 cm/ 1 inch
Left	
2.54 cm/ 1 inch	2.54 cm/ 1 inch
Right	
2.54 cm/ 1 inch	2.54 cm/ 1 inch
Bottom	
2.54 cm/ 1 inch	1.27 cm/ 0.5 inch

Table 10.7 Standard document preparation terms

Term	Definition
Orientation	The default orientation is portrait, as described in Chapter 8; however, some documents require landscape orientation
Paper sizes	The default paper size in word processing is letter size; A4 is also used regularly, especially in government offices, and A5 is the paper size of choice for short versions of business documents
Punctuation policy	There are two punctuation options: open and closed: *open punctuation style* means that certain parts of a letter do not require punctuation marks, even with abbreviated words; *closed punctuation style* includes all required punctuation marks, and is more often used in the indented style of correspondence
Fully blocked/blocked style	The document aligns at the left margin from the beginning to the end of the document; this style uses the open punctuation format
Indented style	A style that allows for varying rules, e.g. the first line of each paragraph is tabbed in 5/6 character spaces from the left margin, or the subject line is centred; additional rules apply to specific documents, and both closed and open punctuation forms can be used in this style
Semi-blocked style	A combination of the blocked style and the indented style; uses either the open punctuation format or the closed punctuation format

Margin options	There are few margin options, except for special display items that require customised margins; most documents are set at a 2.54 cm/1 inch margin all round by word-processing default, but a left or right margin may be changed for a particular reason, e.g. continuing pages or the rules of the business
Line spacing	Most business documents use single line spacing within paragraphs; however, to distinguish content from the line for a signature and also create adequate space, the enter key is pressed 4 or 5 times in letters and 2 or 3 times in other documents
Keying instructions	Indication of how the correct spaces between items in documents are achieved (see the row above); a common instruction is putting in one clear line of space, which indicates a space between paragraphs that is formed by pressing enter twice immediately after the last character in the previous line, or pressing enter 3 times achieves two clear lines of space – note that pressing enter various numbers of times is different from using the tab key (tabbing in) to the achieve the right space
Capitalisation	While some documents require full capitalisation of headings, others require only initial caps, i.e. the first letters of significant words only are in uppercase

Correspondence with internal recipients

In this section, the types of documents that are prepared for correspondence are defined, and standard features and rules of preparation are described. The choices and options of layout, paper size, orientation, margin, line spacing and other rules of document preparation are brought to your attention repeatedly. In all examples, the number of times the enter key is to be pressed to separate the different features of a document is indicated.

General correspondence: memoranda

A **memorandum (memo)** or memoranda (memos) are used for internal communication within and between departments or branches of the same business. Take note of the following rules for preparing memos:

- Memos are prepared in two sizes (long and short memos) and two styles (indented or blocked).
- The appropriate stationery for long memos is A4 or letter size with portrait orientation; for short memos: A5 in landscape orientation.
- The margins for memos are 2.54 cm or 1 inch all around.
- Single line spacing is used, with one clear line of space between paragraphs.
- The font size for the heading may be larger than the rest of the memo, for example 14 pt.
- Main headings can be either spaced caps (M E M O R A N D U M) or closed caps (MEMORANDUM).
- Where main headings consist of several words, spaced caps require 3 spaces between words (N O T I C E   O F   M E E T I N G), while closed caps require 2 spaces between words (NOTICE OF MEETING).

Figure 10.1 shows a memo with the blocked layout style. The bracketed figures represent the number of times the enter key needs to be pressed to separate the different features.

MEMORANDUM

(3)
TO   Mr Anthony Houlder – Finance Department
(2)
FROM   Ms Janine Julien – Purchasing Division
(2)
REF   G1507/jj
(2)
DATE   April 20 2026
(2)
SUBJECT   **RISING COST OF STATIONERY**
(2)
We have been advised by our supplier that, due to the increased costs of shipping and tariffs on all new stationery items, effective June 6, 2026, we will have to pay an additional cost to procure our stationery for all departments within the organisation.
(2)
We hope to negotiate a suitable price for the goods and, if this occurs, we will advise you of the new pricing for these items.

Figure 10.1 Memo showing blocked layout style

Figure 10.2 shows a memo with the indented memo layout style. The bracketed figures represent the number of times the enter key needs to be pressed to separate the different features.

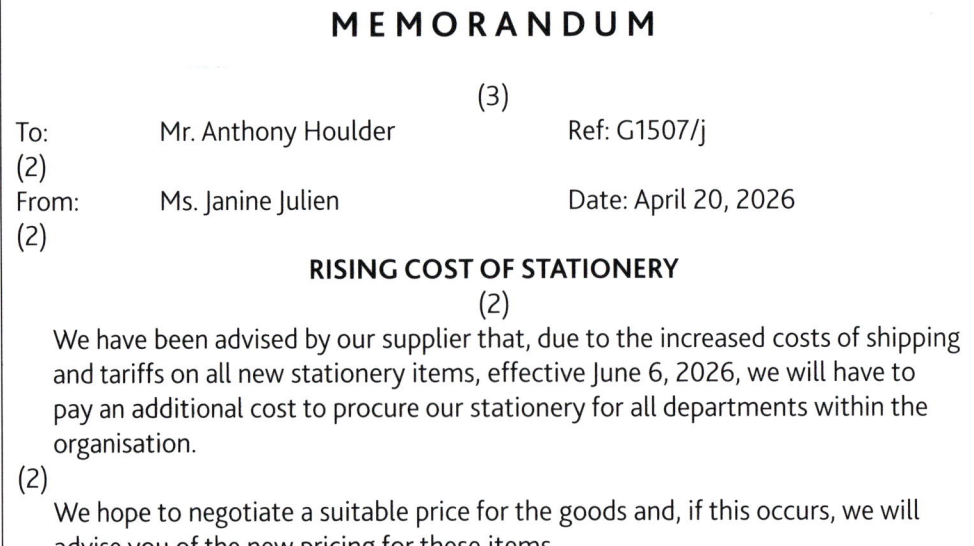

MEMORANDUM

(3)
To: Mr. Anthony Houlder   Ref: G1507/j
(2)
From: Ms. Janine Julien   Date: April 20, 2026
(2)
                    RISING COST OF STATIONERY
(2)
We have been advised by our supplier that, due to the increased costs of shipping and tariffs on all new stationery items, effective June 6, 2026, we will have to pay an additional cost to procure our stationery for all departments within the organisation.
(2)
We hope to negotiate a suitable price for the goods and, if this occurs, we will advise you of the new pricing for these items.

Figure 10.2 Memo showing indented layout style

Activity

Preparing a memo

The administrative assistant of Wyatt Resorts received the following document from her Office Manager, Lily Poultree, on December 20 for urgent action.

1 Using A4 or letter-size paper, 2.54 cm (1 inch) margins all round and single line spacing, create a blocked-style long memorandum following the instructions provided.
2 Proofread and ensure that any spelling, capitalisation and punctuation errors are corrected.

Please see the draft memo below. Several actions need to be taken to improve it. Thank you for getting it out in a timely manner.

MEMORANDUM

TO	Robert - Exec Chef	*(Insert last name 'Devers' and spell out designation)*
FROM	Me – Purchasing Division	*(Insert Lily Poultree)*
DATE		*(Insert today's date)*
SUBJECT	PRIVATE CORP Party	*(Spell out and use all caps)*

(Please be advised)

~~This advises~~ that we have received a request for catering service for a party of

15 *(set out number in words)*

people from MS. Charlene pointdefour, CEO of Pointdefour Industries, one of our highly valued customers.

She requires that: we add Duck and Lamb in Garlic Sauce to our 2026 Corporate Christmas Dinner Package. The dinner is scheduled for December 22 at 6.30 p.m.

All items are to be delivered no later or earlier than half an hour before dinner time. Two people are required for meal service and must be present to receive and set up at the said time. *(Add: 'Kindly note also that' before 'Two people')*

(Use REF No. CP45-15 and place in correct position for a blocked memo)

Correspondence for business meetings

A business meeting is a gathering of two or more people to discuss ideas and objectives that meet the goals of the organisation. Meetings can take place face to face at an office, over the phone or at different locations online. Meetings are held by groups at different levels in an organisation, for example Boards, Managers, Teams, Committees and groups with similar areas of interest, such as societies, associations and foundations.

Some types of meetings are:

- Statutory Meeting
- Annual General Meeting
- Extraordinary General Meeting
- Board Meeting
- Committee Meeting.

Some meetings are formal (they may be structured and recorded), or they may be informal (where simple notes are taken by individuals at the meeting). However, in most instances, documents called a **notice** and an **agenda** (including a special **chairperson's agenda**) are prepared *before* the meeting. Formal **minutes** are prepared *after* the meeting from notes and/or audio recordings taken at the meeting.

Notices

The notice of a meeting advises people of an upcoming meeting, giving the date, time and location of the meeting. The notice is prepared by the secretary of the committee or board, after discussion with the chairperson. The posting of notices of meetings are guided by certain policies. For example, invitees must receive a notice within 14 days, or within 21 days, of the meeting date, depending on the type of meeting and as stated in a constitution (if relevant). Notices are sometimes accompanied by an agenda.

Take note of the following rules for preparing notices, with or without agendas:

- The **layout** of notices is usually on A5 paper in landscape orientation. However, when sent out with an agenda, the notice is prepared using A4/A5 in portrait orientation.
- The heading of a notice identifies the organisation calling the meeting, and is usually in uppercase letters and a larger font size than the body of the notice. A 2.54 cm (1 inch) margin on all sides may be used.
- The blocked style for notices is the most used style of layout. The heading is usually left aligned. However, if using the indented style, the heading should be centred.

Figure 10.3 is an example of an indented layout for a notice. The bracketed figures represent the number of times the enter key needs to be pressed to separate the different features. Identify the features from the bulleted list above.

SIX CREEKS SECONDARY SCHOOL

Banks Road, Six Creeks, San Fernando
Telephone: 555-4538   Email: sixcreeks45@gmail.com

(3)

NOTICE OF MEETING

(2)

A meeting of the Parent–Teachers Association of the Six Creeks Secondary School will be held on Friday September 25, 2026 at the School's Hall at 1700 hours. The agenda will be circulated at a later date.

(4/5)
N. Adams
Honorary Secretary
(2)
September 15, 2026

Figure 10.3 A notice using an indented layout

> **→ Activity**
>
> Prepare a notice with the same information using the blocked style and the information from Figure 10.3.

Agenda

An agenda is a list of items to be discussed at a meeting. The order in which matters are discussed begins with certain statutory requirements, such as a roll call and establishing that a quorum of members is present.

There are three kinds of agenda:

1 An Ordinary Agenda
2 A Chairperson's Agenda
3 An Annual General Meeting Agenda (AGM).

Several styles are available for the heading of an agenda, including:

- using uppercase for the whole word, i.e. AGENDA
- using initial caps, i.e. Agenda
- using spaced caps, i.e. A G E N D A
- using bolding or underscore.

Figure 10.4 shows a fully blocked notice and agenda combination. The bracketed figures represent the number of times the enter key needs to be pressed to separate the different features.

THE KITSON SPORTS ACADEMY

(3)
NOTICE OF MEETING
A meeting of the Selection Committee of The Kitson Sports Academy will be held on Monday March 27 2026, at the North Room of the Galaxy Hotel at 1900 hours.
AGENDA
(2)
1 Roll call
2 Apologies for absence
3 Minutes of the last Meeting
4 Matters arising from the Minutes
5 Confirmation of Minutes
6 Correspondence
7 Business of the Meeting
8 Any other business
9 Date and time of next meeting

(4/5)
R Sampson
Honorary Secretary
(2)
March 13 2026

Figure 10.4 A fully blocked notice and agenda combination

SECTION 3

Chairperson's agenda

The chairperson is expected to guide the meeting and ensure all items on the agenda are completed. A table is the most useful format when creating the chairperson's agenda. The column on the right-hand side needs to be wide enough for notes relevant to the agenda items. The column on the left side of the page shows not only the agenda items, but any relevant information that became available after the agenda was sent out. Figure 10.5 is an example of a chairperson's agenda related to the meeting notice and agenda in Figure 10.4.

THE KITSON SPORTS ACADEMY

(3)
Meeting of the Selection Committee to be held in the North Room of the Galaxy Hotel at 1900 hours on Monday March 27 2026
(2)
CHAIRPERSON'S AGENDA
(2)

	AGENDA ITEM	ACTION
1	Call meeting to order	
2	Apologies for absence Mr. Hinds is unable to attend. Family emergency.	
3	Minutes of the last meeting The increase in fees identified as $250 per year was omitted by Secretary. Apologies for error.	
4	Matters arising from the Minutes Members were reminded to pay their annual subscription by the end of April 20, 2026.	
5	Correspondence Invitation received from Ministry of Education to attend prize-giving ceremony. Representative to be identified.	
6	Selection of applicants Process must be completed before the end of this meeting as the deadline is approaching.	
7	Any other business	
8	Date of next meeting Chairperson is expected to be out of the country on business from April 6–13. Suggest: April 20 as a suitable date for the next meeting.	

Figure 10.5 A committee chairperson's agenda

10 Business documents

The chairperson's agenda is especially important at an Annual General Meeting (AGM), which is a meeting held yearly to discuss the performance of an organisation. The chairperson and directors of the company present the annual report on the operations of the business. At these events, many people who have invested and hold shares in the business (shareholders) may attend (either in-Person or online), and managing the process may be quite difficult. In addition, there are some significant items that are included in the agenda of an AGM that are not usually part of an ordinary meeting. These include matters such as:

- whether dividend payments will be made and, if so, how much
- the selection of auditors of the accounts for the next year
- the retirement and/or election of new members to the board of directors.

Notice of an AGM must be sent out no less than 21 days before the date of the meeting. Figure 10.6 is an example of a notice and agenda for an annual general meeting.

THE KITSONS SPORTS ACADEMY

(3)
NOTICE OF ANNUAL GENERAL MEETING
(2)
NOTICE IS HEREBY GIVEN that the 10th Annual General Meeting of The Kitson Sports Academy will be held at the Conference Room of Lowyatt Hotel, 33 Rongson Road, Port of Spain, on Tuesday 22 December, 2026 at 1000 hours.
(2)
AGENDA
(2)
1 To receive Minutes of the last Annual General Meeting (AGM) held on 19 December 2025
2 To receive Reports for the previous year from the Board of Directors and Committees
3 To receive the Auditor's Report
4 To appoint Auditors for the year 2027
5 To elect two replacement Directors to serve on the Board of Directors
6 To approve Resolutions and Recommendations
7 Declaration of dividend and date of disbursement
8 To transact other business that may arise before the meeting
(2)
**BY ORDER OF
THE BOARD OF DIRECTORS**

(4/5)
R Sampson
Honorary Secretary
(2)
1 December 2026

Figure 10.6 A notice and agenda for an annual general meeting

SECTION 3

> **→ Activity**
>
> Prepare a Chairperson's Agenda from the following information. Use the style given in the Chairperson's Agenda in Figure 10.6.
>
> **DEIDRA'S DANCE SCHOOL**
> (3)
> Meeting of the Selection Committee to be held in the North Room of the Galaxy Hotel at 19.00 hours on Monday 26 March 2026.
> (2)
> **C H A I R P E R S O N ' S   A G E N D A**
> (2)
> 1 **Call to Order**
>   Call meeting to order/Roll Call
> 2 **Apologies for Absence**
>   Mrs. Grant is unable to attend due to personal matters.
> 3 **Minutes of the last Meeting**
>   The increase in fees identified as $250 per year was omitted by Secretary. Apologise for error. Minutes to be approved by a member present.
> 4 **Matters arising from the Minutes**
>   Subscription due date to be extended from May to July 2026.
>   Increase in subscriptions become effective from August 2026.
> 5 **Correspondence**
>   Invitation received from International Dance Academy to compete in the 2027 competition. Suitable dancers to be identified in preparation for this competition. Suggest Ms. Winchester to head selections.
> 6 **Selection of applicants**
>   Ask Mrs. Kanhai on the completion of this process as the deadline is approaching.
> 7 **Any other business**
>   Visit to Jamaica Dance Academy in November.
> 8 **Date of next meeting**
>   Suggest 30 April a suitable date for the next meeting.
> 9. **End meeting.**

Minutes

Minutes of meetings are the official written record of the discussions and decisions taken at a meeting. They are usually recorded by the *Secretary* to the Board or the Committee. Where there are many attendees, for example at conferences and consultations, **rapporteurs** are employed. Both may use either a **verbatim** style of recording (which means word for word, for example 'Ms. Sandra Wells said …') or a summarising style to record the discussions. Preparing minutes (or other documents) from audio files may present some difficulty, due to crosstalk or from lack of clarity or volume when people are speaking.

Today, many organisations use artificial intelligence (AI) programs to make verbatim records of the proceedings of AGMs and other meetings held over the internet.

Minutes are written in the *third* person, for example 'It was reported that …' Minutes are a permanent record of reports and decisions taken, and can be used in legal proceedings. They should be carefully filed for future reference.

10 Business documents

Minutes of a meeting should:

- follow the order of the agenda
- be prepared using A4/legal-sized paper
- be prepared in blocked or indented style in portrait orientation
- use single line spacing, with one clear line between paragraphs
- leave adequate space for the chairperson to sign (created by pressing enter three or four times at the end of the minutes).

Figure 10.7 is an example of the Minutes of the Meeting of the Selection Committee held by The Kitson Sports Academy on March 23. Identify whether you can see the features listed above in Figure 10.7.

Present	Mr. Sherwin Kitson (Chairperson) Ms. Suzette James Mrs. Michelle Hislop Mr. Nicholas Julien Mr. Mark Changkit Ms. Raine Sampson (Secretary)	
Apologies for absence	The Secretary informed members that Mr. Hinds could not attend. He was away on emergency leave.	Action
Minutes of last meeting	Minutes of February 12, 2026 were read, and the omission of the new fee of $250 was corrected. Ms. Sampson moved that the amended Minutes be adopted as correct. The motion was seconded by Ms. James.	
Matters arising from the minutes	Mr. Changkit advised that the tickets for the June Sports and Breakfast Party were selling well and things are in place for the success of the event.	MC
Correspondence	The Secretary reported that they received a quotation for upgrade of the training room for the sum of $10,000.00 from PE Solutions. The members agreed to request a quotation from another contractor.	RS
Business of the meeting	Selected persons for up-coming tournament were advised of training schedule.

List of potential trainers was presented and preliminary selections are to be asked to attend interviews on Saturday April 4.

A letter to be sent to Trophies Are Us for an update on order sent in January. | RS |
| Any other business | The Secretary advised that the upcoming business launch package will be completed and submitted in time for the next meeting. | RS |
| Date of next meeting | The date of the next meeting was set for April 13, 2026. The chairperson declared the meeting closed at 21.00 hours. | |

(4/5)

....
Raine Sampson   Sherwin Kitson
Secretary   Chairperson

....
Date   Date

Figure 10.7 Minutes of a committee meeting

SECTION 3

Action plan

Minutes may include an **action plan** that identifies responsibility points for actions to be taken before the next meeting. In Figure 10.7, initials identify the people responsible for the proposed actions.

Correspondence with external parties

Letters

A letter is a formal method of communication. Recipients may include customers, suppliers, shareholders, banks and government agencies, who are considered external parties. Occasionally, a serious internal matter may warrant the dispatch of a letter within a business. These include disciplinary letters, letters of commendation or promotion letters. As letters represent the organisation, there are several standard features and terms that are expected to be present. Although some are defined in Table 10.4, a review of these terms and the additional terms that are relevant to letter-writing would be useful. These terms are listed and defined in Table 10.8.

Table 10.8 Standard letter features

Standard letter feature/term	Description
Letterhead	Usually includes the name of the business, its address, telephone and fax numbers, email address and its social-media handles, including its website; the heading may or may not include the company's logo
Reference	A combination of letters and numbers that allows both the sender and the recipient to identify, respond to, retrieve and verify a communication
Date/date as postmark	The day, month and year on which the letter was typed, or the date on which it was sent for delivery
Inside address	The address of the organisation and/or person to whom the letter is being sent
Attention line	Identifies the person who is expected to receive and action the letter
Salutation	E.g. Dear Sir/Madam, Dear Mr. Smith, Dear Mrs. Jones
Subject heading	Topic addressed in the letter
Body of letter	Text and objects conveying the message or the matter being discussed
Complimentary close	Choice of: *Yours faithfully*, *Yours sincerely*, *Yours truly*, *Respectfully yours* – all used on different occasions; note that the first letter in the word is in upper case (Y) and the second word is all in lowercase
Signature block	Area is left for the signature of the person authorised to sign the letter
Signatory	Name of the person signing the letter, e.g. Anthony Jones
Designation	Position of person signing the letter, e.g. Marketing Manager
Continuation page	A numbered page containing content that could not fit on the (unnumbered) first page
Circular letter	Also called *form letter*, *standard letter* or *billing letter*; drawn up to provide the same basic information to a group of people, but may have some differences, e.g. names and addresses of recipients, appointment dates and amounts owed

10 Business documents

Tear-off slip	Designed to be detached from circular letters and returned by the recipient to the sender with requested information completed, e.g. a school's permission slip sent out to parents and guardians
Enclosure attachment	A document sent with a main business letter, e.g. a proposal or a quotation for a job sent with a cover letter
Notations	On letters: additional information in abbreviated form, e.g. *post script* (P.S.), *nota bene* (N.B. or note well), Att (attached), Encl. (enclosed), cc (copied to)
	On envelopes: directions for processing, e.g. *Confidential*, *Special Delivery*, *By Hand*
Copy	Sent to other people with an interest in the contents

In this part, you will learn how to create key features of letters and to make the best choice for letter-writing assignments. Samples of different kinds of letters are used to illustrate the options of indentation, paper size, orientation, margin, line spacing and other document-preparation rules. A revisit of Chapters 8 and 9 would be useful at this stage to recall information on formatting, editing and proofreading.

Letterheads

Whether an organisation is large or small, a **letterhead** looks impressive. Many organisations have their letterheads and logos embedded in their computer system so that employees can simply go to that tool and begin their letters. However, in Chapter 9, how to insert a header was explained, and the same procedure allows for the creation of a letterhead with a logo.

To create a letterhead:

1. Go to the insert tab on the Microsoft Word ribbon and click on 'header' in the header & footer subtab.
2. Select a header style or choose 'blank' to create your own style.
3. Create your logo by selecting 'insert pictures'. Choose an appropriate design from your picture folder, or go online to search for free stock pictures.
4. Place your logo in the header and resize to your satisfaction, although it should not be larger than 2.54 cm or 1 inch all around.
5. Add text information for the business: you can change the font size, colour and style, and add borders, shading and other text effects using the dropdown box in the font subtab.
6. Once you have created your letterhead, double-click under it to return to your main document. The letterhead area will fade into the background, but it is still there.

Letter layouts: variations

The layout of the parts of a letter can be any of three variations: *fully blocked*, *indented* and *semi-blocked*. The samples that follow provide guidelines to differentiate between these variations.

The blocked or fully blocked letter style is the most common form of business-letter layout as it is quite simple. Every part of the letter is left-aligned, and it follows the open punctuation layout. In other words, all items begin at the *left* margin and there are *no* punctuation marks except in the body of the letter. Figure 10.8 provides the standard pattern for a blocked letter, while Figure 10.9 displays the same information using an indented style or layout. Pay attention to two major differences between these two styles:

1. In the *blocked* style, *all* parts of the letter begin at the *left* margin, and *open* or *no* punctuation is used;
2. whereas in the *indented* letter:
   - open or closed punctuation can be used
   - the date is in the same line as the **reference** number

Helpful hint

Some organisations may include the names of their board of directors or other standard information about the organisation, or perhaps branded phrases, as a footer on the page.

SECTION 3

- the **subject heading** is centred and bolded
- each paragraph begins with an indent; this means pressing the tab key once before beginning to type the paragraph
- the **complimentary close** and **signatory** line are centred.

ATLAS COMMUNICATIONS
23 Knolly Drive
Kingston 6
JAMAICA

Tel (876) 778-2936   Fax (876) 778-7901
email atlascoms@gmail.com   Website www.atlascommunications.com

(3)
Ref PP/134/tf
(2)
March 17 2025
(2)
The Manager
Atlantic Enterprises
14 Victoria Street
Kingston
JAMAICA
(2)
Attention Ms Janine Julien
(2)
Dear Sirs
(2)
NEW STATIONERY PRICES
(2)
Atlas Communications is grateful for your continued support as we strive to supply you with our leading brands of stationery and office supplies and the best value in service.
(2)
Unfortunately, due to the increased costs of shipping, internal transport and tariffs on our overseas products, we are forced to increase the costs of our goods. These changes will take effect from June 1 2027, as this is the date of receipt of our first shipment of goods at the new prices. We encourage you to take advantage of our remaining stock, which is available at current prices. We have attached a list of items for your information.
(2)
Again, we sincerely apologise for the need to increase our prices; however, this situation is beyond our control.
(2)
Yours faithfully
ATLAS COMMUNICATIONS

(4/5)
Marc-Anthony Matthews
Marc-Anthony Matthews
Sales & Marketing Manager
(2)
Att
(2)
cc   Sales Director

Figure 10.8 A fully blocked style letter

ATLAS COMMUNICATIONS
23 Knolly Drive,
Kingston 6,
JAMAICA

Tel: (876) 778-2936   Fax: (876) 778-7901
email: atlascoms@gmail.com   Website: www.atlascommunications.com

(3)
Our Ref: PP/134/tf
(2)
Your Ref: G1507/jj   March 17, 2026
(2)
The Manager
Atlantic Enterprises,
14 Victoria Street,
Kingston,
JAMAICA.
(2)
Attention: Ms. Janine Julien
(2)
Dear Sirs,
(2)

NEW STATIONERY PRICES

(2)
    Atlas Communications is grateful for your continued support as we strive to supply you with our leading brands of stationery and supplies and the best value in service.
(2)
    Unfortunately, due to the increased costs of shipping, internal transport and tariffs on our overseas products, we are forced to increase the costs of our goods. These changes will take effect from June 1, 2027, as this is the date of receipt of our first shipment of goods at the new prices. We encourage you to take advantage of our remaining stock, which is available at current prices. We have attached a list of items for your information.
(2)
    Again, we sincerely apologise for the need to increase our prices; however, this situation is beyond our control.
(2)
Yours faithfully
ATLAS COMMUNICATIONS

(4/5)
Marc-Anthony Matthews
Marc-Anthony Matthews
Sales & Marketing Manager
Att
(2)
cc   Sales Director

Figure 10.9 An indented-style letter

Figure 10.10 illustrates the *semi-blocked* letter style. This layout is very similar to the blocked-style letter in terms of its normal margin setting and the blocked style of the body of the letter.

SECTION 3

Figure 10.10 also includes the two significantly different features of the indented letter style. Additionally, the complimentary close and signatory line begin from the centre and move to the right of the document.

ATLAS COMMUNICATIONS
23 Knolly Drive
Kingston 6
JAMAICA

Tel: (876) 778-2936　　　　　　　　　　　　　　　　　Fax: (876) 778-7901
email atlascoms@gmail.com　　　　　　　　　Website: www.atlascommunications.com

(3)
Our Ref PP/134/tf　　　　　　　　　　　　　　　　　　　　　March 17 2026
(2)
Your Ref: G1507/jj
(2)
Atlantic Enterprises
14 Victoria Street
Kingston
JAMAICA
(2)
Attention: Ms. Janine Julien
(2)
Dear Sirs
(2)
NEW STATIONERY PRICES
(2)
Atlas Communications is grateful for your continued support as we strive to supply you with our leading brands of stationery and supplies and the best value in service.
(2)
Unfortunately, due to the increased costs of shipping, internal transport and tariffs on our overseas products, we are forced to increase the costs of our goods. These changes will take effect from June 1, 2027, as this is the date of receipt of our first shipment of goods at the new prices. We encourage you to take advantage of our remaining stock, which is available at current prices. We have attached a list of items for your information.
(2)
Again, we sincerely apologise for the need to increase our prices; however, this situation is beyond our control.
(2)
Yours faithfully
ATLAS COMMUNICATIONS

(4/5)
Marc-Anthony Matthews
Marc-Anthony Matthews
Sales & Marketing Manager
(2)
Att
(2)
cc Sales Director

Figure 10.10 A semi-blocked style letter

10 Business documents

> ✓ **Helpful hint**
> Always remember to recheck your work for compliance with letter-writing standards before submitting or sending out your document. This is called *proofreading*.

→ Activity

As the administrative assistant of First Class Cuisine Essentials, you are required to prepare a letter using the information that follows. It is to be signed by the General Manager, Mr. Charles Booby, and the recipient is Ms. Angele Reneaud, Advertising Account Manager of Basseterre Communications, Cotton Ground, St. Thomas Lowland, Nevis for her action.

1 Using A4 or letter-size paper, create a letterhead for First Class Cuisine Essentials, with at least one colour and an appropriate graphic for a logo.
2 Using the letterhead you have created and today's date, prepare a letter in semi-blocked style to send to Ms. Reneaud.
3 Use a suitable 12 pt font and save it as CAD Letter.

> First Class Cuisine Essentials has been in operation from its location at Old Road Town, St. Thomas, Middle Island Parish for twenty years. It has been a profitable company, offering top brands in commercial restaurant equipment supplies, such as True and American-made. The company's focus on prompt response to calls to their telephone number (869) 555 0080, or queries via emails to firstessentials@cuisine.com, has set them apart from competitors.
>
> First Class Cuisine Essentials has decided to host a Customer Appreciation Day on its twentieth anniversary, July 1, from 1.00 p.m. to 4.00 p.m. The theme for the day is 'Thank you for your support throughout the years!'
>
> Customers, who are all restaurant owners or investors, will be treated to refreshments and demonstrations from three chefs, who will be cooking on the newest brand of stoves in stock. One lucky attendee will win a prize of a solar-powered multi-purpose range. Solar-powered ranges are said to be a game-changer in reducing costs of power supplies for restaurants. There will also be a raffle for staff members, and the prize is a gift voucher for dining for a family at The Gourmet restaurant, paid for by First Class Cuisine Essentials.

Short letters

Short letters are brief letters sent to various parties. They may be set out using any of the layouts that you have already met in this chapter; that is, fully blocked, indented or semi-blocked. Short letters use A5-sized paper, with a 2.54 cm (1 inch) margin all around. This is slightly different from regular sized letters.

Figure 10.11 shows a short letter in fully blocked layout.

SECTION 3

ATLAS COMMUNICATIONS
23 Knolly Drive
Kingston 6
JAMAICA

Tel: (876) 778-2936　　　　　　　　　　　　　　　　　Fax: (876) 778-7901
email: atlascoms@gmail.com　　　　　　　Website: www.atlascommunications.com

(3)
Our Ref PP/134/tf
(2)
March 17 2026
(2)
The Manager
Atlantic Enterprises
14 Victoria Street
Kingston
JAMAICA
(2)
<u>Attention Ms Janine Julien</u>
(2)
Dear Sirs
(2)
NEW STATIONERY PRICES
(2)
We at Atlas Communications are grateful for your continued support of our business.
(2)
Unfortunately, due to increased costs, we are forced to increase prices on our goods. These changes will take effect from June 1, 2027. Our sincere apologies; however, the situation is beyond our control.
(2)
Yours faithfully
ATLAS COMMUNICATIONS

(3/4)
Marc-Anthony Matthews
Marc-Anthony Matthews
Sales & Marketing Manager
(2)
Att

Figure 10.11 A short letter in fully blocked layout

> **→ Activity**
>
> Transform the information below into a properly formatted, edited and proofread short letter using a fully blocked style.
>
> | |
> |---|
> | May 19, 2027 |
> | Impossible Made Possible Ad Agency |
> | L'Aimee Road |
> | Gros Islet |
> | St. Lucia |
> | Ref PSRdd19/4/27   Dear Sir/Madam |
> | We hereby submit a request for a quotation for your market services for a period of six months to be used for engaging the public in a 'Clean Up' campaign of 6 major beaches over the period June 2027–December 2027. |
> | Thank you in advance for your prompt response. |
> | Yours Sincerely Lemelle Diavan   Manager |
> | Health Programme for the Environment |
> | Bois Bande Building Castries Saint Lucia |
> | Tel: 758 555 2829 Email Health.Env@govlc |

Continuation pages

One-page letters and the first pages of documents do not carry numbers. However, if documents, including letters, go on to additional pages, these are called **continuation pages**. The continuation pages of letters and other manuscripts are numbered to enable the order of the pages to be identified. *Note that the numbering starts with 2 on the first continuation page.* The name of the **addressee**; that is, the name on the **inside address** and the date of the letter, also appear on the continuation pages. The placement of the name, the page number and the date differ depending on whether the style is blocked or indented. Table 10.9 shows how the continuation page of a fully blocked letter is completed.

Table 10.9 Initial and continuation page of a blocked letter

Keying instructions for heading up a continuation page of a fully blocked letter	Layout at the start of a continuation page in a fully blocked style
1 Type the page number at the top of the page. 2 Press the enter key twice. 3 Type the recipient's name (name of the addressee or name on inside address). 4 Press the enter key twice. 5 Type the current date. 6 Press the enter key three times. 7 Continue with the letter.	2 Mrs. Jacqueline Timothy March 19, 2026

Table 10.10 shows how to type the continuation page of an indented letter.

Table 10.10 Initial and continuation page of an indented letter

Keying instructions for heading the continuation page of an indented letter	Layout at the start of a continuation page in an indented letter
Keying instructions for heading the continuation page of an indented letter At the top of the page type in the page number Enter (1) type in the name of the recipient (name of the addressee or name on inside address. Date is in line with the recipient's name Enter 3 times then continue with the letter.	2 Mrs. Jacqueline Timothy March 19, 2026

To *add value* to continuation pages, it is recommended that the second page should contain more text than the complimentary close and the signature line; that is, at least a paragraph of text. The solution would be to:

- widen the first page margins from 2.54 cm (1 inch) to 5.08 cm (1.5 inches)
- use a larger font, and/or
- change your paper size.

Circular letters

Circular letters (*form letters*, *standard letters* or *billing statements*) are used to communicate similar information to recipients. Schools, banks and utility companies have large numbers of parents or clients, and letters of this nature are sent on a regular basis. The circular letter itself can be prepared:

- using the blocked, indented or semi-blocked style
- with the organisation's colours, associated with their brand, in its letterhead
- without a date (for example a fund-raising letter) so that it can be sent out again at another time
- with spaces left open for entering individualised data, such as:
- the inside address, date, place and information specific to the addressee
- the name and address of the recipient, using a non-specific **salutation** consisting of either 'Dear' followed by a line or 'Dear Customer/Client', 'Dear Parent/Guardian' or 'Dear Participant'
- the amount due or date of appointment, relevant to the named recipient
- with an attachment called a **tear-off slip** that requests the receiver respond by providing some data to the sender; this slip contains space for the requested data, alongside some standard text.

When a circular letter is to be dispatched, the individualised data is entered either manually (handwritten) or by using the *mail-merge* feature available in Microsoft Word.

Figure 10.12 displays a circular letter with a tear-off (permission) slip.

SIX CREEKS SECONDARY SCHOOL

Banks Road, Six Creeks, San Fernando

Telephone 681-4538   Email sixcreeks@gmail.com

Ref EDPM/dwm

May 10, 2026

Dear Parent/Guardian

One aspect of the School Based Assessment (SBA) for the subject EDPM is knowledge of types of office machinery. This includes research on these devices for inclusion in students' portfolios.

In this regard, the Form Five Electronic Document Preparation and Management (EDPM) class will be visiting the Business Museum, located on Lyons Street, Port of Spain. The date carded for the trip is Friday May 22, 2026 from 9.00 a.m. to 12.00 noon.

Please kindly complete and return the following Permission Slip for your child/ward for the upcoming school trip.

Yours faithfully

(4/5)
Riley Michaels
Riley Michaels
Principal III

--✂

I hereby authorise my child/ward to attend the school's EDPM class trip to the Business Museum on Friday May 22, 2026.

………………………………………   ………………………………………
Name of Student (Block Letters)   Parent/Guardian (Block Letters)

………………………………………   ………………………………………
Date   Signature of Parent/Guardian

Figure 10.12 A circular letter with a tear-off slip

Figure 10.13 is an extract from the circular letter that Atlas Communications would prepare to send out to all its customers. Note that the format follows the blocked style. There are spaces left for naming individual customers and for putting in the relevant addresses and the appropriate salutation.

ATLAS COMMUNICATIONS
23 Knolly Drive
Kingston 6
JAMAICA

Tel: (876) 778-2936   Fax: (876) 778-7901
email: atlascoms@gmail.com   Website: www.atlascommunications.com

Our Ref PP/134/tf

March 17, 2026

«Title» «First_Name» «Last_Name»
«Company_Name»
«Address_Line_1»
«Address_Line_2»
«Country_or_Region»

Dear «Title» «Last_Name»

NEW STATIONERY PRICES

Atlas Communications is grateful for your continued support as we strive to supply you with our leading brands of goods.
Unfortunately, due to the increased costs of shipping, internal transport and tariffs on our overseas products, we are forced to increase the costs of our goods.
Again, we sincerely apologise for the need to increase our prices; however, this situation is beyond our control.

Yours faithfully,
ATLAS COMMUNICATIONS

Marc-Anthony Matthews
Marc-Anthony Matthews
Sales & Marketing Manager

Figure 10.13 A circular letter

Key terms

action plan The part of minutes that identifies the person responsible for actions to be taken before the next meeting

agenda/chairperson's agenda A list of items to be discussed at a meeting; a chairperson's agenda contains additional details on certain items to guide them

addressee The name of the person to whom a letter is directed

circular letter A type of letter, also called *form letter*, *standard letter* or *billing statement*, used to communicate similar information to recipients who may or may not be addressed individually

complimentary close A pleasant phrase placed at the end of a letter

continuation page An additional page needed to cover a document's information

correspondence The exchange of information between senders and recipients via memos, notices, letters, emails or other means

date/date as postmark The month, day and year on which a document was typed or sent for delivery

designation The name and position of the person signing a letter

envelope A holder to enclose documents, designed to protect them as well as display a recipient's address

inside address The location of a letter's recipient

layout style A standard way of setting out the content of types of correspondence, i.e. fully blocked, indented or semi-blocked

letter A formal method of business communication

letterhead A type of header used on an ongoing basis for providing information about an organisation, including name, address and contact information

mail merge A feature of an application that provides for the dispatch of similar letters to many recipients at the same time

memorandum (memo) The standard method of communicating on company business with people inside the company

minutes The official written record of discussions and decisions taken at a meeting

notations/special notations Instructions to a mail room, delivery service or post office on how to treat or process an envelope

notices Advice that a meeting is to take place, giving the date, time and location

paper type, size, use The material used to record or print a message to be communicated; paper varies from flimsy to stiff and matte to glossy; sizes vary from the commonly used A4 to business-card size; use varies from the common printer copy to the heavy parchment for invitations and certificates

rapporteur A person assigned to record either verbatim or in summary form what was said at a meeting or conference

reference A combination of letters and numbers included in formal letters to help in tracing the thread of communication between parties and retrieving related correspondence

salutation A greeting for an addressee, such as 'Dear Sir/Madam', placed at the beginning of a letter after the subject line

signatory The name and position of the person signing a letter

subject heading A brief description of the main topic of correspondence

tear-off slip An attachment to a letter that requests that the receiver respond by providing some data to the sender

verbatim A method of recording the exact words of a speaker

SECTION 3

Summary

In this chapter, you have learned to:

- distinguish among paper types and sizes and their uses
- distinguish among envelope sizes and their uses
- create letterheads
- select the appropriate paper size (and envelope), margins, orientation, line spacing and indentation styles for different business documents
- prepare the main types of business documents from skeleton information
- use Word's mail-merge feature.

Practice, research and exam-style questions

Multiple-choice questions

1. Which term is *not* a type of flap on envelopes?
   A Wallet
   B Bullet
   C Square
   D Commercial

2. Which of the following layout styles adopt some of the elements of other types?
   A Semi-blocked
   B Blocked
   C Indented
   D Semi-indented

3. Which one of the following statements is *true*?
   A Memos and notices are the same thing with different headings.
   B A meeting should always follow the order set by the agenda.
   C Minutes must be accompanied by action plans.
   D Businesses use preformatted memo forms.

4. The document that gives details about the occurrence of events in a meeting is the meeting …
   A notice.
   B minutes.
   C agenda.
   D memo.

5. What provides postal personnel with processing instructions?
   A Enclosures
   B Compliments
   C Notations
   D Salutations

6. What is the chief purpose of the reference number in business letters?
   A Maintaining the thread of communication between recipients
   B Indicating the code for the creator and the recipient
   C Providing information on the purpose of the letter
   D Drawing the attention of the people with interest in the subject

7. One line of data and/or the complimentary close alone on a continuation page is not acceptable. Which of these options is *not* a possible solution?
   A Substituting A4 paper for letter size
   B Using Roman numerals for numbering
   C Changing font and/or font style
   D Widening the first page margins

8. In which type of letter is the salutation usually very general or non-specific?
   A Circular letter
   B Merged letter
   C Blocked letter
   D Indented letter

9. If a secondary data source is incorrect, what action will be affected?
   A Efficient use of mail merge
   B Exporting the document
   C Completion of the tear-off slip
   D Communicating with correct recipients

10 Which listing correctly describes a partial sequence for a mail merge?
   A Select recipients, preview results, insert merge fields, finish & merge
   B Prepare main document, amend data list, select recipients, finish & merge
   C Amend data list, prepare main document, preview results, finish & merge
   D Go to mailings, prepare main document, insert merge fields, finish & merge

Exam-style questions

1 Preparing a memo and a notice

> August 19, 2026
>
> Impossible Made Possible Ad Agency
>
> L'Aimee Road
>
> St. Lucia
>
> Ref No:
>
> Dear Tanielle Courvier
>
> Senior Communications Specialist
>
> We are hereby submitting a request for a quotation for your marketing services for a period of six months to be used to engage the public in a vaccination campaign against the coronavirus. The proposed subject will be Developing a Health Campaign Against COVID 2026. Cases are surging again and a national campaign is necessary to prevent the situation from becoming overwhelming.
>
> Thank you in advance for your prompt response.
>
> Yours sincerely
>
> Christopher Fournier Health Education Advisor III
>
> Ministry of Health

The letter above was sent to an advertising agency. Use the information contained in it to:
a prepare a *short memo* to staff of the Ministry of Health's Corporate Communication Division asking them to submit their ideas on the proposed campaign; use a properly formatted and edited blocked style for the memo
b prepare a *notice of meeting* to all staff of the Health Education Division providing the three necessary details that a notice should contain, and apply all the formatting rules appropriately.

SECTION 3

2 Creating a mail merge

Your EDPM class of nine students is having a field trip as part of their School Based Assessment (SBA). Each student's parent/guardian must be formally advised of this activity as they need to give permission for the field trip. The Principal, Ms. Anet Perera, of Fatima Academisch, Meerzog Road, Suriname, must inform the parents of this venture and ensure that she has evidence that permission has been granted. She asks that you, as the teacher, prepare a circular letter with a tear-off slip for her signature. Each parent must sign and return the permission slip before the student is allowed to attend the field trip. Parents and guardians are also to be asked to visit the school's website, www.fatcollacad.edu.sur, for further information.

a Use the appropriate production tool to prepare your primary source (a circular letter with a tear-off slip), giving the following details:
- Destination of trip: Offices of Paramaribo Construction Ltd, Paramaribo City
- Date of trip: February 23, 2026
- Purpose of trip: Observation of general office operations and interview with Office Manager Mr. John Lolydorp
- Travel arrangements: School bus departs 8.00 a.m. Return trip arrives 2.00 p.m.
- Students are to wear proper school uniform and provide their own refreshments
- Tear-off slips are to be signed and returned by February 16, 2026

b Use the mail-merge wizard to send your circular letter, using the following information for your secondary source (database). Use the 'type a new list' function. Stop before the 'finish and merge' action.

SBA parent database				
Parent/Guardian				
First Name	Last Name	Student	Address 1	Address 2
Winston	Oranje	Nickerie	Dominee	Zorg En Hoop Air
Reachel	Zamora	Maagdalen	Neuman	Kekemba
John	Agostini	Zach	Jodenbree	Central Zone
Oscar	Pontbeuit	Flora	Keizer	Wyndham
Vincent	Latour	Anton	Beyroeth	Paramaribo

11 Simple and advanced displays

> ### Objectives
> By the end of this chapter, you will be able to:
> - produce simple displays using the most appropriate stationery and styles
> - produce effective and creative displays given a specific task
> - prepare newsletters using formatting and standards
> - prepare advanced displays given skeleton notes.

Introduction

Office personnel use word-processing extensively. However, the activity is not confined to the production of the business documents described in Chapter 10, but includes the preparation of **displays**. *Displays* include items created for special tasks that are part of the operations of specific businesses, for example menus for restaurants, and flyers that promote special events. Many displays require creativity and innovation as well as adherence to basic rules of presentation. Some advanced displays, such as **flow charts**, require a more technical approach. In both cases, Microsoft Word provides **wizards** to support their creation. Manipulating tabular formats helps to ensure proper alignment and indentation of text and graphics.

Manipulating tables for displays

Once a **table** has been created, you can manipulate it and its content in many ways. The key to changing a table's structure is the 'table layout' subtab (Figure 11.1), which becomes available once your cursor is inside any table.

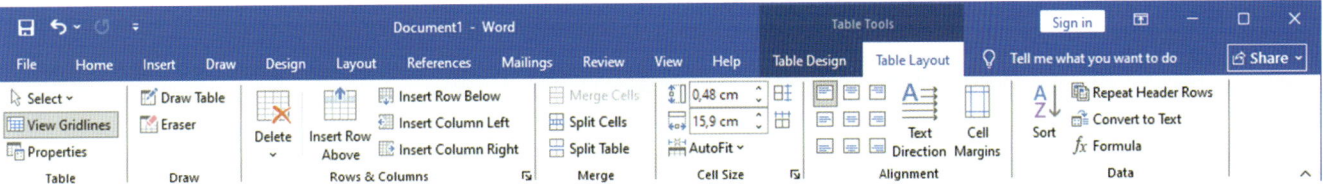

Figure 11.1 Table layout subtab

Place the cursor as directed or highlight the cells to be restructured. The following sections show some of the processes and steps required when using the 'table layout' tool.

Adding rows and columns

To add rows or columns:

1. Place your cursor in a cell that sits in the column or row next to where you wish the additional row or column to sit.
2. Click on the appropriate button in the 'rows & columns' menu as many times as needed.
3. Alternatively, right-click in the existing row or column to bring up the menu for inserting new rows or columns.

SECTION 3

Helpful hint
Make sure you don't delete cells you want to keep. If you do, use the 'undo typing' arrow at the top left of the screen.

Deleting rows and columns
To delete rows or columns:

1 Place your cursor in a cell of the column or row to be deleted or drag the cursor to highlight several cells.
2 Click on the delete button in the 'rows & columns' menu.

Resizing cells
The 'cell size' menu is useful for determining whether cells expand automatically to fit content (*autofit*) or whether cells of equal or different sizes can be created to the user's specifications.

Alternatively, cell borders can be dragged left and right, and up or down as needed. Place your cursor on the border and look for the two-sided arrow cursor. Hold the border and drag to the new position.

Helpful hint
Splitting a table is useful for arranging different cell sizes within a table. Afterwards, use the backspace or delete key to remove the split. The new table will rejoin, while maintaining its new cell sizes.

Merging, splitting and nesting cells or tables
Occasionally, you may need to *merge* several cells to create a header for the cells below them. To merge cells, select the cells to be merged and click on 'merge cells' in the merge menu.

To *split* a table by rows, place your cursor in the row that is to become the first row of the new table. Click on 'split table'. It is also possible to split a cell using the same 'rows & columns' menu.

Occasionally, there is a need to place, or *nest*, a table within a cell of another table. Place your cursor in the destination cell and insert a table of the desired size.

Borders and shading
The 'table layout' subtab and its 'properties' menu provides access to the 'borders and shading' window. Use the borders window to choose different views of outer and inner lines, ranging from all borders to none. You can also vary the thicknesses of the borders.

Shading allows the addition of colour to highlighted cells or the entire table, and you can achieve various degrees of transparency or depth of colour.

Sorting rows and columns
Use the 'data' menu in the 'table layout' tab to shift rows or columns to achieve either descending or ascending alphabetical order.

In the case of rows, place your cursor into any cell row and click on the 'sort' menu.

For a column sort, place your cursor in one of the headers and click on the 'sort' menu. Note that all data in the row or column will move with the sort.

Other table actions

Putting in headings
Row and column headings are very important as they provide a label for the entries in the cells. The headings should be:

- in a slightly larger font size than the table content, with at least one clear line of space before entering text in the next row
- aligned in different positions within the cell; to achieve this:
    - highlight the text in the column headings
    - go to the 'table layout' subtab alignment menu
    - click on your desired position within the cell

11 Simple and advanced displays

- place in a vertical direction, if desired; to achieve this:
  - highlight the text in the column headings
  - go to the 'text direction' button on the 'table layout' subtab 'alignment' menu and click OK.

However, if the text is too long or heavy, it will be broken up to fit the cell. Either change the cell size or drag the line below the header to fit the content. Oblique or slanted headings are easily achieved in a spreadsheet program.

Simple calculations

Word tables can be used for simple calculations, such as counting, adding and finding the average of numbers in a row or column.

1 Click the cell in which the final tabulation is to be placed.
2 In the 'table layout' subtab, choose the data menu, where you can select an icon for 'formula' (fx). A formula dialog box will appear.
3 Choose from =SUM(ABOVE) to find the total of the numbers in a column or =SUM(LEFT) to total the numbers in a row.

Applying formatting rules

Tables 11.1 and 11.2 are examples of a table that was not formatted and the same table after the application of format tools.

Table 11.1 Unformatted table

First Name	Surname	Address	Rent Paid $	Balance Owed $
Trevison	James	Carenage	700	200
Cavonne	Hislop	Scarborough	800	100
Sierra	Mitchell	Tabaquite	900	-
Ronalda	Cedeno	Williamsville	600	300
		TOTAL		

Table 11.2 Formatted table

First Name	Surname	Address	Rent Paid $	Balance Owed $
Ronalda	Cedeno	Williamsville	600.00	300.00
Cavonne	Hislop	Scarborough	800.00	100.00
Trevison	James	Carenage	700.00	200.00
Sierra	Mitchell	Tabaquite	900.00	-
		TOTAL	$3,000.00	$600.00

The featured differences are:

- sorting of data in A–Z alphabetical order based on surname
- shading of column headings
- redirecting the text in the Rent and Balance columns to the vertical direction
- showing financial data to decimal places
- using the formula in the data group to calculate the totals.

> **Helpful hint**
>
> 1 Most of the calculations in Word tables involve money. The standard format is to set out the figures using two decimal places, with all figures right-aligned in a cell.
>
> 2 To include two decimal places in the figures automatically (so you don't need to type them in every time), go to the paragraph subtab, click on 'tabs' under the 'indents and spacing' button and enter 2 in the 'tab stop position'. Click on 'decimal' in the alignment box. Then click OK.

Forms and templates

Tables or tabular formats are not only for arranging, manipulating and comparing data; they also allow you to enter information in ways that control their position. They are therefore useful as the basis of **forms** and *templates*, such as application forms and resumes. Splitting and merging cells and splitting and rejoining tables are useful for achieving various cell sizes on the same page.

Forms

Forms are documents with fixed designs. They are used to collect information from a source, and are often arranged in a user-friendly and logical fashion so that data is easily collated. They can be created then printed as documents or retained as editable digital documents. Some common forms are:

- job application forms
- leave forms, for example sick, casual, vacation
- loan application forms
- questionnaires/surveys
- invoices and credit and debit notes.

Creating forms

A4, letter or legal-sized paper are the most common stationery on which forms are created. The normal margin is 2.54 cm (1 inch) all around. However, some forms use very narrow margins to keep as much data as possible on a single sheet. Where the amount of information to be collected is very limited, A5 paper may be used.

There are two main steps to create a form:

Step 1

- Estimate of the number of columns and rows you may need. You should work this out before creating your table. To estimate the number of rows, pay attention to the name and number of section headings required.
- Establish which section needs the largest number of columns. For example, Figure 11.2 on the next page, requires twelve rows and four columns.
- Prepare to use more than one table if the form must be printed on the reverse side of a document.
- Identify the cells that need to be merged. Column headings are usually placed in cells merging across the row.
- Determine which cells need to be split. Some cells need to be split, or merged and then split, according to the information required.

Step 2

- Enter your text, starting with column headings, and then the details required under each section.
- Adjust row heights and alignment of text as necessary.
- Press enter three times after the text to leave enough space for the person filling out the form.

Figure 11.2 is a sample of a typical application for employment form.

JUICY JUICE LTD

#63 Main Road, Scarborough, Tobago
Telephone: (868) 682 6961 Fax: (868) 682 9662 Email: juice@liquid.org
Visit our website at www.juicyjuice.net

APPLICATION FOR EMPLOYMENT *(Complete all sections)*
State position required:

PERSONAL INFORMATION			
Surname	First Name	Middle Name	Date of Birth

Address:	**Contact information**
	Telephone:
	Email:

EDUCATION		
Institution attended	Level of Examination and year attained	Certificates attained

EMPLOYMENT HISTORY		
Period	Job title	Knowledge and skills attained

REFERENCE		
Name	Job title	Telephone Contact

Signature	Date

Name in block letters

Figure 11.2 Application for employment form

Templates

Templates are like forms in that they are useful for saving time and effort. Templates are for frequent use, for example monthly reports, or a letter or presentation that is branded with the company's information. Templates include placeholders for the insertion of text, numbers or graphics. The most familiar templates are those created for resumes and standard reports.

SECTION 3

Resume

A *resumé* is a formal document prepared by someone seeking employment, and is often requested by employers as part of the jobseeker's application. When preparing your resume, it is important to pay special attention to your grammar and spelling, as this is often used by the employer to evaluate your suitability for the job.

A resumé should contain your:

1 **Contact information:** include your name, address, email address and phone number
2 **Profile, objective or summary:** briefly describe your goals
3 **Experience:** list your relevant work history
4 **Education:** include your educational background
5 **Skills:** highlight relevant skills, tools and certifications
6 **Relevant accomplishments and volunteer work:** showcase any other relevant information
7 **References:** include contact information

> ✓ **Helpful hint**
>
> Ensure that your email address is businesslike. For example, if you wish to be taken seriously by your prospective employer, use your proper name (not one that your friends may call you), such as P.Antoine@gmail.com rather than partygirl@gmail.com.

	RESUME		
Name	Tarelle Frontin		
Address	1 Yearwood Street Valencia		
Telephone	868 620 1814		
E-mail Address	Tfrontin@gmail.com		
Personal Objective	To be the most suitable employee for any tasks given.		
Qualification	English Language	1	
	Mathematics	2	
	Office Administration	1	
	Principles of Accounts	1	
	Electronic Document Preparation & Management	1	
	History	2	
	English Literature	2	
Work Experience	List any holiday jobs, the places worked, dates		
Projects undertaken/ Volunteerism	State if you are a member of any community activities/ church, etc.		
Interests/Hobbies	Blogging, reading, travelling,		
References	Ms. M. Lopez	Ms. A. Pickett	
	Principal	Vice Principal	
	Six Creeks Secondary School	Six Creeks Secondary School	
	868 682 6945	868 620 1418	

Simple displays

Simple displays can be used to create documents such as business cards, index cards, **invitations** and **menus**. In this section, you will be shown how these displays can be created.

Cards

Cards are created for a variety of uses, which depend on the occasion. Table 11.3 shows examples of cards and the sizes that are used for them.

Table 11.3 Card sizes and uses

ISO number	Sizes (cm)	Sizes (inches)	Types of cards
A8	5.2 cm × 7.4 cm	2 inches × 3.5 inches	Business
A6	10.5 cm × 14.8 cm	4.3 inches × 5.83 inches	Index/invitation
A7	7.4 cm × 10.5 cm	3.5 inches × 4.3 inches	
A7	7.4 cm × 10.5 cm	3.5 inches × 4.3 inche	Placeholder/reservation
A6	10.5 cm × 14.8 cm	4.3 inches × 5.83 inches	Postcard/greetings

Index cards

Index cards are used to record significant but brief pieces of data in spaces such as libraries, doctors' offices and on a receptionist's desk. They are used for researchers' notes, recipes, cue cards, flash cards or visual aids for studying or to accompany presentations. Their shape, preset lines and varied colour strips or faces allow easy retrieval of records (Figure 11.3).

Other kinds of cards in everyday use include postcards and greetings cards.

Business cards

Business cards provide information on an organisation like the information on its letterhead. In addition, the name and position of its representative will be included. Business cards are usually small in size as they are made to fit into wallets or card holders. They are often printed in a similar fashion to labels, with a single sheet of paper holding as many as ten business cards. There are many applications, such as Canva® and Placeit®, that provide a variety of templates to help create business cards, and other kinds of cards. Word provides wizards to do the same. Business cards are simple to prepare with and without wizards.

Figure 11.3 Index cards, showing tabs and colours

> ✓ **Helpful hint**
> Wizards are guides for users that simplify tasks by breaking them down into smaller, manageable steps, where the user makes choices from dialog boxes.

Creating cards

Table 11.4 sets out the steps for designing your own business cards with and without a wizard.

Table 11.4 Creating business cards with and without a wizard

Single business card using a Word wizard	Several business cards without using a wizard
1 On a blank document page, click on the file tab, then the 'new' subtab and type 'business card' into the search bar to access many options. 2 Double-click to select a design and make your choice of colours, font styles and sizes. 3 Insert your logo (if any), or insert your choice of a shape or picture from your own folders, or search online by clicking on the insert tab. 4 Enter your information in the appropriate fields, proofread it, then save and/or print your document (or share it with selected people).	1 Open a Word document page, preferably in A4 or letter size. 2 Insert a table of two columns and eight to ten rows. 3 Use narrow margins all around. 4 In the first cell of the table, type in information about the organisation and the representative. Use centre-alignment for most of the text. Place the organisation's logo in a corner of the cell or as background (see Chapter 9). This is the *prototype*. 5 Copy and paste the prototype into the remaining cells. 6 Insert a thick border to allow for cutting. 7 Proofread your work and make any necessary adjustments. 8 Save and print.

Figure 11.4 is an example of producing multiple business cards at once.

 JUICY JUICE LTD

#63 Main Road, Scarborough, Tobago

Telephone: (868) 682 6961
Fax: (868) 682 9662 Email: juice@liquid.org

Visit our website at www.juicyjuice.net

Carla Perreira
Marketing Manager

 JUICY JUICE LTD

#63 Main Road, Scarborough, Tobago

Telephone: (868) 682 6961
Fax: (868) 682 9662 Email: juice@liquid.org

Visit our website at www.juicyjuice.net

Carla Perreira
Marketing Manager

 JUICY JUICE LTD

#63 Main Road, Scarborough, Tobago

Telephone: (868) 682 6961
Fax: (868) 682 9662 Email: juice@liquid.org

Visit our website at www.juicyjuice.net

Carla Perreira
Marketing Manager

 **JUICY JUICE LTD**

#63 Main Road, Scarborough, Tobago

Telephone: (868) 682 6961
Fax: (868) 682 9662 Email: juice@liquid.org

Visit our website at www.juicyjuice.net

Carla Perreira
Marketing Manager

Figure 11.4 Producing multiple business cards

Invitations and menus

> **Did you know?**
> Save the date invitations ask recipients to keep in mind the date of an upcoming event.

Invitations and menus are also found on cards, but their size and purpose vary widely as they depend on user requirements.

Invitations

An invitation is a request for people to attend an event, such as a product launch or other celebrations (Figure 11.5). Invitation designs vary widely, but they are usually printed on paper called *cardstock*. Paper sizes such as A7, A6 or A5, in landscape or portrait orientations, may be used. Invitations contain information on:

- the date, time, venue, type of occasion
- whether formal or informal
- whether there is a need to respond to the invitation (RSVP).

An invitation's artistic elements and themes may reflect the casual, semi-casual or formal nature of the function.

To create your own invitation, with or without using a wizard:

1. Go to the layout tab, then size subtab and select from the preset sizes (for example A5) or from 'more paper sizes', which allows you to design your own custom-sized paper.
2. Choose either portrait or landscape orientation.
3. Select margins appropriate for your paper size and the amount of text to be typed, or choose and enter your own 'custom margin', for example A5 landscape might use 1.27 cm (½ inch) top and bottom and 2.54 cm (1 inch) left and right.
4. Enter your information using suitable fonts and font sizes. Note that if the invitation is to be directed to individuals, then leave space to insert their names.
5. Insert one or more images, pictures or graphics of your choice, if you would like to, and place behind the text using the 'wrap text' tool.
6. You can create a page border using the home tab, paragraph subtab and the 'borders' icon. If you would like to include a border, choose 'borders and shading' and select 'page border'.
7. Save and/or print your invitation.

You can follow similar steps as for business cards to create multiple invitations at once.

Figure 11.5 An invitation

Menus

A menu is a list of food items that are available for purchase at a restaurant. It may also be a list of food items that will be offered at an event. On occasion, invitations are accompanied by menus. In a similar fashion to cards and invitations, artistic elements differentiate menus from one establishment to another; however, inserting a table is helpful for aligning text.

Consider the advice in Table 11.5 when preparing a menu.

Table 11.5 Creating a menu with and without a wizard

Leader characters or tab stops	To create leader characters on a page:
	1. Click Layout, and sub tab Paragraph
	2. Click down arrow and choose tabs
	3. In the tab stop position window, enter the length representing where you wish to end the leader characters.
	4. Select whether the leader characters are to be dots (2), dashes (3) or solid line (4).
	5. Press Ok.
	   i. Note that once set for the first line of the document, it will appear automatically for the following lines.
	   ii. If a list was created beforehand, select all parts that are to show leader characters and follow the process above.
	   ii. Use a section break or above and/or below, if leader characters are not wanted.

Line spacing, margins and borders	• A restaurant menu is often typed in single line spacing, with at least one clear line of space separating the different categories of meals. • Margins may be very narrow to accommodate a lot of text or the margin may be widened to allow pictures of meals to be included. • An attractive outside border may be included. Occasionally, different categories are set apart from each other using inner borders. • The line spacing of a special-event menu is determined by the amount of text to accommodate and the paper size.
Page size and layout	• The heading and/or the meal list may use a centred, horizontal or vertical layout. • Restaurant menus are often printed on a single sheet, or on pages folded to achieve 4/6/8 data spaces. For special events, A5, A4 or letter size is the usual choice. • Items are usually set out on separate lines, with leader characters to the price.
Text effects	• The front of the display or the top heading of the page often uses drop caps on first letters in words or expanded text. This is available on the font subtab of the home tab. Use the down arrow to access advanced font settings. The character spacing window allows you to increase and space the normal font by up to 200%, e.g. **M E N U**. • The word 'Menu' and the heading of each category are often in a different font style and size from the listing of meals. • All fonts should be legible and attractive. • Eye-catching designs and pictures of the choice of meals available for selection occupy borders or are used as background to text.

Use wizard/no wizard	In Word: • From the file tab, click new. Type in 'menus': many templates become available. • Select one, and customise your menu with your chosen information, or choose the customisation options to create your own menu. • Proofread and save your menu.

Invitation with menu combination

Occasionally, invitations to formal events come with a menu. There are some differences to consider when invitations are combined with a menu, including:

- Invitations only may use a landscape orientation, while a portrait orientation is used for the combination.
- Invitations only usually use cardstock of varying colours, while an invitation-with-menu combination may be A5, A4 or letter size, or a customised paper size and quality.
- The text for a combination should be centred horizontally and vertically. To centre the menu horizontally:
    1. Highlight your text.
    2. Go to the paragraph subtab on the home tab.
    3. Click on the centre-alignment button.

To centre your text vertically:

1. Keeping your text highlighted, go to the layout tab.
2. Click the down arrow on the page setup subtab.
3. Click 'layout' in the menu.
4. Click on 'page settings'.
5. Choose 'vertical' in the dialog box
6. Click on its down arrow and choose 'center'.

Figure 11.6 shows a combined invitation and menu.

SECTION 3

INVITATION

Kindly join us for an afternoon of Tea
at

Our Annual **All White** Tea Party
on
Sunday 12th April 2026
3-7 pm
at
The Kenton Hotel
43 Sean Avenue, On the Bay, Maracas

✽✽✽

M E N U
Price: $200 per person

A variety of Teas to choose from
Including our selection of cold drinks and juices

Choose from our array of local and international items
(4 Items per plate)
Cucumber and cream cheese sandwiches
Chicken Salad
Smoke Salmon
Mini Quiches
Pinwheel Cheese sandwiches
Ham and Cheese Scones
Veggies & Dip
Chicken Drumsticks
Mini Bakes and Accra

✽✽✽

THE SWEET STOP
Soursop or Coconut Ice Cream
Strawberry Cheesecake
Red Velvet
Black Fruit cake

✽✽✽

Live Entertainment provided by
Michael Breda & Teja Yung

Tickets available at
Luxury Hotel
Mr. K. Ferrier/Mrs. M. Yarde

Figure 11.6 Combination of an invitation and menu

11 Simple and advanced displays

Programmes

Programmes are lists of activities at events indicating what is to occur and the order in which they take place. They may be created for weddings, graduations, concerts, plays or funerals. Short programmes resemble invitations, where the content is centred horizontally and vertically. Longer programmes are often created in two-column formats, using A4 or letter-size paper folded in landscape orientation. Before you prepare your multi-column programme, develop a prototype of the programme's layout.

1. Hold a blank A4 or letter-size paper in landscape orientation.
2. Fold it in two.
3. Number the outer panels: page 4 on the left and page 1 on the right, as in Figure 11.7. Number the inner panels: page 2 on the left and page 3 on the right. See each side of the folded sheet as two pages, equal to two columns on your screen's table.

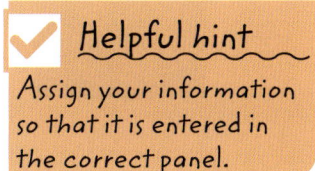

Helpful hint

Assign your information so that it is entered in the correct panel.

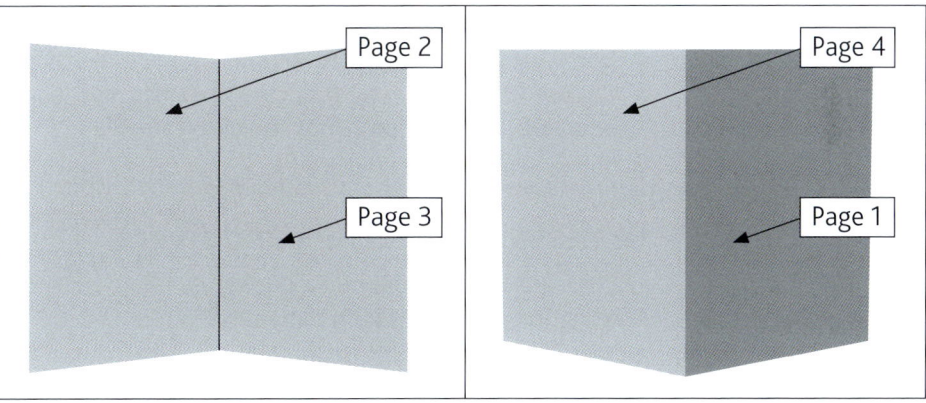

Figure 11.7 Bi-folded paper for visualising a two-column programme

To prepare a programme with two columns:

1. Open a new Word document.
2. Select the layout tab.
3. Change the orientation to landscape.
4. Click on 'columns' in the page setup subtab.
5. Go to 'more columns' and choose the two-column icon.
6. Select the 'equal column width' box and change spacing to 2.54 cm (1 inch).
7. Click OK.
8. Choose your font, font styles and graphics to insert as accompanying images or as background, as appropriate.
9. Type your information for page 4 (the back page) in the column on the left side of the page.
10. When your first column is complete, go to the layout tab, and then 'break' on the menu bar and click 'column break', then OK. (This will move your cursor to the column on the right side.)
11. Type your next set of information for page 1 in the column on the right.
12. When you have completed pages 4 and 1, go to layout, break, page break to get to the next page.
13. Enter the information for page 2 next. Use layout, break, column break to get to page 3.

Helpful hint

Choosing 2.54 cm (1 inch) in the equal column width box ensures that, when folded, information is not lost in the fold.

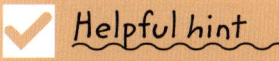

Helpful hint

If there is a lot of data to be entered, insert extra columns to keep your data properly aligned.

SECTION 3

> ✓ **Helpful hint**
>
> Be sure to move your cursor to the next page so you don't print the same page twice. Reinsert the page carefully or you might print over the top of the first print, wasting paper and time!

Printing a programme

As programmes may have information on both sides of the page (Figure 11.8), to print your programme:

1. Ensure that the correct size of paper is in the paper tray.
2. Enable the double-sided printing feature, which reinserts the paper automatically to print the other side.
3. If you do not have the double-sided printing feature, then each side must be printed individually using the 'current page' button, and that sheet must be reinserted, as directed, to print the other side.
4. Go to the file tab and select print.
5. Choose whether you want black and white or colour, and the number of copies.
6. Press print within the window.

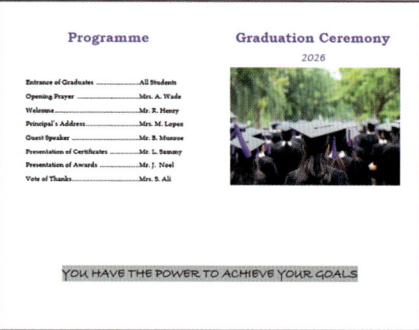

Figure 11.8 A multi-column programme for an event

Leaflets, newsletters and flyers

Leaflets are often used for distributing information on themes such as health matters or cultural or community events. Like programmes, it is useful to develop a sample by folding a single sheet of paper to form panels. When held in a landscape orientation, the page can be folded to show four sides, six sides or eight sides. The larger the leaflet (such as an eight-page leaflet), the larger the size of paper to be used (for example legal-sized paper). Follow the same set of steps as for creating a programme, with each page treated as a column for the placement of text and/or graphics.

Newsletters

Newsletters are used to communicate information in the form of articles about ideas, projects, events and campaigns to a group of people with similar interests. Newsletters can be sent out in print form or virtually via e-mail or other social media platforms, such as WhatsApp, websites and blogs. They are usually created on A4 or letter-size paper in portrait orientation. Newsletters are also prepared using columns. Margin sizes may vary, depending on the design of the newsletter.

Creative headers and drop caps are some of the artistic effects employed in creating a newsletter. A **Drop Cap** is the inclusion of a large capital letter at the start of a paragraph or section (Figure 11.9).

To apply a drop cap:

1. Select the letter to be dropped.
2. Go to the insert tab and the text subtab.
3. Select 'drop cap' and 'dropped' or 'margin' placement.
4. The default drop or margin placement is three lines down. If you prefer fewer or more lines in a drop, go to 'drop cap options'.
5. Click OK.

SIX CREEKS SECONDARY NEWSLETTER

Our third annual treasure hunt took place on March 26 at the school. This event was a great success, and the participants comprised of students of every level, from forms one to five.

The school's next fundraising event will be entitled 'A tribute to Mother'. This is a tea party to be held on May 10, 2026.

Figure 11.9 Extract from a newsletter using drop caps

Flyers

Flyers are created to promote events, such as sales, parties and concerts. They are usually prepared on a single sheet with text on one side only. They use eye-catching and colourful fonts and graphics to attract readers and inform them of the name, date, time and place of the event. Varying paper sizes can be used for producing flyers, and the types of paper can range from glossy to matte.

Special advanced displays

Flowcharts

A *flowchart* is a representation of a process or workflow that identifies the steps to be taken from start to completion of a project. Shapes are used as indicators of the step-by-step approach. These steps include:

1 starting the process
2 obtaining necessary documents and materials
3 carrying out process activities
4 making decisions that change the route or path of the process
5 ending the process.

Table 11.6 shows some of the shapes used in developing a flowchart.

Table 11.6 Flowchart shapes

Process shape	Process identifier	Meaning
⬭	Terminator	Identifies the start and end of the operation process
▭	Process	Identifies a processing activity, i.e. something is underway
◇	Decision point	Indicates that a decision must be made and the choice will affect what happens next. Some decisions are major; some are minor
▱	Document	Identifies a document that is important to process, such as a user manual or a progress report
▱	Data	Identifies the input and output process
→	Flow direction	Indicates the direction of the process
🗎🗎🗎	Multi-document	Indicates types of documents (e.g. material and progress reports) that keep track of expenditures or task completion rates, for example

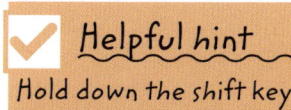

Helpful hint
Hold down the shift key when drawing lines and arrows to keep them straight.

To use shapes to create a flowchart:

1 Open a new Word document and click where your start terminator shape should go.
2 Click the insert tab and go to the shapes menu.
3 Select the flowchart shapes from the menu (Figure 11.10).
4 Select your desired number and types of shapes and place them in the document.
5 Add your text by clicking in the shape, or by right-clicking in the box. You will see 'add text' in the menu.

SECTION 3

6 To align your shapes vertically, go to the start of the diagram and click 'select all' from the editing group.
7 Click on 'layout' on your ribbon and go to page setup; click and the page setup dialog box will appear.
8 Click on the vertical box and click center.

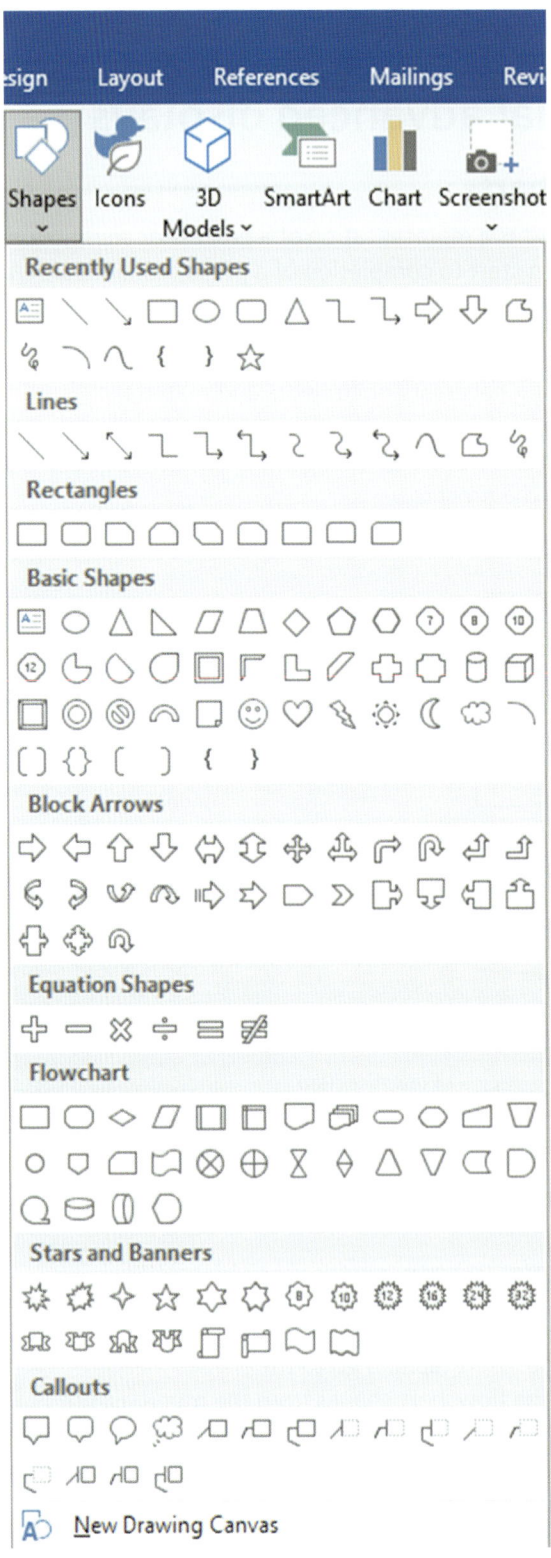

Figure 11.10 Flowchart shapes available from the Microsoft Word Shapes dropdown menu

11 Simple and advanced displays

An example of a completed flowchart is shown in Figure 11.11.

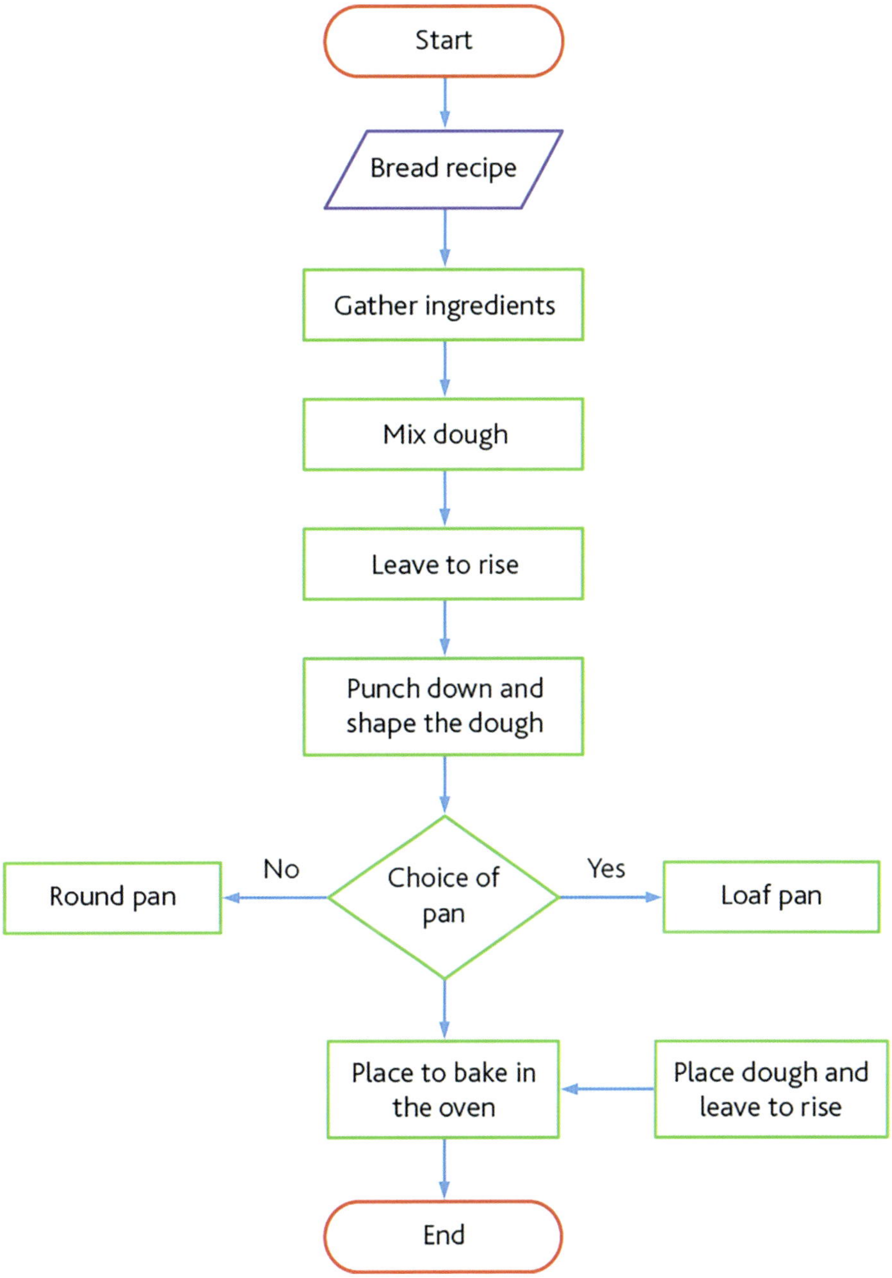

Figure 11.11 A flowchart

> **➜ Activity**
> 1 Which shape is used when a decision must be made?
> 2 Which shape is used to show termination of a process?

Organisation charts

An **organisation chart** is a diagram that shows the governing and hierarchical structure of a related group of people. It shows the reporting relationships within units, sections, departments or companies. Organisation charts are often prepared using landscape orientation.

To use shapes to create an organisation chart:

1 Choose the insert tab and click on 'shapes' in the illustrations subtab.
2 Place your cursor where you want your first shape to be.
3 Select the number of rectangles and the size needed for the organisation chart. Alternatively, continue to copy the first shape and drag the copies into place by holding down the ctrl key.
4 Continue to insert and place shapes as needed.
5 Draw lines to show the reporting lines between people in the organisation.

To use the SmartArt wizard to create an organisation chart:

1 Choose the insert tab and click on the SmartArt menu in the illustrations subtab.
2 Select hierarchy, select a shape from those displayed and click OK.
3 Insert your draft plan information – even including pictures, if you'd like to – by clicking in the boxes.
4 If additional shapes are needed at any level, right-click in an existing box and select the position (above, below, left or right) for the new box.
5 Continue to enter information to complete the chart (Figure 11.12).

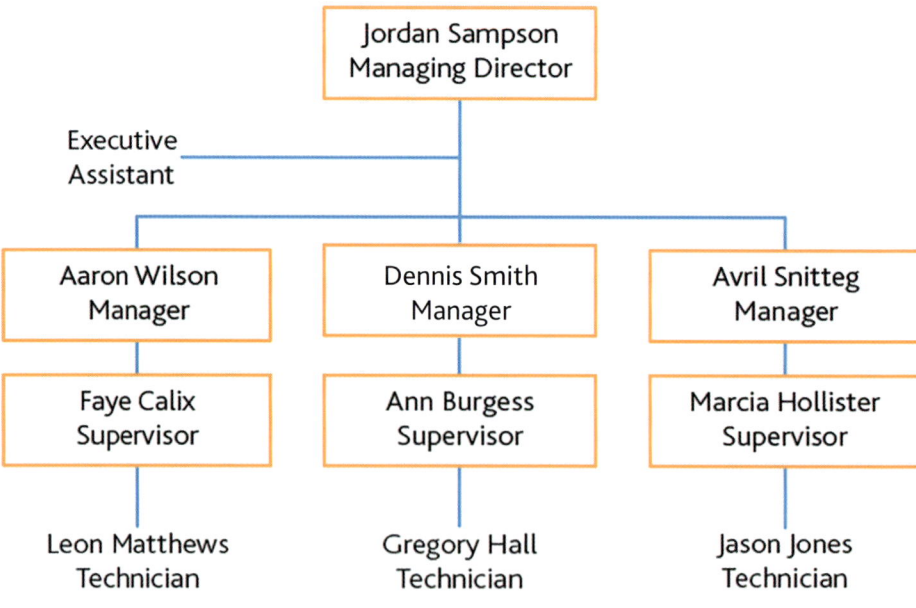

Figure 11.12 An organisation chart

>  **Activity**
>
> Look at Figure 11.11. Can Dennis Smith give an important order to Faye Calix? If not, how can Dennis Smith get his request carried out?

11 Simple and advanced displays

 **Helpful hint**

Change or amend the shapes of your organisation and flow charts by changing their outlines, including with the use of text effects and shape fill, by going to 'shape styles' in the shapes grouping.

Key terms

card A piece of stationery carrying only essential data, which may be embellished by using certain font styles, colours and graphics; business cards, index cards, postcards and greetings cards are some examples

display Any document produced using word-processing functionalities that combine fundamental rules of document production with creative and innovative elements

drop cap A large capital letter that drops several lines (2 or 3) lines at the start of a paragraph or section. These are often used in newspaper articles, books, journals and magazines

flowchart A visual representation of the procedures to be followed to carry out a task from start to end

flyer A single sheet for promoting events, usually prepared with text and graphics on one side of the page only

form A document, designed with fixed placeholders, for collecting information from users for easy collation

invitation A request for the attendance of a person or people at an event

leaflet A single sheet folded in different ways to show four, six or eight sides; used to distribute information on themes such as health or cultural or community events

menu Card of various sizes listing food items for sale or distribution to people at an event

newsletter A number of pages used to communicate information to a group of people with similar interests, in the form of articles about ideas, projects, events and campaigns

organisation chart A diagram that shows the governing and hierarchical structure and reporting relationships of a group of people related in some way

programme A list of activities to be completed in a loose or rigid time frame as part of an event

resume A summary of a person's professional knowledge, skills and accomplishments to accompany an application for a job

table A grid of columns and rows for organising and manipulating content for proper alignment, indentation and line spacing

wizard A programmatic feature of applications that support a step-by-step approach to carrying out processes

 ## Summary

In this chapter, you have learned to:

- prepare displays that require additional planning and creative ideas
- produce displays with and without the use of Word wizards
- create menus, invitations, programmes, leaflets, newsletters and flyers
- use tables or tabular formats to organise and manipulate data for creating properly aligned and professional-looking displays
- produce written text and create visual aids, such as flow charts and organisation charts.

SECTION 3

Practice, research and exam-style questions

Multiple-choice questions

1. Creating displays does not include …
   A advanced word-processing skills.
   B table manipulation software.
   C optical character recognition.
   D advanced language skills.

2. Which of these formatting features for tables is *not* available in Word?
   A Sorting data
   B Merging cells
   C Text effects
   D Oblique headings

3. Which of these features is *not* found in invitations and menus?
   A Artistic effects
   B Informal speech
   C Graphic artistry
   D Calligraphy

4. Which card is most useful for recording client data?
   A Post
   B Business
   C Index
   D Greetings

5. Which of these documents are likely to be produced together?
   A Invitation and menu
   B Flyer and programme
   C Newsletter and leaflet
   D Flowchart and organisation chart

6. Newsletters and leaflets serve to …
   A communicate with specific stakeholders.
   B provide financial information.
   C demonstrate hierarchical arrangements.
   D share national news releases.

7. Which of the following is considered to be an advanced display?
   A Invitation with a menu
   B Leaflet
   C Flowchart
   D Newsletter

8. A visual aid for explaining how a process works is …
   A a bar chart.
   B a flowchart.
   C a pie chart.
   D an organisation chart.

9. Which flowchart shape represents the need to consult a document in the process?

   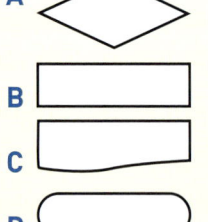

10. Which feature of a computerised environment supports a step-by-step approach to creativity?
    A Form
    B Template
    C Wizard
    D Browser

Exam-style questions

1. Produce three tips on how to complete a professional resumé using various websites, including artificial-intelligence (AI) sites. Try creating your own resumé.

2. Ms. George wants to create a flyer for an upcoming school bazaar. What types and sizes of paper do you suggest she should use?

3 The students of the football club at Cinco Lakes Secondary School are planning a concert to raise funds for their trip to Cost Rica for the CARIFESTA School Games to be held in 2027. The musical concert will be held on July 24, 2027 at the school hall in Grange Road, Tobago.

Prepare a 4-page programme for the concert with the following information:
- Back page: Image of the School with a logo of a football team
- Cover page: Name of School, location, and date of concert with an image.
- Pg 2

5:00 PM – 5:10 PM	Welcome and address by MC – Mr. Richard Pierre
5:10 PM – 5:20 PM	Piano Recital – School students
5:20 PM – 5:30 PM	Classical Indian Dance – Guest Artiste
5:30 PM – 5:40 PM	Medley by School's Junior Choir
5:40 PM – 5:50 PM	Spoken word and poetry reading – Josiah Lawrence
5:50 PM – 6:10 PM	Medley – Classical Instruments – School Students
INTERMISSION	

- Pg 3:

6:30 PM – 6:40 PM	Medley School's Senior Choir
6:40 PM – 7:00 PM	School's Steel Pan Ensemble (Juniors)
7:00 PM – 7:30 PM	Guest Artistes
7:20 PM – 7:40 PM	School's Steel Pan Ensemble (Seniors)
7:40 PM – 7:45 PM	Closing &Thanks – School's Principal – Mrs. P. Worrell

Use leader dots for your reading guide.

12 Specialised documents

> **Objectives**
>
> By the end of this chapter, you will be able to:
>
> - prepare documents that require specific language and formatting standards
> - identify the main features of specialised documents used in well-defined circumstances
> - create templates for specialised documents using wizards in Microsoft Word.

Introduction

At this point, you have engaged in word-processing activities by formatting, editing and proofreading the wide variety of documents used in business, including those that require your creative and innovative skills. In this chapter, your advanced formatting and editing skills will be utilised to produce documents that are important to professional and semi-professional groups. They include *legal documents*, *technical documents* and two examples of the artistic forms called *literary documents*.

Legal documents

A legal document is a written record of the thoughts, actions and wishes of one or more people, which has lawful implications for those people. Several of these represent formal **agreements** between two or more parties, and a legal document becomes a binding **contract** when the two parties have signed it. Examples of legal documents are shown in Table 12.1.

Table 12.1 Types of legal documents

Document type	Description
Agreement	A state of affairs whereby the terms, conditions, rights and responsibilities of two or more parties are fully and truthfully outlined, understood and approved. An agreement can be oral, but it is preferable for it to be documented and witnessed by a neutral third party.
Contract	Most legally binding agreements are called *contracts*. The terms of agreement should be set out in writing and signed by the parties to the contract. Signing indicates acceptance of the terms. Examples of contracts include *hire-purchase agreements* and *employment contracts*.
Conveyancing documents	*Conveyance* refers to the legal process of changing ownership of property from one party to another. It ensures that the agreement to transfer ownership is legal, valid and binding. If there is no conveyance document, called a *certificate of ownership* or *deed*, in the name of the person who wishes to transfer ownership, the conveyance cannot be completed.
Endorsement	The act of signing and the statement being signed are both called *endorsements*, and they are assurances that the document is authentic, valid and legally binding.
Lease	This is a type of contract that outlines the period of time for which a tangible piece of property owned by the *lessor* is to be kept and used by the *lessee* or *tenant*, who will pay a *rent* for the privilege. Examples of leased property include land, buildings, vehicles and equipment. Lease periods can be for short or long periods, but one-year leases are the norm.

Power of attorney	This document gives authority to someone, such as a lawyer or a friend, who is trusted to act in legal matters in a specific situation
Will	The Last Will and Testament (*will*) is the legal document that allows a person, called the *testator*, to decide what will happen to their belongings (*assets*) and how they will be distributed after their death. An *executor* is usually named in the will as the person to manage this process.

Basic standards in preparing legal documents

Table 12.2 outlines the common requirements for the preparation of all legal documents.

Table 12.2 Requirements for the preparation of legal documents

Criterion	Standard
Paper size	Legal-sized paper: 21.6 cm × 35.6 cm (8.5 inches × 14 inches) or A4 paper
Margins	Top 5.08 cm (2 inches); left 3.81 cm (1.5 inches); right 1.27 cm (0.5 inches); bottom 2.54 cm (1 inch)
	If the will goes to a second page, place a 'next page' section break from the layout tab, and change the margins to:
	Top 5.08 cm (2 inches); left 1.27 cm (0.5 inches); right 3.81 cm (1.5 inches); bottom 2.54 cm (1 inch)
Alignment	Full justification
Line spacing	Double or 1.5
Line formatting	There must be no spaces left to the left or right of the margins. Words must not be divided at the ends of lines. Use hyphens or begin text on a new line, so that no additional words can be added later without consent or authority.

Characters	• The following words are always typed in uppercase (capital) letters:
	  – People's names when stated for the first time
	  – Words such as HEREBY, BEQUEATH, WITNESS, DECLARE, BETWEEN.
	• Numbers are typed out in full, for example dates such as 04/15/27 should be typed as the *Fifteenth Day of April Two Thousand and Twenty-seven*, and figures such as $80,000.00 should be typed as *Eighty thousand dollars and no cents*.

Wording required for four legal documents

In this section, the wording and formatting required for four legal documents will be explored. These documents are:

1 a will with an endorsement
2 a contract of employment
3 a hire-purchase agreement
4 a certificate of transfer of ownership (conveyancing document).

Will with endorsement

A will expresses the wishes of a person, who documents their decisions regarding assets left behind upon death. These assets could be in the form of cash, property or investments. It is usually prepared by an attorney and witnessed by a neutral third party. This is a legally binding document.

An example of a Will is shown in Figure 12.1.

THIS IS THE LAST WILL AND TESTAMENT of me **HAROLD ROBERTS** of 43 Milton Street Plaisance Park San Fernando

1. I HEREBY REVOKE all former Wills and testamentary dispositions made by me under the law of the Republic of Trinidad and Tobago and declare that the proper law of this my Will shall be the law of the Republic of Trinidad and Tobago ---------
2. I APPOINT my firstborn son ANDRE ROBERTS to be Executor and Trustee of this my Will AND in case the aforesaid shall die in my lifetime or shall refuse or unable to act in the office of Executor and Trustee then I APPOINT PAMELA STEPHENS of Stephens and Associates, 14 Richmond Street, San Fernando to fill the vacancy in the office of Executor and Trustee hereof --
3. I GIVE the following legacies
   I GIVE to my daughter PORTIA ROBERTS absolutely and free of tax the sum of TWO HUNDRED THOUSAND dollars ($200 000) ----------------------------------
   I GIVE to my son ANDRE ROBERTS absolutely and free of tax the sum of TWO HUNDRED THOUSAND dollars ($200 000) ---
   I GIVE DEVISE AND BEQUEATH the residue of my estate both real and personal of whatsoever nature and wheresoever situated to my wife PETAL JAMES-ROBERTS PROVIDED THAT if the said Petal James-Roberts shall predecease me or fail to survive me by 30 days then I give the residue of my estate or the part of it affected equally to those of my children who survive me---------------------------------------

Signed by the said HAROLD ROBERTS as and for his last Will and Testament in the presence of us both present and we in his and in the presence of each have hereunto subscribed our names as witnesses: ----------------------

Signature of witness

Name of Witness

Address

Occupation

Signature of witness

Name of Witness

Address

Occupation

HAROLD ROBERTS

Figure 12.1 A will

An endorsement often appears in the middle column of a separate sheet of paper from the agreement document being witnessed. It acts as an enclosure for the document being signed and is an easy way of retrieval when filed with others. Figure 12.2 provides an example of an endorsement. Note the clear lines of space between:

- the date
- the term 'Last Will and Testament'
- the word 'of'
- the name of the testator
- the signature line for the witness.

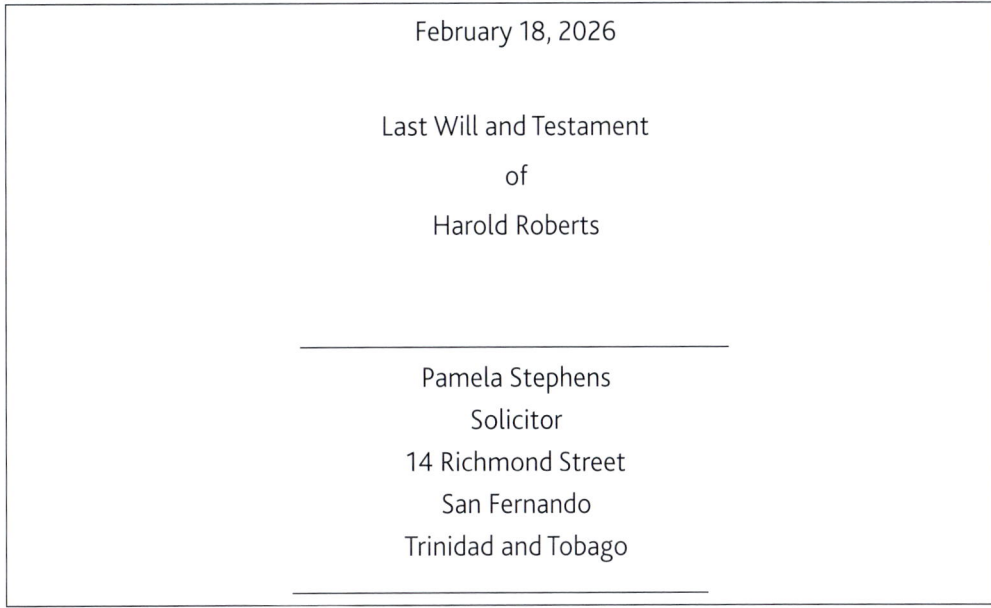

Figure 12.2 An endorsement

Contracts

For a contract to be valid, it must contain certain essential elements. Contracts should be put in writing, with the rights and responsibilities of each party clearly identified to reduce disagreements later on.

Here are examples of two types of contracts:

- A *contract of employment* or *work* sets out the rights and responsibilities of both the employer and the employee (Figure 12.3).
- A *hire purchase agreement* sets out terms and conditions of sale.

SECTION 3

THIS CONTRACT OF WORK is made between EARL ROMA of ATLAS COMMUNICATIONS of #1 Woodray Street, Sangre Grande (hereinafter called 'the Employer') of the one part and ANNA MITCHELL of #3 Circular Road, Nobaire Gardens, Rouca (hereinafter called 'the Employee') of the other part.
WHEREBY both the Employer and the Employee agree to the terms and conditions stated herein:

#		
1	**Employee's Job Title**	Administrative Assistant
2	**Hours and Days of Work**	Monday to Friday from 8.00 a.m. to 4.00 p.m. one (1) hour off for lunch from 12.00 to 1.00 p.m.
3	**Remuneration**	Nine thousand dollars ($9,000.00) per month. The Employer shall pay the Employee on the Twenty-eight (28th) day of every month. Payment shall be made to a bank account; the number of which must be submitted by the Employee.
4	**Duration of Contract**	Two (2) years commencing May 1, 2026.
5	**Job Description**	See attached.
6	**Leave**	The Employee is entitled to two (2) weeks' paid Vacation Leave annually, effective one year from the date of employment, five (5) days' business leave and ten (10) days' sick leave per calendar year. Should the Employee be absent for more than two (2) consecutive work days he/she must submit a medical certificate.
7	**Termination of Contract**	This contract can be terminated by either party giving one month's notice.
8	**Statutory Obligations**	All statutory deductions will be made by the Employer, such as: PAYE, NIS and Health Surcharge. The Employee shall be eligible for registration in the ATLAS COMMUNICATIONS Group Health Plan managed by LATIT Insurance Company.
9	**End of Contract Arrangements**	The Employee is entitled to 1 Two (2) weeks end of contract leave. 2 One (1) month's additional salary (taxed) as gratuity.

IN WITNESS WHEREOF the said parties have herewith voluntarily set their hands on the Twenty-ninth Day of April, Two thousand and twenty-six at Sangre Grande.

Earl Roma on behalf of the Employer
ATLAS COMMUNICATIONS

Anna Mitchell
Signature of Employee

Figure 12.3 A contract of employment

12 Specialised documents

Helpful hint

If you prepare a contract using tables, the information on both sides will line up properly.

Agreements

An agreement should be considered a contractual arrangement. It may or may not be in writing, but it is best to do so, so that all conditions and aspects are clear and understood by all parties. Two examples of documents recording agreements are hire-purchase documents (as shown in Figure 12.4) and conveyancing documents.

This Hire-Purchase Agreement is entered into on this day, February 3, 2026, between:

Mr. Treston Williams
#2 Carol Lane, Topin Road, Chaguanas
(the purchaser)

and

Ms. Tanika Alexis
85 LeeKang Street, Petit Valley
(the seller)

for the purchase of a Black Kia Sorento vehicle No PCF 3977.

WHEREBY it is agreed that Mr. Treston Williams will pay a total sum of Eighty-five Thousand dollars ($85,000.00) to Ms. Tanika Alexis for the purchase of said vehicle PCF 3977. It is HEREBY agreed that an initial payment of Fifty thousand dollars ($50,000.00) will be made to the seller, the balance of which is Thirty thousand dollars ($30,000). The balance of payments will be made in monthly instalments of Two Thousand Dollars ($2,000.00) per month over a period of fifteen (15) months with effect from February 3, 2026.

At the completion of this period of payment for the above-named vehicle, the final transaction for transfer of vehicle PCF 3977 will be formally made at the Licensing Office of Trinidad and Tobago.

This Agreement holds for the said period stated above between Mr. Treston Williams and Ms. Tanika Alexis or any persons so entrusted with her affairs will perform the duties as agreed.

Signed

Treston Williams (Purchaser)	Tanika Alexis (Seller)
Address: #2 Carol Lane, Topin Road, Chaguanas	Address: 85 LeeKang Street, Petit Valley
Witness (Purchaser):	Witness (Seller):
Name:	Name:
Address:	Address:

Figure 12.4 A hire-purchase agreement

A *hire-purchase agreement*, also known as an *installment plan*, refers to an arrangement used for purchasing relatively expensive goods. It is similar to a loan from a seller to a purchaser, who will pay the value of the item plus a certain amount of interest.

Conveyancing

Conveyancing is the act of transferring ownership or title to another person. The agreement in Figure 12.4 proposes to complete the transaction by registering the *transfer of title* at the Licensing Office, a government agency (as is required by law). This is a form of conveyancing. Conveyancing is also carried out in a more formal way when the property being bought and sold is real estate. The **conveyancing document** might be titled a *memorandum of transfer* and consists of:

- the purchase agreement signed by the buyers and sellers
- the certificate of title to the land
- a witness statement, whose signature is affirmed by a Commissioner of Affidavits (also called a Notary Public) or other authorised legal person.

In summary, the conveyancing document should contain the following information, at a minimum:

- the name of the seller (also called the *grantor*)
- the name of the buyer (also called the *grantee*)
- a detailed description of the property (location and measurements; as well as reference to government survey information called a *cadastral sheet*)
- the purchase price
- the date of transfer (and handing over date, if different)
- signatures of witnesses
- notarisation by a legal professional.

Helpful hint
Many technical documents make wide use of tables and text effects.

Technical documents

In this section, you will learn about documents that require technical knowledge for their preparation. Technical knowledge includes that applied in the construction industry. *Specifications*, *bills of quantity*, **scopes of work**, *technical proposals*, *technical reports* and **press releases** require technical knowledge and a methodical approach.

Specifications, bills of quantity and scopes of work

These are examples of documents that seek to ensure mutual understanding of suppliers and clients of what is required for satisfactory completion of a project. Although they are commonly used in the construction industry, they are also used in other industries.

Generally, these documents are prepared using:

- standard paper sizes; that is, A4 or letter size, although organisations may choose other sizes
- standard margins of 3.81 cm (1.5 inches) or 5.08 cm (2 inches) at the top and left, 1.27 cm (0.5 inch) at the right margin and 2.54 cm (1 inch) at the bottom margin
- single line spacing.

Any significant difference in requirements, for example, the requirements for specifications, are highlighted where appropriate.

Specifications

A **specification** is a document prepared by architects and building contractors that sets out the technical requirements of the work to be done. It:

- describes the project
- assigns measurements to the drawings
- lists the materials required for the job
- projects the time frame for completion
- identifies the location of the work site (part of the work may be done off-site)
- outlines the tasks that must be undertaken and the order in which the tasks are to be carried out.

Formatting standards specific to a specification

A specification contains two main parts: the *heading* and the *body*. Although in general either the blocked or indented style, and standard margins and line spacing, are used, there are additional layout rules for preparing specifications. When typing a specification:

1. Type the word *SPECIFICATION* in spaced or closed capital letters at the start of the heading or *introductory paragraph*. The introduction identifies the job to be done and the address of the work site.
2. Indent this paragraph at 6.35 cm (2.5 inches) and type using 1.5 or double line spacing.
3. Indent the name and address of the contractor at 8.89 cm (3.5 inches) and type using single line spacing.
4. Place the date in the left margin, with two clear lines of space between the contractor's information and the date.
5. Type the body of the specification from the left margin with *shoulder* or *marginal* headings. Typical headings are *General Conditions*, *Site Preparation*, *Processes* and, finally, a listing of required tasks, for example *Painting*.

Figure 12.5 is an example of a blocked specification using marginal headings and left-aligned text.

 Activity

Using the information in Column 3 of Table 12.5, create the business proposal, following these instructions:
1. Using A4 paper, create your own suitable letterhead with an appropriate look.
2. Use fully blocked style, with 3.18 cm (1.25 inch) left and right margins and 2.54 cm (1 inch) top and bottom margins.
3. Use double spacing.

SPECIFICATION of work to be done and materials to be used for the construction of two (2) gates at 94 Victoria Street, Grenville for Mr. Patrick LaBadie to the satisfaction of:

FYR Builders
20 Brizan Drive
Prospect
ST. PATRICK

July 15 2026

GENERAL CONDITIONS

<u>Site visit</u>	The contractor shall visit the site to become familiar with the location and surroundings before the start of the project.
<u>Environment</u>	The contractor shall ensure that the worksite be free from all hindrances and all areas be kept in a clean and safe environment.
<u>Site preparation</u>	The contractor shall remove all grass and other surroundings which may impede the construction of the gate. The contractor shall also deconstruct previous gates and clear all materials which may remain following the removal of the gates.
Steel work	Pre-designed pattern in metal to be added to base of gate Cut tubes in measurements of 2 ft × 2 ft square pieces Cut steel tubing to size Weld steel tubing together Create gate hinges Add expanded steel sheeting Create gate's sliding bolt lock and latch
Paint and finish	2" paint brush × 2 ½" paint brush × 2 4" rollers × 2 Sand gate using fine-grit sand paper Rust converter primer – grey oxide paint 1 L Metal paint – black – 1 gallon 2 × rollers and 2 × paint brushes of 2" and ½" sizes

Figure 12.5 A specification (blocked with margin headings and left-aligned)

Bills of quantity

A *bill of quantity* is a detailed listing of the quantity and cost of each item needed to complete a project. Details included in a bill of quantity are the:

- name, address and contact information of the company completing the project
- heading (bill of quantity)
- details of the customer, such as their name, address and contact number
- name of the task/job to be performed
- date
- quantities and costs of materials
- labour cost.

Figure 12.6 is an example of the bill of quantity for the specification in Figure 12.5.

FYR BUILDERS
#20 Brizan Drive, Prospect, St. Patrick GRENADA
Phone: (473) 702-0101   Fax (473) 702-0120   Email: build@fyrbuilders.org

BILL OF QUANTITY

Project:	Construction of 1 Wrought Iron Gate
For:	Mr. Patrick LaBadie of #94 Victoria Street, Grenville
Date:	25 February 20..
Order No:	FYR 2554

Item No.	Description	Quantity	Unit Price $	Cost $
1	Pre-designed pattern and base	1	4,000.00	4,000.00
2	Chop saw Disc	2	38.00	76.00
3	4" Grinding Disc	2	11.00	22.00
4	Gate guide	1	70.00	70.00
5	Red Oxide	1 quart	58.00	58.00
6	Black paint	2 quarts	43.00	86.00
7	Etching Primer	1 quart	80.00	80.00
8	Labour			3,300.00
			TOTAL	$7,692.00

Estimated cost: (*subject to change*) $7,692.00

Estimated completion time: 5 days

Franklyn Richards
Contractor

Figure 12.6 A bill of quantity

Scopes of work

A *scope of work* (SOW) is used to outline clearly what is to be done and the resources to be used, with deliverables and timelines for the completion of a project in greater detail than the specification. A proper SOW can avoid misunderstandings between the contractor and the client, and ensure that the project is completed within the specified time to the satisfaction of the client. The terms and conditions of the SOW must be agreed to by both parties.

Details included in a scope of work are the:

- identification of the project goals
- tasks to be performed (using a phased approach)
- deliverables to comply with the goals
- establishment of delivery dates
- agreement on payment terms
- signatures of parties to the agreement.

Figure 12.7 shows a scope of work based on the specification in Figure 12.5.

SCOPE OF WORK	
Statement of work	Construction, installation and painting of one steel Gate. 7 ft. tall × 15 ft. wide Sand and prime gates using fine grit sand paper and grey oxide primer Neatly paint gates using black matte paint – colour code 12456. Quantity 1 L.
Client information	Mr. Patrick LaBadie
Client address	#94 Victoria Street, Grenville
Client contact information	Phone: (473) 298-7542 Email: PLabadie@hotmail.com
Effective date	July 15, 2026
Completion date	July 18, 2026
Deliverables	
Phase 1	One (1) well-constructed steel gate combining a predesigned panel, measuring 3 ft by 15 ft with a solid steel base panel measuring 4 ft by 15 ft to be completed in one (1) day from start
Phase 2	Properly installed gate bolted on concrete pillars with sliding bolt lock and latch to be completed in one (1) day after completion of Phase 1
Phase 3	Properly painted gate in black to be completed in one (1) day after completion of Phase 2
Delivery dates	Phase 1: July 16, 2026 Phase 2: July 17, 2026 Phase 3: July 18, 2026

Project cost	Materials	4,692.00
	Labour	7,200.00
	TOTAL	$11,892.00
Method of payment	Downpayment of 50% before commencing project with balance on completion of project	
Signature Project Manager	Signature Customer	

Figure 12.7 A scope of work

Proposals, reports and press releases

The contents of *proposals*, **reports** and **press releases** vary widely as they are prepared by people responding to the demands of individual events. However, there are standard formatting rules that many follow. Generally, these documents are prepared using:

- paper sizes such as A4, letter or legal
- margins that are 2.54 cm (1 inch) for left, right, top and bottom of the page, although the left margin may be increased to leave room for binding the finished document
- 1.5 or double line spacing
- shoulder headings (or none)
- a table of contents (optional but useful in large documents).

Developing a table of contents using a wizard

Proposals and reports often contain a table of contents (TOC) at the beginning of the document. By matching text with page numbers, readers can navigate through documents that might be hundreds of pages long.

You can insert a TOC manually or automatically in your document from the references tab. However, you must first format your shoulder headings using the Styles subtab on the home tab. To do so:

1 Select your first heading (usually the title) in your report or proposal.
2 Right-click on the 'heading 1' menu and choose 'modify'.
3 Enter your format choices in the windows: font, font weight, font size, font colour. At the bottom left of the menu, click on 'format' to make additional formatting choices.
4 Click OK, and OK again. Your choices become the template for all headings that will be described as level 1 headings (see the APA guide in Table 12.3).
5 Repeat the sequence for paragraph headings by right-clicking on the heading 2 choice for level 2 headings. Level 2 headings have different formatting choices from level 1.
6 Repeat the sequence for level 3 headings.

Table 12.3 Examples of APA heading styles

Level 1	'The leader in me' business proposal	Centred, bold, capitalise major words
Level 2	Design your title page Write your problem statement Identify your proposed solution State your costs, payment schedule and delivery conditions Draft the executive summary Write your conclusion	Left-aligned, bold, capitalise major words
Level 3	*Method and goal* *Proposed target group* *Dedicated resources* *Proposed timeline*	*Left-aligned, bold and italics, capitalise major words*

Note that the table uses different fonts, different font sizes, and different font colours.

When you have styled your headings at the different levels, select your entire document and click on the 'table of contents' subtab. Choose automatic No.1 or 2. If you choose 1 for the business proposal shown in Table 12.3, your table of contents will look like Figure 12.8.

> **Helpful hint**
> Accommodate additions and deletions to headers in tables of contents by clicking on 'add text' for new headers and 'update table' for including the changes in the contents.

Contents
Title page	1
Executive summary	3
Problem statement	4
Proposed solution	5
Method and goal	6
Proposed target group	6
Dedicated resources	6
Proposed timeline	6
Terms and conditions	7
Conclusion	7

Figure 12.8 Table of contents

Business proposals

A *business proposal* is a type of technical document sent to a prospective client to show how the business can solve a customer's problem. The proposal demonstrates the proposer's technical expertise in treating the problem. Tables 12.4 and 12.5 list types of business proposals and a step-by-step approach to preparing proposals.

Table 12.4 Three types of proposals

Soliticed	A proposal requested by the public or selected people or organisations
Unsolicited	A proposal submitted to a prospective client without a request – it must attract a client's interest to receive a positive response
Internal	A proposal developed by employees, usually a team, to solve a company's problem or create a new path for the company

12 Specialised documents

Table 12.5 A step-by-step approach to preparing a business proposal

Proposal Section	Contents	Example
Title/Cover page	Create a title that grabs attention and reflects the purpose of your proposal. Include the client's name, and your company's name and contact details. Use graphics, colours, font styles and text effects to stand out from other proposals.	**THE LEADER IN ME: UNDERSTANDING YOUR INNER LEADER** Sweetie Pie Baked Goods Business Proposal August 20 Atlas Solutions 23 Knolly Drive Kingston 6 JAMAICA Tel: (876) 778-5555 Fax: (876) 778-5556 Email: atlassols@gmail.com Website: www.atlassations.com

Table of contents	Use the references tab and table of contents subtab to create the contents after completing the proposal.	Contents
		Title page 1
		Executive summary 2
		Problem statement 3
		Proposed solution 4
		    Method and goal 5
		    Proposed target group 6
		    Dedicated resources 7
		    Proposed timeline 8
		Terms and conditions 9
		Conclusion 10

Executive summary	Provide a short summary that highlights what your proposal is about and how the client will benefit. Offer to discuss further at a meeting. Create this section after completing the proposal.	Atlas Solutions was established in 2015 to train people in business skills including leadership. Our proposal is designed to develop the leadership potential that exists in your middle managers. Our solution is a one-day workshop that provides information, guidance and opportunities for leadership. Our costs are reasonable given the expertise of our team members. Atlas Solutions looks forward to working with your team.
Problem statement	State what you interpret is the problem or issue to be solved. If the proposal is unsolicited, state what your research into the industry or company has revealed.	Your company means to find your future leaders from among your people. We believe leaders can be taught and we can help.
Proposed solution	Outline your ideas and how they can solve the client's problem. Details about your solution, such as methods, goals, target groups, the resources that will be used and timelines, can be stated here.	• Method and goal The proposed one-day workshop is entitled 'The 10 qualities, 5 skills and 8 powerful strategies of great leaders: How many do I have and how do I get the rest?' • Proposed target group A minimum of 10 divisional senior supervisors. • Dedicated resources Our team of 2 facilitators, Dr. Randolph Grey and Mrs. Shirley Warsing of the Business Department at Roblo University, bring 15 years of training others to develop their leadership skills. • Proposed timeline Our team proposes to mobilise and deliver the one-day workshop from 9.00 a.m. to 5.00 p.m. within 5 business days of your signed acceptance of the proposal.

SECTION 3

Financials	Clearly provide a costing (per hour, per trainee, per event), payment terms (downpayment and balance due times) and any other conditions (e.g. responsibility for venue and meals)	**Cost**	$2,400 per trainee
		Payment schedule	65% downpayment on contract signing; balance within 5 business days of completion of assignment
		Venue and accommodation	To be supplied by the client
		Delivery conditions	No refund if client cancels; rescheduling is negotiable
Conclusion	Restate how your proposal meets the client's needs and why you are the best choice. Refer to the title on the cover.	Atlas Solutions' workshop helps people recognise their inner leadership potential.	
Appendices (optional)	Add any extra details, e.g. the team lead's resumé or any evidence of expertise in the proposed area, as this provides support for your proposal.	See references from two satisfied customers.	

Technical reports

A technical report is a response to a request for information on a topic, incident, event or exercise. Reports can be created after investigations, observations or other research activities. Table 12.6 lists different types of technical reports.

Table 12.6 Types of technical reports

Academic reports	To test a student's knowledge of a topic, e.g. SBA Research Report, book reports, biographies
Business reports	To provide information and analyses of business results to assist in creating or amending business strategies, e.g. SWOT analyses, feasibility studies, marketing reports
Event reports	To provide key information about an incident or accident, or feedback to organisers indicating the results of specific company initiatives, to be used as confirmation of business decisions or improvements in the future
Scientific reports	To provide the results of scientific investigations or research through papers and articles in subject-specific journals or magazines

Written reports are detailed and comprehensive and may become the source document for Microsoft PowerPoint presentations.

12 Specialised documents

Reports may show some of the elements set out in Table 12.7.

Table 12.7 A step-by-step approach to preparing a technical report

Element	Description
Cover letter (optional)	• Might be separate or included at the front of the report • Follows the usual letter writing blocked or indented style, open or closed punctuation style • Makes reference to the purpose of the report and provides the final conclusion of the report writer.
Executive summary	Provide a short summary that highlights what your report is about, including conclusion and recommendation(s).
Introduction/ Context	Provides some background information so that the reason or purpose for the report is understood.
Body	Describes the details of the incident or how the investigation or research was done.
Findings/ Conclusion	Lists what the investigator, observer or researcher found.
Recommendations	Lists any proposals to prevent the incident, improve the situation, solve the problem or further actions that might be taken.
Signature of report preparer	All reports should be signed by one or more of the persons who worked on the activities and the document.
References	Any newspaper or journal article, previous report or book that was used as justification for carrying out the actions should be cited.

Many technical reports, such as incident reports, are simpler; containing the minimum amount of information. The activity provides information for an incident that might occur at your school.

> **Activity**
>
> On Tuesday March 26 2026, at 7.45 am, Nathaniel Adams of Form 4, Six Creeks Secondary School was in the school hall with his friends, Jhene Gomez, Hunter Cedeno and Amarie Mendoza. They were preparing for their upcoming drama presentation. While hanging a prop, the ladder under Hunter slid across the floor and he fell injuring his right shoulder. The drama teacher who was present, Ms Roquel Pemberton, contacted Hunter's parents and called for an ambulance which arrived at 8.15 am. Hunter was taken to the nearest health facility accompanied by Ms Pemberton. On her return, Ms Pemberton prepared an incident report. In her report, she recommended that greater care must be taken to ensure that all equipment are in good order before use.
>
> You are to:
> 1. Prepare the Incident Report with the title, Student injury at school – Hunter Cedeno using shoulder headings for:
>   • Date
>   • Time
>   • Location of incident
>   • Name and designation/s of person preparing the report
>   • Person injured
>   • Names and designation/s of Witnesses
>   • Description of incident
>   • Actions taken by persons
>   • Recommendation
> 2. Use A4 or letter-size paper, single spacing, blocked style with 2.54 cm (1 inch) margins at the top, bottom and right, and a 3.81 cm (1.5 inches) margin on the left.

SECTION 3

Press releases

A press release (also called a *news release*, *press statement* or *media release*) is sent to media outlets such as radio and television stations, newspapers, websites and magazines. It is used to promote news, such as the launch of new products or services, company events or company milestones.

Press releases are carefully worded announcements containing approximately 300–500 words to stimulate interest from journalists, reporters and the public. Official statements may be issued via press releases. For example, government institutions may give updates on situations as they occur. Table 12.8 provides a step-by-step approach to preparing a press release, including explanations and examples of its technical elements.

Table 12.8 A step-by-step approach to preparing a press release

Element	Description	Example or explanation
Heading	Summarises the topic of the release	West Indian Airlines launches new route to Nevis
Notes to editors	Notes about whether the press release is to be held for a later time or for use immediately; placed at the top of the document	**MEDIA RELEASE** **FOR IMMEDIATE DISSEMINATION**
Images	Images and/or logos with captions	*A WIA PRODUCTION*
Dateline	Sets out the date when and location where the release was prepared	Bridgetown, Barbados, November 12, 2026
Opening paragraph	Summarises the core message	**Bridgetown, Barbados** – West Indian Airways announces the launch of a new service between Bridgetown, Barbados and Charlestown, Nevis with effect from January 1, 2027.
Additional paragraphs	Additional information on the topic	This is an all-economy flight and is set to operate twice weekly, on Wednesdays and Fridays. This new route is aimed at increasing tourist visits to the island and enhancing connectivity for passengers travelling between Barbados and Nevis. Flights between Bridgetown and Charlestown will be available for booking by December 1, 2026 through our website www.west-indianairways.com, as well as through our travel-agency partners. There will be a special introductory price for all customers who may be interested in booking between December 1 and December 27, 2026.
Quotation	May include a quotation or opinion statement from one or more people or a group who have information on the matter	"We are thrilled to introduce this new route between Barbados and Nevis, enhancing connectivity and supporting tourism between these beautiful islands," said Michael Johnson, CEO of West Indian Airways. "We remain committed to providing affordable and convenient travel options for our customers."

Contact details	Contacts for further information	For more information, visit our website at www.west-indianairways.com or Facebook, TikTok or Instagram **@flywestindianairways** for up-to-date news and offers. This release has been issued by West Indian Airways Limited Corporate Communications Department Tel: 1 (246) 668-8000 Ext 1245
Boilerplate	A brief section of one or two lines indicating the nature, purpose or history of the organisation issuing the press release, and its products; a standard part of all press releases, the text is usually in a much smaller font size than the body of the news release	Established on June 18, 2001, West Indian Airways Limited began its full service on August 23, 2002. We offer service links to passengers to our smaller Caribbean islands with a fleet of seven ATR72-700 aircrafts and with professional and skilled support staff. Jointly owned by the people of the Caribbean Region, our headquarters is in Bridgetown, Barbados. As a Caribbean airline, we are proud of our safety standards and reliable service.

While the heading for a press release is brief and straightforward, the company's logo, colours or other brand elements should be included in the release.

Literary documents

Literary work is comprised of written or spoken pieces of art that are characterised by themes and compositions that aim to provoke thought, express creativity and reflect on human experiences.

Types of literary works include:

- fictional stories
- nonfiction stories
- poetry
- plays, scripts (part of the play) and scenarios.

Poems

A poem uses language that expresses the poet's feelings, desires and experiences. The words usually form a pattern that may possess a rhyming structure. Some poems are set to music, and their lines are known as *lyrics*.

Layout for typing a poem

- The body of a poem is typed in single line spacing and centred horizontally and vertically on the page.
- Poems usually start with capital letters at the beginning of each line.
- When alternate lines rhyme, the second line is indented two or three spaces.
- No indentations are used when successive lines rhyme, or when the lines do not rhyme at all.
- Always follow the precise punctuation and capitalisation from the original.

Figure 12.9 is an excerpt from poem 'Digital Devolution' by Liesl van Dreau.

This section describes the instructions for typing poems and plays, as they differ significantly from other types of literary documents.

> **The Digital Devolution**
> *by Liesl van Dreau*
>
> [It begins with a ghost on a screen
> A beating cursor, tabs set, font chosen
> A word, a phrase, a heading boldly unfurls …]
>
> **Words in a gilded cage**
>
> [And suddenly – a flurry of fingers, a tapdance on tiles
> Sentences flow like water …
> A paragraph precipitates from thin air
> Digital alchemy!]
>
> In dusty rooms, in years gone by,
> Writing was fashioned with fanciful feathers
> Dipped deliberately in indelible ink
> Etched on the hide of handmade paper
> Carefully carried over
> L e t t e r   f o r   l e t t e r
> As if they were precious cargo
> On a voyage through crushed lapis
> And borders gilded with beaten gold.
> Painstaking, time-taking works of art
> Distilling beauty into substance.
>
> But now – in these modern ages
> Our gilded pages
> Are but gilded cages
> Uploaded in stages
> To metal mages
>
> [Formatted, Named, Saved and Foldered]
> But the words no longer sing as sweet.

Figure 12.9 Layout of a poem excerpt

Plays

A play is a composition or written work designed to be performed before an audience. It narrates a story, and is composed of dialogue between characters, with major divisions called *acts* and changes in scenery or locations called *scenes*. The document in which the play is set out is called a *script*.

Layout for typing a play's script

- All plays, whether for theatre, television or radio, are typed on A4 paper with the left margin set at least 3.81 cm (1.5 inches).
- The front sheet of the document outlines the:
    - title of the play
    - author's name
    - subtitle (if any)
    - brief description of the period (for example 1970s) and location (setting) of the story
    - cast list (the names of actors assigned to the various characters/roles/parts).

- The main body of the play includes the:
  - names of characters (shown in full throughout the play)
  - spoken words
  - unspoken material; that is, actions and stage directions (identified by underscoring, enclosure in parentheses and red font).

Figure 12.10 is an example of the layout of Act 1 of a play's script.

ACT 1
MONICA'S LIVING ROOM

<u>The kettle whistles and Monica heads to the kitchen to make a cup of tea for herself and her friend Althea who is visiting from the Caribbean.</u>

Monica	This is my last year at this apartment here in Arizona. I must leave as times have become challenging. Give me one good reason why I should change my mind?
	<u>(Monica places the cups of tea on the table)</u>
Althea	What are you going to do then? You have been here for over 30 years and times are difficult everywhere. I know you cannot stand the cold climates of other parts of the region, so where are you planning to go?
	<u>(Althea gets up from her chair and takes her cup of tea)</u>
Monica	I just checked the weather and again it is going to be a high of 102°, and it's only June. I'm so tired of this constant heat, I need to find a cooler climate, perhaps back home in Dominica.
	<u>(Monica moves from her seat in the living room to the window)</u>
Althea	That sounds like a marvelous idea. We can be closer to each other now that we are both retired.
	<u>(Althea sips her cup of tea)</u>
Monica	I'm serious you know, I shall soon be making arrangements to look for a piece of property back home where I can retire.

Figure 12.10 Layout of the script of a play

Key terms

academic report A document that outlines a writer's knowledge of a topic, such as book reports and research studies

agreement/contract An arrangement, either documented or oral, where the terms, conditions, rights and responsibilities of two or more parties are fully and truthfully outlined; contracts such as hire-purchase agreements are documented agreements, witnessed and approved by signatures and stamps

business report Information and analysis of business results to assist in creating or amending business strategies, such as marketing reports

conveyancing document *Conveyance* is the legal process of changing ownership of property from one party to another; *conveyancing documents* include certificates of ownership, deeds, titles of transfer, memoranda of transfer

endorsement An assurance that a document is authentic, valid and legally binding

event report Feedback, analysis and recommendations for improvement of specific company initiatives

SECTION 3

internal proposal Detailed suggestions from employees for solving a company's problem or creating new direction for a company
lease A type of contract that outlines the period of time, usually 1 year, for which a tangible piece of property, such as equipment, owned by a lessor is to be kept and used by a lessee or tenant, who will pay rent
legal document A written record of thoughts, actions and wishes that requires execution in accordance with the law
literary document A written record of artistic thought or creative expression of human thought and experience
power of attorney A document that gives authority to someone, for example, a lawyer or a friend, who is trusted to act in legal matters in a specific situation
press release Also called a *news release*, *press statement* or *media release*; a carefully worded announcement sent to media outlets to share news and/or stimulate interest in a company
scientific report The results of scientific investigations or research
solicited proposal A response to requests to the public or to selected people or organisations for the supply of goods and/or services
specification/scope of work A document that sets out the technical requirements of work to be done in measurable detail, including what, where, when and with what resources
technical document A document that required technical knowledge and a methodical approach in its preparation, especially when becoming a source of information for contracts
unsolicited proposal A detailed suggestion for the supply of goods or services, although the prospective client made no request
will/testament A legal document that sets out, in the presence of a person called the *witness*, how the belongings (*assets*) of a person (*testator*) will be distributed after their death by another person (*executor*)
form A document, designed with fixed placeholders, for collecting information from users for easy collation
innovation The ability to combine existing elements to create a new element
invitation A request for the attendance of a person or people at an event
leaflet A single sheet folded in different ways to show four, six or eight sides; used to distribute information on themes such as health or cultural or community events
menu Card of various sizes listing food items for sale or distribution to people at an event
newsletter A number of pages used to communicate information to a group of people with similar interests, in the form of articles about ideas, projects, events and campaigns
organisation chart A diagram that shows the governing and hierarchical structure and reporting relationships of a group of people related in some way
programme A list of activities to be completed in a loose or rigid time frame as part of an event
rough draft A sketch or outline of content to provide a choice of display elements to influence decisions before actual creation

Summary

In this chapter, you have learned to:

- prepare certain legal, technical and literary documents by applying specific techniques to achieve the required appearance
- appreciate the role of customisation as companies make formatting choices to distinguish their brand from those of competitors.

Practice, research and exam-style questions

True or false?

1. An endorsement is set out on the next blank page at the end of a will.
2. Typically, a will includes the testator's name, the beneficiaries and witnesses' signatures.
3. Long-term rental agreements are called *leases*.
4. A contract of employment guarantees the employee the job indefinitely.
5. A hire-purchase agreement allows use but not ownership.
6. A hire-purchase facility is similar to a loan only if interest is charged.
7. Conveyance is the act of transferring a title.
8. A bill of quantity sets out the total cost of construction materials only.
9. A scope of work identifies the tasks to be performed by the contractor.
10. A business proposal that responds to a request for specialised services is a type of technical proposal.
11. A technical report focuses on research topics only.
12. A news release usually has a section for boilerplate information.
13. Poems always have rhyming words.
14. A radio event that tells a story with dialogue and characters is considered to be a play.
15. An underscored line in parentheses and red font indicates inaudible words in a play.

Exam-style questions

1. List the *six* essential aspects required for a contract to be valid and legally binding.

2. **Group project**

   Mr. Selwyth Marshall is planning to add a 10 ft × 12 ft concrete platform, 4" thick, and a garage 15 ft × 15 ft to his house in Montrose, Chaguanas. He makes a list based on the contractor's information. The contractor, Rose Mohammed, has indicated that her crew consists of herself and two labourers for a labour cost of $15,300.00; 75% to be allocated to the platform. Mr. Marshall undertakes to find out unit costs for himself. After calling several nearby hardware stores, he compiles the following list of unit costs.

Item	Amounts	Unit cost
Steel poles	4	$285.00
I-beams, purlins and angle irons	Misc.	$5,487.00
Galvanise (grey)	5	$210.25
Lengths of guttering	4	$201.00
Nails, screws, bolts	Misc.	$130.35
Bags of cement	25	$61.00
Load of gravel	1	$1,200.00
Roll 6" × 6" BRC wire	1	$310.10
Lengths of boxing board 1" × 4" × 12 ft	8	$60.00
Roll of polyurethane	1	$175.00
Tins of paint – rust proofing and colour grey	3	$85.00
Transport	2	$250.00

Mr. Marshall and Ms. Mohammed draw up a simple contract using the details provided, agreeing that:
- the job would begin on March 1, 2026 and would be completed in 10 days
- Mr. Marshall would order and pay for all materials and other costs
- Mr. Marshall would make a downpayment of 50% of labour costs on March 1, 2026 by transferring funds to Ms. Mohammed's account at First Citizens Bank
- the remainder would be paid on completion of the job by March 11, 2026 or before.

Your group is asked to:
a. Prepare a specification for the proposed project for Ms. Mohammed.
b. Prepare a bill of quantity and a scope of work as appendices to the specification. Use shoulder headings to separate the platform costs from the garage costs.
c. Insert your own ideas where necessary, such as:
   - addresses for parties to the specification
   - the name and contact information of a witness.

13 Basic spreadsheet techniques

Objectives
By the end of this chapter, you will be able to:

- list instances where a spreadsheet application is useful
- explain key terms associated with the use of spreadsheet tools
- describe the purpose and location of the basic components of a named spreadsheet application
- construct basic tables from information provided
- apply spreadsheet formatting to basic tables
- apply spreadsheet sort and filter techniques
- create charts and graphs from basic tables
- use features of a spreadsheet application to enhance presentations.

Introduction

Spreadsheet tables form grids comprising columns, which run vertically from top to bottom, and rows, which run horizontally from left to right. Cells are formed where rows cross columns and vice versa.

Popular spreadsheet applications include Microsoft Excel, Google Sheets™ web-based spreadsheet program, and Apple Numbers®. Other spreadsheet software are created for professions such as Accounting (QuickBooks®) and Project Management (Microsoft Project).

Microsoft Excel provides access to pages called worksheets or sheets formatted into grids or tabular forms. Each sheet has access to tools on its ribbon that make Microsoft Excel very useful in many ways. Microsoft Excel's usefulness is increased with functions such as sorting and filtering of data and creating charts and graphs.

Some uses of spreadsheet applications

Spreadsheets can be used in many tasks in your personal and professional life. They:

- provide a format that makes it easier to analyse data by transforming it into statistics for comparisons and into visual aids for making better, data-driven decisions
- create charts and graphs that make Microsoft Word documents and Microsoft PowerPoint presentations more informative and attractive
- keep track of earnings, expenses and savings
- create to-do lists and schedules for projects and events.

To take advantage of Microsoft Excel's benefits, you should be able to describe its basic components, which are listed in Table 13.1.

Table 13.1 Microsoft Excel key terms and features

Tool/feature	Description
Workbook/spreadsheet	A Microsoft Excel file composed of a large number of worksheets
Worksheet/sheet	A page in a workbook consisting of: • columns, rows and cells • white data spaces for data and information entries • a ribbon with menu tabs for operations

13 Basic spreadsheet techniques

Microsoft Excel ribbon	• A display of menus/tabs familiar from Word, e.g. home, insert, page layout, review, view • However, Microsoft Excel has two new tabs: formulas and data
Tab/menu	Indicates the location of a selection of related buttons, commands and tools for use when entering varying data types in individual worksheets, as well as settings controlling the overall workbook.
Data space	• A space where information (processed data) may appear automatically as instructed by a command from the spreadsheet application • Other data spaces are available for manual entry of data
Column identification/name/address/reference	• Columns are labelled using the letters of the alphabet or combinations of letters, e.g. the very first column is labelled A, followed by B, C, etc. • When all 26 letters have been used, the next column is labelled AA, then AB, AC, AD, etc. • After AZ, BA follows, then BB, BC, etc. all the way to XFD
Row identification/name/address/reference	Rows are labelled using numbers from 1 to 1 048 576
Cell identification/name/address/reference	• Each cell has its own name or address made up of the column letter and row number, e.g. A1, B14, AB34 • When you enter data, you enter, or *input*, it into a cell at a particular address
Row range	A selection of two or more cells that are next to each other in the same row
Column range	A selection of two or more cells that are next to each other in the same column
Block range	A selection of cells identified by its rows and columns ranges
Active cell	A cell that has been selected for use by clicking on it
Name box	Where the address of the currently active cell appears
Formula bar	• Initially, the formula bar displays the content of the active cell • It can also be used to enter additional data, remove unwanted data or correct errors in the active cell • If a formula is entered, the desired calculation is performed on the numerical data in the active cell
Column/row heading	A term or label that describes the common aspect of the values in the column or row, e.g. a column labelled 'Products Manufactured' indicates that the rows beneath contain the names of products manufactured by the business
Colon	Punctuation sign (:) in between the addresses of two cells, which describes the row or column range of the table
Graph	Displays mostly numerical data to show trends and patterns over time or another variable
Chart	Displays numerical and textual data in the form of bars, lines or pie slices to make it easy to compare categories or values

Manipulating the workbook

Manipulating the workbook begins with opening a blank worksheet. You can then prepare Microsoft Excel documents by entering data of different types in cells to create, format and edit tables. Accessing dropdown boxes in subtabs and menus helps to create properly formatted and edited Microsoft Excel tables.

SECTION 3

Opening, naming and populating the worksheet

Opening and naming

First, click on the Microsoft Excel icon in the taskbar at the bottom of the screen and choose 'new'. A blank worksheet labelled 'Sheet 1' will appear. Figure 13.1 shows the opening page of a Microsoft Excel workbook.

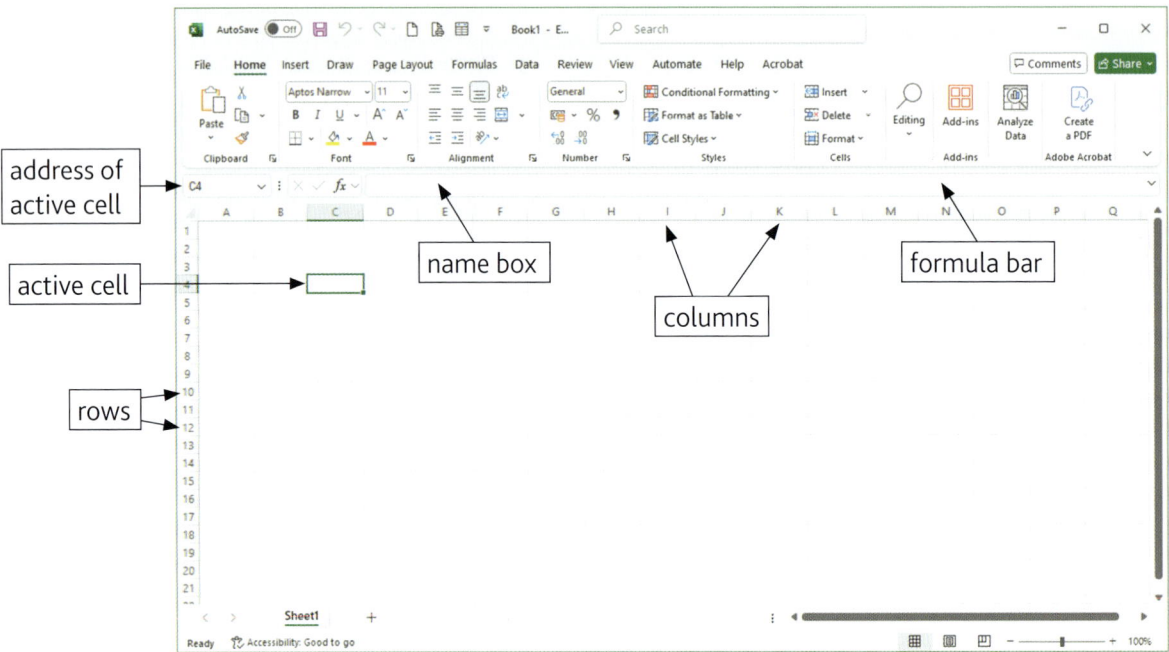

Figure 13.1 A blank Microsoft Excel worksheet

> **Did you know?**
> There are 16 384 columns and 1 048 576 rows in Microsoft Excel, giving you over 17 billion cells available for data entry.

Name your worksheet to distinguish it from another worksheet in the same workbook: Right-click on 'Sheet 1' and choose rename. You can also apply a colour to the tab.

To open another worksheet, click on the encircled plus sign (+) located at the base of the screen.

Entering data

Place your insertion point in a cell to enter data. Recall from Table 13.1 how to identify or reference a cell, for example A1 or C5.

Data may consist of any of these data types: text; numbers; combinations of numbers and text; dates and times; and formulas. Note that, while text, alphanumeric characters and formulas are aligned to the left margin of a cell, numeric data (numbers) are aligned to the right margin of a cell – see Table 13.2 and Figure 13.2, which provide some examples of each type.

Table 13.2 Data types

Data category	Types of data	Examples
	Text	• First and last name of customer, e.g. Jane Doe • Expense per month, e.g. Electricity
	Numbers	• Price of a gas stove, e.g. $4,001.00 • Age of winners, e.g. 18 • Number of tickets sold in the last month, e.g. 224

13 Basic spreadsheet techniques

CONSTANT	Alphanumeric characters (treated as text by spreadsheet tools)	• Student IDs, e.g. AB001 • Combining gender and age, e.g. F36 (female, 36 years)
	Date and time	• Year, e.g. 2011 • Date, e.g. 01/28/2026 • Time, e.g. 8:00 AM or 800 hours
FORMULAIC	Formulas	• Calculate, e.g. SUM (total of expenses paid last month) • Calculate, e.g. AVG (average number of hotel guests for the carnival season)

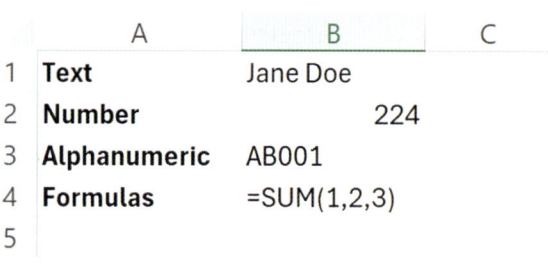

Figure 13.2 Data types

> **→ Activity**
> Refer to Figure 13.2 to answer these questions.
> 1 Which data type is located in cell B3?
> 2 Which category of data is located in cell B4?

Move to the next cell by left-clicking in it to enter more data.

Additional data entry options

While in a cell, right-clicking allows access to a dropdown box of several features for manipulating both the worksheet and the data. For example, while typing a long entry, the data will appear to continue into other cells, but in fact it remains in the selected cell. To avoid the false appearance, highlight the data and select 'wrap text' on the alignment subtab on the home tab (Figure 13.3). Other data-placement options can be found on the alignment subtab (Figure 13.4). You can choose to place the data in the top, middle, or bottom of a cell or text can be oriented at different angles or degrees.

> **Helpful hint**
> In Microsoft Excel, the shape of the cursor or pointer changes as you perform different tasks. You should become familiar with the various forms.

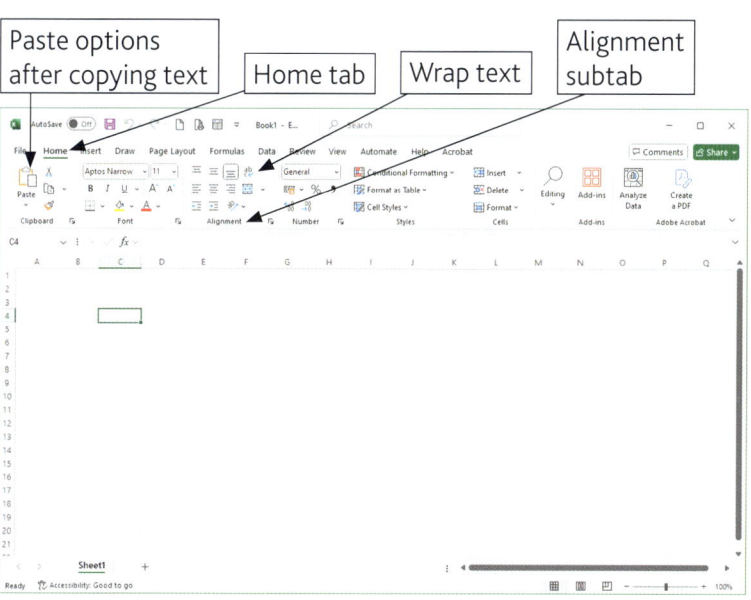

Figure 13.3 Data alignment options

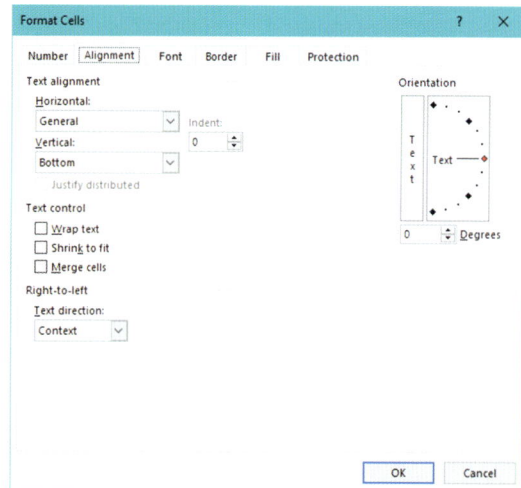

Figure 13.4 The alignment subtab and dropdown box

SECTION 3

Moving and deleting data

Whole blocks of data can be cut or copied and pasted into new worksheets, new parts of the same worksheet and or images by highlighting the data and right-clicking to get the dropdown box to cut or copy (Figure 13.5). The dropdown box shown as Figure 13.6 offers several ways to paste into the new location according to the type of data.

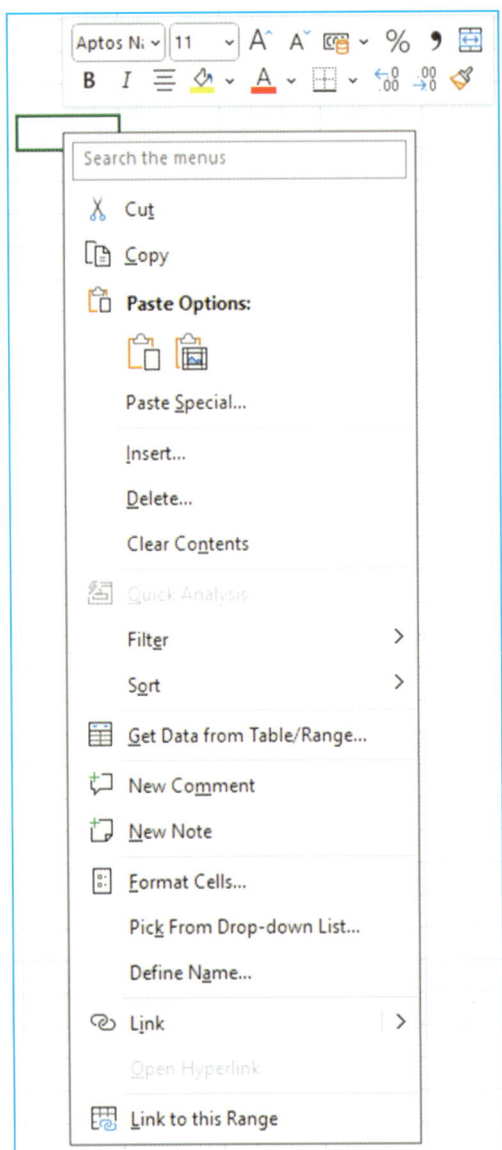

Figure 13.5 Table-manipulation menu and dropdown box

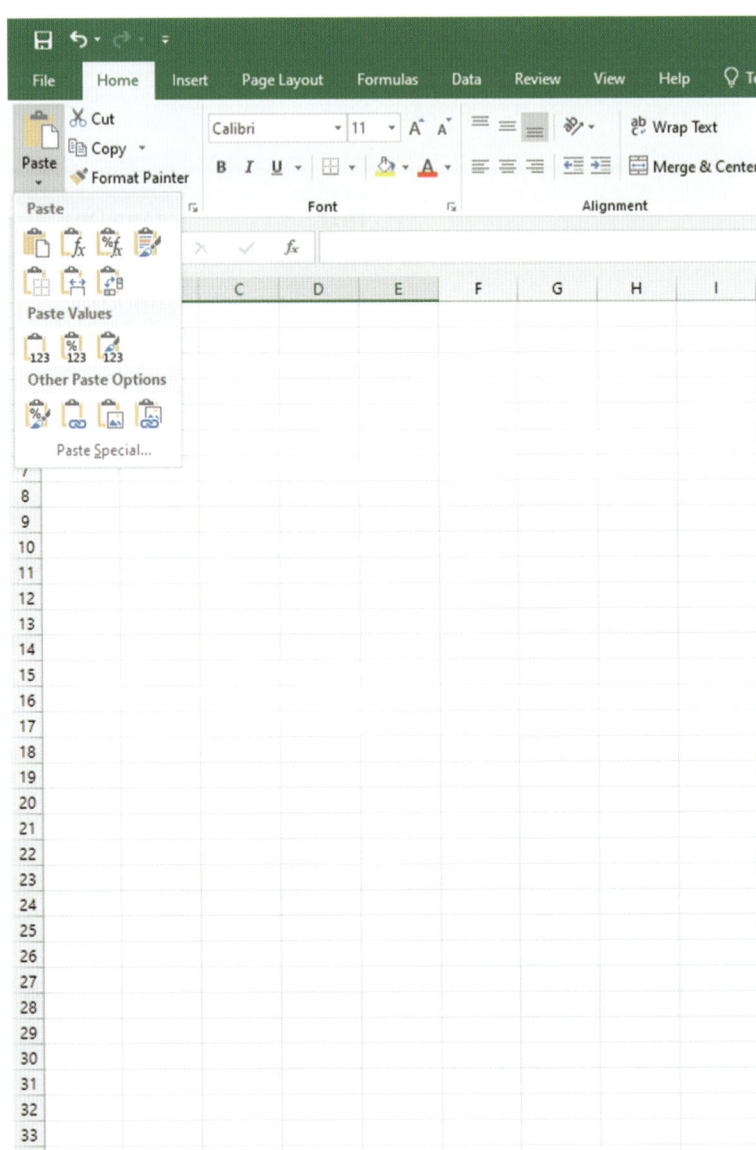

Figure 13.6 Different paste options

The paste will automatically occupy the number of cells needed.

Widening rows and columns

While typing a long entry the data will appear to run on to other cells, but in fact it remains in the selected cell. This is an example of Microsoft Excel table cells expanding automatically to accommodate data entry. However, on occasion the column or row may need to be expanded. There are several ways to adjust the cell width:

1 Hover the cursor over the right gridline of the column head labelled A, B, and so on – (cursor shape changes to ↔) when you are in the right spot, drag the line to the right (for columns). Or double click on the column head (A, B, and so on). For rows you must go to the numbered row and drag downwards to the appropriate width.
2 Click on the *Cells* subtab on the *Home* tab and click on *Format* to see options that specify row height and column width the default row height setting for cells is 14.4 and width is 8.11.

Using Wrap Text

Some column entries are much longer than others and therefore require to be placed within the cells to accommodate the data. This is where 'Wrap Text' is used.

There are 2 ways this can be achieved.

1 Enter your text, (which will go past your cell width)
2 Click outside of the filled cell then return to the cell and
   a Go to Alignment subtab
   b Click the 'Wrap Text' box and text will automatically fill within the adjusted cell.
   Or
   c Before typing information into the cell, click the 'Wrap Text' in the Alignment subtab box and begin typing your data into the cell

There are other data placement options on the Alignment subtab including placing text at the top, middle or bottom of a cell.

Moving and deleting data

Whole blocks of data can be cut or copied and pasted into new worksheets, new parts of the same worksheet and/or images by highlighting the data and right-clicking to get the dropdown box to cut or copy.

To remove a value (that is, clear content) from a cell, select the cell with the unwanted data and either press delete or type in the new value. Look at the formula bar to ensure that no part of the unwanted value remains.

Creating row, column and block ranges

Sheet 1 is a blank table. You should have some idea of what data will be entered into your table, and how you plan to manipulate the data. When you have determined the size of your table, you will need to define a *row range* and a *column range*; together, they will create a *block range*.

Figure 13.7 displays each type of range using coloured cells.

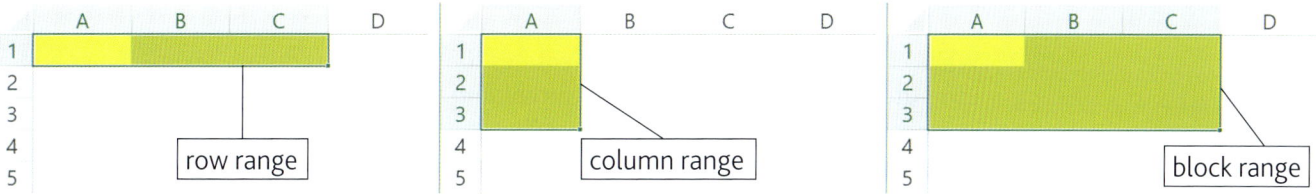

Figure 13.7 Types of Microsoft Excel table ranges

SECTION 3

> **Helpful hint**
>
> A *row range* crosses more than one column; a *column range* crosses more than one row, while a *block range* spans multiple rows and multiple columns.

> **Activity**
>
> Create a copy of the table in a Microsoft Excel worksheet, and using different colours, highlight the following ranges. (Clue: go to the Font subtab and the Paint button on the Home tab.)
> a the row range 2
> b the column range F
> c the block range A3 to E5

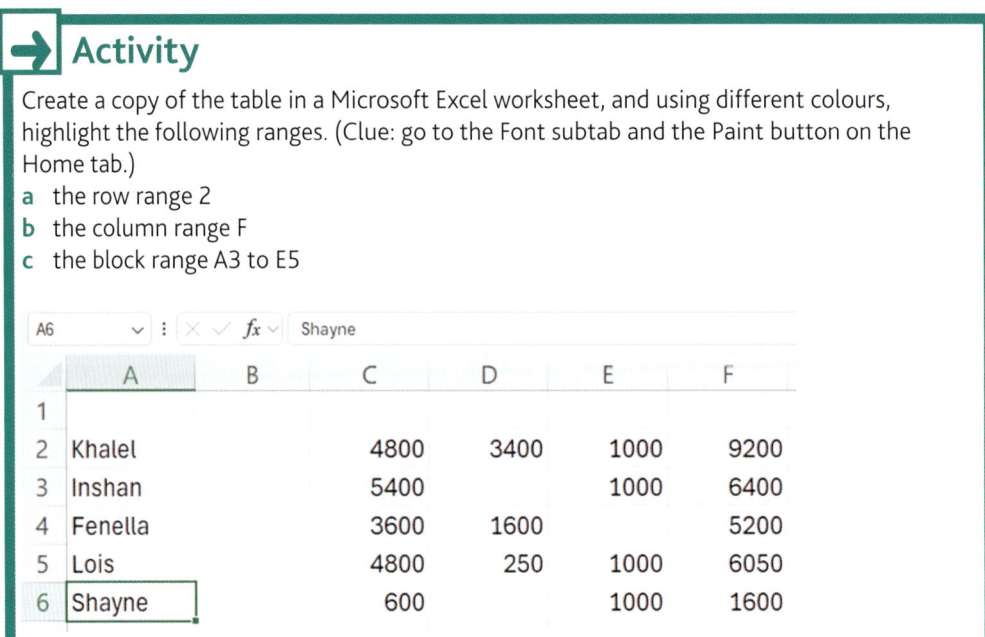

Entering headings and naming tables

One requirement for creating a basic table in a Microsoft Excel sheet is entering headings. *Headings* are titles or labels that indicate the classification of all the entries in a particular column or row. Different headings will appear in every column in the row range and in every row of the column range.

Figure 13.8 shows two kinds of headings:

1 'Product name' is at the top (A1) of text-type headings in A2, A3 and A4.
2 2017, 2018, 2019 are year headings in cells B1, C1 and D1.

PRODUCT NAME	2017	2018	2019
Printers	2000	2500	1000
Fax Machines	4000	5000	5000
Computer Screens	6000	7500	9000

Figure 13.8 Basic Microsoft Excel table with row and column headings

While cell A1 in Figure 13.8 clearly identifies that products (printers, fax machines and computer screens) will be shown in the column range, the purpose of the year headings in the rest of the row range is less clear. This is an indication that the whole table needs to be *named*. For example, if a new row is added and the title 'Units of Products Sold in 2017–2019' is entered in the new row 1, the purpose and usefulness of the table would be clearer.

Adding and deleting columns and rows

If data is omitted or misplaced, you need to insert or delete a column or a row inside your initial block range. The steps to insert new columns and rows or delete unwanted columns and rows are:

- **To insert a new row:** Left-click on the row number address, for example, #13, to select the row *below* the place where you want to add the new one. Right-click and choose the insert option from the dropdown menu. A new #13 row will be added. Note that the row that was #13 is now named #14.
- **To insert a new column:** Left-click on the letter address, for example, F, to select the column *after* where you want to add the new one. Right-click and choose the insert option from the dropdown menu. A new F column will be added. Note that the column that was F is now named H.
- **To delete a row or column:** Follow the sequence above, but right-click on delete in the dropdown box.

> 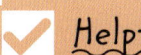 **Helpful hint**
>
> Note that a new row or column is always inserted *above* in the case of a new row, or *before* in the case of a new column, and can be achieved from the cells subtab on the home tab, as well as by right-clicking.

Formatting tables and cells

Formatting options are available on the home tab and styles subtab for tables and cells, but the cells subtab is the most versatile for formatting data in cells.

- The format menu and format cells dropdown box offer formatting options for presenting data in different fonts and font styles and in various orientations (horizontal, vertical or oblique) and different weights of borders and fills.
- Numeric data can be preformatted to appear in a uniform way, for example:
  - the number of decimal places can be preset
  - accounting values can always be shown with a $ sign.
- Dates can be presented in a standard format, for example mm/dd//yy or mm-dd-yy. (Note that a cell with both text and digits, for example CA4/11/25, will not be recognised as a number.)

Filtering and sorting data

Filtering and *sorting* data are basic analytical tools of spreadsheet applications. The subtab 'sort & filter' on the data tab provides different views of the same data by rearranging it according to selected criteria. Let us look at an example of the usefulness of both tools to demonstrate how the process works.

Mr. Pendleton, an analyst with Noreiga Bolts and Screws Limited, has created a Microsoft Excel table containing a dataset (also known as a *database*) of a range of information about the 40 employees of the company. A new manager wants to make some human-resource decisions. He has been asked for the following information from a 20% sample from the database:
- a quick view of how many people are in each department's sample
- who has the highest and lowest salary within each department.

Mr. Pendleton produces Table 13.3, which is an extract from his database.

Table 13.3 Extract from a Microsoft Excel database

Name	Department	Salary
Allan	Marketing	10,000
Simon	Office	45,000
Avni	Production	26,000
Beth	Marketing	11,500
Simeon	Sales	22,000
Leslie	Production	18,000
Carla	Sales	18,000
Tristan	Office	12,000

He will sort his data to:
- show all people in the same department in close proximity to each other
- apply a 'next level' sort that will show who has the highest and who has the lowest salary in each department.

For his response, Mr. Pendleton:
1 Selects his table, including the headings
2 Clicks on the Data tab and Sort subtab
3 Selects department, cell values and A–Z in the 'Sort by' windows
4 Selects 'Next level'
5 Selects salary, cell values and largest to smallest in those windows.

Table 13.4 shows the result of the database sorted by department and salary.

Table 13.4 Extract sorted by department and salary

Name	Department	Salary
Allan	Marketing	11,500
Beth	Marketing	10,000
Tristan	Office	45,000
Simon	Office	12,000
Leslie	Production	26,000
Avni	Production	18,000
Carla	Sales	22,000
Simeon	Sales	18,000

If Mr. Pendleton needs to rank the entries to show the highest and lowest salary earners overall, he can select his table, including the headings (note that, if only the salary column is selected, only that column will be sorted), and click on the data tab and the filter subtab to access filter buttons (Figure 13.9).

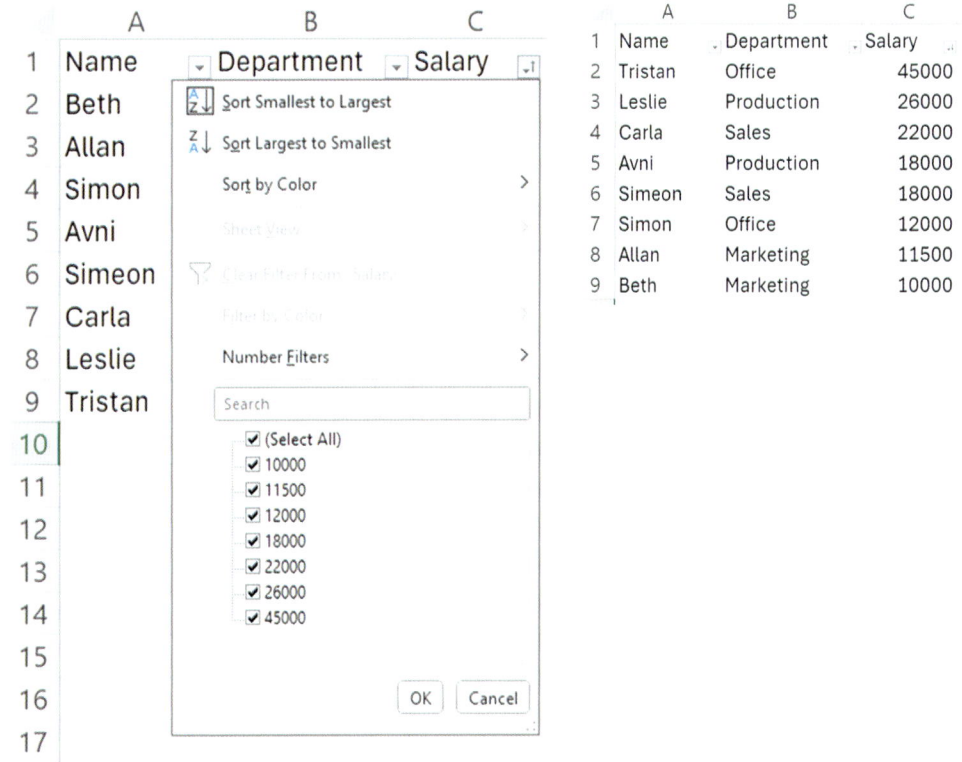

Figure 13.9 Dropdown box showing the filter buttons

Finally, if Mr. Pendleton selects the 'largest to smallest' filter, the table is filtered immediately. (Note that, if a column contained text, it would filter alphabetically.) Table 13.5 shows the result of Mr. Pendleton's filter.

Table 13.5 Salaries ranked from highest to lowest

Name	Department	Salary
Simon	Office	45,000
Avni	Production	26,000
Simeon	Sales	22,000
Leslie	Production	18,000
Carla	Sales	18,000
Tristan	Office	12,000
Beth	Marketing	11,500
Allan	Marketing	10,000

Charts and graphs

Data may also be presented as a **chart** or *graph*, which can help with understanding patterns or trends more clearly than reading a table. The observations made from charts and graphs provide answers and support decisions. They can also be copied and pasted into other applications to enhance presentations and reports.

The most common types of charts are *bar charts*, *pie charts* and *line charts* (or *line graphs*), which are different ways of presenting data.

To create various types of charts:
1 Select the completed table or the range of data for your chart.
2 Position your cursor where you want your chart to appear in the worksheet.
3 Click the Insert tab on the ribbon. In the Charts group, select your desired chart type (such as Column, Line, or Pie) and click on a specific chart style.
4 The chart will appear on your worksheet. Drag it to your selected position in the worksheet.

Bar charts

Bar charts are most useful for comparing values across different categories. Most spreadsheet tools enable presentation in two ways: either the bars are horizontal (*row charts*) or the bars are vertical (*column charts*). Let us look again at the table that shows product sales for the years 2017–2019 and create examples of the different charts and graphs using that data (Figure 13.10).

PRODUCT NAME	2017	2018	2019
Printers	2000	2500	1000
Fax Machines	4000	5000	5000
Computer Screens	6000	7500	9000

Figure 13.10 Basic Microsoft Excel table with row and column headings

The Sales analyst at the company has been tracking the number of products sold every year in a spreadsheet. He thinks he sees a pattern, and wants to show his supervisor. He decides to create a *vertical bar chart* to show the data.

1 Select the completed table or part of the table or the range of data you want to include in the chart.
2 Position your cursor where you want your chart to appear in the worksheet
3 Click Insert on the ribbon, go to the Charts group, select your chosen chart or graph, and then click Insert.
4 Drag your chart or graph to your selected position in the worksheet.

The result is shown in Figure 13.11.

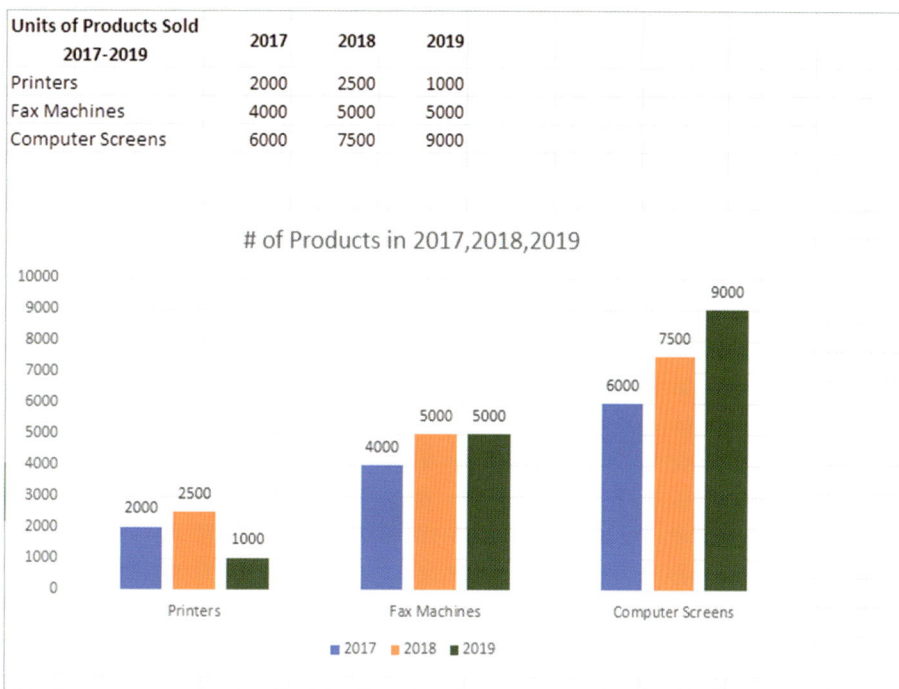

Figure 13.11 Simple vertical bar chart

The analyst can also present part of the data using a different layout, such as a *horizontal bar chart*. He uses the 2019 product sales, as shown in Figure 13.12.

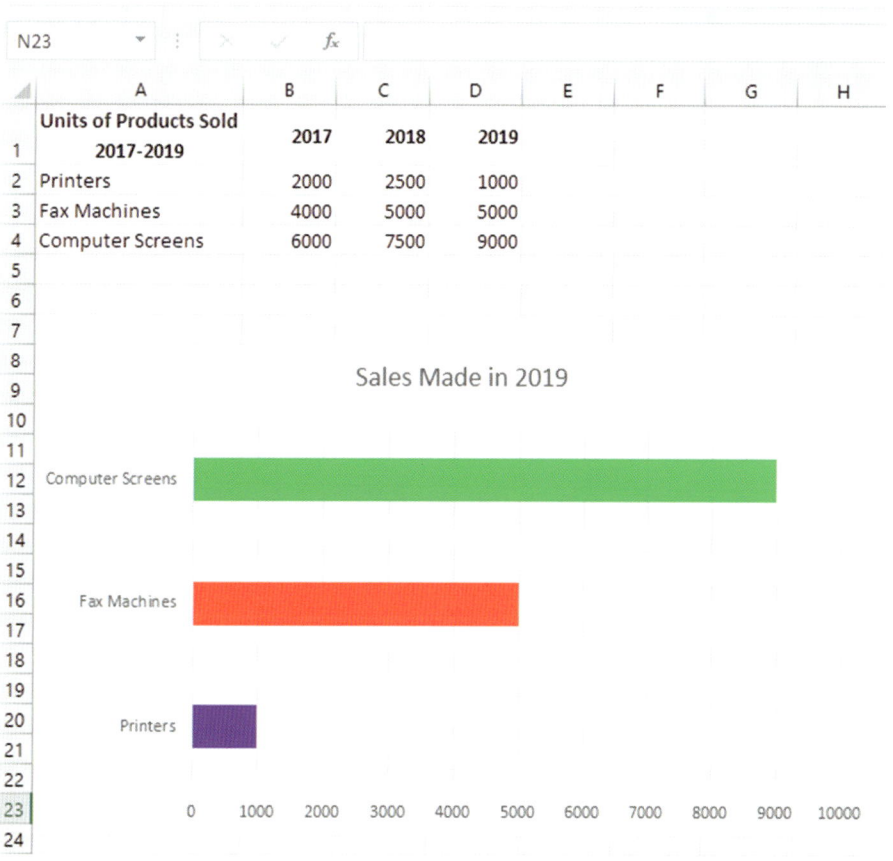

Figure 13.12 Simple horizontal bar chart

>  **Activity**
>
> If you were part of the team preparing advertisements for 2020, which product would you give most attention?

Pie charts

Pie charts are best for highlighting the percentage of a total taken up by each item. The concept is that of a circle cut into slices. They work best when there are no more than four categories as, otherwise, the pie slices become too small to show any meaningful pattern.

> The Sales analyst wants to show how much of the company's sales are from computer screens versus the other products. A pie chart summarises and displays the results for all products, as in Figure 13.13.
>
>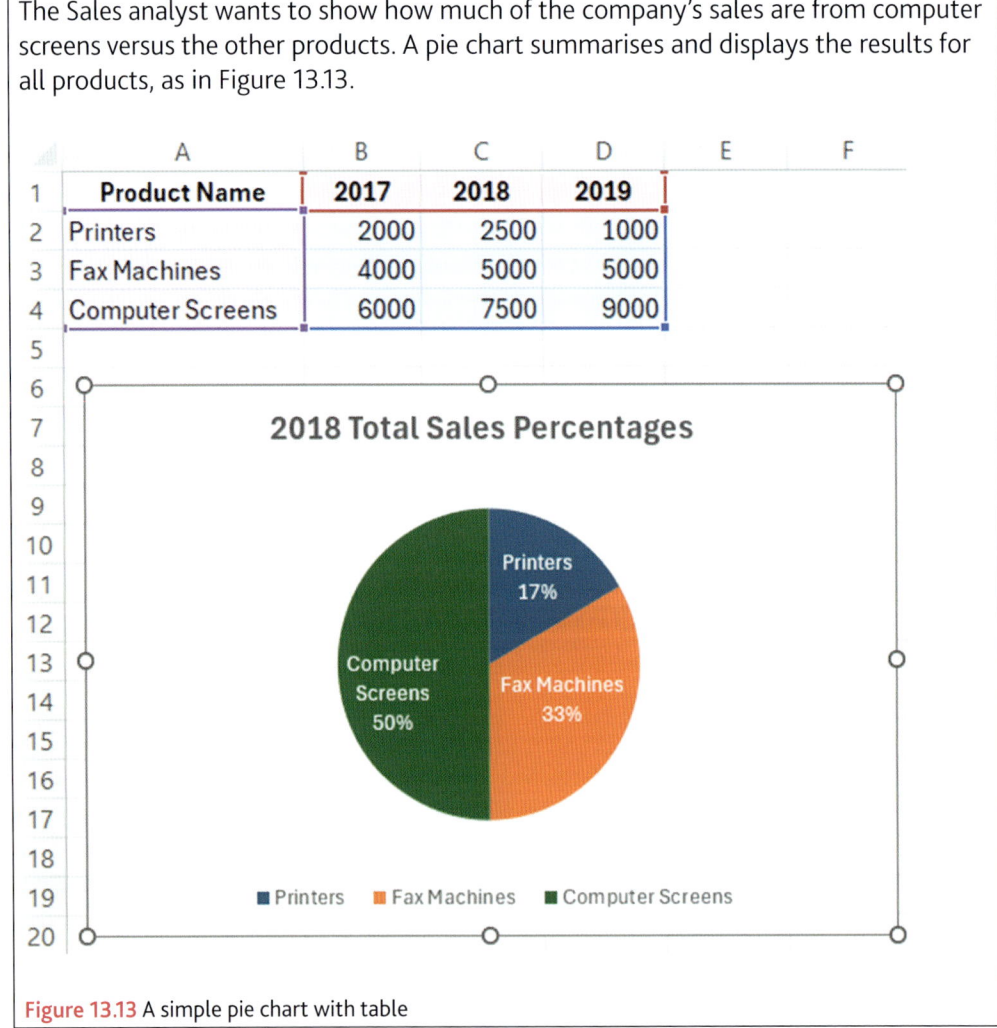
>
> Figure 13.13 A simple pie chart with table

Line graphs

Line graphs or *line charts* are best used for showing trends or patterns over time, such as months or years. The lines can have markers included as circles or other shapes that pinpoint the associated time period.

The supervisor looked at the analyst's first bar chart and saw that computer screens had the highest sales, and they had kept growing from 2011 to 2019. She asked the analyst to prepare a line graph to show the trend over the years.

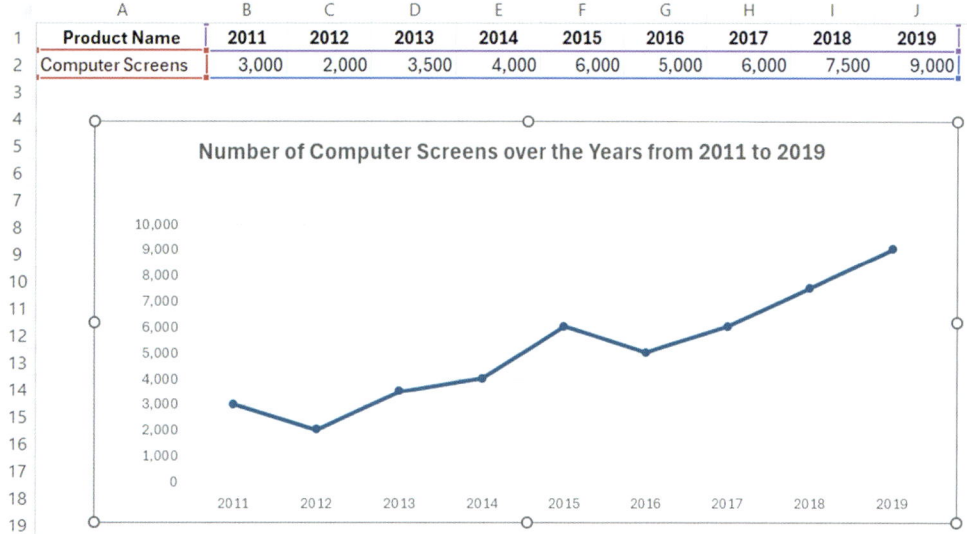

Figure 13.14 A simple line graph

Figure 13.14's line graph confirms the supervisor's observation, but also shows years of decreased sales.

Creating a chart

Now that you have seen the value of charts and graphs, follow the steps to create your own chart.

Activity

1 Using the data given below, create a table in a Microsoft Excel worksheet, using three columns with headings labelled First Name, Last Name and Final Test Score. Begin your table from cell B4.

Table 13.6 Final test scores

		Final test score			Final test score
1	Pamela Guthrie	77	5	James Proudstar	90
2	Emma Frost	93	6	Anna-Marie LeBeau	61
3	Scott Summers	56	7	Kamala Khan	79
4	Ororo Munroe	50	8	James Bradley	97

2 Select your table including the headings. Go to the Insert tab and click on the *Insert Column or Bar Chart* icon in the Charts subtab.
3 Choose the 2-D bar chart from the bar chart menu. You may need to drag the chart from on top of the table to a position next to your table. Your vertical bar chart should look like Figure 13.15.

SECTION 3

> ✓ **Helpful hint**
> Use your table to create pie charts and line graphs of various kinds.

Including chart titles and data labels

Charts and graphs should include appropriate titles.

To include a *chart title*, double-click on the 'chart title' space on your chart and edit the words to 'Comparison of Students' Final Scores'. If the space for the chart title is not visible, click on any blank space of the chart and a plus sign (+) will appear next to the chart. Click it, check the box next to chart title to select it and the title space will appear for your editing.

To include *data labels*, which show the scores on the bars themselves, click on any blank space of the chart and a plus sign (+) will appear next to the chart. Check the box next to data labels. You can also show the original table on the chart if you check the 'data table' box.

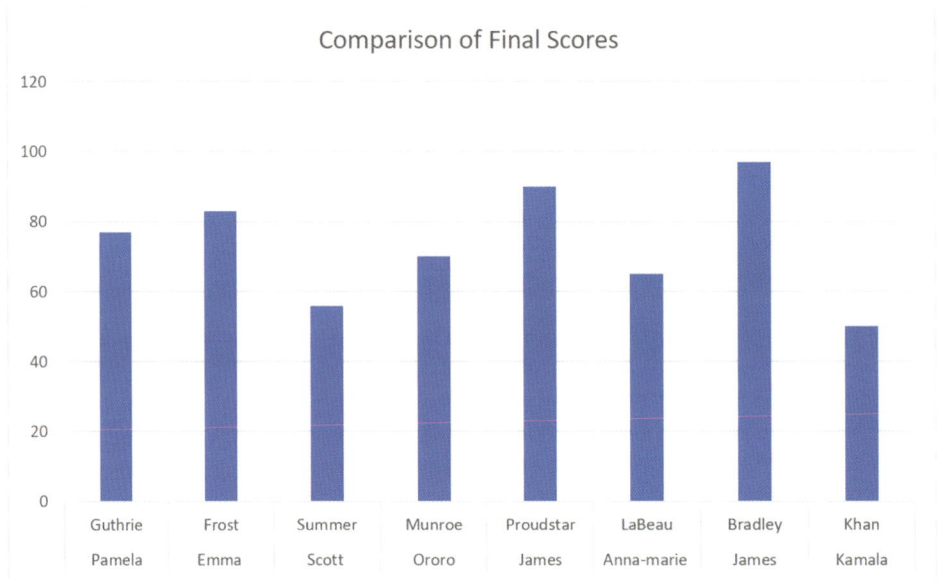

Figure 13.15 A vertical bar chart comparing final scores

Formatting the chart

Charts can be made more attractive by inserting contrasting colours or patterns.
To do so:
1. Click on the chart to activate the Chart Tools. This will display the Chart Design and Format tabs on the ribbon.
2. Click on the Chart Design tab to change the colours, select a preset chart style, or change the chart type altogether.
3. Click on the Format tab to access various formatting options for chart elements, such as shapes, text, and effects.

Resizing to fit a document or presentation

Click on any blank space in the chart and circles will appear on the borders. Select one, and drag it either horizontally or vertically to fit the allotted space in your document. When you are satisfied, click the 'Save as' button on the file tab, name your file appropriately and close it.

13 Basic spreadsheet techniques

Adding a chart to a document or presentation

A report or a presentation will benefit from the addition of visual aids such as charts or graphs. To add a chart or graph:

1 Copy the graph that is on your Microsoft Excel worksheet.
2 Open your Microsoft Word document or Microsoft PowerPoint presentation.
3 Insert a text box and paste the copied chart or graph in the appropriate space. (The paste may appear to cover text or other images.)
4 To resize your chart to fit the allotted space, click on any blank space in the chart and circles (called control buttons) will appear on the borders.
5 Select one and drag it either horizontally or vertically to fit the allotted space in your document.
6 When you are satisfied, click the 'Save as' button on the file tab, name your file (if needed) and close it.

> ### Key terms
>
> **active cell** A cell that has been selected for use
>
> **block range** A selection comprising a column range and a row range that forms a quadrilateral space
>
> **cell identification** A cell's name/address/reference, made up of the column address and row address
>
> **chart** A display of numerical and textual data in the form of bars, lines or pie slices to make it easy to compare categories or values or show trends and patterns over time or another variable
>
> **colon** A punctuation mark (:) that describes a row or column range when placed between the addresses of two cells
>
> **column identification** Labels that use the letters of the alphabet or combinations of letters; also known as *name*, *address* or *reference*
>
> **column range** A selection of two or more cells that are next to each other in the same column
>
> **data space** A space where data or information (processed data) may appear, either from manual entry or from computer instruction
>
> **formula bar** A window that allows the user to manipulate data in the active cell, including entering manual formulas for operating on numerical data
>
> **graph** A display of numerical and textual data in the form of bars, lines or pie slices to make it easy to compare categories or values or show trends and patterns over time or another variable
>
> **heading (column/row)** A label used to describe the common aspect of the values in a column or row
>
> **name box** A window that displays the address of the currently active cell or the first cell to be clicked in a block range
>
> **resizing** The action of manually or automatically allowing a row or column to change dimensions to accommodate data inside cells
>
> **ribbon** A display of familiar **menus/tabs**, such as home, insert, page layout, review, view, with two additional tabs in Microsoft Excel – formulas and data – which provide tools for the manipulation of data, especially numeric data
>
> **row identification** Labels that use numbers from 1 to 1 048 576, also known as *name*, *address* or *reference*
>
> **row range** A selection of two or more cells that are next to each other in the same row
>
> **workbook** A spreadsheet application that provides a file composed of a large number of worksheets
>
> **worksheet/spreadsheet/sheet** A page in a workbook composed of cells, data spaces and a ribbon

SECTION 3

 **Summary**

In this chapter, you have learned to:

- use a spreadsheet application (Microsoft Excel) to tabulate, manipulate, sort and filter data
- transform various data types into different formats, such as charts and graphs
- appreciate how data reformatted into Microsoft Excel tables supports data-driven decisions
- choose the format that adds value to presentations and reports.

Practice, research and exam-style questions

Multiple-choice questions

1. Which of these actions is *not* suited to a spreadsheet application?
   A Budgeting
   B Trend identification
   C Performance rating
   D Letter-writing

2. Which statement is *inaccurate*?
   A The intersection of a column and a row is called a *cell*.
   B A grid of cells makes up a worksheet.
   C A worksheet is a single page in a spreadsheet.
   D A spreadsheet table is the same as a word-processing table.

3. Which option has *no* value in a spreadsheet application?
   A Symbols
   B Formulas
   C Text
   D Numbers

4. Which term is *not* relevant when creating a table in a spreadsheet application?
   A Row range
   B Cell address
   C Field property
   D Block range

5. Which data type is normally aligned to the right margin of a cell?
   A Text
   B Number
   C Alphanumeric character
   D Formula

6. The cell reference C5:C13 refers to cells located in …
   A Column C, rows 5 and 13
   B Column C, namely C5 to C13
   C Row C, columns 5 to 13
   D Row C, columns 5 to 13

7. Cell headings can be in all these alignments *except*:
   A Horizontal
   B Arched
   C Vertical
   D Slanted

8. A spreadsheet application is the best tool for …
   A analysing sales performance.
   B increasing sales performance.
   C designing discounted sales flyers.
   D preparing memos for sales agents.

9. Pie charts provide …
   A slides.
   B lines.
   C slices.
   D bars.

10. Which statement represents the *correct* sequence of some of the actions to produce a chart?
    A Open a worksheet, create a basic table, select block range, press the insert tab
    B Press the insert tab, open a worksheet, select block range, create a basic table
    C Open a worksheet, select block range, create a basic table, press the insert tab
    D Press the insert tab, open a worksheet, select block range, create a basic table

Research activities

1. For each option, list *two* things it can do in a Microsoft Excel table.
   a Font
   b Alignment
   c Chart design

2. List *three* reasons why naming tables carefully is important.

3. What are *two* quick ways to add rows and columns?

4. List *two* advantages of converting data to a bar graph.

Exam-style question

You are the facilitator for a two-day workshop. You are asked to submit a budget. Prepare a spreadsheet to record the information on the right, following *all* the instructions.

1. Start the spreadsheet in cell C3 and work out the block range.

2. Name the spreadsheet 'Resources for Workshop', using Arial 18 pt bold and caps.

3. Use the column headings 'Equipment', 'Materials' and 'Total Cost' in Arial 14 pt bold.

4. Enter the data in Arial 12 pt in initial caps only.

5. Use shoulder headings to separate the two categories of equipment and materials.

6. Create a pie chart for the Hardware category.

7. Create a bar chart for the Expenses category.

HARDWARE	
ITEM	COST
Multimedia projector and screen	$3,000
Microphones (3)	$6,000
Speakers (2)	$1,600
Whiteboards (4)	$4,000

EXPENSES	
ITEM	COST
Folders (200)	$3,000
Pens (250)	$750
Writing pads (200)	$1,200
Whiteboard markers (100)	$500
Meals (210)	$10,500

14 Advanced spreadsheet techniques

Objectives

By the end of this chapter, you will be able to:

- prepare financial source documents and financial statements using Microsoft Excel features
- perform basic arithmetical operations using simple formulas or predefined functions on financial documents
- use predefined functions on financial documents to arrive at basic statistical information.

Introduction

In this chapter, the focus will be on preparing financial documents using Microsoft Excel's formatting and editing tools. In addition, various arithmetical and statistical operations can be applied to these documents to calculate important subtotals, totals and statistics that can be displayed in charts and graphs.

Advantages of Microsoft Excel tables

Microsoft Excel tables are considered to be more advanced because the data in their cells (called the *values*) can be manipulated to produce answers to important questions. There are other advantages to using Microsoft Excel tables rather than Microsoft Word tables too:

- Microsoft Excel tables are easier to organise and can be updated quickly where there is a lot of data that spans many rows or columns.
- You can auto-populate table cells with data or **formulas** by dragging the cursor across columns (that is, within the same row) or downwards across rows (that is, within the same column).
- You can quickly remove unwanted or irrelevant data, or add data; the table will automatically contract or expand and will apply the same formatting and formulas to new cells.
- Cell addresses are used in formulas as references, making them easy to apply across the dataset.
- You can update the appearance of presentations, using built-in formatting styles that add highlighting, colour, borders and alignment, to make your tables, charts or graphs look cleaner and more professional.

Preparing financial documents

There are many special terms used by accountants and other financial experts who work with financial documents. The three categories of financial documents for preparation are:

1. source documents
2. working papers
3. financial statements.

14 Advanced spreadsheet techniques

The preparation of financial documents involves understanding the key terms in this specialised area, using various layouts and formatting features for the different documents and calculating missing values. Study this list of financial terms in Table 14.1 carefully.

Table 14.1 Financial terms

assets	Items with monetary value, e.g. property, machinery, equipment (**fixed assets**) and **stock**, and money in the bank (**current assets**) that a business uses to operate and make profits; **debtors** (or *receivables*) are people sold goods and/or services on credit
balance sheet	Also known as the *statement of financial position*; sets out the assets and liabilities of the business, including the amount owed to owners
bank statement	A document issued by a bank to its customers to provide details of the amounts deposited and the amounts withdrawn during a period
capital	Also known as *owner's equity*; the amount provided by the owner to start the business – capital increases with profits and reduces with losses
expense/expenditure	Represents *outflows* of cash for the purpose of making and selling goods for a profit, e.g. purchases, salary, wages, insurance, interest on loans
income/revenue	*Inflows* of cash from sales or other sources; service businesses use terms such as *fees*, *commissions* and *subscriptions* for their source of income
invoice	A document that provides details of items purchased or sold, including amounts, descriptions and costs
liabilities	Amounts owed to individuals and other companies, including lenders such as banks (loans) and people who provide goods and/or services on credit (*creditors*/payables)
loss	The difference between income and expenditure, when expenditure is greater than income, which reduces capital
profit	The difference between income and expenditure, when income is greater than expenditure, which increases capital
profit and loss account	Also known as **income** and **expenditure** account; matches the total of all income against the total of all expenditure to calculate either a profit or a loss – if a trading account has been done, it starts with the balance (gross profit or gross loss) from that account to calculate *net profit* or *net loss*
receipt	A document that provide evidence of payment for goods or services rendered
trading account	Focuses on the sales income and the cost of goods sold to calculate gross profit or gross loss
trial balance	A list of all assets, expenses (in the debit column on the left side) and all liabilities and capital (in the credit column on the right side); ensures that both columns are equal

Preparing source documents

Source documents are created to record **transactions** with stakeholders including customers, suppliers, insurance companies and banks. Three often-used source documents are *receipts*, *invoices* and *bank statements*. All of these make use of spreadsheets to align and format text, including merging cells, adding shapes and performing calculations.

Receipts

Businesses purchase and sell goods and/or services on cash or **credit terms**. When cash is received, businesses issue receipts. Receipts come in several forms: handwritten pages in a receipt book, cash-register stubs and electronically prepared and issued receipts (e-receipts). Both the stubs and e-receipts make use of spreadsheet-type applications:

- A cash-register stub is a list of items sold and their individual and collective total costs calculated.
- E-receipts use a company's template with headings and spaces to fill in with relevant details, including totals and subtotals.

Figure 14.1 provides samples of an e-receipt, a receipt-book page and a cash-register receipt. Take note of details that are usually included, such as dates and reference/account numbers and a description of the item/service being paid for.

****

RECEIPT

****

COMPANY NAME

Address:	Lorem Ipsum 8/24
Date:	MM/DD/YYYY
Manager:	Lorem Ipsum

Description	Price
Orange Juice	$2.15
Apples	$3.50
Tomato	$2.40
Fish	$6.99
Beef	$10.00
Onion	$1.25
Cheese	$3.40
Tax	
TOTAL	$29.69

THANK YOU

****

123456778963578021

Amount: 300.00	Account number
	CRM_000151379
Date	
Sat Apr 4, 2026	
Issuer	Confirmation number
Atlas Communications Limited	ACOB_004051671

CASH RECEIPT

No. ______________ Date: ____________________

Received from ____

The sum of ____ dollars

($______________)

being payment for ____

Signed ____________________

Figure 14.1 An e-receipt, a cash receipt page and a cash-register receipt

14 Advanced spreadsheet techniques

Helpful hint
One company's sales invoice is another company's purchase invoice.

Invoices

Although some businesses issue receipts labelled *cash invoices*, invoices are more often prepared to record credit transactions. Another type of invoice is the pro forma invoice, which is sent to inform a customer of the estimated cost of a good or service. Two types of credit invoices are *sales invoices* and *purchase invoices*.

Invoices list details about the:

- date of transaction
- names and addresses of buyer and seller
- units of products sold (or purchased)
- costs per unit
- total costs
- overall cost
- service charges
- value added taxes (VAT)
- discounts given to customers.

Figure 14.2 shows a sample invoice as well as the details that usually appear on it.

SALES INVOICE			
Samosas To Go, 111 Main Road, Sads Village, San Juan			
Order No: 54			Date: 9/12/26
Sold to:			
V Paularal - 129 Rosa Avenue, Headstown, San Pedro			
Quantity	Description	Unit Price/dozen $	Total Cost $
2 Dozen	Potato samosas	$ 96.00	$ 192.00
3 Dozen	Chicken samosas	$ 180.00	$ 540.00
2 Dozen	Lamb samosas	$ 240.00	$ 480.00
	Total Cost		$ 1,212.00
	Down payment (9/12/26)		$ 606.00
	Balance due (9/13/26)		$ 606.00
Credit terms: 50% down payment; remainder on collection of order			

Figure 14.2 Sales invoice

The pro forma invoice will not have as many details.

SECTION 3

> **→ Activity**
>
> Lamy is a small caterer who recorded the following transactions during the month of June. Name each source document that would have been used for Lamy's transactions.
>
> | Date | Transactions | Source document |
> |---|---|---|
> | June 2 | Bought a tank of gas for the stove; paid $200 in cash | |
> | June 4 | Bought $2,000 in grocery items from Chin Wong; agreed to pay on July 5 | |
> | June 4 | Sold baked items for $1,000 in cash | |
> | June 12 | Sent estimate to customer for $6,200 worth of meals to be paid for at end of July | |

> **✓ Helpful hint**
>
> A bank statement usually includes the logo and name of the bank or other financial institution.

Bank statement

A *bank statement* is a record of a person or company's transactions with its bank. The bank statement is a table of five columns with these headings:

1 Transaction date
2 Transaction description
3 Debit entries (withdrawals)
4 Credit entries (deposits)
5 Balance (after every transaction)

However, the number of rows depends on the number of transactions over the stated period.

Figure 14.3 displays an incomplete bank statement for Noreiga's Bolts and Screws for the period November 2, 2026 to December 30, 2026.

> **→ Activity**
>
> 1 Create a Microsoft Excel table from the information in Figure 14.3 on the next page.
> 2 Save the file as Bank Statement.

> **Helpful hint**
> Although there are usually more debit entries than credit entries, the value of the entry is more important, or the business will have overdrawn its balance at the bank.

\	NOREIGA'S BOLTS AND SCREWS			
\	BANK STATEMENT			
\	for the period November 2, 2026 to December 30, 2026			
Date	Details	Debits ($)	Credits ($)	Balance ($)
Nov-02	Opening balance			13,890
Nov-08	Cash deposit		8,060	
Nov-23	Withdrawal – wage disbursement	11,850		
Nov-30	Bank fees	1,000		
Dec-05	Direct deposit from Customer Nandaram		13,700	
Nov-30	Standing order payment: Creditor: Lee	3,000		
Dec-08	Cash deposit		15,955	
Dec-15	Withdrawal – foreign purchases	21,850		
Dec-30	Withdrawal – wage disbursement	11,850		
Dec-28	Standing order payment: Creditor: Lee	3,000		
Dec-30	Bank fees	1,000		
Dec-30	Closing balance			

Figure 14.3 Incomplete bank statement

Preparing working papers

Working papers include trial balances, payroll documents, revenue calculations and budget documents. These documents make use of Microsoft Excel tables in their preparation, with the number of rows and columns determined by the amount of detail required. In this section, draft working papers are to be prepared and saved. These draft papers are then used for practising mathematical and statistical operations in the following section.

Trial balances

A trial balance is prepared before **financial statements** to check for errors and ensure that the records are in balance. A table of three columns with the headings 'Items', 'Debit entries' and 'Credit entries' makes up a trial balance.

Figure 14.4 shows an incomplete trial balance as at December 31 for the business Noreiga's Bolts and Screws, as it appears in a Microsoft Excel worksheet of three columns and fourteen rows.

NOREIGA BOLTS AND SCREWS
Trial Balance as at 31 December 20xx

ITEMS	DEBIT($)	CREDIT($)
Land and buildings	68960	
Vehicles	15000	
Bank overdraft balance		16340
Petty cash in hand	120	
Equipment	58000	
Gross profit		91350
Closing stock	8670	
Salaries and wages	118500	
Miscellaneous expenses	2320	
Accounts receivable	8110	
Accounts payable		14990
Capital		157000
	xxx	xxx

Figure 14.4 Incomplete trial balance

> **Activity**
>
> 1 Create a Microsoft Excel table using the information in Figure 14.4.
> 2 Save the file as Noreiga's Trial Balance.
> 3 Close the file.

Paysheet

A **paysheet** is the most important payroll document, as information from other documents, such as clock cards and work tickets, are entered here. Using a Microsoft Excel worksheet to prepare a paysheet allows for quick calculations of pay information for each employee, such as gross pay and deductions for tax and national insurance payments, as well as calculations of total expense items for the business.

The number of rows and columns used for the paysheet is determined by the amount of detail needed.

Figure 14.5 shows some pay information for eight employees of Noreiga's Bolts and Screws for the week ending May 31, 2026.

NOREIGA'S BOLTS AND SCREWS							
Paysheet for the week ending …							
First Name	Last Name	Department	Hourly rate of pay ($)	Total hours worked	Gross pay ($)	Tax ($) @ 25%	Net pay ($)
Starr	Fayard	Production	20	40			
Brownie	Delpino	Production	30	25			
Shivani	Marcus	Production	30	30			
Lionel	Trooper	Production	20	50			
Marion	Vinicius	Marketing	30	40			
Nathaniel	Gomez	Marketing	30	35			
Ayanna	Furstan	Marketing	20	40			
Vernon	Mitchell	Marketing	20	25			

Figure 14.5 Pay information

>  **Activity**
> 1. Create a Microsoft Excel table using the information in Figure 14.5.
> 2. Save the file as Noreiga's Paysheet.
> 3. Close file.

Revenue/income calculations

Businesses that earn revenue/income from various sources may also use an Microsoft Excel worksheet to keep track of these funds. Headings might include a reference number, an item description, a name for the source of funds, the value of the source and the percentage of the value that the business earned.

Budget

Businesses and individuals might plan ahead for revenues and expenses connected to projects. Using headings such as item name, quantity, unit cost and total cost in a Microsoft Excel worksheet, with shoulder headings to indicate categories or departments, would provide subtotal and total values for various aspects of a project.

Performing mathematical and statistical operations on financial documents

In this section, the tables will show the usefulness of Microsoft Excel's advanced features, and the performance of:

- *mathematical* (arithmetical) operations: addition, subtraction, multiplication and division
- *statistical* operations: average, maximum and minimum values in a data set, and percentages.

These calculations can be performed by using either:

- typed-in formulas applied to cell references
or
- predefined functions available under the formulas tab on the Microsoft Excel ribbon.

General guidelines for using formulas include:

- Place your cursor in the cell where you want the answer to appear (the active cell), or it will appear in the next empty cell after your last value. The typed formula and the answer will also be shown in the formula bar.
- When typing in formulas manually, use the cell references to describe all the rows in a particular column (column range) or all the columns in a particular row (row range) that you need to use for your results.
- Start each formula with an equal sign (=) so that Microsoft Excel recognises it as a formula.
- Do not place different data types in the same column or row and try to apply formulas.
- When using predefined (built-in) formulas, look for the **function library** subtab in the formulas tab – see Figure 14.6.

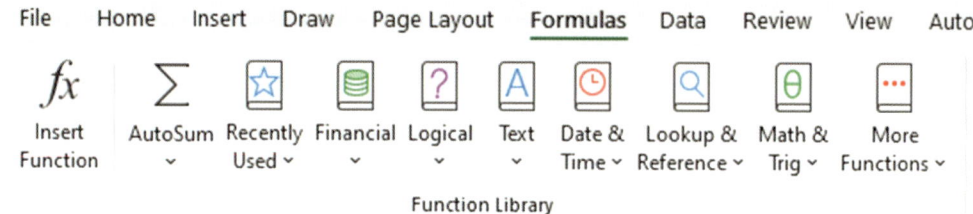

Figure 14.6 Microsoft Excel's formula tab's function library subtab

How Microsoft Excel's arithmetical features work

Manual entry mode

Table 14.2 explains how to use the manual entry mode for arithmetic.

Table 14.2 Using the manual entry mode mathematical operations

Addition +	The formula =(A1+B1) will find the *total* or *sum* of all the values that are in column A row 1 and column B row 1. The formula =(A5+A17) will find the total of all the values that are in column A row 5 and column A row 17.
Subtraction −	The formula =(A1-B1) will calculate the total of *subtracting* the value in cell B1 from the value in cell A1. The formula =(A5-A17) will subtract the value that is in column A row 17 from the value in column A row 5, even if the answer is a negative number.
Multiplication ×	The formula =(A1*B5) will calculate the total of *multiplying* the value in cell A1 by the value in cell B5 or vice versa.
Division ÷	The formula =(A1/B5) will calculate the total of *dividing* the value in cell A1 by the value in cell B5. Note that this is *not* the same formula as =(B5/A1).

14 Advanced spreadsheet techniques

Note:

- If the formula needs to be written as a series of cell references, the punctuation marks colon (:) or comma (,) can be substituted for the mathematical symbols, for example instead of =(A3+A4+A5+A6+A7+A8+A9), you can enter the formula as =SUM(A3:A9) or =SUM(A3, A4, A5, A6, A7, A8, A9) – this format is most useful when the data set is long
- For subtraction, use the format =(A3–D3) where the items are in the same row or =(A3–A4) if the items are in the same column.

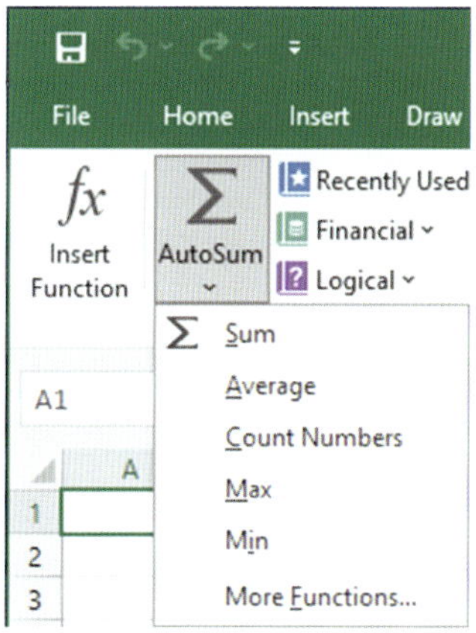

AutoSum mode

Adding and subtracting can also be performed with the use of the built-in formula called **AutoSum**.

1 In the Editing tab on the Home ribbon, observe the icon for various mathematical operations. Click on the formulas tab and the subtab AutoSum.
2 Alternatively, click on SUM from the menu (Figure 14.7). An option box =SUM() will appear.
3 Select all the cells whose values you wish to add, noting that this works best where the values lie next to each other
   or
   Type in the cell references within the parentheses, noting that, if you are subtracting values, you need to use a minus sign before the parenthesis that encloses the second cell reference.
4 Place your cursor where you want the answer to appear (the active cell) and press enter.
5 The total of all selected values will appear.

Figure 14.7 The AutoSum icon and dropdown box

Applying the operations to financial documents

Balancing a trial balance

A trial balance should show the same total at the end of the debit and the credit column (trial balance).

1 Open your saved file: Trial Balance.
2 Place your cursor in the next empty cell at the bottom of the Debit column. Either type in the formula to add using =(first value in column+last value in column) and press Enter. The total of all the values will appear in the Total row.
   OR
   Highlight the cells from first value to last value in the column and click AutoSum in the formulas tab.
3 Follow the same steps for the Credit column.
4 Save the file as Trial Balance.

SECTION 3

Completing a bank statement

A bank statement usually shows an individual's or business's balance at the bank after every transaction. To populate the balance column from Figure 14.3 (the incomplete bank statement), take note of the following:

1. Place your cursor in the first empty cell in the Balance column (below the opening balance) and enter a formula that will add the credit value to the balance, for example =(E5+D6) will give a new balance of $21,950 in cell E6.
2. Open your saved file: Bank Statement
3. To calculate new balances, you will need formulas to add and subtract. For example, to calculate the balance of $10,100, the formula would be =(E7-C8). Place your cursor in cell E8 and enter this formula. Now follow the same steps to complete the bank statement balances.
4. Save the file as Bank Statement.

> **Helpful hint**
> Entries in the credit column *increase* the balance, while entries in debit column *decrease* the balance.

Figure 14.8 shows the first three correct balances.

	NOREIGA'S BOLTS AND SCREWS			
	Incomplete Bank Statement			
	for the period November 2, 2026 to December 31, 2026			
Date	Details	Debits ($)	Credits ($)	Balance ($)
Nov-02	Opening balance			13,890
Nov-08	Cash deposit		8,060	**21,950**
Nov-23	Withdrawal – wage disbursement	11,850		**10,100**
Nov-30	Bank fees	1,000		**9,100**
Dec-05	Direct deposit from Customer Nandaram		13,700	
Nov-30	Standing order payment: Creditor: Lee	3,000		
Dec-08	Cash deposit		15,955	
Dec-15	Withdrawal – foreign purchases	21,850		
Dec-30	Withdrawal – wage disbursement	11,850		
Dec-28	Standing order payment: Creditor: Lee	3,000		
Dec-30	Bank fees	1,000		
Dec-30	Closing balance			

Figure 14.8 Partially completed bank statement

> ###  Activity
> Find the closing balances of total debits and total credits using the AutoSum function.

Completing a paysheet

The paysheet is completed by calculating the gross pay, deductions (such as tax) and net pay for each employee.

1 Open your saved file: Paysheet.
2 Place formulas in appropriate active cells to calculate these amounts for each worker:
   a The formula is total hours worked × hourly rate of pay.
     Gross pay (hours worked × hourly rate) Place the cursor in empty cell F4, then create the formula. For employee Fayard Starr, use =SUM(D4*E4). The answer is $800.
   b The formula is gross pay × 25%.
     Tax (25% of gross pay)
     For Fayard Starr, place the cursor in cell G4 and type in =(F4*25%). The answer will be $600.
   c The formula is gross pay minus net pay:
     Net pay (gross pay − tax)
     For Fayard Starr, place the cursor in cell H4 and type in the formula =(F4-G4). The answer is $640.
3 Complete the paysheet by calculating gross pay, tax and net pay for the remainder of employees.

> **Activity**
> 1 Work out total gross, total tax and total net pay using the AutoSum function.
> 2 Create a pie chart that compares total taxes with total gross pay.

Statistical operations

Spreadsheets are useful for finding answers in the form of statistics. A paysheet prepared using Microsoft Excel may be used to calculate statistics that are important to the business.

Average

To find the average of a set of values in a table, add all the values together and then divide the sum by the number of values. Using Microsoft Excel, you can enter the formula that does the same operation. For example, =SUM(B1:B4)/4 will find the average of all values in column B between rows 1 and 4. Note that:

- The formula will ignore any empty cells between the cell references.
- Placing the parentheses is very important as you want all values to be added *before* the dividing operation takes place.

To practice, return to your Paysheet file and calculate the *average weekly tax* paid by the workers.

Alternatively, the AutoSum subtab can be used to carry out the same operation quickly, especially with large data sets.

1 Highlight or enter the cell references for all the values you wish to include in the calculation.
2 Click on the AutoSum subtab.
3 Select 'average' from the dropdown box.
4 The answer will appear in the next empty cell.

SECTION 3

Helpful hint

The answer to a question on average, min or max is highlighted and becomes part of the next calculation you perform, so select all the cells carefully — even the empty ones — before applying the formula.

Helpful hint

If you ever forget how to use a formula, go to the formulas tab and hover over the function or start typing a formula in the formula bar. The spreadsheet tool will show you a toolkit, which is a quick summary of how to use the function.

Helpful hint

Accurate results depend on accurate inputting of data. If data-entry errors are made, especially at the initial stage, all the final accounting calculations and statements will be incorrect.

Minimum (min) and maximum (max)

To find the *minimum value* or the *maximum value* among the values in a spreadsheet, you can use two additional functions in the AutoSum subtab's menu. The *min*, which finds the smallest value in the selected cells, and the *max*, which finds the largest value in the selected cells, are listed below sum and average. The steps are the same as finding the average:

1. Highlight or enter the cell references for all the values you wish to include in the calculation.
2. Click on the formulas tab and the subtab AutoSum.
3. Select max or min, as required, from the menu.
4. The answer will appear in the next empty cell.

To practise:

1. Return to your Paysheet file and calculate the *maximum* amount of net pay earned and the *minimum* of next pay earned.
2. Return to your Bank Statement file and calculate for the month:
   a. the *average* value of balances
   b. the *maximum* amount deposited (*credit* column)
   c. the *minimum* amount collected (*debit* column).

Financial statements

Financial statements report the end results from records of transactions. The trial balance, which lists all aspects of the business, is the major source of information for the preparation of the **Profit and Loss** (P&L) account. Another name for the P&L is the *income and expenditure account*. Together with the **Balance Sheet**, these documents use spreadsheet tables in their preparation and make use of the mathematical and statistical functions for calculating totals and subtotals.

Profit and loss account

This document is prepared using the last or closing balancing figure from a **Trading Account**. Figure 14.9 is a Trading Account for Noriega's Bolts and Screws. Note that the statement refers to 'for the period ended'.

NOREIGA'S BOLTS AND SCREWS
Trading Account <u>for the period ended</u> December 31, 2026

	$	$
Sales		137,025.00
Less: Cost of goods manufactured and sold		
Opening inventory	3,860.00	
Purchases	50,485.00	
Cost of goods manufactured (includes production wages of $44,000)	54,345.00	
Less: Closing inventory	(8,670.00)	
Cost of goods sold		(45,675.00)
Gross profit		91,350.00

Figure 14.9 Trading account

Figure 14.9 demonstrates a **vertical style** layout where:

- All text is in column 1
- The values that represent sales-related expenses (for example cost of goods sold and wages) are in columns 2 and 3, and are shown to two decimal places
- A shoulder heading is used to indicate the calculation of a subtotal
- The values that represent income (for example from sales and fees) are placed in column 4
- The figure for total costs is subtracted from the figure for total for sales income to calculate the gross profit or gross loss. This is the last value to be entered in the Trading Account and the first value in the Profit and Loss Account.

Figure 14.10, the Profit and Loss Account, is set out as a table of four columns but using a *horizontal style* layout. The words 'gross profit' are entered in column 3 and the value is entered in column 4. Expenses in the Profit and Loss Account are entered in columns 1 (text) and 2 (value).

NOREIGA'S BOLTS AND SCREWS

Profit and Loss account <u>for the period ended</u> December 31.

	$		$
Salaries and non-manufacturing wages	118,500	Gross profit	91,350
Miscellaneous expenses	2,320	Net loss	29,470
	120,820		120,820

Figure 14.10 Profit and Loss account

Activity

On the next page is the horizontal-style trading and profit and loss account for Nandaram's Building Solutions at the end of their *accounting cycle* (*financial year*), which is June 30, 2026. The company buys and sells types of glue for wooden furniture.

SECTION 3

	Nandaram's Building Solutions		
	Trading and Profit and Loss Account		
	For the year ended June 30, 2026		
	$	$	$	$
Opening inventory	800.31		Cash sales	5,900.56
Add: Purchases	6,850.34		Credit sales	16,317.04
Subtract: Closing inventory	550.10			
Total of cost of goods sold (COGS) –(B4+B5-B6)		xxx		
Gross profit (Sales – COGS)		15,117.05	Total sales	xxx
		xxx		=(E5+E6)
Subtract: Expenses			Gross profit	xxx
Insurance				
Interest				
Salaries and wages				
Total expenses		xxx	Net profit	xxx
		xxx		xxx

Produce this Trading and Profit and Loss Account in a spreadsheet and calculate these figures. (Remember to place the cursor in the appropriate cell next to the label.)
1. Total sales
2. Cost of goods sold
3. Gross profit
4. Net profit
5. Net profit as a percentage of sales

Balance Sheet

The *Balance Sheet* has three sections: the asset section, liabilities section and a special section for the owner's capital or equity. Like the Profit and Loss Account, the Balance Sheet can be set in a vertical or horizontal style.

The balance sheet makes a distinction between the assets that will be part of the firm over more than a year (*fixed assets* or *long-term assets*) and those assets that will be cashed in within one year of the date at the top of the balance sheet date: *current* or *short-term assets*. The same distinction is made for liabilities: *current liabilities* and *long-term liabilities*.

The following activity shows two versions of the same balance-sheet information. In both styles, the final figures are equal or *balanced*.

14 Advanced spreadsheet techniques

→ Activity

Type the balance sheet shown for Liguanea Bed and Breakfast into a worksheet and calculate the missing figures using a Microsoft Excel worksheet using formulas to calculate the missing figures.

Liguanea Town Bed and Breakfast
Balance Sheet as at October 31, 2026

	$	$	$
Fixed assets			
Machinery	18,250.00		
Delivery van	16,500.00		
Total fixed assets		xxx	
Current assets			
Inventory	4,500.00		
Receivables	2,450.00		
Bank	7,350.00		
Total current assets		xxx	
Total assets			xxx
Current liabilities			
Wages owing	1,620.00		
Payables	2,890.00		
Total current liabilities		xxx	
Long-term liabilities			
5-year bank loan		5,000.00	
Total liabilities			xxx
Total assets – total liabilities			xxx
Owner's equity			
Capital		35,000.00	
Net profit		5,000.00	
Total owner's equity			xxx

Key terms

assets Items with monetary value used to operate a business

AutoSum A feature in spreadsheet applications, such as Microsoft Excel, that automatically inserts a formula to calculate the sum of a range of numbers

bank statement A document issued by a bank to its customers to provide details of the amounts deposited and the amounts withdrawn during a period of time

capital Also called *shares* or *owner's equity*; the value provided by the owner to start the business (owners might be sole traders, partners or shareholders in limited liability companies or government agencies; capital is increased by profits and reduced by losses)

creditor Also called *payable*; a current liability – the people and businesses a business owes for goods or services received on credit

credit terms When payment takes place some time *after* goods or services are sold or purchased

current assets Assets that do not remain the same during the accounting year, such as stock, debtors, bank and cash balances

debtor Also called receivable; a current asset – the people and businesses who owe a business for goods or services they received on credit terms

expense/expenditure Outflows of cash for the purpose of making and selling goods/services for a profit

financial statement A document that conveys information about a company's operational results (profit or loss) and its financial position (assets and liabilities) over a stated period and at a given date

fixed assets Assets that are owned for more than one accounting year, such as property, machinery, equipment

formula A method for calculating a value for a range of values or a dataset, given the mathematical or statistical operation required

function library The subtab in a spreadsheet app that holds the built-in formulas and functions that perform mathematical or statistical operations

income Also called *revenue*; inflows of cash from sales of goods and services; service businesses use terms such as *fees*, *commissions* and *subscriptions* for income

invoice A document that provides details of items purchased or sold, including amounts, descriptions and costs

liability Amount owed to lenders and people who provide goods and/or services on credit; a long-term liability (such as a 5-year loan) has a payback period of more than a one year, while a current liability (such as payables/creditors) must be paid back within the accounting year

loss The difference between income and expenditure when expenditure is greater than income; it reduces capital

paysheet A document prepared to collect and calculate employee payroll information

profit The difference between income and expenditure when income is greater than expenditure; it increases capital

profit and loss account Also called *income and expenditure account*; matches the total of all income against the total of all expenditure to calculate either a profit or a loss; if a trading account has been created, the P&L account starts with the balance of that account (gross profit or gross loss) and adds any additional non-sales income against all other expenses to calculate net profit or net loss

receipt A document that provides evidence of payment for goods or services bought for cash or credit

stock Also called *inventory*; a current asset: items purchased for sale and kept on shelves and in warehouses until they are sold

trading account Matches sales income against the cost of goods sold to calculate gross profit or gross loss

transaction An exchange of goods and/or services for money

trial balance A list of all assets, expenses (placed in the debit column on the left side) and all liabilities and capital (placed in the credit column on the right side) and ensures that both columns are equal in total

vertical style One of two standard layouts used in producing a company's financial statements

14 Advanced spreadsheet techniques

> **Summary**
>
> In this chapter, you have learned:
>
> - that spreadsheet applications' tabular format is especially useful in the preparation of financial documents
> - to prepare samples of source documents, working papers and financial statements
> - to use Microsoft Excel's capacity for quick and accurate calculations of subtotals, totals and statistics by applying typed-in formulas and preset functions.

Practice, research and exam-style questions

Multiple-choice questions

1. Which statement describes a feature of Microsoft Excel tables that tables in word-processing applications do *not* possess?
   A Copy-and-paste feature
   B Font-style selections
   C Oblique headings
   D Auto-populating cells

2. All values in all the cells in a table are called the ...
   A dataset.
   B Microsoft Excel feature.
   C logical condition.
   D function library.

3. Which function of a spreadsheet application is used to arrange data in alphabetical order?
   A Sort
   B Rank
   C Sum
   D Read

   Look at the table and answer the following two questions.

	D	E	F	G	H
1	17	23	25	18	
2	24	28	15	22	
3	34	12	32	09	

4. Which formula will show the total of the series if the answer is automatically placed in cell H1?
   A =SUM(E1:H1)
   B =SUM(D1:D3)
   C =SUM(D1:G1)
   D =SUM(D1:G3)

5. Which will be called the *active cell* for this purpose?
   A H1
   B H3
   C H2
   D H0

6. Which sign is *not* recognised by the formula library?
   A *
   B \
   C /
   D +

7. Which sign tells the application that a formula will be inserted?
   A =
   B :
   C /
   D €

8. Which spreadsheet function produces the largest number in a series when data is manipulated?
   A Statistical operation or 'max'
   B Logical operation
   C Arithmetical operation
   D Alphanumeric operation

221

SECTION 3

Exam-style questions

1. Jhene Vasco is a real-estate agent with Pierre Realtors. She has been very busy and has only recorded the value of her sales over the last three months, without calculating her commission of 20% on residential properties and 25% on commercial properties.

   Her notes look like this:

Dates	Property	Selling price
May 5	Residential	450,600.00
May 14	Commercial	850,000.00
May 29	Commercial	2,800,900.00
June 10	Residential	558,500.00
June 12	Residential	657,200.00
June 22	Commercial	978,000.00
June 29	Residential	750,160.00
July 17	Residential	80,990.00
July 21	Commercial	358,000.00

   She has asked for your help, so you need to carry out the following tasks:

   a Type the information into a spreadsheet following all instructions below.

   b In column 2, sort the items into residential and commercial. Leave one empty row between categories.

   c Insert one column to the right of the 'Selling price' column and label it 'Commissions'.

   d Use formulas to show:

      i the total value of sales in each category

      ii the commission earned on each property

      iii the total value of commissions earned in each category

      iv the maximum amount earned on any property.

   e Using any two colours, show Jhene's most successful month and her least successful month.

   f Save the document as 'Commissions for the period May–July 2026'.

2. Seymena's Mini-mart provides you with the following records and values:

	Dec 31, 2026
	$
Accounts receivable	1,760
Accounts payable	420
Purchases	17,440
Sales	15,290
Delivery van	4,000
Closing stock	330
Electricity bills	2,100
Data expense	1,200
Bank	4,360
5% per year bank loan	2,110
Land and water rates	570
Concrete shed, shelves and fittings	8,000
Capital: Sandra Walker	6,210

   a Identify these items using the letter code:

      i Assets (A)

      ii Liabilities (L)

      iii Expenses (E)

      iv Income (I)

      v Capital (C).

   b Produce a properly formatted trial balance and use the SUM function of Microsoft Excel to balance it.

Practice questions

1. Use the template to create a Microsoft Excel worksheet with oblique column headings.

NAME	Base hours	Base pay rate	Total base pay	GROSS PAY
	40			
	40			

2. Enter the values using the information provided.

Builder: Peter	100 hours	Base pay $150 per hour
Labourer: Natey	40 hours	$50 per hour
Labourer: Zach	120 hours	$50 per hour

3. Using appropriate formulas, calculate:

   a the total earnings of each person

   b the total wages expense for the period.

4. Save the file as Labour Costs.

15 Database applications

> **Objectives**
>
> By the end of this chapter, you will be able to:
> - list instances where the basic and advanced features of a database-management application are useful
> - explain key terms associated with databases and database-management applications
> - construct a simple database from information provided
> - respond to simple queries with reports

Introduction

Individuals and businesses accumulate a lot of data. In the past, filing cabinets, file jackets and paper records were necessary to keep information stored and organised. Today, **databases**, data lakes and data warehouses are required, as there is even more data to be retrieved and managed. In this chapter, you will learn about the terms used in **database management** and how to create a simple database, recognise relationships between items in a database, and produce queries and reports.

What is a database?

A database is an organised system or folder that stores collections of related data files. The usual way to organise the items in a file is in the form of a table. Organisations usually create and maintain several databases. If a relationship can be seen among tables, a relational database can be created, and a name given to the new database. Note that there are other ways of arranging databases. In this chapter, you will learn to use the database-management system (DBMS) Microsoft Access for the following actions:

- data entry
- data retrieval
- data display
- data manipulation
- information production
- report generation.

> **Did you know?**
>
> A data lake stores raw, unprocessed data, while a data warehouse stores structured, processed data.

Key terms in database management

Table 15.1 identifies some key terms in database management and provides real-world example of a school.

SECTION 3

Table 15.1 Some key terms in database management

Key term	Definition	Example
Item/Entity	A single unit for which data is collected.	A school will have information for each student, each teacher, each office staff member etc.
Record/Tuple	The attribute or characteristic an organisation chooses to collect for each entity of interest.	A school might collect the following for each teacher: ID No., Last name, First name, Date of birth, Teaching subject, Other skill/s. In a list, a comma will be used to separate each attribute. E.g. 231, Fai, Zion, 10/01/2003, EDPM, Football Coaching.
Table	A structure that allows each attribute for each record to be shown in individual cells formed by columns and rows. Columns (aka *fields*) are used to name the common or unique attribute of all the entities in a table. Rows (aka *records*) are used to hold the information of each entity in a table.	Examples of fields | ID#	Last Name	First Name	Date of birth	Teaching Subject	Other skill/s
---	---	---	---	---	---
231	Fai	Zion	10/01/2013	OA	Football Coach	
Database management system (DBMS)	The electronic folder containing a collection of related tables or database must be useful, responsive and comprehensive and properly managed.	Students and teachers are placed in various groups and different tables constructed e.g. Form 1 students 2026–2027, all teachers of General/Integrated Science or all Form 4 students who are taking EDPM. Some entities appear in more than one group/table. All tables are part of the school's database and may require a dedicated person to manage it.
Field definition	The data in the cells of a particular column or field must be set out or *defined* using the same type and format to be recognisable or the application will perceive an error.	Text data can be at maximum 255 characters but is usually limited to 30 or 40 characters; numeric data may have many digits like bank account numbers or a few like ID numbers. Currency figures may show up to 2 decimal places while dates of birth may be written as text, numeric or alphanumeric forms.
Primary and Composite Keys	This is a field that has a unique entry for every entity in a table. Every record must have an entry in that particular cell so that it becomes a primary key. The field cannot be empty. A table may have more than one primary key made up of two or more fields.	The most common unique identifier in a database table is an assigned ID number. This becomes a primary key for filtering and sorting information and answering questions about entities in that table. Mr. Fai's Form 4 OA class table will have his name as a field that is a unique identifier and his individual student's ID as another unique identifier; together they form a composite key to answer queries about that class.
Relationship	The link between two tables in a database that allows the use of a **foreign key** (a field, linked from another table, in which it is a primary key) to answer questions.	The school's database will have many tables and its DBMS can be used to identify links and answer queries, for example, the date of birth of students in Form 4 who are members of the cricket team to ensure that no one is overage for a category.
Relational database	Tables can be linked in 3 ways. One-to-one, one-to-many and many-to-many.	
Query	A tool to retrieve or manipulate data inside of the database.	The manager may instruct the app (called making a query) to process or analyse the sales data to get it in a certain order or result e.g. sales totals by month.

15 Database applications

Constructing a database

This section describes the actions needed to create and populate a database using the example of a school's DBMS.

Populating tables

Schools collect and save data on students, teachers, administrators, ancillary staff, subjects, classes and classrooms. A few examples of these tables are shown in Table 15.2.

Table 15.2 Examples of tables in a database

FORM 4 STUDENTS

ID NO.	First Name	Last Name	Date of Birth	Subj	Subj	Extra-curricular activity
1003	Marilyn	Abbott	20-May-10	EDPM	French	Football and Lifeskills
1324	Denzil	Jackson	25-Nov-12	EDPM	Biology	Football and Lifeskills
2018	Daniel	Greg	20-May-10	EDPM	French	Lifeskills and French club

TEACHERS

Status	First Name	Last Name	ID No	Gender	Teaching Subject	Additional Responsibility
Mr.	Edgar	Adams	37	Male	EDPM	Football and Lifeskills
Mrs.	Savi	Ramlal	14	Female	French	Lifeskills and French club

>  **Activity**
>
> Look at Table 15.2.
> 1. How many database tables are there?
> 2. How many fields are there in each table?
> 3. How many records are there in each table?
> 4. What field should be used as the unique identifier (the primary key) in each table?

Establishing the nature of a relationship between tables

When populating a database, the relationships among elements in tables should be established. There are three relationship types in a relational database. Table 15.3 provides information about these types.

Table 15.3 Types of relations between table elements

Type	Description	Example
One-to-one	One record in a table can link to only *one* record in another table	Denzil Jackson from the Students table can only attend a class once. His ID number would only appear once in a list of the students in the class e.g. 'Class Roster' table.
One-to-many	One record in the table is linked to many records in another table	Edgar Adams from a Teachers table teaches EDPM to multiple classes which could be in a Classes table. His ID number could appear multiple times.
Many-to-many	Multiple records in a table can appear multiple times in a second table. We often use a third table to clear any confusion.	Marilyn Abbott attends both EDPM and French classes alongside Daniel Greg. A Class Roster table can be created to prevent them from being signed up twice for the same class.

Using a DBMS application

Before creating a database, it is important to know how many tables you will need, and what sort of data you will store in them. For example, the school may need tables in its database such as:

- Students' information
- Teachers' information
- Classes for teachers
- Subjects offered and who teaches them.

Steps for creating the database table 'EDPM Students' will be described and explained below.

Step 1: Create the Database

The first step is the creation of the database that will hold all the tables.
To create the database:
1. Open the Access application.
2. Choose New Blank Database.
3. Enter the word School as the name of the database (Figure 15.1).

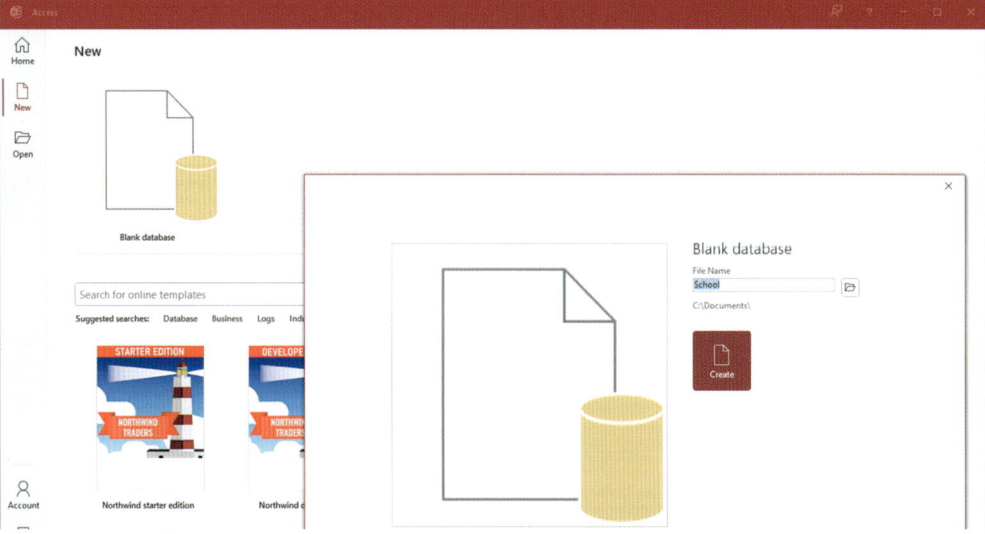

Figure 15.1 Opening and naming a new database

Step 2: Open a Blank Datasheet
Click Create to open a blank datasheet, as shown in Figure 15.2.

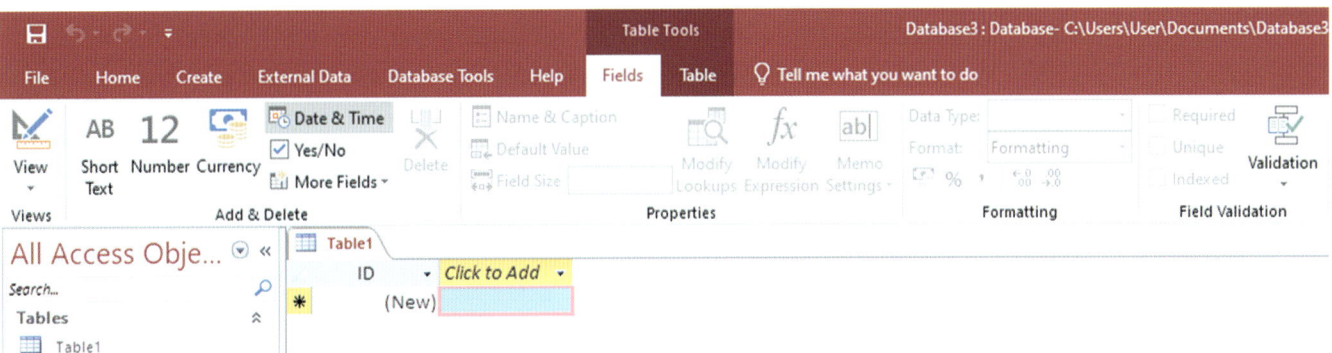

Figure 15.2 Blank 'Database View' screen

Notice that on the left side of the screen, there is a pane labelled All Access Objects. This pane will display a list of items called objects. An example of an object is a new table. Every time a new table is created or a report is generated, it will be listed in this pane.

At this point, the only object is the empty table form on the right, called Table1, so these words appear in the All Access Objects pane. Table1 will be used to enter data to create the EDPM Students table.

Step 3: Use Design View
When creating a table, you need to consider how many fields are required and what data types and formats should be used. Some examples of fields and their appropriate data types and formats for the EDPM table are as follows:

- Last Name – *a short text field*
- First name – *a short text field*
- Student's ID number – *Number*
- Student date of birth – *Date and time field*
- Parent's contact – *Alphanumeric field*
- Male or female – *Yes/No field*
- Registration fee paid – *Currency field*

Step 3.1: Create a Field Definition Table in Design View
To access the Design View screen:
1 Click on the View dropdown arrow.
2 Select Design View.

The Design View screen will appear with preset column headings, which include Field name, Data Type and Description (Optional). The EDPM Students table will consist of 4 Fields; *Student ID*, *First name*, *Last name* and *Date of Birth*. Additional fields such as Subjects, Scores and Attendance can be added later.

SECTION 3

Step 3.2: Create the EDPM Students Field Definition Table

1 Enter the chosen field names in the Field Name column, one field per row. (Note the data type recommended for each field, which will appear automatically. This can be changed manually if needed. Additional data types can be selected by clicking the down arrow at the bottom right corner of the Data Type cell.)
2 Select options from the Field Properties table below. This table is used to further define the fields. For example, the First Name field can be limited to a maximum size, such as 30 characters. A student's date of birth may be entered as 23/05/2010 or 23rd May 2010. Once a format is chosen, all dates of birth must be entered consistently in that format, or Microsoft Access will consider it an error (See Figure 15.3 for how this appears in Design View).

Table 15.4 shows the field information collected for each student for the EDPM Students table.

Table 15.4 Field information table

Student_ID	First Name	Last Name	Date of Birth
1001	Sean	John	25-Jan-11
2116	Jackson	Michael	29-Jan-10
1003	Marilyn	Abbott	20-May-10
1324	Denzil	Jackson	25-Nov-15
2018	Daniel	Greg	20-May-10
2017	Danielle	Steele	06-Aug-10
1115	Sean	John	07-Oct-11
1239	Curtley	Ambrosia	30-Apr-11
1003	Jason	Bourne	02-Jan-12
3018	Lisa	Stone	3rd September 2012

Table 15.5 is a manual version of the field definition table prepared for the information above.

Table 15.5 Manual version of the field definition table

Field Name	Data Type	Description	Properties
Student ID	Number	Unique identifier for each student	Field Size: Long Integer
First Name	Short Text	Student's First Name	Field Size: 30
Last Name	Short Text	Student's Last Name	Field Size: 30
Date of Birth	Date/Time		Format: Medium Date

Step 3.3: Set the Primary Key

It is necessary to identify the primary key. This may be done automatically, often by setting the field name in the first cell of row 1, such as Student ID, which is usually the unique identifier for each record. However, this can be changed or supplemented (to create a composite key) by highlighting another field name and clicking the Primary Key button (the key icon located at the top left of the Design View ribbon). A key symbol will appear to the left of the selected field name(s).

15   Database applications

Figure 15.3 shows how the field definition table appears in Design View.

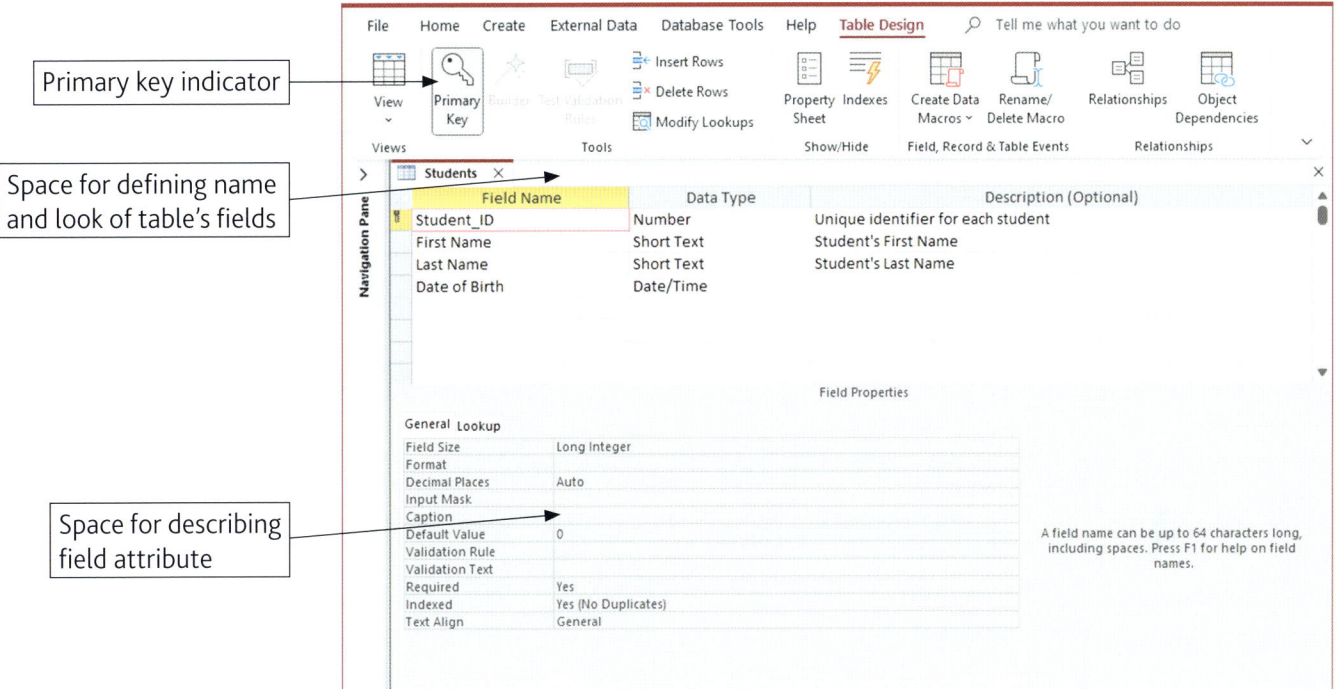

Figure 15.3 Field definition information in Design View

Step 3.4: Name the Table
Name the table EDPM Students, then save and close it.

Step 4 Populating a Table in Datasheet View
The following steps will create the table that forms part of the database:
1 Refer to Table 15.4, which contains information collected for 10 students in the EDPM class.
2 Click the View dropdown and select **Datasheet View** (a table labelled EDPM Students with the field headings created in Design View will appear).
3 Note that there will be only one empty row below the heading row. Begin entering data for the first student (Sean John) to complete the record.
4 Create similar records for all 10 students.
   (If you try to enter information that Access recognises as an error, you will not be able to proceed. For example, two students have the same ID number in Table 15.4, so one number must be changed. Also, the date of birth for one student, Lisa Stone, does not follow the Design View data type format. Change the format to match the one defined in the Field Definition table. Figure 15.4 shows the completed and corrected table in Datasheet View.)
5 Save the table.

SECTION 3

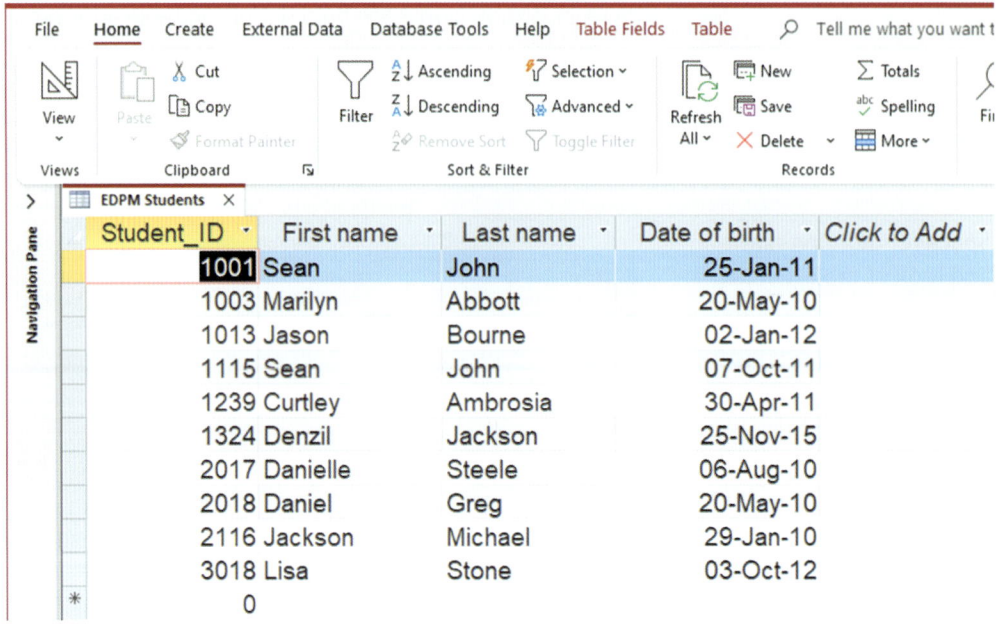

Figure 15.4 A completed datasheet view for EDPM Students

Using the query tools

The database tool Query exists to access, sort, filter, and manipulate data to obtain answers without manually searching through numerous tables. Establishing relationships between tables helps in responding to queries and producing reports.

There are three major types of queries, as shown in Table 15.6.

Table 15.6 Types of queries

Query type	Used for	Example: You are asked to …
Action	Adding, adjusting or deleting records in tables	add information from forms filled out by two new Form 4 students, as well as from three change-of-address forms for other Form 4 students
Crosstab	Pre-defined mathematical tasks such as calculating Sums, Averages, and so on	prepare a report on the average pass rates in the end-of-year test over all Form 4 subjects for the last three years, highlighting in red all those below 50%
Select	Retrieving specific data from your database using specific criteria, such as the first and last names of all students in Mr Adams' classes, or all Form 4 Students with Parent/Guardian's names and addresses, or all students whose DOB is after 1-Jan-2001.	prepare a list of all students in Form 4, with last name first, followed by first name, the name and address of the student's primary care giver, their date of birth and the subjects they have signed up for

15 Database applications

The Select query is usually the most commonly used type, as it focuses on retrieving data from across the database. You must enter your query by specifying criteria using the correct format, which is important to obtain the desired results.

Query criteria

In Microsoft Access, queries are designed to help filter and search for specific information within the database. They can produce any type of information needed to complete a task. Guided by your requirements, query criteria can be set within a range of data, using specific descriptive terms called values and operators.

For example, you may search for all female students in a table where gender is a field. By entering Female as your criterion, the query will return a list of only female students. Alternatively, if your criterion is an address, such as 'all persons with Trincity addresses', the query will list all students whose address includes Trincity.

The different symbols used for query criteria are shown in Table 15.7.

Table 15.7 Symbols used for different query criteria

Symbol	Example
=	Anything which is equal to that which is listed as the criterion. If $200.00 is given as the value, only students who have paid this amount will be produced on the query table.
< Less than	If the age of less than 17 years is the criterion, then any student that is not yet 17 years will be named on the query response.
> Greater than	This criterion will select students over the age of 17 years.
>= Greater than	This criterion will select any amount that is more than or equal to the quantity stated. E.g. >= $200.00 will produce figures from $200.00 and more.
<= Less than or equal to	This criterion will select any amount that is less than or equal to the quantity stated. E.g. <= $200.00 will list students who have paid less than or exactly $200.00.

Although Microsoft Access has a wizard that provides a step-by-step guideline for queries, you can also perform a query without the wizard, as shown in the following section.

Steps to run a query using the wizard:
1. Open your saved database.
2. Click the Create tab on the ribbon.
3. In the Queries group, click Query Wizard.
4. The New Query dropdown will appear. Choose Simple Query Wizard and click OK.
5. Select the table or query from which you want to retrieve data.
6. Select the fields you want to include in your query. Use the single arrow (>) to select individual fields or the double arrow (>>) to select all fields.
7. Click Next.
8. Choose whether to open the query to view information or to modify the query design. If you choose to modify, click Finish.
9. To refine or narrow your search, you need to enter a criterion in the field of your choice within the Query Design View. For example, if you wish to find all students over the age of 17, in the 'Age' field's Criteria row, you can type >=17 and then click Run (the red exclamation mark) in the Results group on the Query Design Tools Design tab.

Steps to run a query without the wizard:
1. Click the Create tab on the ribbon.
2. Click Query Design.
3. In the Show Table dialog box, select the table containing your data and click Add.
4. Click Close to close the Show Table dialog.
5. The list of fields from the selected table will appear in the top pane.
6. Double-click or drag the fields you want to include in your query down to the query grid below.
7. To sort the results, select Ascending or Descending in the Sort row for the relevant field(s), such as Last Name or First Name.
8. Enter any criteria in the Criteria row to filter the data (for example, Female in the Gender field).
9. Click Run (red exclamation mark) on the ribbon to execute the query.
10. The query results will be displayed in Datasheet View.

 **Activity**

Complete the entire process of creating a table in Microsoft Access and perform queries on the results:
1. Open Microsoft Access on your computer.
2. Click New Blank Database (not just the create symbol).
3. Name the database Six Creeks Secondary and click Create.
4. In the new database, go to the Create tab and click Table Design to create a new table.
5. Name the table Upper School Students.
6. Use the following field names and assign appropriate data types to create the field definition table:
   - Last Name
   - First Name
   - Address
   - Address 2
   - Age
   - Male/Female
   - Telephone Number
   - Form
7. Enter the following data into the table (each comma separates a field):
   Samara, St Carr, 16, 15 Apple Drive, Santa Rosa, Female, Form 4, 892-5338
   Arianne, Construct, 17, 14 Cherry Street, Trincity, Female, Form 4, 779-6352
   Rebecca, Maharaj, 17, 23 Almond Crescent, D'Abadie, Female, Form 4, 217-9365
   Shiva, Jagdeo, 17, 34 Circular Drive, Arima, Male, Form 4, 678-6697
   Kerry, Ganesh, 18, 19 Orange Crescent, Santa Rosa, Female, Form 5, 786-2347
   Amanda, Alleyne, 19, 32 Mango Drive, Trincity, Female, Form 5, 438-9654
   Darren, Mitchell, 18, 32 Cherry Drive, Trincity, Male, Form 5, 678-6098
   Curt, James, 17, 49 Sorrel Crescent, Tacarigua, Male, Form 5, 623-8765
   Nicholas, Gomez, 19, 47 Whim Farms Road, D'Abadie, Male, Form 5, 246-3684
   Vernessa, Adams, 17, 67 Bankers Row, Trincity, Female, Form 5, 787-3574
8. After creating and saving the table, perform the following queries:
   - Sort all names in ascending order (by Last Name, then First Name).
   - Filter to show all female students.
   - Filter to show all students aged 17.
   - Filter to show all male students in Form 5.

Reports

Reports compile information from tables or queries in ways that make them suitable for review or printing. Microsoft Access provides a Report Wizard to guide you through the steps. For example, you may be asked to produce a report showing the names of the top five performing students based on final exam scores. The process is similar to creating a query.

You can present the information in a Word document, formatted and edited to the specifications of the recipient. Use Report View to see how the report will appear, and switch to Design View to make edits before printing. Figure 15.5 shows a query result displayed as a report.

EDPM Class List — Saturday, 07 June 2025, 15:42:30

Class_Name	First Name	Last Name
Adams EDPM 2	Marilyn	Abbott
Adams EDPM 2	Daniel	Greg
Adams EDPM 2	Denzil	Jackson
Adams EDPM 2	Sean	John
Adams EDPM 2	Sean	John

Figure 15.5 Query result in report view

Advanced database use

Some advanced database uses include using forms and responding to crosstab queries.

Forms

Data entry is important for database creation, but avoiding data-entry errors is crucial. A form is easy to understand and can be edited to look exactly like a paper form, thereby reducing errors when collecting initial data. In addition, a form allows for data entry directly into one or even multiple tables.

You can use the Form Wizard to create a form in a similar fashion to the Report Wizard. After clicking the Create tab and following the steps, you can change the views of the form by using the Form Layout Tools and then the Design tab. Use the Form View to enter data, the Design View to alter the look of the form, and Layout View to edit where fields and field names are placed or to add a field if you have accidentally deleted one.

Performing Mathematical Operations

Collecting numerical data within a database holds similar advantages to using it within a spreadsheet. Expressions, such as additions and subtractions, or complex formulae like functions, can be used to summarise data and retrieve insightful information. This can be executed in crosstab queries or even in reports.

Advantages and disadvantages of a DBMS

Advantages
- Large amounts of data can be stored, saving paper and storage space.
- Records are quick and easy to find.
- It is easy to modify records and add fields as needed without having to redesign the table.

- Passwords can be used to keep data secure.
- Data can be entered quickly and easily.

Disadvantages
- Some databases can be complex and difficult to use and maintain, so trained and often costly expertise must be hired.
- A lot of time and money may be needed to train employees how to use the system effectively.
- If there is a power outage or malfunction, you cannot use the database.
- Viruses may corrupt the database or stop it from working effectively.

Key terms

column/field A single, specific piece of data about an item in a table
composite key A primary key made up of two or more fields
database An electronic folder, which contains a collection of related files set out in tables
database management The actions carried out to use databases efficiently
datasheet view A screen that looks like a normal table of rows and columns, which can be manipulated like a normal table; suitable for entering, reviewing or extracting data
design view A screen that lists the fields required for designing a table as well as the formats that will be used to create (i.e. define) the fields
field definition Description of the field attributes, i.e. how the data in the field will appear, such as by putting limits on the number of characters in the field
foreign key A primary key in one table when treated as a field for linking/identifying a relationship in another table
primary key A field that uniquely identifies a record, such as individual ID numbers (N.B. a primary key must be chosen for database management and can never be empty/null)
query A tool for retrieving and manipulating data inside the database
relationship The link between two tables in a database
report A visual representation of information prepared for external viewing or printing; this is the processing result shown as a text document, chart table or other format
row/record A collection of all the data about an item in a table, which therefore crosses multiple fields

Summary

In this chapter, you have learned how to:

- Define key terms in database management
- Create a simple database with one table
- Utilise the functions of the Design View
- Complete the database table in Datasheet View
- Perform simple queries with and without the wizard
- Appreciate the use of reports, forms and mathematical operations in database management

Practice, research and exam-style questions

Multiple-choice questions

1. In Microsoft Access, data is stored in …
   A tables.
   B forms.
   C queries.
   D reports.

2. Microsoft Access *cannot* store …
   A images.
   B text.
   C dates.
   D numbers.

3. Uniqueness is a necessary quality for a …
   A data storage system.
   B primary key nomination.
   C criteria search base.
   D query and report system.

4. Which option is *not* an example of a field attribute?
   A yy-mm-dd
   B Short text
   C Short integer
   D Names

5. Which type of key is *not* used for identification of a unique record?
   A Composite key
   B Primary key
   C Table key
   D Foreign key

6. Which tool is necessary for completing a query that requires information in the records of *two* separate tables?
   A Foreign key
   B Composite key
   C Primary key
   D Design key

7. In Microsoft Access, forms are data …
   A collectors.
   B queries.
   C formats.
   D reports.

8. Two or more tables can be linked if they have …
   A a relationship.
   B a responsiveness setting.
   C current formatting protocols.
   D a similar execution.

9. A query …
   A retrieves data only.
   B retrieves and filters data.
   C adjusts fields for new information.
   D adjusts displays in reports.

10. A report can be …
    A filtered.
    B sorted.
    C formatted.
    D queried.

SECTION 3

Exam-style questions

1. What is a relational database?

2. Your family sells varieties of lettuce to mini-marts in your area. Answer the questions on various pieces of data that follow the table.

Types of lettuce	Colour	Catalogue_ID number	Taste	Growing time (weeks)
Muir	green	182	leafy	4
Oakleaf	spotted-green	212	crunchy	6
Romaine	light green	47	crunchy	5
Iceberg	light green	23	sweet	6
Butterhead	yellow green	110	smooth	5
Cress	olive green	56	bitter	4

   a What fields are shown in the table?
   b Which field should be used as the primary key, and why?
   c In which View will this table appear?
   d Which tool on the Microsoft Access ribbon would be useful to answer questions based on the table?

3. Answer the following questions using the field definition table.

Field name	Data type/format	Description	Properties
Name	Short text	Lettuce variety name	Field Size: 15
Colour	Short text	Shades of green	Field Size: 10
Catalogue_ID	Number	Unique identifier	Field size: long integer
Taste	Short text	Adjective	Field Size: 20

   a Use the table definition provided above and the data provided in Question 1 and create a table in the Datasheet View.
   b Name the table 'Lettuce'.
   c What field should be used to form the primary key in this table?

4. a Which field should form the primary key for a table based on the following information?

Name	Store type	Address	Contact_number	Purchases (units)
Rincon	Minimart	Coehlo_Rd	789-1050	130
Negril	Minimart	Elroy_St	789-1275	212
Vertige	Minimart	Pitre_St	789-4571	145
San Juan	Minimart	Coehlo_Rd	789-6908	260

   b Create an appropriate field definition table using the relevant data type or format: number, short text, short text.
   c What would be an appropriate name for this second table?
   d Recreate the Datasheet View of this table.
   e Run a query to identify purchases greater than 200.

16 Presentation and graphic applications

> **Objectives**
>
> By the end of this chapter, you will be able to:
>
> - list instances where the basic and advanced features of a presentation application are useful
> - list and explain key terms associated with presentation applications
> - describe the basic and advanced features of a presentation application
> - construct a simple presentation from information provided
> - identify the purposes or role of graphic software in creating digital media
> - discuss five considerations when selecting graphical images
> - amend or adjust graphics to suit content and context in a given situation.

Introduction

In this chapter, you will learn how to use the presentation application Microsoft PowerPoint. Other presentation applications, such as Prezi and Google Slides™ web-based presentation program, provide blank canvases called *slides* for your content. Presentations are created for concepts, ideas, key features and results shown on slides using tables, charts and graphs from spreadsheets and databases or graphics from applications such as Adobe Photoshop, Canva® and Photoroom. If additional information is needed or a point is to be emphasised, a term, phrase or image can be hyperlinked to an external file or site or another slide in the same presentation.

Usefulness of presentation applications

Presentations are particularly useful in online and offline business meetings, lectures, seminars, training workshops and public speeches.

Table 16.1 will help you gain understanding of how to create presentations.

Table 16.1 Key terms in presentation and graphics software

Term	Explanation
Presentation	The file that contains compiled information to share with an audience; also referred to as a *slide deck*
Presenter	The person speaking and controlling the pace of presentation **delivery**
Slide	A page in landscape orientation that contains a portion of content for display
View	The presentation format of slides, which varies depending on the need to develop, navigate or edit the presentation; all views can be accessed from the view tab on the Microsoft PowerPoint ribbon
Normal view	View that provides for navigation and editing; broken into three sections: outline pane, layout pane (or *slide development pane*) and notes pane
Slide sorter view	View that provides large **thumbnails** of slides, allowing the order of the presentation to be seen; a particular slide to be found quickly; or the slides rearranged by highlighting and dragging to new positions

Slide show/ presentation view	View that shows the slides in full screen mode; each mouse click or press of the directional arrows on the keyboard moves to the next slide or back through the presentation
Hide slide	Particular slides in a slide deck that are not shown to an audience, for customising a presentation
Placeholder	A space on a slide reserved for inserting, manipulating or amending text, pictures, graphics, videos and more; new placeholders can be inserted as needed
Outline pane	A thumbnail view of all the slides; allows viewing and rearranging slide order easily, and is similar to **slide sorter view**
Notes pane	A space for the presenter to add notes or important points for discussion, not visible to the audience as it is hidden in slide show view; can be printed separately for the presenter's use
Layout pane	Where placeholders or slots are used to enter different types of content
Design template	A predetermined set of styles in a presentation; can include the size and types of fonts, background designs and colour schemes – a default set of options is provided under the design tab
Transitions	The movement of slides during the full presentation, as determined by the presenter, who chooses from options such as automatic fade, accompanying audio, timing between slides, use of mouse clicks or keyboard presses
Animations	The movement of content on a slide, e.g. to appear or fade in
Hyperlinking	Introducing a clickable link to enable additional information in a presentation
Graphics	The representation of data through images, photographs, artworks, tables, charts and graphs; also called *graphical data*, it helps viewers to understand relatively large datasets

> ✓ **Helpful hint**
>
> With multiple monitors, for example a laptop and a projector screen combination, the presenter can have their slideshow as full screen on the projector screen plus a preview of upcoming slides and notes on the laptop.

Developing a presentation

In this section, you will follow steps to create a presentation in Microsoft PowerPoint of this passage:

> Technology Education (Tech Ed) is currently one of three subjects that is offered at the lower secondary level in most of the secondary schools of T&T that can be considered as technical and vocational in nature. The two others are Home Economics and Agricultural Science. Tech Ed is a channel for teaching the knowledge and skills that are necessary for living in the 21st Century. These include problem-solving, innovative thinking, information management and communication, among others. Tech Ed students are taught to identify 2 or 3 aspects or issues of a problem or task, define each aspect, explore and assess possible solutions, choose and test one solution and evaluate whether or not it worked. Technology Education is therefore a method for the delivery of desirable skills, competencies and attitudes that should be the focus of schooling and education today.

Step 1: Opening the presentation application

Click on 'file' to open a blank presentation slide, and examine the tabs and subtabs, which are defined in Table 16.1. Blank **title slides** are also available under the layout subtab of the home tab, while preset designs with patterns and colours that make your presentation attractive are available in the design tab (Figure 16.1).

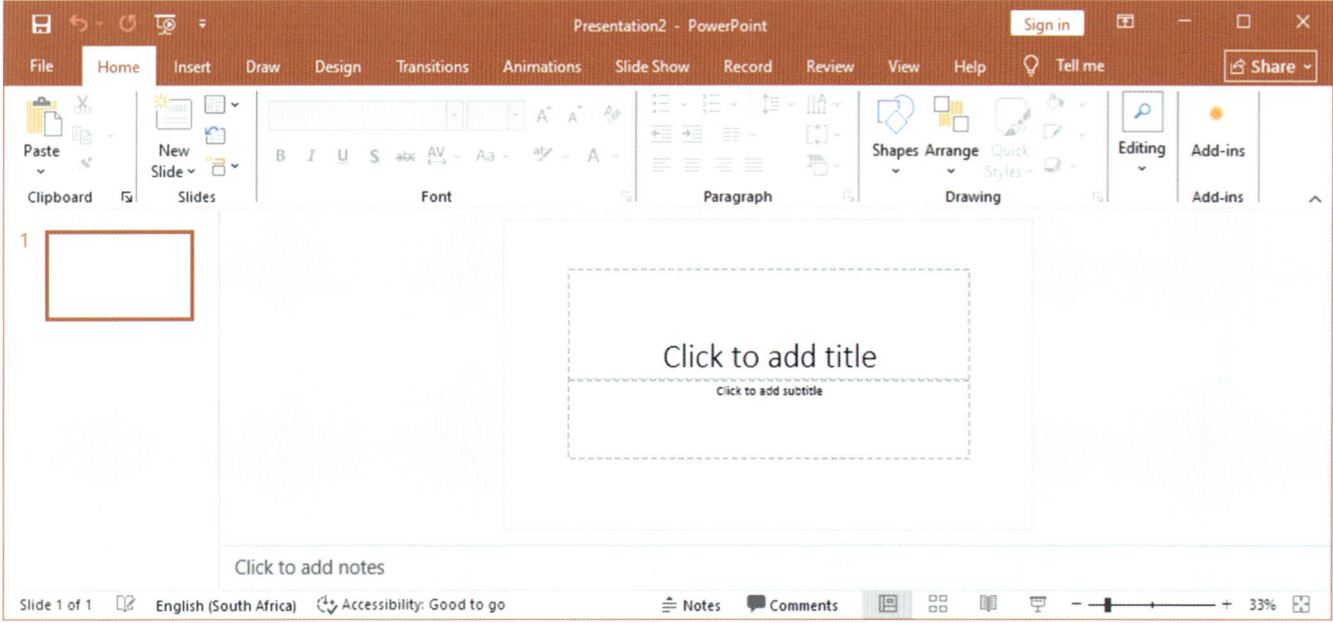

Figure 16.1 Title slide view showing placeholders, tabs and subtabs on the Microsoft PowerPoint ribbon

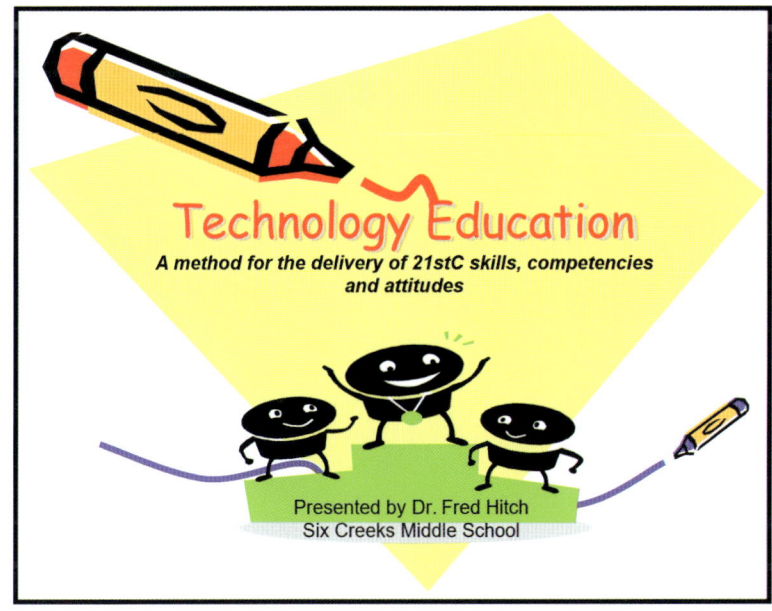

Figure 16.2 A formatted title slide

Step 2: Completing the title slide

a Think of a suitable title for the presentation using the topic sentence of the passage (this is often the first sentence) or any repeated term or phrase in the passage or the manuscript. Click to add the title in the placeholder.

b Decide whether to include a subtopic or brief description of the topic.

c Use another placeholder to enter information about the presenter.

d Format the title slide with your choice of colours, shapes, fill and font styles.

Figure 16.2 shows a possible title slide based on the passage.

Step 3: Creating additional slides

From your second slide and subsequent slides, you need to:

- make a choice of *layout* and design
- create content consisting of the points from the passage.

Layout choices

Click on New Slide or Layout on the home tab and slides subtab to choose slides with different layout options. If you want to change to a new layout during the presentation, click on the dropdown arrow. The slide layout that you are using at any point will be highlighted.

Figure 16.3 shows the selection of preset layouts with placeholders for content such as text, pictures, charts, shapes, symbols, forms, templates, videos, tables and online images. Some slides have slots called *icons* that indicate where specific digital media should be placed. You can also choose a blank layout template and add your own placeholders from your saved files or from online **sources**.

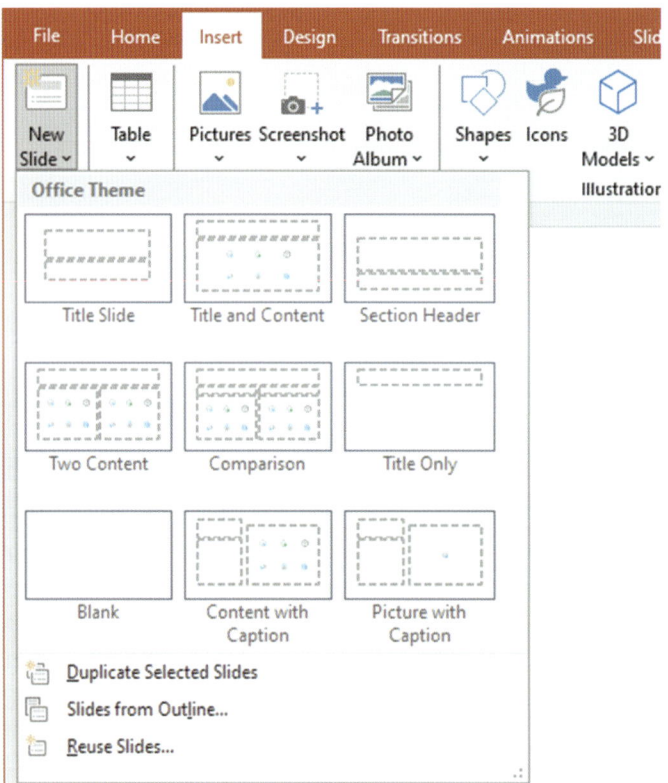

Figure 16.3 Presentation layouts

Design choices

Many of the formatting and editing features available in other Microsoft applications are also available in Microsoft PowerPoint.

> **Activity**
>
> Name *two* formatting and editing tabs from Microsoft PowerPoint that also appear in other Microsoft applications.

Preset themes, as shown in Figure 16.4, are available from the design tab. Every slide in the deck will maintain the colours and/or pattern of the theme. Other themes are available online.

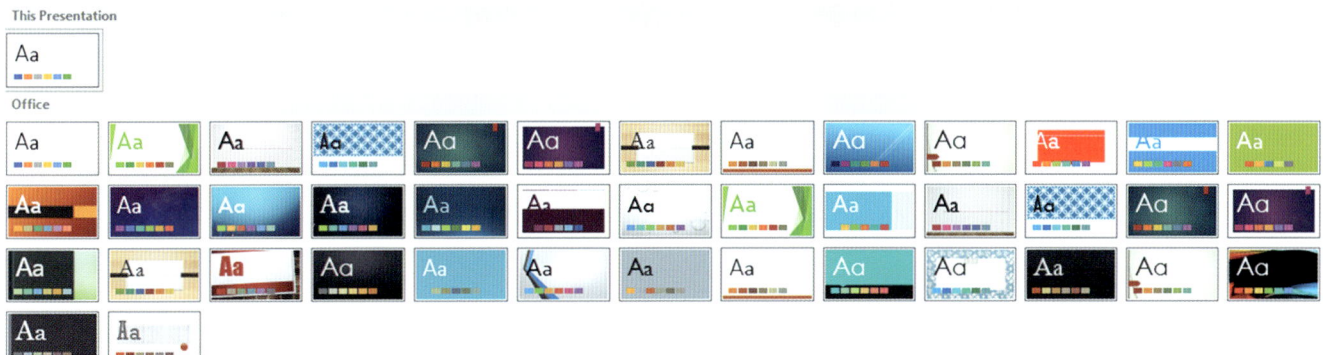

Figure 16.4 Preset themes available in the design tab on the ribbon

Content creation

Your second slide should set out the two to three objectives of the presentation. Your third and subsequent slides should be based on an analysis of your source of information (manuscript, report, research notes).

Figure 16.5 provides one way of analysing text for your slides.

 **Helpful hint**

A good method of analysis is to:
- make a bulleted list from each sentence or section heading
- create short expressions from key sentences with new information
- avoid repeated ideas or points and opinions
- remove unnecessary words
- combine similar points, if possible.

- Technology Education (Tech Ed) is currently one of three subjects that is offered at the lower secondary level in most of the secondary schools of T&T that can be considered as technical and vocational in nature.
- The two others are Home Economics and Agricultural Science.
- Tech Ed is a channel for teaching the knowledge and skills that are necessary for living in the 21st Century.
- These include problem-solving, innovative thinking, information management and communication, among others.
- Tech Ed students are taught to look at a task or problem and:
  ○ identify 2 or 3 aspects or issues
  ○ define each one
  ○ explore and assess possible solutions
  ○ choose and test one solution and evaluate whether or not it worked.
- Technology Education is therefore a method for the delivery of desirable skills, competencies and attitudes that should be the focus of schooling and education today.

Figure 16.5 Passage converted to a bulleted list

Completing the process

Enter your points using bullet points or numbers, as appropriate. The concluding slides will:

- restate the objectives
- make recommendations for action, if the purpose of the presentation requires this
- indicate the end of the presentation, and may invite questions or comments from the audience.

Figure 16.6 shows a series of four slides that would appear after analysis of the passage. A design from the Design tab has been chosen and applied.

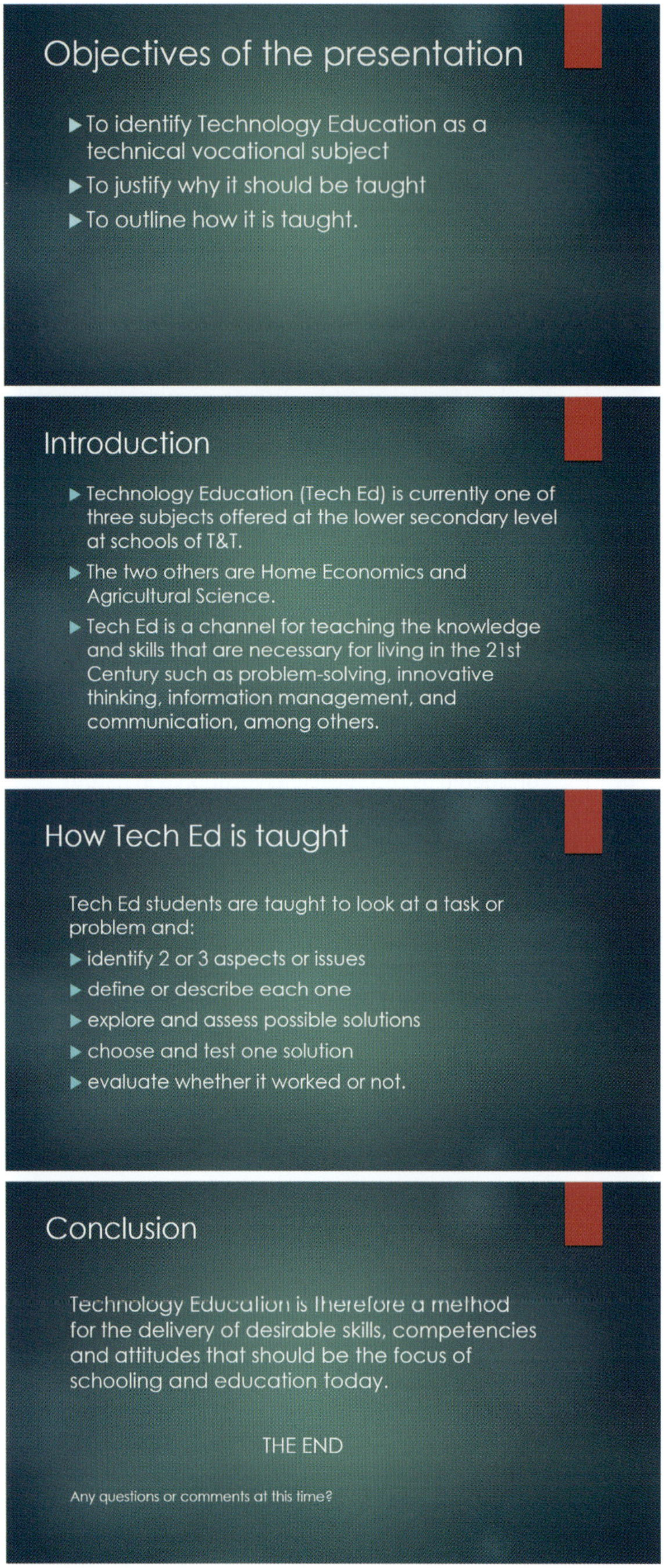

Objectives of the presentation

- To identify Technology Education as a technical vocational subject
- To justify why it should be taught
- To outline how it is taught.

Introduction

- Technology Education (Tech Ed) is currently one of three subjects offered at the lower secondary level at schools of T&T.
- The two others are Home Economics and Agricultural Science.
- Tech Ed is a channel for teaching the knowledge and skills that are necessary for living in the 21st Century such as problem-solving, innovative thinking, information management, and communication, among others.

How Tech Ed is taught

Tech Ed students are taught to look at a task or problem and:
- identify 2 or 3 aspects or issues
- define or describe each one
- explore and assess possible solutions
- choose and test one solution
- evaluate whether it worked or not.

Conclusion

Technology Education is therefore a method for the delivery of desirable skills, competencies and attitudes that should be the focus of schooling and education today.

THE END

Any questions or comments at this time?

Figure 16.6 Presentation of four slides after passage analysis and choice of design theme

Step 4: Selecting, importing and editing graphics

Selecting graphics

Graphical data consists of images, icons, symbols, art, pictures, line drawings, doodles, tables, charts and graphs.

Some things to consider when selecting graphics include:

- the source of the graphics
- their relevance to the content and context
- their clarity, simplicity and readability.

Source

The source of graphics may be your personal collection of family or work pictures; company-owned logos, charts, graphs and trademarks; or commissioned artwork or stock pictures that are available for free or for purchase on the internet.

Licensed images usually require credit or acknowledgement to the original creator, if known.

Relevance to content and context

Consider the appeal of the graphical data in terms of its placement, size and colour to the characteristics of the audience. Younger age groups prefer fewer words and bright colourful graphics. Balancing the appeal to both boys and girls might be important to an audience. Older people might find graphs and charts with colours used to highlight key data points more interesting.

Consider where and how the audience will be viewing the presentation. Graphical data that can be seen very clearly in online meetings might be less visible to attendees at the back of a venue in an offline meeting.

Clarity and simplicity

Make sure that the features of objects on the slide are properly labelled. The illustrating of some ideas may be less straightforward and better explained in words.

Graphics should work with the text in and around it to present clear and simple messages. Neither the picture nor the font style should overwhelm the slide nor distract from the information being presented.

Activity

List *five* criteria for selecting graphical data appropriate for presentations.

Importing graphics into presentations

Click on the 'insert' tab to see all the subtabs available for inserting graphics and other objects. You can also drag and drop images and videos from your own computer. The 'pictures' subtab allows importation of images from online sources.

The 'insert' menu and 'media' subtab include video, audio and even screen-recording options. Choosing 'online videos' will allow you to use a video URL to preview and import into your presentation.

SECTION 3

Using hyperlinking

Inserting too many forms of digital media into your presentation reduces the goal of being brief and simple. Inserting a hyperlink helps you to include additional information and objects, and even to go back or forward to other slides in the same presentation.

To insert a hyperlink:

- Place your presentation in a folder with the documents, other presentations or objects that you will hyperlink from your presentation.
- Open your presentation, select a suitable word or phrase on the relevant slide and either right-click on the selection or click on the 'insert' tab, look for the 'links' subtab and choose 'link'.
- A window will open that shows all files that are in the same folder as your presentation. Click on the one that contains the relevant additional data. Alternatively, browse for information online.
- Once you are satisfied that you have established a link with the relevant details, click OK to insert the link.

Figure 16.7 shows a hyperlink in a presentation, whereas Figure 16.8 shows hyperlinked text.

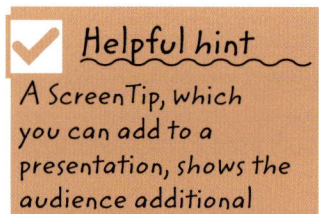

Helpful hint

A ScreenTip, which you can add to a presentation, shows the audience additional information when the presenter hovers over it.

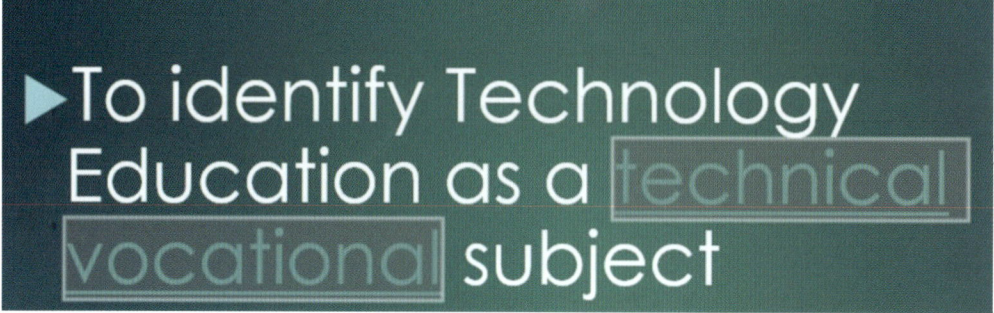

Figure 16.7 A hyperlink in a presentation

TECHNICAL AND VOCATIONAL EDUCATION is a term that refers to the study of technologies and related sciences and the acquisition of the practical skills, knowledge and attitudes related to occupations in various sectors of the economy and society.

Figure 16.8 Hyperlinked text

Editing graphical data

After insertion, graphical data may need to be relocated, resized, amended or enhanced with special effects. Microsoft PowerPoint provides wizards and specially shaped cursors for these actions.

Table 16.2 Table 16.2 summarises the essential techniques for editing and formatting graphics to ensure they are positioned and styled correctly within a document.

Table 16.2 How to edit graphics

Edit	Action	Pointer image
Relocating an image	• Hover over the selected image until the cursor transforms into a four-sided arrow. • Click to hold and drag it to the desired location on the slide or page. • Be careful not to cover other images, as it might become difficult to separate them. • If the new location is in the midst of text, use the 'align' text feature on the 'paragraph' subtab on the 'home' tab to place the text in a different position. • To transform the graphic into a background feature, right-click on the graphic. Choose 'picture format' from the 'arrange' menu on the 'drawing' subtab, or right-click and choose 'send to back' to place the graphic behind the text on the page.	
Resizing/reshaping	Right-click on the graphic. Place the double-pointed cursor on the control button on the corner or side to shorten, widen or lengthen the graphic.	

Cropping and background removal	• Change the shape or remove unwanted aspects of an image by right-clicking on the image. The crop icon appears below the menu.
	• Drag the bolded edges of the picture until the unwanted aspects of the photo are covered. Click outside of the image or press enter to keep the wanted parts.
	• To remove the background of a picture:
	  – click the 'picture format' tab and 'background removal' subtab
	  – choose between 'mark areas to keep' and 'mark areas to remove'
	  – select and accept changes.

Add effects	• Right-click on the image and select the 'format picture' subtab (Figure 16.9). The menu appears on the right-hand side, with options such as colour, appearance and a change from a 2-dimensional look to a 3-dimensional look. • The insert tab provides access to illustrations, text and other subtabs. Textboxes, WordArt and other text effects can be added anywhere on the slide. • The 'picture format' tab provides many tools to blur, glow, correct colour, apply texture and add borders, as well as predefined stylistic looks and edits in the 'artistic effects' menu.	Format Picture 

SECTION 3

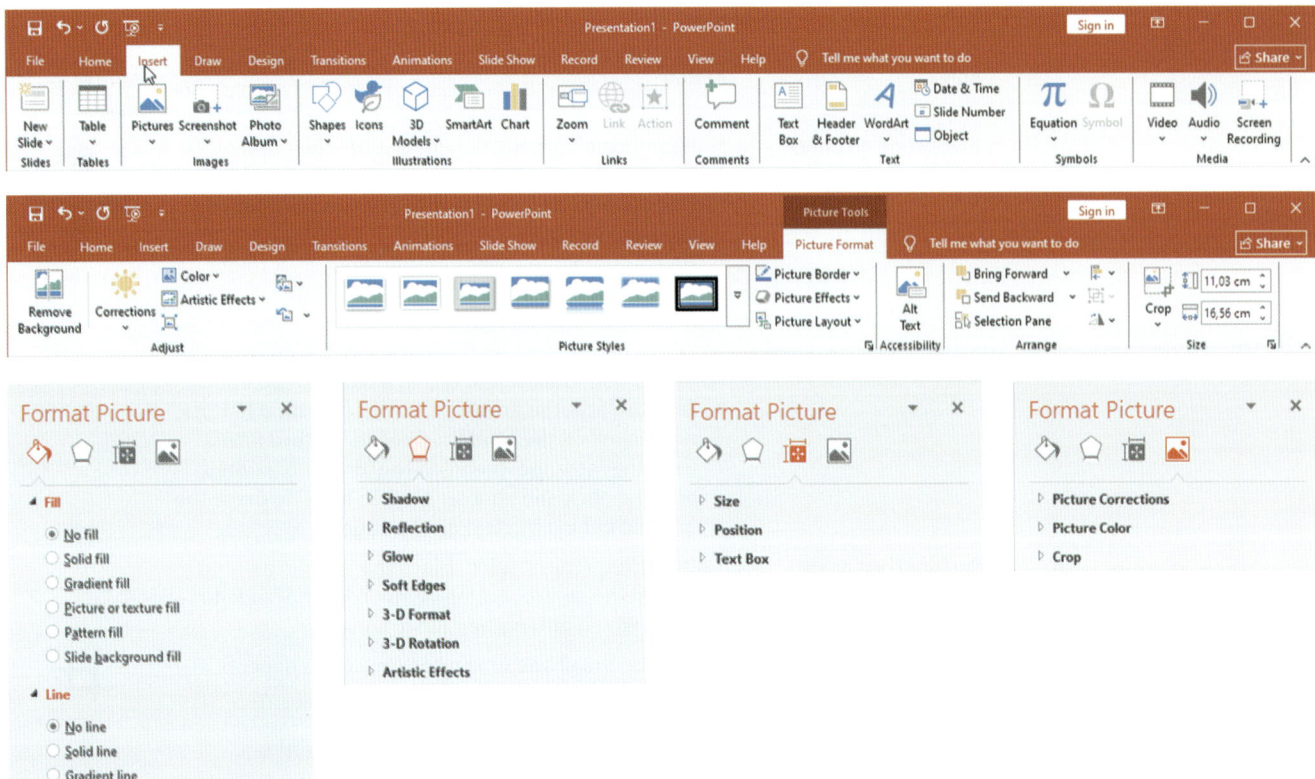

Figure 16.9 The 'insert' tab and subtabs, and the 'picture format' tab and subtabs

Advanced features

Several tools in Microsoft PowerPoint can be used to enhance the preparation and delivery of a presentation. These include:

- using the 'slide show' tab
- making the transition from slide to slide more exciting
- animating the text and objects on slides
- providing printed documents (*handouts*) to reinforce the message or provide access to your sources of information.

The 'slide show' tab

The 'slide show' tab is used for the delivery of presentations (Figure 16.10). Slides appear in full-screen mode, allowing the audience to focus on each slide individually. There are two modes for delivery of the slide deck:

1. The first mode requires the manipulation of the slides one by one, starting with either the 'from beginning' button or 'from current slide' button on the 'start slide show' subtab. The presenter can click through the slides or use the left and right arrows on the keyboard to navigate through the slides.

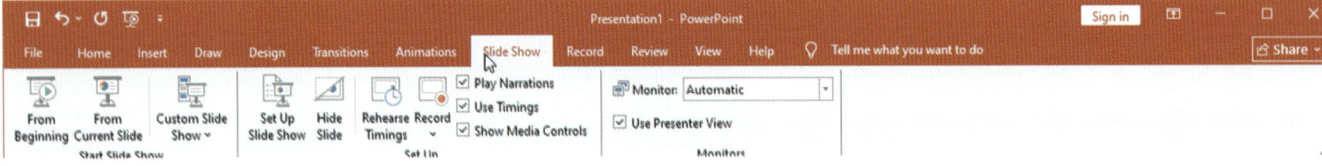

Figure 16.10 The 'slide show' subtab menu

2. The second mode is to set up an automatic delivery of the slide deck using the 'set up' subtab.
   - The slides will move through their sequence according to preset timings and accompanying narrations.
   - Recording the presentation beforehand helps the presenter know how it looks and sounds from the view of the audience.
   - It can also be exported as a video after saving it under the 'record' tab on the ribbon.

Transitions and animations

Using transitions and animations enhances the delivery of a presentation.

After you have decided on a theme and entered your content, you can add features to improve audience engagement. Two tools – transitions and animations – on the ribbon help make the presentation more interactive and/or activate or change the focus of the audience.

Transitions

A *transition* is the movement of the slides through the presentation. Microsoft PowerPoint comes with a number of default transitions grouped by descriptive themes, as shown in Figure 16.11.

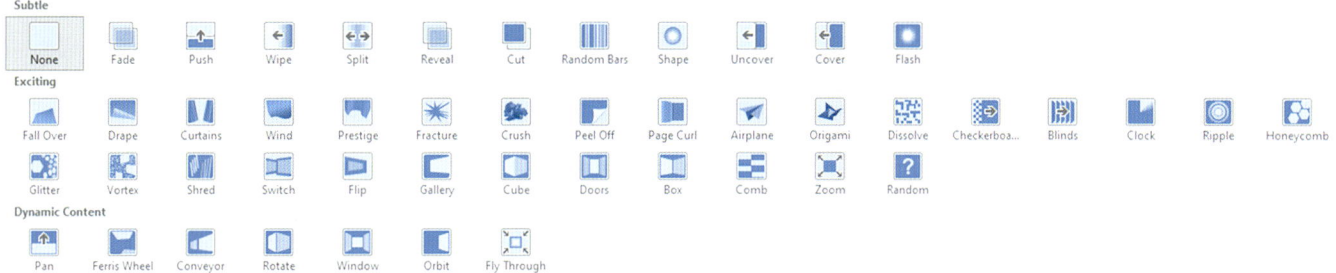

Figure 16.11 Options for transitioning slides

To use transitions, go to the thumbnail of slides (the outline pane) and add each transition option individually, or select some or all slides and click 'apply'. Alternatively, click the 'apply to all' button.

Transitions can be customised by adding sound, changing the duration of the transition effect or even setting the slide to move to the next slide automatically after a period of time.

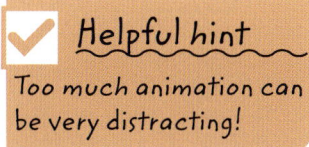

Helpful hint

Too much animation can be very distracting!

Animations

The animation tab allows you to add actions that are similar to transitions, but they apply to the content of a slide. The animation tab also allows you to change the order that content appears on a slide, or make timing changes, among other features. Figure 16.12 shows the animation options available in Microsoft PowerPoint.

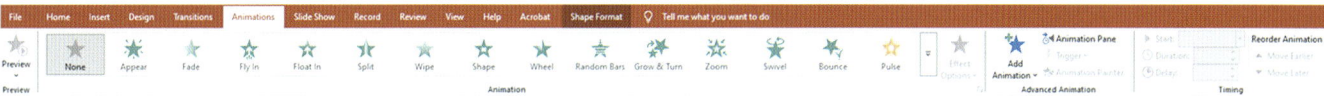

Figure 16.12 Options for animating slide content

SECTION 3

Speaker notes and handouts

Speaker's notes

To deliver an effective presentation, limit the number of details on each slide and, instead, expand on the information orally. This means simplifying your presentation by not including long texts on slides.

Using speaker's notes – brief text in the notes pane feature found at the bottom of each slide – can help with this. Edit the text with bold for words you want to emphasise and use bullet points for clarity. If the notes pane is missing, click the view tab and show subtab for the notes to appear.

Handouts

Delivering your slide show might involve printing the slide deck (with or without your speaker's notes) and giving physical copies/handouts to the audience.

To print the presentation:

- click the file tab and select 'full page slides – print 1 slide per page' from the drop-down box
- select from the various options of how you would like the handouts to appear.

Figure 16.13 provides information on these options.

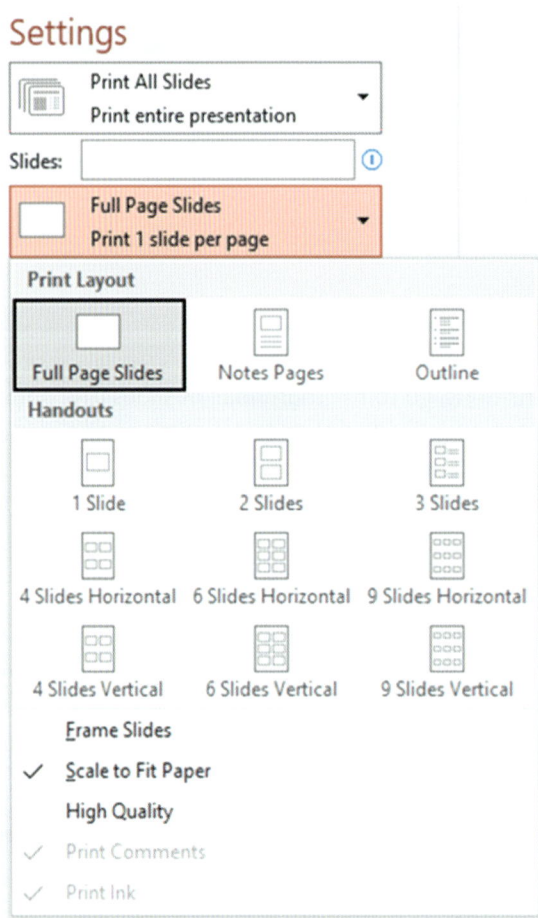

Figure 16.13 Handouts print options from the file tab

Key terms

animation The application of a tool that causes text, icons, pictures, other graphics or whole slides to appear to move, to attract or maintain the attention of viewers of presentations

delivery The act of explaining, expanding on or displaying text and graphics of a presentation to an audience

design The choice of preset options or personal choice of colours, font styles, etc. that appear on every slide of a presentation

graphics Pictures, images and text effects, such as WordArt, used to enhance a document or presentation

layout pane Also called the *slide development pane*; used to develop the look of slides by determining the content and its placement

normal view The main view for navigation and editing a presentation, which is generally broken into three sections: outline pane, layout pane and notes pane

notes pane A space that allows a presenter to add speaking notes, such as important points they want to say, without having the audience read it

outline pane A quick thumbnail view of the slides that make up a presentation; allows you to see your slide order and quickly rearrange it, similar to the slide sorter view

placeholder A preset space on a slide for text, art, videos or more; additional placeholders can be inserted

presentation/slide deck The file that contains the compiled information for sharing with the audience

presenter The person delivering a presentation, i.e. speaking and controlling the pace of information delivery

relocating/reshaping/resizing The manipulation of graphics or other objects in a document or presentation

slide A page inside a presentation that contains content for display; generally laid out in landscape orientation

slide show view/presentation view The view that audiences see, with slides in full screen mode free from thumbnails and speaker notes; each mouse click or keyboard press (except the escape key) moves forward or back through the presentation

slide sorter view Provides large thumbnails of slides, allowing you to see the order of your presentation and quickly rearrange it

source The original creator, website or location of information; graphics of other copyrighted products

thumbnail A small version of all slides, which sits on the left of the screen for seeing which slide comes next and allowing quick navigation to a specific slide

title slide The first slide in a slide deck; supplies key referential information on the presentation, for example, topic and presenter's information

transitions A tool that helps determine the order, sequence and flow between slides

Summary

In this chapter, you have learned about:

- basic and advanced features of Microsoft PowerPoint, a presentation application
- presentations that use slides to provide information at business meetings and in educational contexts
- constructing presentations by summarising data into informative titles and bulleted points, while using hyperlinking to provide additional information
- making presentations more engaging with graphics and special effects, such as slide transition and content animation, suitable for content and context
- preparing speaking notes and handouts to ensure effective delivery.

SECTION 3

Practice, research and exam-style questions

Multiple-choice questions

1. Presentation software can …
   - A manipulate numbers to create graphics.
   - B display calculations and graphics.
   - C manipulate tables to answer queries.
   - D store graphics for easy retrieval.

2. A collection of related slides is called a slide …
   - A sort.
   - B view.
   - C deck.
   - D field.

3. Which term is *not* relevant to presentation-software use?
   - A Cell reference
   - B Notes pane
   - C Normal view
   - D Placeholder

4. Other than the layout tool, which presentation software tools provide layout options?
   - A New slide
   - B Clipboard
   - C Page setup
   - D Reset

5. Which term applies to graphics manipulation?
   - A Salutation
   - B Rotation
   - C Presentation
   - D Function

   These options are for questions 6 and 7:
   - A Transitions
   - B Animations
   - C Design template
   - D Slide sorter

6. Which option adds a form of special effects to the contents on a slide?

7. Which option ensures that the same features appear across slides in the same presentation?

Research questions

Work in groups of three or four to carry out the following.

1. Using any source of information, carry out brief research to create an attractive title slide for any one of these topics:
   - Gaming today
   - Cyberbullying
   - Space travel today

   Your creation should:
   - use one of the preset title page layouts provided in a presentation application
   - display a suitable title
   - include a subtopic
   - identify a fictitious presenter/organisation.

2. Using your researched topic from question 1, create five more slides to form a six-slide deck. Your second slide should contain at least *two* objectives for your presentation. Your final slide should invite questions or comments and include an appropriate shape, icon or symbol.

   a Using the information provided in Table 16.2, import at least *one* suitable graphic into each of slides 3 and 4 of your slide deck.

   b i Choose and apply a transition effect to your slide deck.

   ii Apply an animation effect to the content of at least *one* slide other than the title slide.

   iii Save and label your file with a suitable name.

   iv Print *one* copy of your slide deck to be used as a handout for each member of your group.

Section 4

CHAPTER 17 Electronic communication
CHAPTER 18 Document management

17 Electronic communication

> **🏠 Objectives**
>
> By the end of this chapter, you will be able to:
>
> - define the term *electronic communication*
> - describe two categories, with examples, of electronic communication
> - compare new and emerging communication technologies
> - identify the distinct features of electronic mail
> - use various features of email in communicating with other people
> - sort and store emails by applying efficient file-organisation methods
> - select electronic-communication media based on various factors
> - identify the advantages and disadvantages of different forms of e-communication.

Introduction

The increased demand for information-sharing, intelligence-gathering and record-updating has meant a greater need for networks of computers and different means of electronic communication. The features of emailing systems appear to be the most useful for business and personal purposes, but new and emerging communication-technologies channels have their advantages.

Definition of electronic communication (e-communication)

E-communication is the use of input and output devices, such as the computer, smartphone, tablet, other devices and computer networks, with their processing and storage capacities to exchange messages, in the form of digital multimedia.

> **Did you know?**
>
> E-communication architects love abbreviations and the creation of new words!

The methods and protocols of e-communication

The existence of computer networks, especially the internet, and billions of pieces of content set out on webpages on those networks, mainly the World Wide Web, are part of what is described as *e-communication architecture*. Rules, standards and techniques that enable and govern interconnectivity, and allow access, use and amendments to content, are also part of this architecture.

Another term used in the computerised environment is inter-accessibility, which occurs via *websites*. The most famous and extensive network is called the internet, and the major source of information is called the *World Wide Web (www)*.

The internet and the World Wide Web. A **net** or **network** refers to the capacity of computers to communicate with similar devices. It may be confined to one organisation *(intranet)* with a public access point *(extranet)* or one geographic space *(Local Area Network or LAN)*, or it may be found across many organisations in many countries (internet). The World Wide Web describes huge amounts of information, located on independent computers across the world, that is freely available via links and keywords.

17 Electronic communication

Web addresses or *domain names* for websites are needed for adding *webpages* of information to, or accessing information from, the web. When an address is input into a computer with access to the internet, a web **browser** (such as Chrome™ browser or Firefox) or search engine (such as Google™ search or Microsoft Bing) searches for keywords or domain names and takes the user to a list of possible information sources or directly to the named website.

Key terms used for describing e-communication architecture are examined in Table 17.1.

Table 17.1 Important e-communication terms

E-communication term	Meaning
Bandwidth	The capacity of a channel to carry a certain volume of data
Browser/search engine	An application that allows you to find, see and send webpages; send and receive **email**; participate in conferences; chat; and shop online – some popular browsers are Chrome™ browser, Microsoft Edge and Firefox
Communication channel	E-communication channels include those that are attached or wired (such as via coaxial cables or fibreoptic wire) and those that use wireless technologies (such as radio signals from satellites, Wi-Fi® channels, Bluetooth® technology, hotspotting, mobile phone networks)
Local Area Network (LAN)	A net or network of computers that are located in a relatively small geographic space such as in one building
Locators	Ways of finding data (content/websites) and their sources using address protocols, such as the Internet Protocol (IP), the Universal Resource Locator (URL), domain names, **email addresses**
Protocol	The rules for formatting and processing data so that different software and hardware combinations can understand messages and reply to them, such as: • HyperText Transfer Protocol (**http**) provides instructions for sending plain text data between parties • https is the version that ensures encrypted data is sent securely
Wide Area Network (WAN)	A network of computers that are far apart in geographic terms

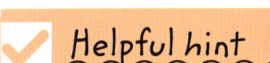

Helpful hint

When a top-level domain name is followed by a separator and space, it turns blue and underlined, which allows access to a website or an email server via ctrl and a left-click of the mouse.

An example of a locator is the URL for a website, for example: https://www.mform.edu/centre/tvettraining/assessor-manuals.html. This organisation does not exist but, if it was real, the URL would provide the information in Table 17.2.

Table 17.2 Requirements for a URL

https	The name of the Internet Protocol that gives access to the website; note that the 's' at the end gives assurance that the site's information is encrypted for safe transmission of data – other IPs include FTP and TCP/IP
www	The server computer that holds or hosts the organisation's web pages
.mform	The sub-domain name, which indicates the name of the organisation; often, the organisation uses an appropriate abbreviation of its name
.edu	Top-level domain name, which indicates that this is an educational institution; two other top-level domain names are .com (commercial enterprise) and .gov (government agency)
centre	A subdirectory, i.e. the special part of the organisation that owns the website

tvettraining	Term that identifies the part of the centre with that particular purpose; in this case, they offer training in technical and vocational skills (EDPM can be considered a TVET subject)
assessor-manuals	Indicates the type of documents in the tvettraining folder; trainer-manuals might be substituted in another URL
html	Abbreviation of *Hypertext Markup Language*; indicates that the documents are written in a format that is standardised and easy to read
/ (separators)	Help the browser redirect the search to the exact location of the item

The contexts and purposes of e-communicators

Electronic communication can be divided into two groups. Each grouping serves different purposes, depending on the context:

- Group 1 can be described as the exchange of digital media for personal, professional or commercial reasons. The mechanisms include electronic mail (email); *instant messaging*/text messaging; audio and videoconferences; and **streaming platforms**.
- Group 2 includes electronic media that are used to connect people with similar interests or who aim to develop such relationships. These are **online communities**, discussion forums, **chat groups**, weblogs and web vlogs, e-newsletters, message boards, **webinars** and **podcasts**.

New and emerging communication technologies

Instant messaging (IM/SMS), emailing, creating and posting content, browsing and chatting have become very familiar to us. Other familiar network-enabled mechanisms include online collaborative software, software using Voice Over Internet Protocol (VOIP) and the evolving functionalities of social media networks/platforms.

Online collaborative software

Online collaborative software includes applications that allow managers and workers, remote or in office, to coordinate and cooperate to accomplish numerous daily and project-based tasks. Table 17.3 provides information on the features of collaborative applications.

Table 17.3 Some tasks, functions and applications of collaborative software

Task	Collaborative function	Popular applications
Document-sharing and file-sharing	• Documents can be worked on simultaneously, with every insertion of additional digital media or any suggested change alerting other contributors • Files that need approval after editing or where confidentiality is important can still be shared in a secure manner	• SharePoint • Google Docs™ • Google Workspace™ • Microsoft OneDrive • Office 365 • Dropbox
Automatic scheduling of invitees to conferences	Online-meeting tools, such as presentation-sharing, side-bar chatting, raising a hand, reactions, AI-enabled recording and note-taking, help ensure smooth and efficient meetings	• Zoom • Google Meet™ • Microsoft Teams

17 Electronic communication

Project collaboration and status-sharing	Project-management applications that include access to emailing facilities, document-sharing, time- and work-tracking and other **collaborative tools**	• Microsoft Project • Trello • Basecamp
Intelligence and information collection	• Applications exist to collect information and feedback to boost research and development and marketing activities • Monitoring and responding to social-media users ensures that businesses understand their consumers as well as their competitors	• Google Docs™ • Sprout • Qualaroo

Enhanced instant messaging

WhatsApp and Telegram are examples of downloadable software that offer almost instant access to text, visual and audio forms of communication to anyone who can connect to the internet and have downloaded the apps. Using VOIP, both telephone calls and data in video formats are transmitted between computers. The messages are encrypted so that confidential information is available only to the designated receivers in a chat group. Many businesses have WhatsApp-enabled smartphones separate from the traditional cellular phone and landline. Administrators add or remove people by adding or deleting mobile numbers in the chat.

> **→ Activity**
>
> Name an application used for group chats.

Social media networks/platforms

Social media platforms have become significant tools for e-communication between individuals, private groups, government agencies and businesses, who exchange information by creating content, posting other people's content and commenting on content on a wide range of topics. Platforms such as TikTok, Instagram, YouTube and Facebook are the most popular with users. Digital media can range from eight-hour long compilations of information to shorts and reels a few seconds long.

New and emerging communication technologies include those listed in Table 17.4.

Table 17.4: New and emerging communication technologies

Communication technology	Description
Artificial intelligence (AI)	Tool that allows computers to communicate in an almost human-like manner by responding to direct queries transmitted orally or in writing; works by collecting possible responses from information available on the World Wide Web and making suggestions to questioners with rapid speed
Machine learning (ML)	Branch of AI that trains machines to follow the path of how humans learn and respond; consequently, the communication and performance of computerised machinery and facilities improve
Blockchain technology (BT)	Application that maintains and distributes records of transactions or digital events to those who have permission for access; rapid and secure transmission of financial data is the most popular use of the technology

SECTION 4

> **Did you know?**
> Users of the same server may not be allowed to duplicate names already in use according to server's index of email addresses, so you might become patjones56824@gmail.com because Pat Jones might be the name of many other email owners.

5G	Used in cellular communication; offers faster download speeds of data-heavy messages, for example, videostreaming, virtual-reality scenarios and the internet of things
Internet of things (IoT)	Applications that encourage communication directly between computers without human intervention; supports the development of robotics, smart homes and automated processes, connected to smartphones

While some businesses continue to use older e-communication technologies, such as the facsimile machine, the various features of electronic mail (email) makes it the most popular modern form of e-communication in the world today

Using the email function

There are many features available for using and managing a company's email system, including sign-in to email, email management and email communication.

Sign-in to email

Signing in to an email system requires knowledge of the email address of the owner. The email address refers both to the name chosen to represent the owner and to the server that is hosting the owner's communications. For example, the owner of a business called MforM Portfolio Solutions may have a business email such as m4msol@mformsolutions.org, which is hosted by the company's in-house server. His private email may be hosted by a global server, for example Google, and be something like jamesbond49@gmail.com.

When you have succeeded in signing in, you will see the *inbox view*. This screen shows all the messages that have been sent to you; both those you have *read* (shown without any letters in bold) and those that remain *unread*. The date and time when the email was received are also available. Currently, some servers show the last message received as part of a **thread** or group of connected messages between you and another email user.

Email management

Managing emails requires consistent monitoring to prevent cluttering the inbox and sent folders until you are warned of approaching maximum storage. Several actions are necessary for preventing the situation where important correspondence remains unread or responses are repeated because they are lost in the clutter. Sorting, saving, deleting and archiving are proactive measures for preventing this situation and achieving efficiencies.

Figure 17.1 Preset folders for saving sorted and unsorted emails

In the email environment, messages are saved in labelled, preprogrammed folders (Figure 17.1). Other subfolders can be created via user-set criteria called *filters*. These subfolders can help organise correspondence by such categories as work-related versus personal; action required; importance (high/medium/low); and keywords (for example subjects, names, assignments, projects). There are applications that can help remove unnecessary emails and prevent future clutter.

Table 17.5 Roles of email folders

Folder type	Role
Inbox	Holds all messages received since the email system was established; you may have thousands of messages there, unsorted except by date and time received
Sent	Holds all messages sent by you, arranged according to date and time
Drafts and snoozed	Holds new messages that are incomplete or must be delayed for some reason, such as waiting for approval before delivery
Starred/pinned (receiver) Important/priority (sender)	Holds emails copied from the inbox in accordance with criteria or filters set by the receiver or the sender of messages; these criteria are used to *prioritise* or *sort* emails so that due attention is paid to them on a timely basis
Spam/promotions/updates	Holds emails sent as part of a general marketing effort and identified as 'spam' by the server; opportunities to *report* spam email or *block* or *unsubscribe* from the senders are usually provided, but occasionally a message from a new source may be treated as 'spam' – it is worth checking your spam folder occasionally in case a new contact has sent you an email you might not have been expecting
Trash/bin	Holds email scheduled for permanent deletion after a set number of days

Monitoring

Notifications and alerts ensure that the communication channel remains open and the relationship between sender and receiver is maintained. An alerts system can be installed to inform whether emails that have been sent were read or remain unread. **Notifications** are automatic messages that inform you whether an email message has been received or a potential receiver is out-of-office (OOO). Some billing companies use notification emails to inform customers of their credit status or of some activity on their account. Notifications can also be used to inform you of a scheduled meeting by providing date, time, location, agenda items and the names of other attendees.

The second type of email monitoring focuses on tracking employee use of the email system. *Email logs* record the emails sent, to whom, their subjects and the dates and times.

Archiving

Archiving is a deliberate action taken to preserve and protect messages received or sent. Archiving means you can:

- recover emails that were accidentally deleted
- access emails that contain valuable information that is needed years after the email was sent
- keep records attached to emails if required for preservation under a country's law.

SECTION 4

In the computerised environment, archiving can be done automatically or by dragging the email to the icon that looks like a file box.

Email communication

Composing an email requires you to use many of the same techniques and skills as in composing letters and memos, as well as being familiar with the functionalities of the email system.

Creating an email

Above the inbox folder in the inbox view page, the command *compose*, *create* or *new email* will appear. When opened (left-click), a new page will open (Figure 17.2).

Figure 17.2 Email page features

17 Electronic communication

The available features and functions of an email page are shown in Table 17.6.

Table 17.6 The features of an email page and their functions

Feature	Functions
Status indicators	These make a distinction among recipients of the message: • TO – *identifies the recipient/s who will receive the message directed for their information and necessary action.* • CC – *a copy of the email is sent to other person/s. This message may be used for the recipient(s) information and or action.* • BCC – *(Blind copy) identifies additional recipient/s who must be informed on a private or anonymous basis and therefore remains unknown to those who received the email as TO or CC.* Note that the sender's address will appear in the email Inbox folders of all recipients.
Summoning Contacts list	After clicking on the (To) in the email page. The folder collects the names and email addresses of all people with whom you would have communicated over time. When entering information in a status indicator, the system will suggest possible recipients based on the first few letters of the contact's name. It will also suggest additional contacts associated with the first contact to allow bulk emailing to take place.
Subject line	Indicates/ the purpose of the information in the message. A distinctive subject line will make recovery easier after archiving activities.
Creating text message	The main portion of the new page is for entry of a text message with any available formatting feature
Attaching additional information/ messages	• Upload documents from storage media using the paperclip icon. • A scanned document can be sent directly to an email address or several addresses at once. This is especially useful for urgent messages. If the attachment is too large, and saved in some form of Cloud storage, the icon that resembles a hard drive will attach a link to the file.

>  **Activity**
>
> Draw a version of any symbol or icon that is used to attach items to email messages.

Selecting the best communication medium

With e-communication, individuals, groups and companies must select appropriate devices and software. Factors in selection include the purposes of the communication; the desired relationship between senders and receivers; and a comparison of the advantages and disadvantages of one medium over another.

Advantages of electronic communication

- Devices allow speedy, cost-effective and convenient messaging directed to selected individuals or groups. New and emerging software enables a variety of communication modes.
- The portability of devices allows access to scanned files and emails and supports remote work and increased productivity. Alerts and notifications keep e-communicators in touch with one another.

- Through social media networks, software and online collaborative tools, people can concentrate on relationship-building as managers utilise e-comm media for direct and ongoing access to customers and employees, and vice versa.
- Subordinates and supervisors are helped by being able to email or instant message each other quickly with precise information on companies' goals and current positions; this helps to motivate workers.
- Interest groups interact with like-minded people, and innovative and inventive ideas and information are easily shared.
- E-communication systems are also major sources of employment as there is a need for network professionals, technicians, and support personnel.

Disadvantages of electronic communication

- The dependence of devices on networked spaces poses a major disadvantage where access to the internet especially is unstable or non-existent.
- Systems such as browsers and cloud storage are users of large volumes of electric power and are therefore major sources of unhealthy emissions.
- Continuous accessibility to workers through devices and software applications pose health risks to work–life balance from constantly being connected or compelled to check emails and notifications.
- Workers are easily distracted by software that poses both health and security risks to businesses and personal affairs.
- Businesses or customers may find their privacy invaded, especially where cyber-security issues cause publication of confidential information, such as secret formulas, passwords and bank-account details.

Key terms

bandwidth The data-transfer capability of a network, usually measured in kilobits per second or megabits per second

browser An application used to find places on a network of computers, particularly the internet

chat group Also called a *forum*; a limited gathering of people in an online space who are encouraged to interact over topics of mutual interest

collaborative tool A project-management application that includes access to emailing facilities, document-sharing and document-editing that aims to improve the effectiveness and efficiency of teams

email Electronic messages sent to individual accounts at email addresses, with or without attachments

email address A method of locating recipients using the form uniquename@emailprovider.com

html Hypertext Markup Language; a structured method of coding widely used on the internet; it makes documents standardised and easy to read

http Hypertext Transfer Protocol; a series of rules that dictates how html is shared over the internet

instant messaging A popular form of quick transmission of text, images and voice notes between two people
locator A way of finding data (content/websites) and their sources using address protocols such as the Internet Protocol (IP), the Universal Resource Locator (URL), domain names and email addresses
notification Also called an *alert*; a sound, vibration, action or image intended to draw attention to the receipt of an e-communication
online community An internet-based social gathering of individuals with common interests
podcast An audio-based delivery of topical information over several episodes; the word is an amalgamation of *iPod* and *broadcast*
protocol A set of rules that dictates how data is shared across a network
search engine An online tool used to find information quickly by accessing databases across the internet
separator A few punctuation marks, such as forward slash and period, that help a browser redirect a search to the exact location of a web address and an item at that address
status indicator (to, cc, bcc) An email feature that allows a sender to distinguish between intended recipients of a message in the communication process
streaming platform Online media-sharing tool that allows users to consume shared content without having to own or download it
thread A series of message exchanges between people based on a single topic
webinar An online information dissemination tool that provides information and encourages broad-reaching collaboration

Summary

In this chapter, you have learned that:

- electronic communication is the use of computers and computer networks for the exchange of messages
- rules, standards, techniques and applications have been developed to make e-communication the preferred channel for information-sharing, intelligence-gathering and record-updating
- electronic mailing systems (email) provide quick, easy and cost-effective forms of e-communication, but they must be well managed for greatest efficiency
- people with similar interests find e-communication the best means for collaborating using social media platforms; new and emerging technologies are very supportive of this demand.

SECTION 4

Practice, research and exam-style questions

Multiple-choice questions

1. What is the difference between http and https?
   - A Http provides instructions for sending visual data between parties.
   - B Https provides instructions for sending encrypted data between parties.
   - C Http provides a language in which to write text for easy transmission.
   - D Https provides a channel for sending multiple texts at the same time.

2. Before transmission, electronic mail must be …
   - A printed.
   - B directed.
   - C saved.
   - D faxed.

3. In the URL http://www.leavenbread.com, the term *.com* represents …
   - A the type of organisation.
   - B the name of the business.
   - C the name of the host server.
   - D the language used in the webpages.

4. The use of the CC field in an email means the person's address in that field …
   - A will not be seen by the recipient.
   - B will be seen by the recipient.
   - C will be the main recipient.
   - D will be replied to by the recipient.

5. Successful sign-in will show the …
   - A owner's password.
   - B inbox view.
   - C recipient's name.
   - D subscriber folder.

6. One convenient feature for an organisation who must send emails to different groups of people at once is the …
   - A contacts folder.
   - B inbox folder.
   - C sent folder.
   - D categories folder.

7. What is a factor when sending financial information to a recipient?
   - A Speed
   - B Confidentiality
   - C Clarity
   - D Value

8. A podcast is an example of …
   - A teleconferencing.
   - B traditional broadcasting.
   - C social media use.
   - D blogging.

9. Which list includes only new/emerging technologies?
   - A streaming platforms
   - B artificial intelligence
   - C facsimile
   - D short messaging

10. Which email folder delays delivery until an approval is given for delivery?
    - A Inbox
    - B Drafts
    - C Snoozed
    - D Priority

Short-answer questions

1. a Define the term *e-communication* using another source other than your text.
   b Write brief notes on these terms:
      i Input devices
      ii Output devices
      iii Processing capacities
      iv Storage capacities
      v Computer networks
      vi Digital multi-media

2. List *two* abbreviations used as top-level domain names to indicate the type of organisation.

3. a What is the difference between blogging and vlogging?
   b What is the difference between a webinar and a podcast?

4 Lisa Trudo, Research Assistant at Manley Enterprises, has been late to work on more than four days during May 2026. This is a concern, as she was previously spoken to about her tardiness last month.

She is being given a formal letter regarding this matter, which will be placed in her personnel file. The letter is to be signed by her immediate supervisor, Mr. Theo Raidy. Additionally, a copy of the letter will be sent to the Human Resources department and copied to Ms. Crystal Ritchie, Manager of the Research Department.

Write an email to Ms. Lisa Trudo from her Supervisor advising her that a letter is being placed in her personnel file due to her unpunctuality during the period of May 12–15, and again on May 19, 21 and 27, 2026.

Send a blind copy (BCC) of this email to the manager, Ms. Crystal Ritchie, and a copy (CC) to Ms. Shelly Fields, Human Resources Manager, for their information.

For reference, the email addresses are as follows:
- Lisa Trudo: Ltrudo@ManleyEnterprises.com
- Theo Raidy (Supervisor): Traidy@ManleyEnterprises.com
- Crystal Ritchie (Manager): Critchie@ManleyEnterprises.com
- Shelly Fields (HR Manager): Sfields@ManleyEnterprises.com

18 Document management

> **Objectives**
>
> By the end of this chapter, you will be able to:
>
> - compare manual and electronic filing systems
> - identify the advantages and disadvantages of manual and electronic filing systems
> - organise files, folders and directories in a hierarchical structure
> - identify issues affecting file integrity and outline appropriate electronic, physical and cyber solutions
> - describe issues related to document versioning, retention and traceability and outline appropriate responses
> - identify types of word-processing documents in terms of their features and purpose.

Introduction

Businesses gather documents all the time. Many of these documents need to be stored on drives and in the cloud. Other documents need to be printed and made available for physical use. Copies of these documents might be stored manually for legal and accounting obligations but, in a computerised environment, an e-document management system should be used. Issues such as how to keep files intact and safe, how long to keep documents and how to find relevant documents must be resolved. Finally, the problem of non-compliance, which exposes businesses to information loss and hackers, requires policies and compliance strategies.

Using a Document Management System (DMS)

Features of an effective DMS

Whether manual or electronic, a DMS must provide a system:

- for storing different *types* of documents
- for registering and **indexing** multiple documents, including different versions of the same document
- for retrieving and **archiving** documents, including real-time access to approved users.

The cost of setting up, operating, securing and maintaining a manual DMS (MDMS) versus an electronic DMS (EDMS) system must be considered. Some businesses must maintain both types of system.

An *MDMS* places paper-based documents into labelled cardboard/manila folders (called *files*), which are then placed into hanging folders (with appropriate titles). These are then located in a filing/storage cabinet (directory). Files may be registered on index cards, which are stored in another filing cabinet. An elaborate system may be needed for auditing and tracking down the correct version of a file that is no longer in everyday use.

An *EDMS* stores a wide variety of files, including audio, video, images and text-based files in computer storage. Some businesses consider storage of external hard drives as another version of a manual system.

Advantages and disadvantages

Both manual and electronic systems have their advantages and disadvantages, in terms of space; costs; safety and security; and efficiency (Table 18.1).

Table 18.1 Advantages and disadvantages of manual and electronic DMS

	Manual filing systems	Electronic filing systems
Space	• **Advantage:** Files may be placed in a central filing area or kept in relevant departmental facilities for people who require access to paper-based files. • **Disadvantage:** Filing cabinets take up a lot of physical space.	• **Advantage:** More documents can be stored in a smaller space. • **Advantage:** Storage capacity, especially in the cloud, is scalable and agile. • **Disadvantage:** Legal and accounting regulations may require printed copies of certain documents.
Costs	• **Disadvantage:** Set-up costs may be expensive, and even more so to extend storage capacity, including holding duplicates and for file **retention** (archiving). • **Disadvantage:** Staff may need to be hired to manage the file room's work flow (registering, indexing, checking in and checking out files).	• **Advantage:** Less costly, as internal and external storage facilities are easily available and comparatively cheap. • **Advantage:** File creators and users can manage documents easily if processes are standardised and communicated, and implementation tracked.
Safety and security	• **Advantage:** Hardcopies are safe from computer hackers and viruses. • **Advantage:** Files are still available in case of electricity outages, computer failure or network instability. • **Disadvantage:** Files can be destroyed by fire or flood.	• **Advantage:** Protective structures, devices and features can be installed to keep records safe, to restrict access and provide alternative power sources. • **Advantage: Backup systems** can be automated. • **Disadvantage:** Can be prone to hacking and **malware**, which may result in information being changed, stolen or destroyed. • **Disadvantage:** Electronic files can be easily lost if deleted in error.

Efficiency	• **Advantage:** Employees may need little training for retrieval of files if operations are small. • **Disadvantage:** Takes a lot of time to organise, find and retrieve documents. • **Disadvantage:** Documents can be easily misfiled or lost. • **Disadvantage:** Records are usually available to only one person at a time.	• **Advantage:** Locating and retrieving documents is much faster. • **Advantage:** Allows access to documents by more than one person at a time and in real time. • **Advantage:** Increased portability and duplicability for large volumes of information. • **Disadvantage:** Scanning of paper documents into a computer system is time-consuming but may be necessary for quick transmission. • **Disadvantage:** If there is a power failure, records may not be accessible. • **Disadvantage:** Poor folder organisation may result in delays in workflow.

Filing in a computerised environment

In a well-organised EDMS, the second level of organising files is placing them in folders. These large capacity folders, often named *Desktop*, *Downloads*, *Documents* or *Pictures* by default, may be called *directories*. You are usually prompted to save your documents in the main folder – *Documents* – during and at the end of processing.

A well-organised EDMS will have subfolders inside the directories containing files that are related in some way. The categories for placing files into subfolders will be determined by the organisation. Individual files are the lowest level in the DMS, but should still be properly named before being saved in relevant folders.

In summary, a properly structured DMS uses a **hierarchical** or **tree structure**. An example of such a structure is shown in Figure 18.1.

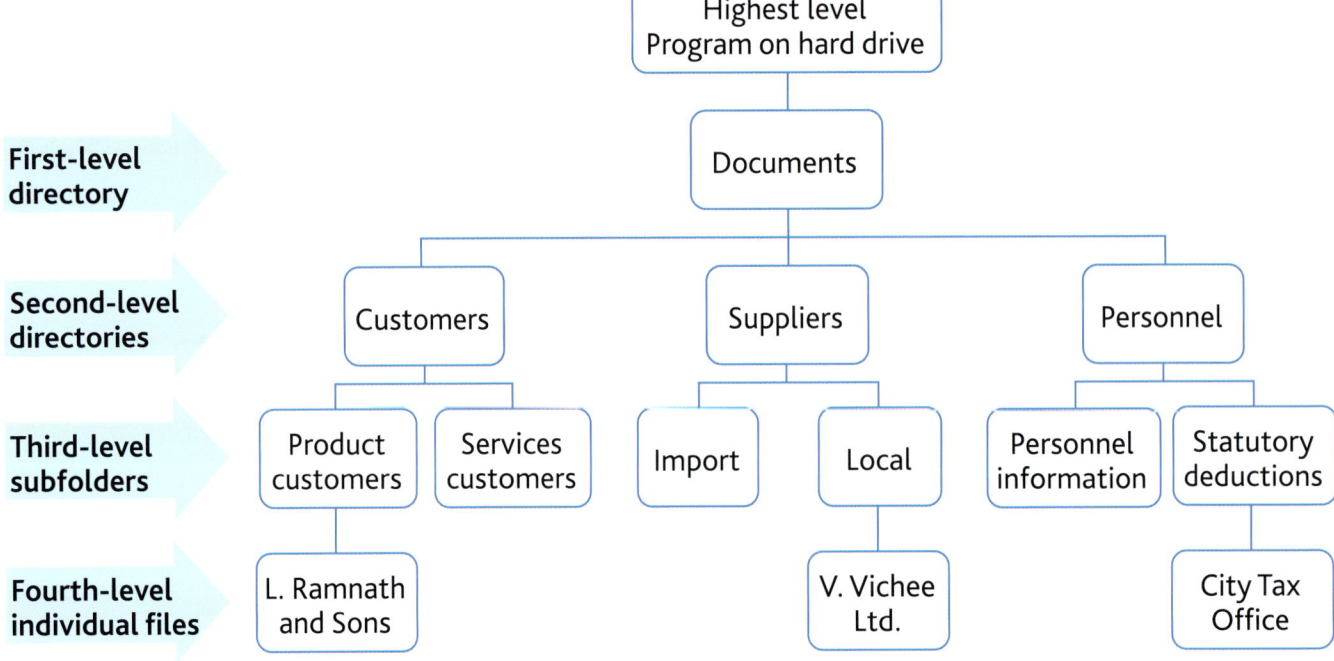

Figure 18.1 A hierarchical (or tree) structure for filing in a computerised environment

18 Document management

> **Did you know?**
> File-integrity analysts call themselves CIA defenders. CIA stands for Confidentiality, Integrity and Availability.

File integrity and security

Putting a file into a folder and then into the external hard drive may interfere with the *integrity* of the file, especially if there are a lot of graphics included with the text. A file that is inaccurate because of storage, transmission or unapproved changes has reduced reliability and usability. Companies must ensure that the system is safe from unauthorised access, alteration, tampering or destruction of records by installing a file-integrity management system.

File Integrity Management System (FIMS)

A *FIMS* (Figure 18.2) is a combination of policies and applications that work by:

- controlling access (using passwords, personal identification numbers [PINs] and **encryption**)
- preventing unapproved changes (applying read-only access and overwrite protection)
- implementing **disaster-recovery strategies** (backing up of files to external hard drives and storing drives in waterproof, fireproof cabinets)
- implementing **cybersecurity** measures (**metadata** restrictions, antivirus programs, firewalls.)

> **Helpful hint**
> In some countries, emails are allowed as evidence in legal situations. They contain information in their metadata and in their body. Email metadata includes information on the subject, the sender, the recipient, the date and time sent, and the host server. The text in the message itself may also contain valuable evidence.

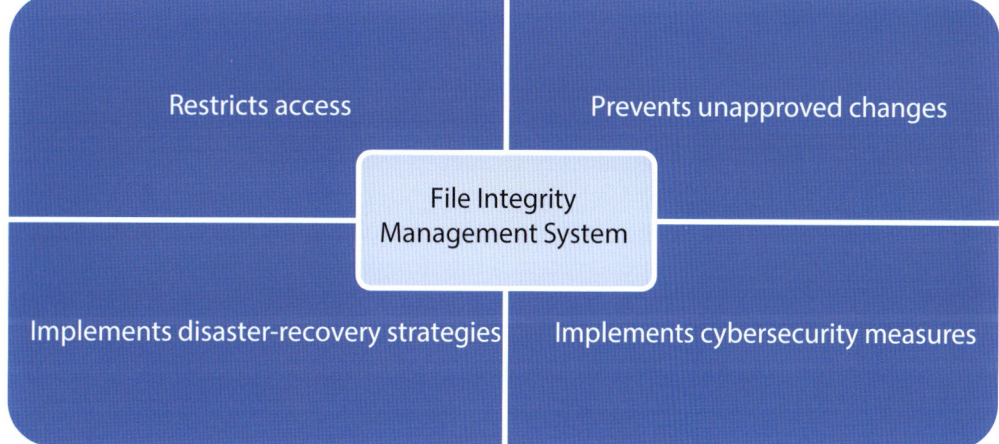

Figure 18.2 A FIMS action grid

FIMS strategy 1: restricted access

In many organisations, some records have restricted access; that is, only certain approved personnel may view them (Figure 18.3). These records may include confidential information such as human-resources data (for example employees' personal information) and accounting records. Other files under restricted access include production methods under patents and proposals for marketing plans. Those people who are approved for access may be provided with passwords, PINs or (at higher levels) dencryption programs.

Figure 18.3 Some records have restricted access

SECTION 4

Helpful hint

Remember that passwords are case-sensitive and that spaces and punctuation marks are considered characters.

Helpful hint

If a password is lost or forgotten, access to content is lost permanently unless a DocRecrypt application is installed beforehand. A PIN is usually recoverable or easily replaced.

Did you know?

It is wise to store a list of passwords and their related files in a safe place.

Did you know?

- Not every file needs a password.
- Try not to use the same or similar passwords every time.

Password protection

An ideal password is a mixture of at least eight but no more than fifteen characters, and is used to access sensitive files. A PIN acts like a password in numbers and is usually much shorter. PINs are usually assigned by the company, or the user may select their own PIN. Most people who use an ATM (automatic teller machine) have their own PIN, which is used to transact business while shopping or to receive monies from the banks' machines.

To password-protect a file:

1. Open the file.
2. Go to the 'file' tab and the 'info' subtab.
3. Click on the 'protect document' menu and click on the 'encrypt with password' button.
4. A window will open for you to enter a password combining letters, numbers and symbols.
5. Click OK.
6. Another window will open for you to repeat the sequence of characters you have used for your password.
7. Click OK.

Encryption

Encryption is the process of scrambling the instructions (code) from the application that was used to create a file so that it appears in a different pattern. An encryption key is the sequence of characters that is used to scramble the code. This makes the file impossible to read unless a decryption measure is taken, which requires access to the encryption key. The file may be used only if it is *decrypted* and *restored* to its original code.

Encryption is the strongest form of file protection for sensitive information that is provided by the Windows operating system. It is also used to protect information such as a customers' personal details and credit-card numbers, especially when conducting business online.

FIMS strategy 2: preventing unapproved changes

A second method for reducing the incidence of intentional and unintentional changes to files is applying read-only access (*overwrite protection*).

Read-only access (overwrite protection)

The operating system (OS) of a computer sets out various permissions for users that vary from full control to read-only access. When read-only permission is applied to a file for one or more users, they cannot modify, erase, copy or move the file. This lack of permission (also called *write-protected*) can be applied to files, folders or hard drives. Read-only permissions help to avoid anyone making changes to the file's information, whether it is done purposely or accidentally. To apply read-only access to a file (Figure 18.4), follow these steps:

1. Right-click on the saved file in its folder or subfolder.
2. Go to Properties in the dropdown box, go to the General tab and choose Read-only.
3. Click Apply and then OK to save the changes.

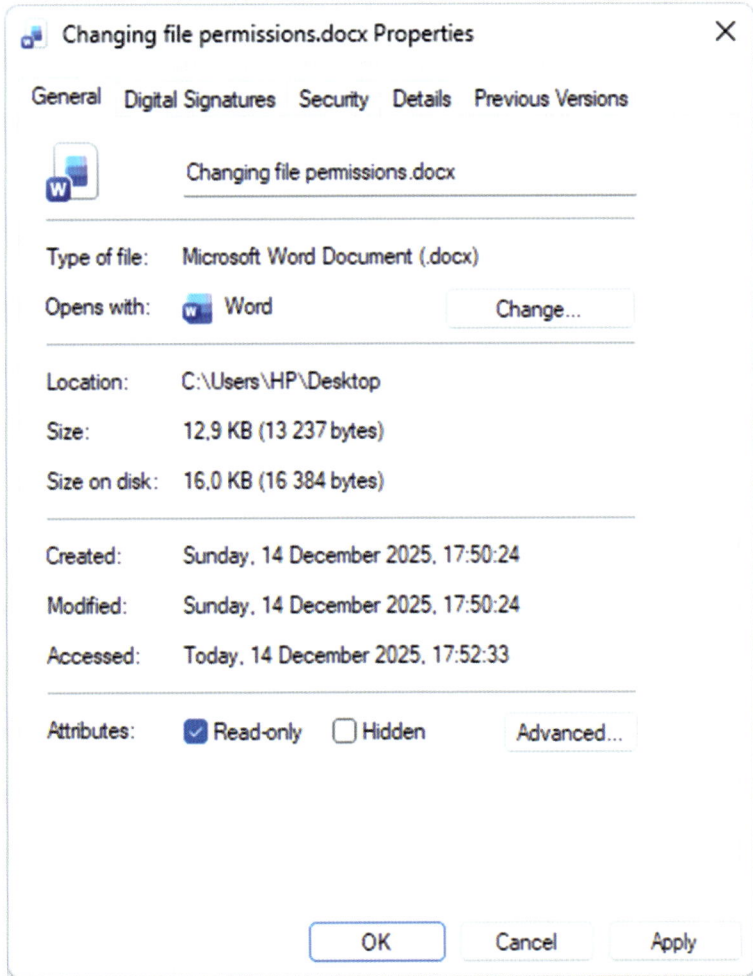

Figure 18.4 Applying read-only access to a file

FIMS strategy 3: implementing disaster-recovery strategies

Disaster-recovery is the manner and timeframe in which regular operations are resumed after a disaster has occurred. There should be a predetermined disaster-recovery plan that gives a detailed set of procedures intended to reduce the time it takes for an organisation to resume normal operations. The most important step is to develop a backup system, and the second step is to store the duplicates in either an off-premises location with sturdy waterproof and fireproof cabinets or in the cloud.

Backup systems

A computer's backup system comprises external devices that hold copies of important information, including the operating system. If the original data on a hard disk is lost or damaged, the copy can be used to restore the material on the hard disk. It is vital that businesses ensure strict compliance with the company's protocols for the backup system.

Fireproof and waterproof storage

A proactive disaster-recovery strategy is to have good-quality waterproof and fireproof cabinets for storing disks, tapes and optical media (Figure 18.5). Should any damage occur to the computer system, any information that is backed up can be safely stored in these safes or cabinets.

FIMS strategy 4: implementing cybersecurity measures

Cybersecurity is a vital consideration in **document management** as cyberattacks on a computer's OS can be detrimental for a business. These attacks range from corruption of files and their metadata to rendering files inaccessible on storage devices, and even destruction of sensitive files.

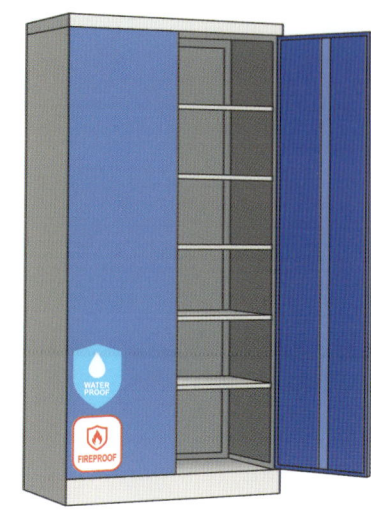

Figure 18.5 A waterproof/fireproof cabinet

Preventing metadata access

Metadata is described as 'data about data' because it provides information *about* the file, folder or directory that has been saved on a computer. Microsoft Word collects metadata about files that tells you who the author is, who modified the data, when it was modified and even where it is stored, which may be on an internal hard drive or on a USB flash.

If hackers collect enough metadata, they may be able to generate adequate knowledge to make a document-management system unsecure. As such, preventing access by encrypting metadata is part of good document management.

Antivirus programs

A *virus* (also called *malware*) is a piece of software that can result in very serious damage to a computer's system and connected computers and external devices. Antivirus software is used to detect, recognise and eradicate other viruses. Unfortunately, hackers frequently make or build robust malware, and companies are therefore always trying to keep ahead by subscribing to antivirus software suppliers such as McAfee®, Norton AntiVirus Plus, Bitdefender and AVG AntiVirus. Some viruses remove access to files or the system as a whole. Some hackers threaten, while others simply want to disrupt the workflow for 'fun'.

Firewalls

A firewall is a barrier between an organisation's interior network and access to exterior networks (Figure 18.6). It searches through digital media coming in from outside and filters it according to rules and criteria set by the business. This helps to prevent unwelcome data and programs from entering.

> **Did you know?**
> Malware is a shortened version of the term malicious software.

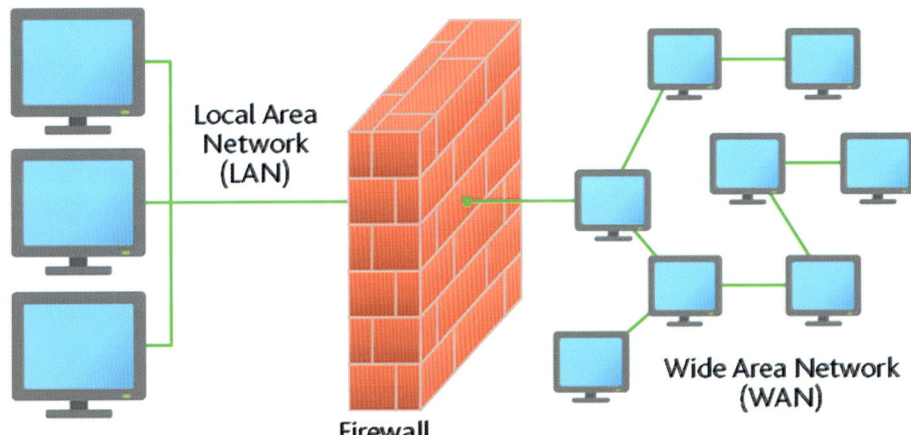

Figure 18.6 A firewall between a Local Area Network (LAN) and a Wide Area Network (WAN)

Version control and retention obligations

The integrity and security of files may be compromised when multiple versions of a file are created. This may occur on complex projects and/or when employees are working from home and accessing files remotely, and may result in a breach in compliance regulations. Version control is vital for reducing or eliminating loss of data, duplicated work and wasted resources. It also increases traceability and compliance with retention regulations.

Versioning

Versioning is the process of renaming a document each time changes are made, while retaining the original document. Versioning can be done easily without losing information contained in the original version, and users can identify/trace one version of a document from another.

There are different techniques that may be used for tracing document versions:

- Using version numbers, for example you can name and save your first typed document: '2-page letter 1'. When you have made any amendments, name and save the new version '2-page letter 2'. If there is another amendment and it is the last one, name this third version '2-page letter Final'. Note that all three versions will remain in the folder in which they were saved.
- Using the date the document was created to distinguish it from the date it was modified, for example the name '2-page letter – January 27 2026' is a different version from '2-page letter – January 19 2027'.

Version control

Version control is a system that uses a standard file-naming convention and version-management rules that all staff should use consistently.

One such rule is setting permissions so that new versions are produced by personnel who have been allowed access to modify and save newer versions. Preventing overwriting and accurate version retention should be accompanied by regular reviewing of the DMS to update indexes and archive files by trained and experienced staff.

The final responsibility of such staff is ensuring that the business meets the regulatory requirements for retaining certain types of processed data.

Archiving and retention

Data-archiving is the exercise of storing data that is no longer required for daily use but must be retained due to *financial*, *legal* or *administrative* **obligations**. It involves moving data from primary storage to secondary storage, including to the cloud. Examples of the types of data that are subject to retention action include databases and emails.

Legal and regulatory obligations

By law, some records must never be destroyed. These are permanent records, and include:

- business formation documents
- operating and partnership agreements
- employment contracts
- non-disclosure agreements
- client contracts
- terms and conditions
- privacy policies
- intellectual property agreements.

File-retention policy

A comprehensive file-retention policy ensures that information is accessible and secured for future reference (see Table 18.2).

Table 18.2 File-retention criteria

Criterion	Reason
Method of classification	Whether files are permanent, temporary, current or inactive, based on their purpose and retention period
Limitation period for retention	States for how long files should be kept before being destroyed: In many countries, business correspondence must be kept for at least three years, and financial records for a minimum of seven years; the reason for placing limitation periods for keeping files is that some records can be used as part of evidence in court proceedings (a legal requirement)
Method of indexing for traceability	An inventory of archived files should be maintained
Period for review and updating	Active and archived files should be examined at a predetermined time to determine their appropriate status: active, archived, or disposed. Criteria for decision-making include: • how often the records are used • what type of information is in the file • what laws govern the time for keeping files • how useful the information will be for future decision-making
Policy on file disposal	This includes what files are to be disposed of and how; several methods are available, including shredding, burning, pulverisation and degaussing

When an organisation creates a planned retention system that deals with files efficiently, it benefits the business since it becomes easier to retrieve files, save space and ensure good accounting practices.

Activity

Describe *two* items that should be included in a file-retention policy.

Types of documents in data-processing

Data-processing, including keyboarding, scanning and other forms of digitisation, allows the placement of records into electronic filing systems. *Machine-readable documents* can be read directly and opened by the computer in response to the suffixes at end of the name of the file. These suffixes are called **file extensions**, and they identify the type of file that is being created or retrieved. Table 18.3 describes some well-known file formats and the basic structure of how different data types are stored.

Table 18.3 File-extension types

Data type	File-extension type
text	.doc, .docx, .pdf, .rtf
tabular	.csv
images	.jpeg, .png, .gif
audio	.mp3, .wav, .wmv
video	.mp4, .avi
web page	.html
application	.exe, .c, .java
compressed file	.zip

> **Did you know?**
> What is happening if a png comes into your inbox? Someone has sent a picture to you!

Some businesses have converted human-readable (analog) documents into machine-readable documents through *digitisation*. Examples include *source documents* and *turnaround documents*.

Source documents

Source documents are created to record the elements involved when a business engages in financial activities.

Examples of source documents for *external* business transactions include quotation letters, sales and purchases invoices, delivery notes and receipts.

Internal source documents include pay slips, bank-reconciliation statements and petty-cash vouchers.

These financial records are used by accounting staff, and need to be organised properly for business efficiency and legal reasons.

Turnaround documents

Turnaround documents are produced by a computer to compile data to be input into the same or another system. For example, copies of a credit sales invoice will have to be sent to the billing department and the payment department.

A standard survey form collects data that needs to be entered into a computer for analysis and report. However, when these forms are created as turnaround documents, manual data-entry becomes unnecessary. An optical character reader can enter the data immediately into the computer without the potential errors of manually re-entering data. Furthermore, if a barcode or QR code is part of the digitised version, an analyst can search for a particular form among the many in the folder. Examples of turnaround documents include travel boarding passes, barcodes on products and cheques.

SECTION 4

> **Key terms**
>
> **archiving** Storing files that are no longer required for daily use but must be kept stored and accessible/traceable as part of a retention policy
>
> **backup system** Saving copies of important files and folders, including operating system instructions, for disaster-recovery purposes
>
> **cybersecurity** Methods of protecting computer systems, individual devices and data from intentional and unintentional threats; methods include antivirus programs, anti-hacking systems, firewalls, overwrite protection and various forms of restricted access
>
> **disaster-recovery strategy** A detailed set of procedures for resumption of normal operations after cyberattacks or lack of compliance with security rules by internal users
>
> **document management** Also called *file management*; describes the rules and activities governing the safe production, naming, registering (for traceability), access, use, storage, retrieval, disposal and archiving of files and folders
>
> **document type** Types of documents in a computerised environment are machine-readable, source and turnaround documents
>
> **encryption** Scrambling the instructions from an application that was used to create a file so it becomes impossible for the computer to read
>
> **file extension** Short suffix at the end of a filename, such as .docx, .pdf, .jpeg and .mp3, which identify the type of file that is being manipulated
>
> **file integrity** Refers to terms describing the conditions of files, such as 'uncorrupted' or 'available', which make digital media usable and reliable
>
> **file-monitoring** Examining files, folders, directories, databases and systems on a constant or scheduled basis to ensure file integrity
>
> **hierarchical/tree structure** A file-saving arrangement of different levels, with the highest level being the operational programs and the lowest being files created for individual entities
>
> **indexing** A process that organises files in a directory or folder to ensure that they are easily traced
>
> **malware** An application, such as virus, trojan or worm, developed to deform, steal or destroy information or cause serious damage to a business's computer system
>
> **metadata** Information about the author of a file, folder or directory; when the item was modified; and where it is stored (whether on an internal hard drive or a USB flash)
>
> **obligation** A requirement of a legal, financial, administrative or other regulatory nature
>
> **retention** Storing files that are no longer required for daily use but must be kept stored and be accessible/traceable
>
> **turnaround document** The result of formatting a collection of data by a computer such that it is inputted to all relevant subsystems automatically
>
> **versioning** Renaming a document each time changes are made, while retaining the original document

Summary

🏠 **Summary**

In this chapter, you have learned that:

- businesses create machine-readable records that must be easily and securely stored, while maintaining integrity and traceability
- manual filing of hardcopies may be necessary for legal and regulatory purposes, an electronic filing system's hierarchical structure for storage takes up less space, costs less and recovers more easily from disasters
- disasters include fire and water damage, successful cyberattacks and failed file-protection policies
- water and fireproof cabinets, backing up records in external hard drives and strong file-protection and monitoring systems should be operated and enforced consistently across organisations
- other management policies cover version control, as well as file-retention and file-disposal requirements.

Practice, research and exam-style questions

Multiple-choice questions

1. What is a *disadvantage* of manual filing systems?
   - A Managing the file room
   - B Procuring cabinets
   - C Indexing files
   - D Digitising files

2. What is an *advantage* of electronic filing systems?
   - A Access for users is easier
   - B Passwords are secure
   - C Encryption keys are available
   - D Access restriction is easier

   The following questions refer to the hierarchical structure used for storage.

3. Which file path represents a label for a stored image file?
   - A C:\Documents\Family.doc
   - B C:\Pictures\Family.jpeg
   - C C:\Documents\Family.exe
   - D C:\Pictures\Family.pdf

4. Which piece of text represents the drive in a storage address?
   - A The first piece before the initial backslash
   - B The piece immediately after the initial backslash
   - C The piece after the second backslash
   - D The piece describing the file extension

5. A *disadvantage* of undisguised metadata is …
   - A the availability of information for cyberattacks.
   - B its accessibility from any location.
   - C receiving bulk mail from unknown sources.
   - D that the speed of delivery may overwhelm the system.

6. Which strategy would *best* reduce the risk of malware infection?
   - A Installing computer security devices
   - B Hiring a systems manager
   - C Monitoring employee emails
   - D Installing antivirus programs

7. Degaussing is a method of file …
   - A disposal.
   - B detection.
   - C retention.
   - D retrieval.

8. The process of renaming a file after amendments is called …
   - A version control.
   - B versioning.
   - C accounting.
   - D internal control.

SECTION 4

9 Which option is *not* an internal word-processing product?
  A Source documents
  B Turnaround forms
  C Index cards
  D Machine-readable documents

10 Which options are *not* likely to be discussed in the same paragraph?
  A Barcodes and turnaround documents
  B Accounts and source documents
  C Document management and posture
  D File extensions and machine-readable documents

Short-answer questions

1 What might be a reason for your OS to apply read-only access to a file, folder or external drive?

2 Name *two* pieces of information that improve the traceability of a document.

3 What are the meanings of these abbreviations for file extensions:
  a .rtf
  b .jpeg
  c .png
  d .html

4 List *two* differences between manual filing systems and electronic filing systems.

5 a List *two* criteria that should be part of a comprehensive file-retention policy.
  b Name *one* reason why a business might retain a file.

Section 5

CHAPTER 19 Work standards and ethics in the business environment
CHAPTER 20 School-based assessment

19 Work standards and ethics in the business environment

> **Objectives**
>
> By the end of this chapter, you will be able to:
>
> - list and describe desirable work standards, habits and attitudes for appropriate interactions in the online and offline business environment
> - define terms relevant to applying ethical standards in the business environment
> - list and describe guidelines for avoiding unethical behaviours.

Introduction

The workplace of the 21st century may be a workstation on the 21st floor of a skyscraper building in the capital city of your country, or it may be a space set aside at home for you to work remotely. This chapter is about the knowledge and application of desirable *work standards*, *habits* and *attitudes*, including maintaining *ethical standards* in the workplace.

Desirable work standards and/or habits

Successful businesses usually produce manuals for employees that set out their work standards. A *work standard* describes the business's processes or procedures that employees are to adhere to. Four such categories are described in this chapter.

1 Document preparation and management standards

The first category of *work standard* includes the rules for the preparation of different documents. For example, some rules are standard for creating letters; other rules exist for proofreading manuscripts. A company may develop electronic document-management rules for naming, saving, archiving and retaining documents.

2 Work-process standards

A second type of work standard is a *policy*. This work standard may be described in text and/or in a graphic that describes or shows:

- the *why*, i.e. the purpose or objective of the standard
- the *what*, i.e. the scope of work; the sequence of steps may also be shown
- the *who*, i.e. who is to carry out the steps (this may be one person or a team); who will provide the instructions or specifications for the job; and who will check that the quantity and quality specifications are being met (*quality assurance*)
- the *where*, i.e. where the steps or tasks are to be performed
- the *how*, i.e. the *machinery* or *technology* to be utilised
- the *which*, i.e. the *health* and/or *safety measures* to be taken, such as mandatory breaks from computer use or mandatory use of personal protective equipment.

Employees are expected to know and conform to the business's guidelines, and that expectation is best met if the company has documented these standards.

One major work standard that should be documented is the company's policy on internet use:

- The use of the internet for private business, for example reading personal emails; scrolling through personal social media; accessing blogs, vlogs, forums, gaming sites or other inappropriate sites, is generally not acceptable during work hours. This should be clearly documented and any allowance, such as during breaks or lunch periods, should be expressly stated.
- The rules of conduct or **netiquette** when engaging in online interactions for business purposes or even in personal time should also be addressed. Unacceptable behaviours, such as poorly written or addressed emails; inflammatory or offensive comments; or posts that are disrespectful of the diverse nature of the modern workplace, must be clearly stated in the company's policy/handbook (Figure 19.1). Your manager/supervisor is usually responsible for monitoring compliance of netiquette rules. Failure to follow this rule may result in suspension or dismissal, depending upon the severity of the matter.

> **Did you know?**
> Netiquette is a made-up word that combines the words *net* and *etiquette*. Etiquette is a word for the rules of a polite community.

→ Activity
1. Who is usually responsible for monitoring compliance with netiquette rules?
2. Name *one* penalty that might be applied for a violation of a rule.

3 Performance standards

A third type of work standard comprises the universally accepted ways of performing one's job. These are also known as *performance standards* and include:

- being *punctual* and *regular* and calling your supervisor if you will be late or absent – this is considered **professional behaviour**
- being *courteous* to your peers and those in authority – this demonstrates your ability to work with others and as a member of a team
- *organising your workstation* and making to-do lists to assist in ensuring compliance with your work schedule
- *prioritising tasks* – priority might be given to reading emails, as they may include instructions for the day's work or may alert you that a task needs to be done earlier rather than later in the day; follow-up reminders might include notes to yourself or setting notifications on your computer that will prompt you to check on unfinished tasks
- practising good *time management* to meet deadlines for assignments consistently, or accounting for failures or disruptions in schedules
- maintaining a balance between speed and accuracy by employing procedures such as *proofreading* and *independent eye checks* before sending correspondence
- being *proactive* and *anticipatory* by thinking of possible issues and solutions before they occur
- maintaining *confidentiality* so that there is no unauthorised sharing of content or revealing company secrets
- engaging in good *hygiene* and *grooming*.

SECTION 5

> **Did you know?**
> It is important to look well-groomed even in online meetings with colleagues and supervisors.

Figure 19.1 The performance-management process

> **→ Activity**
>
> Name *two* examples of professional behaviour for office workers.

These positive behaviours should become personal work *habits*. Exemplary work habits are achieved by nurturing positive *work attitudes*. These attitudes become your *attributes*.

4 Desirable work attitudes

Your work attitudes are a combination of personal characteristics, ways of thinking and behaviours; they reveal an approach to work that should add value to the business. Here is a list of examples of work attitudes that businesses desire in employees:

- An awareness of personal strengths and weaknesses
- A sense of responsibility
- A preparedness to cooperate with others
- A willingness to work
- An inclination to keep learning
- A kindness that recognises and respects diversity

A sense of obligation to one's employer and positive *work ethic* are very important as more and more people work remotely (Figure 19.2). Many firms have employees that are working from home, located far from the main offices, speak different languages and work on different timelines. Robust protocols must be put in place so that teams apply acceptable etiquette and netiquette practices in their interactions with others, whether face to face or online.

> **✓ Helpful hint**
> Scheduling meetings that may start or end in the early morning hours for some team members working remotely is poor netiquette.

Figure 19.2 A work-from-home employee

Ethical standards

Working standards include the maintenance of ethical practices. When preparing documents, one major ethical practice is adhering to **intellectual-property rights**. These include moral rights and commercial rights. *Moral rights* refer to economic rights, meaning that the creator/owner should be able to earn money from the creation arising from their intellect. *Commercial rights* refer to the legal right to earn benefits from the creation's use, for example as promotional material.

Intellectual property (IP) refers to audio recordings, printed works, filmed works, artworks, technological inventions and processes originating from someone's ideas that were turned into forms that others can recreate or copy, use as a template or manufacture (see the examples in Table 19.1).

Table 19.1 Examples of intellectual-property rights

Intellectual property	Examples
Audio recordings	Songs, audio books, spoken-word poems, speeches
Printed works	Books, magazines and newspapers that display stories, poems, pictures, graphics, plays and lecture notes
Filmed works	Full-length and short films made for cinemas, streaming services, such as Netflix and Prime Video, and television stations; videos on social media platforms such as Facebook, YouTube, TikTok and Instagram
Artworks	Paintings, photographs, sculptures
Technological inventions	Microchips, memory drives, solar panels, hybrid and electric cars
Processes	Recipes; manufacturing, refining and processing methods

Figure 19.3 CCL logo

Figure 19.4 OER logo

Types of permission to use IP

There are occasions when the creator gives *anyone* the permission or licence to use their work under specific terms. This permission is called a **Creative Commons License (CCL)**, as shown in Figure 19.3.

Some CCLs are issued to encourage collaboration and creativity in other people for a special purpose. Lesson plans, lecture notes, learning activities, textbooks and audio and video recordings may be created and shared freely as **Open Educational Resources (OERs)**, as shown in Figure 19.4. In this case, the creators give up the rights to their creations to increase access to good educational content.

Some CCLs require only that the creator is named or acknowledged, but the person with the permission can modify the form and even earn money from it. Other CCLs are very strict and the form cannot be altered in any way nor used in commercial ways.

> ###  Activity
> List *two* creations that carry any kind of CCL and **two** pieces of OERs.

Ownership of, or intellectual property rights to, creations may be registered and documented in the form of **patents**, **trademarks**, **business names** and domain names. A fee is paid to obtain exclusive rights for different time periods. It also allows the originator of the work to benefit financially from their inventions and creations. Having a **copyright** for paintings, songs, poems, designs and symbols, and a licence to use copyrighted works, are treated differently. The first is protected by IP law, while disputes over the second are dealt with under contract law. Table 19.2 describes the different types of licences and Figure 19.5 gives example of well-known trademarks.

Table 19.2 Types of copyright licences

Licence	Description
Patent	A grant of exclusive rights, for a stated period, by a government authority to people who have invented a design, process, application or device
Trademark	Government authorities use laws to protect inventions of brands, logos, business names and slogans registered with them; trademark infringements are not tolerated by trademark holders
Copyright	Original works of art, sculpture, literature, songs, musical arrangements, music lyrics, music beats, music samples, fabric patterns, fashion designs, professional names, code sequences and other created works do not *have* to be registered but *should* be to be protected by national laws and international agreements from misuse
Licence	A grant from a patent-holder to someone for the right to use the property under specified conditions; the licence usually pays royalties for the grant depending on whether the grant is exclusive to the licence-holder or non-exclusive – a non-exclusive licence means other people can use the invention
Franchise licence	A more restrictive grant than other licences as it is usually accompanied by rules from the patent-holder, which must be strictly followed; usually granted in service-type industries, and the franchisor maintains the right to monitor compliance and withdraw permission with little notice
Domain names	Website addresses for businesses; usually comprise the business name and an extension, such as .com, .org, .edu or .gov. – these names are bought from domain registers, who ensure that they are protected from copying

Figure 19.5 Well-known trademarks

 Activity

Identify the standard symbols used for the following types of IP: Copyright, Patent, and Trademark.

Plagiarism

Plagiarism is the practice of using someone's ideas, words or products without acknowledging that they were not created by the secondary user. Ideas expressed in public forums; published works, including self-published books; digital content, including songs, phrases and photographs should not be copied without acknowledgement that the ideas, words, and so on are not your original work. If you have previously published your work, that must be stated.

Plagiarism may be found in reports, manuscripts and speeches, so the document preparer, editors, proofreaders and reviewers must:

- check for it and remove it; a number of applications have been developed to help ensure that copyrights are not violated
- ensure that quoted words or ideas are properly indicated using quotation marks and cited and shown in the reference list appropriately; this includes quotations from previous documents created by the document preparer
- ensure that permission/approval for use is obtained or at least sought from authors or creators, if they are known.

 Activity

You have an urgent school assignment, and it is a repeat of your sibling's assignment. Would it meet ethical standards if you changed the cover and submitted it as your own? If not, what term would be used to describe your action?

> **Did you know?**
>
> Creators using social-media sites often acknowledge that a photograph, video or piece of music they are using is not their own creation and simply make a general statement crediting the unknown creator.

SECTION 5

Key terms

business names/trademarks/logos Examples of terms, phrases and graphics that are protected by law from copying, defacing or other undesirable actions

copyright The right to claim ownership of intellectual property by the creator or licence-holder, once available in physical form

Creative Commons License (CCL) A form of 'permission to use' called a *licence* that provides different degrees of access to the intellectual property of others

ethics The standards that determine whether an action is moral, good, wrong or acceptable in a particular environment

intellectual property (IP) The result of creative efforts of one's mind that may or may not assume tangible form, but can be formulated enough to be protected by law

intellectual-property rights Moral rights or economic rights to IP, i.e. the capability for earning benefits and commercial rights, which are the legal rights to earn benefits

netiquette/internet-use policy The general rules of conduct for people engaging in online interactions, such as emailing or online meetings, outlined and customised in a policy document

Open Educational Resources (OERs) Creations, such as lesson plans, lecture notes and learning activities, shared, free of property rights, to increase access to good educational content

patent A grant of exclusive rights, for a stated period, by a government authority, to people who have invented a design, process, application or device

plagiarism The use of someone's written or recorded ideas, words or products without acknowledgement, permission or licence

professional behaviour/performance standards Desirable work standards, habits and attitudes for appropriate interactions in the online and offline business environment; includes adherence to punctuality, regularity, hygiene, time management, work-ethic confidentiality, quality work, proactive approaches

 ## Summary

In this chapter, you have learned about:

- desirable work standards, habits and attitudes for appropriate interactions in the online and offline business environment
- terms relevant to applying ethical standards in the business environment, including respect for intellectual property and copyrights
- some guidelines for avoiding unethical behaviours.

Practice, research and exam-style questions

Multiple-choice questions

1 Which statement about performance standards is *false*?
   A Independent eye checks will ensure that eyes are rested from the screen every 20–30 minutes
   B Calling your supervisor if you will be late or absent is considered professional behaviour
   C Good time management ensures accounting for failures or disruptions
   D Your attributes are recognised from work habits and attitudes

2 A firm's policy will generally include which of these pieces of information?
   A The name of the maker
   B The length of the document
   C The purpose of the work standard
   D Follow-up procedures

3 Keeping distractions to a minimum helps with all these actions *except* …
   A time management.
   B meeting deadlines.
   C work–life balance.
   D meeting work standards.

4 All these actions are professional expectations of employees *except* …
   A maintaining confidentiality.
   B a willingness to collaborate.
   C a sense of responsibility.
   D sharing personal stories.

5 A trademark infringement results when someone copies …
   A a slogan.
   B an invention.
   C a book.
   D a pattern.

6 Which option describes the right to be paid for use of one's intellectual property?
   A Economic rights
   B Moral rights
   C Legal rights
   D Ethical rights

7 Copyright can be recognised *only* when the creator …
   A applies to a government authority for recognition.
   B has written or recorded the idea.
   C registers the idea with a copy shop.
   D gives permission for limited copies to be made.

8 OER is an acronym for …
   A Other Electronic Output.
   B Open Educational Resources.
   C Overwrite Electronic Optics.
   D Open Experimental Reserves.

9 Social media posts containing another person's photographs might have committed …
   A trademark infringement.
   B patent deregistration.
   C licence withdrawal.
   D plagiaristic action.

10 Pat, a commercial publisher's proofreader, spots a paragraph of ten lines that she has seen in a self-published book. Which assurance indicates to Pat that plagiarism was *not* committed? The new document's author …
   A is allowed to repeat something she heard.
   B believes that it is permitted to copy up to 10% of a book.
   C is the person who had self-published the earlier book.
   D has included an acknowledgement of original work.

SECTION 5

Group research questions

CrestFall Limited has won a contract to proofread a series of three mystery novels from a first-time author. A contract has been signed, which details the scope, with a timeline of three months from the contract date, and fees have been agreed.

1. What is the importance of knowing that there are three books to proofread in three months?

   Alex, the proofreader on the project, has been supplied with the 'Work Policy for Proofreading Manuscripts'.

2. List *one* purpose that might be stated in the policy.

   All people hired for proofreading tasks must confirm in writing that they have the required language and technical skills to meet the client's requirements.

3. Name *three* language skills and *three* technical skills Alex might need as a proofreader (see the Proofreading section in Chapter 9).

4. As a proofreader, Alex must:
   - sign a non-disclosure agreement
   - work away from unauthorised people.

   Give one reason for each of these restrictions on Alex.

5. As an employee, Alex must
   - utilise only the company-provided laptop
   - ensure that the assigned laptop is loaded with a strong antivirus program.

   Give one reason for each of these actions expected of Alex.

6. Name *one* word-processing application and *one* strong antivirus program that Alex might use.

   All work will be carried out using the digital platform Google Docs™.

7. What are *two* benefits to a supervisor when Alex uses the digital platform Google Docs™?

   Alex is expected to take mandatory breaks of 15 minutes for every two hours of computer use.

8. What is the general purpose of instructions such as this?

9. Suggest a similar instruction that might be part of the policy.

   Alex will be supervised by a senior proofreader who will act as manager, quality-assurance person and client liaison.

10. Copy and complete the table with the senior proofreader's responsibilities.

Role	Responsibility
Manager	
Quality-assurance person	
Client liaison	

11. List *two* possible responsibilities of the client who awarded the contract to Crestfall Ltd.

20 School-based assessment

> **Objectives**
>
> By the end of this chapter, you will be able to:
>
> - suggest approaches for completing the SBA
> - identify the areas that require careful planning to achieve goals
> - simplify the research process for students and groups
> - examine the requirements for the portfolio.

Teacher notes

School Based Assessments (SBA) are an integral part of the final assessment of all that students have learned and experienced. The completion of these assignments involves:

1. identifying resource requirements
2. scheduling
3. student-supportive approaches.

> **Helpful hint**
>
> A printed copy of a student's submission might be a useful way to detect all errors and apply the mark scheme.

Resources required for students' SBA

Students need to supply or be supplied with a means of external storage, such as jump/flash drives with their initials. On each student's drive, there should be at least four folders for storing:

1. draft and practice documents for their portfolio
2. their final portfolio pieces
3. contributions to their research group's efforts
4. their final Research Paper.

Each folder, as well as the files inside the folder, should be properly labelled and include the year of submission.

Due to the fear of viruses, you might create a dedicated email address to receive draft documents and return the documents with your feedback on amendments. Students should be provided with your support 'until the desired standard is achieved'.

Scheduling

Realistic scheduling is required for completing the demands of the SBA. Because of the time factor and varying issues that students tend to experience in researching their topics, it is suggested that work on the School Based Assessment should commence at the start of the second term in Year 1. If students are exposed to the demands of the SBA from Term 2 of Year 1, it can be more hopeful that students will receive adequate time to complete their Research Paper, and give you time to make the corrections and amendments needed. However, preparation of the items for the portfolio cannot be neglected, so some general recommendations follow.

General recommendations

1 Identify the foundational knowledge and skills of this subject and ensure that students cover all that is required before attempting the initial elements of the research assignment.
2 Take all or most of the first term to develop mouse techniques and keyboarding skills.
3 Have students create their personal dictionary of terms with their own explanations, definitions, drawings, pictures and research notes in a sketchpad or journal. These can be compiled from various sources.
4 From Term 2 Year 1, dedicate time every week to guiding students on their SBA elements; this applies not only to their Research Paper, but also to creating and saving drafts of entries for their portfolio. These items can be refined later as skills are developed.
5 Collecting actual data could be done during Term 3 of Year 1. Therefore, the development of questionnaires or interview schedules and the identification of participants should be completed before the end-of-term tests. Hopefully some, if not all, groups will be ready with their findings by the first month of Year 2.
6 Introduce students to the basic features of spreadsheet, database and presentation applications. (Students enjoy moving beyond applying word-processing skills to developing presentations.)
7 The optimistic goal is a complete draft of the Research Paper from each group by November or December of Year 2, with finished Papers and Portfolios by February of students' second year.

Addressing the specific needs of the Research Paper Assignment (RPA)

The content, format and focus areas of the Research Paper are set out clearly on page 40 of the syllabus. The length of the Paper, the items to be included and even mark-scheme guidelines set useful limits to guide you. Each step throws up issues that require solutions and decisions. Table 20.1 provides recommendations for actions by individuals and groups.

Table 20.1 Challenges and solutions for the RPA

	Issue	Possible solutions	Actioning with student groups
1	Starting out in an organised fashion	• Discuss with students techniques for working in a group. • Show students how to create a one-column Word table, with a row for each of the content headings and a row to enter relevant text, as needed. • Encourage them to enter text into the appropriate row or section as they continue their research efforts. • Teach students about citing readings and keeping a reference (for citations) and bibliography list on index cards.	• Ensure students select a leader and a record-keeper for action items. • They should make meetings efficient by completing the task assigned to each student. • They need to draft a table, label the file 'EDPM Research Assignment' and place it in an 'EDPM SBA Research Assignment' folder. • Each group member should share materials of all work they have done via email or a WhatsApp chat. • Each group member should choose a different-coloured index card to show individual contributions to group assignments.

2	Framing the topic into a Statement of Topic	• One challenge in beginning the Research Paper effort early is that, if the syllabus is your scheduling guide, certain topics would not have been taught. This should not be a setback if students are guided into understanding the topic as a research area rather than a conduit for learning technical skills. • Direct students into thinking of a problem, i.e. the context or background to one of the suggested areas.	• Each group should choose a suggested topic statement or create one approved by you. • Groups should turn their suggested topic into a Problem Statement, for example, 'Cellphone calls have become so constant in today's world that they affect family life' or 'In today's world, family life is affected by constant cellphone calls'. (Note how important it is to omit judgmental/evaluative words at this point.)

		• 'Many people are complaining that the cellphone has become so intrusive that it is affecting their family life – Section 7 (Electronic Communication)'
		or
		• 'The most frustrating thing is trying to find an important item on your smartphone – Section 8 (Document Management)'
		or
		• 'Sampling other people's musical lines and beats without acknowledging them is very prevalent in the music industry today – Section 9 (Ethics)'
		or
		• 'Small-business owners must be tired from having to do everything for their business, including preparing specialised documents like financial statements. How do they cope? – Section 6 (Specialised Document Preparation)'.
		• Alternatively, develop or source a short case study or article on a topic that can be turned into a Problem Statement and then Research Question.
			• Each group member should read at least *one* article on the topic and make at least *three* points on an index card indicating *what* is happening (people's experiences), *where* it is happening (setting, such as country/community), to *whom* (population characteristics) and the writer's opinion on *why* it is happening.
			• The group meeting will indicate:
			  – that the problem exists and the Problem Statement can stay
			  – there are at least 1–2 pieces of evidence that support the existence of the problem (evidence should agree that there is a trend that has led to the problem)
			  or
			  – the group has to make a new choice and repeat (*no more than once*).
			• Work with students to identify the key terms in the Statement of Topic and define them, such as 'cellphone calls', 'constant', 'family life'. This will help students draft their Context/Background and Purpose of Research sections.
			• Students should draft the response under the first and second headings in their template.

3	Defining the purpose/ importance of the research	Encourage students to state *why* the topic is of interest, for example, personal experience, family-member experience, a message on TikTok, a song by their favourite artist, a discussion with peers.	Possible thoughts from students: • Interesting problem from hearing the statement/similar comment • Experienced it personally or observed it somewhere and saw the consequences • Would like to find out the truth or extent of the problem • Would like to contribute to solving the identified problem

SECTION 5

4	Drafting Research Questions that suit the chosen methodology	Quantitative and qualitative methodologies have different aims and therefore different action verbs are used. • Quantitative asks *what* and *why*, i.e. about causes and influences. • Qualitative asks 'What does [participant] think is happening', 'How and where and when is it showing up in [participant]'s life/the world' and 'How is it affecting [participant]?'	Ask the groups to: • research both methodologies and make a table of *three* differences, then to state which choice they are making, and why, in two or three sentences • use the appropriate first word that reflects their choice and draft at least *two* Research Questions, as follows: | Quantitative	Begin with the words *what* (to establish the features of the thing being looked at) and *why* (to look for a probable cause–effect relationship between the concepts in the topic statement)
---	---
Qualitative	Begin with the words *what* and *how* is (the thing you want to find out) being felt by participants (put a title to the group, such as students, teachers, parents, etc.) in the setting (such as a named or made-up school)	
5a	Designing your data-collection instrument so that the data is easy to collate and patterns or trends appear, i.e. how to ask for data so that you have some data to analyse	• Quantitative data looks at something only if it is *objectively* measurable and observable. It will likely use a questionnaire with close-ended questions and will count or create tables, charts or graphs of findings. • Qualitative data looks at how the individual is *subjectively* measuring and observing and whether there is a pattern of belief or experience emerging. It will likely use interview questions, or an open-ended questionnaire, to collate similar points, and tell stories as evidence.	Students can design their own questionnaires using tables, Google Docs™ or SurveyMonkey to: • share and collect participant information/bio-data • create closed (yes/no) or rating (agree/disagree) questions that help to respond to the hypothesis and be a source for a chart or graph or • create open-ended questions for descriptions of experiences and/or • set up interviews with three or more people using a preset interview schedule, with questions that require more than yes/no answers (at least three will give more chances of common-experience data) – they can use a smartphone to record what participants say, while trying to keep the participant to the point, and take a photo if they have consent (a picture of a participant's hands adds value to a qualitative presentation if no consent is received for a photo of their face) • prepare a permission letter with a tear-off slip for participants' consent • research online articles or a book on the subject.
5b	Ensuring ethical behaviour	• The permission letter requirement could be a circular letter ('Dear participant, the bearer is a student at …') with a consent tear-off, which would have been taught by the end of the second term of Year 1 among the word-processing items. • The questionnaire or interview schedule should state the specific purpose of the research at the beginning, starting with 'Dear Participant'.	

6a	Outlining the characteristics of who you will ask (population) and afterwards who you asked (sample)	Both methodologies collect biodata on participants, i.e. from a questionnaire or interview schedule.	Make sure the questionnaire or interview schedule will collect descriptions of interviewees.
6b		Students should write up the first part, and the second part after data collection.	Use tables to display information, for example, for cellphone use research:

	Total number	Male	Female
< 30 years			
> 30 years			
Employed			
Has company cellphone			
Lives in family home			

7	Data analysis and synthesis	Students will need assistance with the next stage: presentation, discussion and interpretation of findings. Data-collection instruments should be created in a manner that the student is able to collect the information, and people participating understand what is being asked. The following words and phrases should be connected to the particular methodology: *Quantitative*: • perhaps influenced by • may be caused by • on average, most participants/few participants *Qualitative*: • felt that • experienced • wished for • reacted to	If quantitative, the group can: • create an Excel table for different types of questions • calculate percentages and averages; produce pie charts for yes/no questions; produce bar graphs for rating-scale questions; use one that answers the main Research Question. If qualitative, the group can: • use a colour to pick out similar words in interviewees' answers to the same question (*coding*), such as 'work forever calling even on weekends' is coded 'does not like the calls from work', which shows feelings or experiences • make a concluding statement about how prevalent certain comments are and use a quotation like the one in the previous bullet as evidence • discuss what that says about the issue, *not* the participants. Advise students not to try to chart or discuss everything. Encourage them to write broad sentences that show possible conclusions from the data.
8	Recommendations and implementation strategy	This is a challenging area for new researchers. Remind students of the perceived problem and their purpose. Recommendations could be on either: • how participants/researchers/experts in articles see how the problem could be solved and/or proposed solution implemented. • what more could be researched to help solve the problem.	Student groups need to listen, discuss and agree on at least *one* recommendation from each of the categories.

SECTION 5

9	Conclusion	Remind students of: • their starting perception of the problem • the purpose they identified for the research • the context/setting • the participants they worked with • the advantage of their methodology and instrument. Then ask them: • what conclusions their findings lead to • the benefit of their recommendations.	Review the entire document and write sentences on some or all the listed sections, keeping the word count in mind.
10	References and appendices	Remind students to keep a list, which should have at least two entries and show the pattern used for APA style references. Note that neither references nor appendices are counted in the word count.	Students can look up the APA style source as a reference, if they wish. There is a wizard for creating an APA-style reference list in the References tab. Appendices would include the questionnaire or interview schedule, an interview transcript, the permission letter with tear-off slip, additional charts.

Closing tips to share with students

Students should use apps' built-in facilities (that is, wizards) as much as possible. Table 20.2 provides an overview of wizards and tips relevant to frontmatter, endmatter, and samples.

Table 20.2 Wizards and tips for frontmatter, endmatter and samples

Cover page	Click on 'insert'. To the furthest left, there is the 'page cover' icon. Click the down arrow and select the cover page of choice. Some schools have designed their own cover page for uniformity, and this can be included.
Title page	Ensure that the title page is suitably labelled by using a slightly larger font and/or bolding and underscoring; alternatively, use the 'heading styles' from the 'styles group' in the ribbon.
Table of contents	Creating a table of contents can be done on completion of the Research Paper; however, if students begin early, they can keep updating the table with additions or deletions.
Examination samples	Encourage students to look at past papers to see examples of possible items to be produced for their portfolio, for example, include worksheets for financial information such as paysheets.
References or bibliography	The APA style is to be used for referencing work. The 'references' tab is useful for ensuring compliance with the APA style. Students should ensure they cite their sources of information correctly. They need to keep a record of their sources (most likely from online research) to ensure that the referencing is correct. However, they should avoid using too many direct quotations. They should try wherever possible to use their own words to avoid plagiarism.

Portfolio

A portfolio is a collection of students' work displaying the knowledge and skills required to produce properly prepared documents. The foundational skill is speedy and accurate keyboarding, and it is recommended that focus is placed on achieving suitable keyboarding skills from Term 1 Year 1. The required samples are often a choice between items requiring similar knowledge and skills, but some are more advanced than others. Students may need guidance to choose wisely.

From Term 2 Year 1, students should begin preparing their portfolios, as it is recommended that, as each item for the portfolio is taught, students should begin preparing samples of the work.

The syllabus requires a total of 9 samples, which ensures that skills in using all four recommended applications are included. In alignment with the approach taken in this text, it is suggested that the flow of work starts with students:

1 being urged to prepare the simpler choices from straightforward Word documents, such as displays for Committees and legal documents, for example, students might prepare the notice of a meeting with an agenda, for storing in their dedicated folder
2 moving on to spreadsheet-application skills, with the preparation of tables (with vertical or oblique headings), charts, graphs and a financial document; look at the syllabus to see what are accepted as financial documents, and refer to past-paper questions to see the range of documents accepted as financial documents
3 following up with the creation of organisational charts or flow charts
4 then pursuing a mail-merge exercise – remember that students need to understand the primary documents and data source, as well as the positioning of the fields (especially when creating a letter) and the creation and saving of the database using the fields as needed (*customise columns*)
5 keeping on track with the use of the database application Microsoft Access may then be introduced, as it relates to the database creation used in mail merge
6 getting to do an eight- to ten-slide presentation (including title slide and end slide), using information from their Research Raper – the headings or quotations could be animated and used to create or import one or two appropriate images, or the charts created for the Paper could become part of the presentation; the Research Paper would also be the source of brief notes for PowerPoint's speaker's notes pane.

Final tips to share with students

- Label every sample clearly, for example, 'Minutes of a meeting with action items'.
- Place your name as a header on your page.

Conclusion

The SBA presents many challenges for you the teacher and your students. However, when students achieve a properly completed SBA, it is a major step in attaining a good grade in their final examination. You may feel that you are more invested in having them do well than they are! However, be assured that most students do appreciate the effort you put into nurturing their life and career skills during the period spent with them.

Glossary

A

abacus A very early device for computing, i.e. processing numbers

academic report A document that outlines a writer's knowledge of a topic, such as book reports and research studies

action plan The part of minutes that identifies the person responsible for actions to be taken before the next meeting

active cell A cell that has been selected for use

adapted input devices Devices redesigned to meet the needs of users with disabilities or specialised interests such as gaming, such as joysticks, trackballs, eye-tracking cameras, gesture-recognition devices and speech-to-text generators

adapted output device A device that is modified or redesigned to meet the special needs of users; includes Braille readers and speech generators

addressee The name of the person to whom a letter is directed

agenda/chairperson's agenda A list of items to be discussed at a meeting; a chairperson's agenda contains additional details on certain items to guide them

agreement/contract An arrangement, either documented or oral, where the terms, conditions, rights and responsibilities of two or more parties are fully and truthfully outlined; contracts such as hire-purchase agreements are documented agreements, witnessed and approved by signatures and stamps

alignment Where and how texts are placed in relation to the edges of a page

analog computer A computer that uses physical properties to carry out computer operations

animation The application of a tool that causes text, icons, pictures, other graphics or whole slides to appear to move, to attract or maintain the attention of viewers of presentations

antivirus application Software that monitors and filters incoming and outgoing data and prevents unwelcome data from entering and corrupting a computer system

application software (app) A set of instructions for the computer that uses specially-written code to execute input, processing, storage and data exchange tasks

archiving Storing files that are no longer required for daily use but must be kept stored and accessible/traceable as part of a retention policy

assets Items with monetary value used to operate a business

audio card Also called a *sound card*, *audio adaptor* or *sound adaptor*; an I/O device that receives signals from a computer, converts recorded or generated digital data into a vibrational pattern and transmits the pattern to other output devices, such as speakers or headphones

AutoSum A feature in spreadsheet applications, such as Microsoft Excel, that automatically inserts a formula to calculate the sum of a range of numbers

B

background An image that appears behind a document's text for visual appeal

backspace The key that removes a single character

backup system Saving copies of important files and folders, including operating system instructions, for disaster-recovery purposes

balance sheet Also called the *statement of financial position*; sets out the assets and liabilities of a business, including any amount owed to owners

bandwidth The data-transfer capability of a network, usually measured in kilobits per second or megabits per second

bank statement A document issued by a bank to its customers to provide details of the amounts deposited and the amounts withdrawn during a period of time

barcode reader A device that reads barcodes, which are lines of various thicknesses that contain basic details about products

biometric reader An I/O device that collects biological information, such as face and retinal scans and fingerprints, to ensure that access to a business's computers is limited

blank document The first page of a new Word file available for keying in characters

block range A selection comprising a column range and a row range that forms a quadrilateral space

Blu-ray Disc™ A portable item that companies and individuals use to store large files such as videos and movies

bold A stronger emphasis than *italics*; may be used to emphasise key words, technical terms or action items in a passage or presentation

borders Lines of different thicknesses and patterns placed around selected text to add visual appeal or to indicate importance

Braille embosser A type of impact printer that converts text on a computer screen into the raised dots on special paper

Braille reader A device that allows users to feel and read computer text in Braille as it appears on a monitor; it is programmed to push round-tipped pins through holes in the flat surface of the Braille terminal as the text is converted into Braille line by line

break A way to manipulate whole pages, such as keeping text separate through page breaks or changing orientations through section breaks

browser An application used to find places on a network of computers; particularly the internet

bulleting A tool to manage lists of items, points or other content using a non-sequential method

business names/trademarks/logos Examples of terms, phrases and graphics that are protected by law from copying, defacing or other undesirable actions

business report Information and analysis of business results to assist in creating or amending business strategies, such as marketing reports

byte The smallest unit of measurement for assessing storage capacity; the amount of storage required for a single character of text

C

cache memory Extremely high-speed volatile memory used for faster manipulation of data

capital Also called shares or *owner's equity*; the value provided by the owner to start the business (owners might be sole traders, partners or shareholders in limited liability companies or government agencies; capital is increased by profits and reduced by losses)

caps lock key The key that allows every letter typed to appear in uppercase form

card A piece of stationery carrying only essential data, which may be embellished by using certain font styles, colours and graphics; business cards, index cards, postcards and greetings cards are some examples

cell identification A cell's name/address/reference, made up of the column address and row address

central processing unit (CPU) The main compilation of electronic circuitry that understands coded instruction for processing digital data

centre-aligned Text centred on a page, but not at equal distances for every line, which may result in ragged lines at the left and right of the paragraph

characters Shapes (letters/numbers), marks (punctuation), pieces of code, sounds or symbols (icons) that devices and software convert into computer-readable language

chart A display of numerical and textual data in the form of bars, lines or pie slices to make it easy to compare categories or values or show trends and patterns over time or another variable

chat group Also called a *forum*; a limited gathering of people in an online space who are encouraged to interact over topics of mutual interest

check Function that automatically assesses spelling, grammar and use of language against built-in resources, such as dictionary, thesaurus and grammar rules

circular letter A type of letter, also called *form letter*, *standard letter* or *billing statement*, used to communicate similar information to recipients who may or may not be addressed individually

click Push down on the moveable parts (*buttons*) of a traditional mouse; there is one on the right and one on the left of a rolling ball or wheel

cloud-based storage (CS) The facility provided by an extremely large storage capacity of connected data centres

code The language used by programmers to 'speak' to computers – to tell them what to do and in what order – in the form of different combinations of the digits 0 and 1

collaborative tool A project-management application that includes access to emailing facilities, document-sharing and document-editing that aims to improve the effectiveness and efficiency of teams

colon A punctuation mark (:) that describes a row or column range when placed between the addresses of two cells

column identification Labels that use the letters of the alphabet or combinations of letters; also known as *name*, *address* or *reference*

column range A selection of two or more cells that are next to each other in the same column

column/field A single, specific piece of data about an item in a table

compact disc (CD) A portable item that companies and individuals use to store large files such as videos and movies

complimentary close A pleasant phrase placed at the end of a letter

composite key A primary key made up of two or more fields

computer system A set of physical and non-physical components that work together to carry out computational, data-processing and communication tasks automatically and efficiently

computerised environment The modern office space, comprising workstations furnished with electronic devices, mainly computers and wired and wireless peripherals

content Forms of digital media that include documents, pictures, images, videos and even audio information that can be prepared through access to applications via keyboarding

continuation page An additional page needed to cover a document's information

conveyancing document *Conveyance* is the legal process of changing ownership of property from one party to another; *conveyancing documents* include certificates of ownership, deeds, titles of transfer, memoranda of transfer

copyright The right to claim ownership of intellectual property by the creator or licence-holder, once available in physical form

correspondence The exchange of information between senders and recipients via memos, notices, letters, emails or other means

Creative Commons License (CCL) A form of 'permission to use' called a *licence* that provides different degrees of access to the intellectual property of others

credit terms When payment takes place some time *after* goods or services are sold or purchased

creditor Also called *payable*; a current liability – the people and businesses a business owes for goods or services received on credit

current assets That do not remain the same during the accounting year, such as stock, debtors, bank and cash balances

cursor/runner A shape that moves horizontally or vertically across a monitor or screen in response to a user's manipulation

cybersecurity Methods of protecting computer systems, individual devices and data from intentional and unintentional threats; methods include antivirus programs, anti-hacking systems, firewalls, overwrite protection and various forms of restricted access

D

data Material that can be converted to a digital form and processed by a computer; *information* is processed data, but is treated as raw data when it is to be subjected to further processing

data centre A building that hosts large and powerful mainframe computers or servers for storage

data protection Methods including firewalls, antivirus programs and backup storage for preventing loss, corruption and unintended access to data

data space A space where data or information (processed data) may appear, either from manual entry or from computer instruction

database An electronic folder, which contains a collection of related files set out in tables

database management The actions carried out to use databases efficiently

datasheet view A screen that looks like a normal table of rows and columns, which can be manipulated like a normal table; suitable for entering, reviewing or extracting data

date/date as postmark The month, day and year on which a document was typed or sent for delivery

debtor Also called receivable; a current asset – the people and businesses who owe a business for goods or services they received on credit terms

delete The key that removes text or images entirely

delivery The act of explaining, expanding on or displaying text and graphics of a presentation to an audience

design The choice of preset options or personal choice of colours, font styles, etc. that appear on every slide of a presentation

design view A screen that lists the fields required for designing a table as well as the formats that will be used to create (i.e. define) the fields

designation The name and position of the person signing a letter

desktop computer A standalone and compact computer

digital computer A computer with electronic circuits on boards that use codes to trigger actions

digital media Data that has been processed, which takes the form of text, numbers, images, sounds/audio or a combination of these, such as videos; also called *output* and *information*

digital video disc (DVD) A portable item that companies and individuals use to store large files such as videos and movies

diode Semiconductor that allows electricity to flow in one direction only, which makes it suitable for visual displays

direct-thermal printer A printer that applies pressure and heat to printheads, which strike special heat-sensitive paper causing many black dots to form the letters or images

disaster-recovery strategy A detailed set of procedures for resumption of normal operations after cyberattacks or lack of compliance with security rules by internal users

display Any document produced using word-processing functionalities that combine fundamental rules of document production with creative and innovative elements

document A type of digital media that is the main product of keyboarding in applications; while some are printed, others remain in electronic format for saving, manipulating and/or retrieving

document management Also called *file management*; describes the rules and activities governing the safe production, naming, registering (for traceability), access, use, storage, retrieval, disposal and archiving of files and folders

document type Types of documents in a computerised environment are machine-readable, source and turnaround documents

drives Long-term, non-volatile, internal and external storage devices, such as hard disk drives, solid state drives jump drives, pen drives, memory cards, and flash drives

drop cap A large capital letter that drops several lines (2 or 3) lines at the start of a paragraph or section. These are often used in newspaper articles, books, journals and magazines

E

e-communication Sharing digital media with others using the capabilities of computers and computer networks

electronic circuit A network of different physical parts through which electricity flows in ways that enable processing and conversion of signals

electronic document preparation and management (EDPM) The art and science of performing clerical and administrative document preparation and management tasks knowledgeably, skilfully and competently in the computerised environment

email Electronic messages sent to individual accounts at email addresses, with or without attachments

email address A method of locating recipients using the form uniquename@emailprovider.com

encryption Scrambling the instructions from an application that was used to create a file so it becomes impossible for the computer to read

end A navigational key that takes the insertion point to the end of a line

endnotes Short notes placed at the end of chapters in academic and technical books, papers, journals and reports to provide additional information, explanations, comments and citations

endorsement An assurance that a document is authentic, valid and legally binding

enter The key that moves text or images down to a new line

envelope A holder to enclose documents, designed to protect them as well as display a recipient's address

ergonomic A description for an office space and its furniture that has been designed for human efficiency, safety and comfort

ethics The standards that determine whether an action is moral, good, wrong or acceptable in a particular environment

event report Feedback, analysis and recommendations for improvement of specific company initiatives

expense/expenditure Outflows of cash for the purpose of making and selling goods/ services for a profit

external hard disk drive (EHDD) The most popular form of secondary storage, attached to a computer for power using a USB cable plugged into a port; if it is large it may not be very portable

extranet A series of computers, connected with or without physical wires for communicating with one another; open to public access

eye-tracking camera A camera that performs actions or moves a mouse pointer by following a user's eye movements

F

field definition Description of the field attributes, i.e. how the data in the field will appear, for example, by putting limits on the number of characters in the field

file extension Short suffix at the end of a filename, such as .docx, .pdf, .jpeg and .mp3, which identifies the type of file that is being manipulated

file integrity Refers to terms describing the conditions of files, such as 'uncorrupted' or 'available', which make digital media usable and reliable

file tab Tab on the left side of a window that has at least four major subtabs: open, save, print and close

file-monitoring Examining files, folders, directories, databases and systems on a constant or scheduled basis to ensure file integrity

financial statement A document that conveys information about a company's operational results (profit or loss) and its financial position (assets and liabilities) over a stated period and at a given date

firewall Software that monitors and filters incoming and outgoing data and prevents unwelcome data from entering and corrupting a computer system

fixed assets Assets that are owned for more than one accounting year, such as property, machinery, equipment

flash memory Memory that sends rapid messages to microchips

flowchart A visual representation of the procedures to be followed to carry out a task from start to end

flyer A single sheet for promoting events, usually prepared with text and graphics on one side of the page only

fn A key that affects the action of another key when they are pressed in the same motion

font A form of writing of different geometrical shapes, sizes, weights and slants from the vertical

footers Ways of communicating standard information about an organisation by repeating text or marks at the bottom of each page in a document

footnotes Short notes placed at the bottom of pages in academic and technical books, papers, journals and reports to provide additional information, explanations, comments and citations

foreign key A primary key in one table when treated as a field for linking/identifying a relationship in another table

form A document, designed with fixed placeholders, for collecting information from users for easy collation

format and edit Manipulate different types of digital media by applying rules or specifications and making changes as required

formatting The use of tools to organise the layout and appearance of characters, sentences, paragraphs or the whole of a document

formula A method for calculating a value for a range of values or a dataset, given the mathematical or statistical operation required

formula bar A window that allows the user to manipulate data in the active cell, including entering manual formulas for operating on numerical data

fully justified Text spaced so that it goes completely across from left to right of a document and aligns neatly and evenly within both left and right margins

function keys Operating system keys, labelled F1–F12, located at the top of a keyboard and used for predetermined tasks, for example, controlling the speaker volume

function library The subtab in a spreadsheet app that holds the built-in formulas and functions that perform mathematical or statistical operations

G

gigabyte 1 billion bytes

Global Positioning System (GPS) Technology that shows the location of a device by using satellites that orbit the Earth

graph A display of numerical and textual data in the form of bars, lines or pie slices to make it easy to compare categories or values or show trends and patterns over time or another variable

graphic tablet An I/O device that allows the creation and display of drawings and sketches

graphics card See *video card*

graphics Pictures, images and text effects, for example, WordArt, used to enhance a document or presentation

H

hard drive A storage area for a computer's memory

hardware The physical and tangible parts of a computer

headers Ways of communicating standard information about an organisation by repeating text or marks at the top of each page in a document

heading (column/row) A label used to describe the common aspect of the values in a column or row

heading Indicates the main subject matter of a passage, located at the start of the text it refers to; differs in font size, use of capitalisation, and alignment from the page margin

headphones Device that allows one user to listen to audio generated by a computer

hierarchical/tree structure A file-saving arrangement of different levels, with the highest level being the operational programs and the lowest being files created for individual entities

highlighting Emphasising parts of content by adding a colour, shadow, reflection or glow to selected words or phrases

home keys The central row of keys on a standard keyboard (**A**, **S**, **D**, **F**, **G**, **H**, **J**, **K**, **L**, **;**) where fingers are positioned before beginning to type

home tab Tab on the left side of a window that has five major subtabs or menus: clipboard, font, paragraph, styles and editing; each menu has its own submenu of commands

html Hypertext Markup Language; a structured method of coding widely used on the internet; it makes documents standardised and easy to read

http Hypertext Transfer Protocol; a series of rules that dictates how html is shared over the internet

I

impact printer A printer whose printheads (metal pins engraved with letters and special characters) strike an inked ribbon; the ribbon transfers the engraved words onto paper

income Also called *revenue*; inflows of cash from sales of goods and services; service businesses use terms such as fees, *commissions* and *subscriptions* for income

indexing A process that organises files in a directory or folder to ensure that they are easily traced

inkjet printer A printer that sprays droplets of black, red, blue, yellow and cyan ink from cartridges onto materials at great speed, while the material moves through a series of rollers

innovation The ability to combine existing elements to create a new element

input device/peripheral An internal or external device, connected to a computer via a cable or wire through the appropriate port or wirelessly using Wi-Fi® or Bluetooth®, that deciphers users' movements into instructions for the computer

input/output (I/O) device A devices that takes in raw data and displays processed data almost simultaneously

insert tab A menu with eight submenus, including commands for inserting tables, pictures, page numbers and other items used frequently when creating Word documents

insertion Formatting feature that includes pre-keyed text, page numbers, headers and footers, breaks and links

insertion point A tiny blinking vertical line indicating the active point for inputting data on a page

inside address The location of a letter's recipient

instant messaging A popular form of quick transmission of text, images and voice notes between two people

intellectual property (IP) The result of creative efforts of one's mind that may or may not assume tangible form, but can be formulated enough to be protected by law

intellectual-property rights Moral rights or economic rights to IP, i.e. the capability for earning benefits and commercial rights, which are the legal rights to earn benefits

interface Boundaries or points on devices that allow the exchange of information for computer operations to occur between the computer and users as well as between computer parts

internal hard disk drive (IHDD) The tangible, non-volatile storage device that is embedded in the motherboard and stores all digital media in a permanent form

internal proposal Detailed suggestions from employees for solving a company's problem or creating new direction for a company

intranet A series of computers, connected with or without physical wires for communicating with one another; limited to a particular organisation

invitation A request for the attendance of a person or people at an event

invoice A document that provides details of items purchased or sold, including amounts, descriptions and costs

italics Emphasis used to draw attention to a significant word within a sentence or to introduce a section of quoted content

K

keyboard Input device made up of knobs called *keys* or letters, numbers and special characters

keyboarding The set of knowledge and skills demonstrated through mastering the many features of computers and a range of applications

L

landscape orientation When the longer side of the page runs horizontally and the slightly shorter side runs vertically

laptop Portable computer that is smaller and lighter than a PC and lower processing power

laser printer A printer that uses an electrical charge to press coloured inky material, called toner particles, onto paper and then applies pressure and heat to fuse the ink onto the paper permanently

layout pane Also called the *slide development pane*; used to develop the look of slides by determining the content and its placement

layout style A standard way of setting out the content of types of correspondence, i.e. fully blocked, indented or semi-blocked

layout tab A menu that includes the submenus 'page setup', 'paragraph' and 'arrange', which help with the orderly and effective presentation of information on a Microsoft Word page, according to specifications for different types of documents

layout The structure or format of a document or presentation

leaflet A single sheet folded in different ways to show four, six or eight sides; used to distribute information on themes such as health or cultural or community events

lease A type of contract that outlines the period of time, usually 1 year, for which a tangible piece of property, such as equipment, owned by a lessor is to be kept and used by a lessee or tenant, who will pay rent

left-aligned Text starts at the left margin and moves to the right, resulting in an uneven right margin

legal document A written record of thoughts, actions and wishes that requires execution in accordance with the law

letter A formal method of business communication

letterhead A type of header used on an ongoing basis for providing information about an organisation, including name, address and contact information

liability Amount owed to lenders and people who provide goods and/or services on credit; a long-term liability (for example, a 5-year loan) has a payback period of more than a one year, while a current liability (for example, payables/creditors) must be paid back within the accounting year

line spacing The function that separates lines of text for reading purposes, preset to range from single line spacing to triple line spacing

link A method of providing additional information on a topic by inserting a highlight on a word or phrase that sends the reader to that other source of information

literary document A written record of artistic thought or creative expression of human thought and experience

locator A way of finding data (content/websites) and their sources using address protocols such as the Internet Protocol (IP), the Universal Resource Locator (URL), domain names and email addresses

locator technology A program that allows a network of computers connected to satellites to determine the specific location on the Earth's surface of a receiving device, such as a smartphone or another computer; Global Positioning System (GPS) is the best-known locator system

loss The difference between income and expenditure when expenditure is greater than income; it reduces capital

lower row The keys below the home row, consisting of the letters and punctuation marks **Z, X, C, V, B, N, M, ,, ., /**

M

magnetic input device A magnetic ink character reader or magnetic strip reader, which use sensors to detect magnetic fields or magnetic inks

magnetic ink character recognition (MICR) reader A device that reads characters printed in magnetic ink, commonly used by banks to process cheques quickly and accurately

magnetic strip reader A device that uses sensors to detect and decode information

mail merge A feature of an application that provides for the dispatch of similar letters to many recipients at the same time

mailable document The final version of a document that conforms to specifications free from spelling and grammatical errors, following the process of proofreading

mainframe A huge standalone computer with the capab**ility to process a huge amount of data in a short time**

malware An application, such as virus, trojan or worm, developed to deform, steal or destroy information or cause serious damage to a business's computer system

manuscript A text-filled document, which used to be written by hand

margins The clear spaces around the text and graphics in a document; they control the length of lines of text and prevent run-off text at either edge of the page

memorandum (memo) The standard method of communicating on company business with people inside the company

menu bar A row of terms and icons in an app that allows the user to find and use tools to complete tasks

menu Card of various sizes listing food items for sale or distribution to people at an event

metadata Information about the author of a file, folder or directory; when the item was modified; and where it is stored (whether on an internal hard drive or a USB flash)

microcomputer A stationary computer that is hardly ever moved; often called a personal computer (PC) or desktop computer

microphone An input device that collects sound waves or vibrations from speech, music or other sources for conversion to electrical and then digital formats by specialised software

minicomputer Smaller in size than a mainframe but with similar features, such as a high capacity for storing data and information

minutes The official written record of discussions and decisions taken at a meeting

monitor A device that provides visual displays of information using either liquid crystal or light-emitting diodes

motherboard The main board or compilation of electronic circuitry into which other units or boards such as the CPU, power supply, fan and peripherals are connected and controlled

mouse An input device that is clicked or rolled to move a companion image called a cursor to access any feature available on a computer ribbon or active page

mouse techniques A description of the manipulation of a mouse to instruct the computer by clicking, rolling, dragging, selecting and dropping

N

name box A window that displays the address of the currently active cell or the first cell to be clicked in a block range

naming convention The process, used consistently, to name a file or folder before first save, using a brief descriptive word or phrase, date of creation or modification based on a standard format and version numbers where relevant

negative effects The disadvantages to people and business relationships from overusing computers in office environments; these include poor physical and psychological states, as well as lowered productivity and costly fixes

net/network A series of computers, connected with or without physical wires, designed to communicate, or *inter-operate*, with one **extranet** – the most widely used is the **internet**

netbook/notebook Portable computer that is smaller and lighter than a PC and with lower processing power

netiquette/internet-use policy The general rules of conduct for people engaging in online interactions, such as emailing or online meetings, out**lined and customised in a policy document**

network-attached storage (NAS) A data storage location placed on either a company's intranet or on an extranet and stored on large and powerful mainframe computers or servers housed in buildings separate from the companies using them

newsletter A number of pages used to communicate information to a group of people with similar interests, in the form of articles about ideas, projects, events and campaigns

non-volatile Memory tool that does not lose data even after the electrical supply is disconnected

normal view The main view for navigation and editing a presentation, which is generally broken into three sections: outline pane, layout pane and notes pane

notations/special notations Instructions to a mail room, delivery service or post office on how to treat or process an envelope

notes pane A space that allows a presenter to add speaking notes, such as important points they want to say, without having the audience read it

notices Advice that a meeting is to take place, giving the date, time and location

notification Also called an *alert*; a sound, vibration, action or image intended to draw attention to the receipt of an e-communication

num lock key Key that enables access to the digits on the number pad

number keys The keys 0–9

numbering A way of ordering a list when the order of things in the list should be followed, for example, instructions

numeric keypad The keys labelled 0–9 and symbols for arithmetical operations (**+**, **-**, ***** and **/**) that form a keypad on the right side of a keyboard

numeric keys Keys labelled 0–9 that form a number pad on the right side of the keyboard

O

obligation A requirement of a legal, financial, administrative or other regulatory nature

online community An internet-based social gathering of individuals with common interests

Open Educational Resources (OERs) Creations, such as lesson plans, lecture notes and learning activities, shared, free of property rights, to increase access to good educational content

operating system (OS) Major application or program that acts as a platform for other applications to work efficiently and smoothly for users

optical drive Portable items such as CDs, Blu-ray Discs™, which have had lasers store information on their magnetic tapes

optical input device Use a combination of photosensitive cells to convert real objects and documents into images and pictures that are machine-readable

optical mark recognition (OMR) reader A special scanner that processes large numbers of forms

organisation chart A diagram that shows the governing and hierarchical structure and reporting relationships of a group of people related in some way

outline pane A quick thumbnail view of the slides that make up a presentation; allows you to see your slide order and quickly rearrange it, similar to the slide sorter view

output devices/peripherals Devices that display information to the user in their desired form, including text, audio and video

output peripheral Hardware for displaying data, which includes display screens or monitors, printers, speakers and projectors

overtyping A tool that allows the erasure of words to the right of the cursor while keying in new words

P

page down A navigational key for moving the insertion point to the bottom of the page

page numbering A tool that places sequential numbers on designated pages, providing an order that can be used as a reference or to find information in a manuscript easily

page up A navigational key for moving the insertion point to the start of the page

paper type, size, use The material used to record or print a message to be communicated; paper varies from flimsy to stiff and matte to glossy; sizes vary from the commonly used A4 to business-card size; use varies from the common printer copy to the heavy parchment for invitations and certificates

patent A grant of exclusive rights, for a stated period, by a government authority, to people who have invented a design, process, application or device

paysheet A document prepared to collect and calculate employee payroll information

peripherals Devices created to utilise the capabilities of the computer by employing its input, output, processing, and storage mechanisms

phablet A combination of a phone and a tablet; larger than a smartphone but smaller than a tablet

placeholder A preset space on a slide for text, art, videos or more; additional placeholders can be inserted

plagiarism The use of someone's written or recorded ideas, words or products without acknowledgement, permission or licence

plates/platters Circular disks in hard disk drives coated in magnetic material; information to be stored is converted by electrical impulses to electrons that can 'reside' on the plates

plotter printer A printer whose computer program instructs it to draw continuous lines to produce large-format text, images of many different colours and graphics on large sheets of paper, vinyl, cardboard, fabric, plastic, plywood or aluminium

podcast An audio-based delivery of topical information over several episodes; the word is an amalgamation of *iPod* and *broadcast*

port A physical or digital point of entry or access between a computer and peripherals

port Slot on the side of a computer that acts as a point of connection for peripherals to the motherboard

portable storage device Self-contained storage devices that can be easily transported between locations and connected to a computer using a physical port, such as memory sticks or jump drives

power of attorney A document that gives authority to someone, for example, a lawyer or a friend, who is trusted to act in legal matters in a specific situation

presentation/slide deck The file that contains the compiled information for sharing with the audience

presenter The person delivering a presentation, i.e. speaking and controlling the pace of information delivery

press release Also called a *news release*, *press statement* or *media release*; a carefully worded announcement sent to media outlets to share news and/or stimulate interest in a company

primary key A field that uniquely identifies a record, for example, individual ID numbers (N.B. a primary key must be chosen for database management and can never be empty/null)

primary storage Internal storage, essential to computer functioning

printer A device that places text, images, graphics, special characters or combinations of these on paper or other materials by different means, including thermal (direct/transfer), impact, inkjet, laser and plotter

professional behaviour/performance standards Desirable work standards, habits and attitudes for appropriate interactions in the online and offline business environment; includes adherence to punctuality, regularity, hygiene, time management, work-ethic confidentiality, quality work, proactive approaches

profit and loss account Also called *income* and *expenditure account*; matches the total of all income against the total of all expenditure to calculate either a profit or a loss; if a trading account has been created, the P&L account starts with the balance of that account (gross profit or gross loss) and adds any additional non-sales income against all other expenses to calculate net profit or net loss

profit The difference between income and expenditure when income is greater than expenditure; it increases capital

programme A list of activities to be completed in a loose or rigid time frame as part of an event

projector A device that shines a beam of light through different lenses shaped as prisms to project an image or video onto a surface

proofreading Checking a document for quality and clarity, including freedom from spelling and grammatical errors; repetition; and typographical and punctuation errors

protocol The standard rules that govern how data is formatted, transmitted and received by other computers

punctuation keys The keys for typing punctuation characters, which are part of the writing system that separates written language into units to simplify and clarify what is being expressed

Q

query A tool for retrieving and manipulating data inside the database

QWERTY keyboard The type of keyboard whose name describes the arrangement of the first six letters on the upper row of the most commonly used keyboard for those writing in English

R

random-access memory (RAM) Short-term, volatile, internal storage space for files and programs that are in current use or recently used

rapporteur A person assigned to record either verbatim or in summary form what was said at a meeting or conference

read-only memory (ROM) Non-volatile memory that stores data and instructions that allow the computer to start up

receipt A document that provides evidence of payment for goods or services bought for cash or credit

reference A combination of letters and numbers included in formal letters to help in tracing the thread of communication between parties and retrieving related correspondence

relationship The link between two tables in a database

relocating/reshaping/resizing The manipulation of graphics or other objects in a document or presentation

report A visual representation of information prepared for external viewing or printing; this is the processing result shown as a text document, chart table or other format

resizing The action of manually or automatically allowing a row or column to change dimensions to accommodate data inside cells

resume A summary of a person's professional knowledge, skills and accomplishments to accompany an application for a job

retention Storing files that are no longer required for daily use but must be kept stored and be accessible/traceable

ribbon A row of terms and icons that show the range of capabilities provided for EDPM by individual applications; A display of familiar **menus/tabs**, such as home, insert, page layout, review, view, with two additional tabs in Microsoft Excel – formulas and data – which provide tools for the manipulation of data, especially numeric data

rough draft A sketch or outline of content to provide a choice of display elements to influence decisions before actual creation

row identification Labels that use numbers from 1 to 1 048 576; also known as *name*, *address* or *reference*

row range A selection of two or more cells that are next to each other in the same row

row/record A collection of all the data about an item in a table, which therefore crosses multiple fields

S

salutation A greeting for an addressee, such as 'Dear Sir/Madam', placed at the beginning of a letter after the subject line

saving and retrieving Storing documents in files, folders and directories, and reopening stored documents

scientific report The results of scientific investigations or research

search button Feature for finding devices and applications easily

search engine An online tool used to find information quickly by accessing databases across the internet

secondary storage device External storage, not necessary for the computer's operation but helpful to users

separator A few punctuation marks, such as forward slash and period, that help a browser redirect a search to the exact location of a web address and an item at that address

server computer A large and powerful computer arranged in a system with a high volume of memory

shortcut A way to bypass the mouse by combining the modifier/control keys with alphabet keys, enabling the quick performance of frequent tasks, for example, copy and paste

signatory The name and position of the person signing a letter

sleep A mode that allows a computer to conserve energy

slide A page inside a presentation that contains content for display; generally laid out in landscape orientation

slide show view/presentation view The view that audiences see, with slides in full screen mode free from thumbnails and speaker notes; each mouse click or keyboard press (except the escape key) moves forward or back through the presentation

slide sorter view Provides large thumbnails of slides, allowing you to see the order of your presentation and quickly rearrange it

smartphone A highly computerised cellphone

smartwatch A highly computerised watch

software The instructions or commands that make a computer's system operational

solicited proposal A response to requests to the public or to selected people or organisations for the supply of goods and/or services

solid state drive (SSD) A small, portable drive, such as a memory card, flash drive, jump drive, or pen drive

sound card See *audio card*

source The original creator, website or location of information; graphics of other copyrighted products

space bar Key that places one space between words and sentences each time it is pressed

speaker A device that reproduces sounds generated by a computer

specification/scope of work A document that sets out the technical requirements of work to be done in measurable detail, including what, where, when and with what resources

speech-to-text generator An input device that types or turns sounds into text for entry into a computer system

standing desk A heightened desk that allows a user to stand while using a computer

start button A virtual button that gives access to apps that ensure the smooth operation of the computer, such as task manager, disk manager and device manager

status indicator (to, cc, bcc) An email feature that allows a sender to distinguish between intended recipients of a message in the communication process

stock Also called *inventory*; a current asset: items purchased for sale and kept on shelves and in warehouses until they are sold

streaming platform Online media-sharing tool that allows users to consume shared content without having to own or download it

subject heading A brief description of the main topic of correspondence

subtabs Access to the several capabilities of tabs – some contribute to one main task, while others provide a number of options or menus for EDPM; common subtabs include 'clipboard' and 'font'

supercomputer An extremely powerful computer that can perform millions of calculations quickly; often used for scientific and engineering functions

symbol A common or uncommon mark or shape for interpretation by the reader

symbol keys The keys for typing special characters; mainly located above the number keys and include @, #, $, %, &, (,)

T

table A grid of columns and rows for organising and manipulating content for proper alignment, indentation and line spacing; Tool that holds the data on a subtopic in overall subject matter, divided into rows and columns; a collection of similar records

tablet A portable, lightweight computer with a touchscreen and built-in keyboard, camera and microphone

tabs Major features on ribbons of all applications that provide key capabilities for creating, formatting and editing digital media; common tabs include file, home, layout and insert, and each tab contains subtabs and menus

taskbar An element of a computer's OS that allows the user to see and work with important applications simultaneously and efficiently

tear-off slip An attachment to a letter that requests that the receiver respond by providing some data to the sender

technical document A document that required technical knowledge and a methodical approach in its preparation, especially when becoming a source of information for contracts

template A form comprising standard text queries and placeholders for responses; created for frequent replication with expected changes in data; A page that has fixed formatting features, for example, places to hold predetermined information in specific ways, such as dates

terabyte 1 024 gigabytes

text movement A way of manipulating text, images and objects, including tools to cut, copy, paste, drag and drop, delete, insert, find and replace; items are selected using either the left-click and drag method or the select button

text box A facility that allows the placement of text anywhere on a page by overriding line spacing and margin defaults

text-to-speech generator A device that converts computer text into sound so that partially sighted people can hear the information they want to read

thermal-transfer printer A printer that melts wax or resin of a single colour onto thermal paper

thread A series of message exchanges between people based on a single topic

thumbnail A small version of all slides, which sits on the left of the screen for seeing which slide comes next and allowing quick navigation to a specific slide

title slide The first slide in a slide deck; supplies key referential information on the presentation, such as topic and presenter's information

touch typing The placement and movement in a particular order and direction of fingers to assigned keys

touchscreen technology Technology used to input data based on the ability of physical forces to respond to the electric currents produced by the body, especially at the fingertips

trading account Matches sales income against the cost of goods sold to calculate gross profit or gross loss

transaction An exchange of goods and/or services for money

transitions A tool that helps determine the order, sequence and flow between slides

trial balance A list of all assets, expenses (placed in the debit column on the left side) and all liabilities and capital (placed in the credit column on the right side) and ensures that both columns are equal in total

turnaround document The result of formatting a collection of data by a computer such that it is inputted to all relevant subsystems automatically

types of computers Two main types of computers are analog computers and digital computers

U

unsolicited proposal A detailed suggestion for the supply of goods or services, although the prospective client made no request

upload and download The actions of saving and retrieving digital media to or from web addresses or to personal electronic storage places

upper row The keys above the home row, consisting of the letters **Q**, **W**, **E**, **R**, **T**, **Y**, **U**, **I**, **O**, **P**, tab and some punctuation marks

usability A method of rating computer peripherals and features in terms of their efficiency and ease of use

user interface (UI) The point at which information is exchanged between users and computers; between computer components; or between computers and peripherals

V

verbatim A method of recording the exact words of a speaker

versioning Renaming a document each time changes are made, while retaining the original document

vertical style One of two standard layouts used in producing a company's financial statements

video adaptor See *video card*

video card Also called a *graphics card* or *video adaptor*; an I/O device that contains a graphics processing unit (GPU) for instructing a computer to assemble thousands of picture elements (*pixels*) into an image or video via a monitor

virtual keyboard Software that shows a keyboard as characters on a screen

virtual-reality controller An input device operated by turns of the head, arm, chin, foot, lip or even tongue

volatile Memory that loses data when the electrical supply is lost

W

watermark An image that appears behind a document's text as an identifier, security measure or copyright protection

webinar An online information dissemination tool that provides information and encourages broad-reaching collaboration

will/testament A legal document that sets out, in the presence of a person called the *witness*, how the belongings (*assets*) of a person (*testator*) will be distributed after their death by another person (*executor*)

wizard A programmatic feature of applications that support a step-by-step approach to carrying out processes

workbook A spreadsheet application that provides a file composed of a large number of worksheets

working papers Documents such as trial balances, budgets and paysheets, created to ensure that information and calculations are complete and correct before being placed in financial statements

worksheet/spreadsheet/sheet A page in a workbook composed of cells, data spaces and a ribbon

workstation A computer more powerful than an ordinary PC because of its greater speeds and memory

World Wide Web (www) Huge amounts of information located on independent computers across the world, which is freely available via links and keywords

Index

A

abacus 2, 11, 294
Academic reports 178, 183, 294
active cell 187–8, 201, 212–3, 215, 221, 294, 297, 299
agenda 114, 116, 122–5, 127, 140–1, 257, 293
AGM (Annual General Meeting), 121, 123, 125–26
alignment 83–6, 91, 93, 95, 143, 146, 161, 165, 189, 191, 202–4, 293–4, 297, 302
alphanumeric keys 55–6, 58, 64–6
alt 51–3, 55–6
analog computers 2, 11, 14, 294–95
animations 238, 247, 249–50, 294
antivirus 4, 14, 42, 267, 270, 274, 295
APA style 176, 292
application software, 4, 11, 44, 294
archiving 256–8, 264–5, 272, 274, 278, 294, 296
assets 38–9, 165, 184, 205, 218–20, 222, 294, 297, 303–4
audio adaptor/card 28, 30–3, 294, 302
AutoSum 213–16

B

backgrounds 47, 83, 96, 99–100, 109–11, 150, 152, 155, 289, 294
backup systems 265, 269, 274, 294
balance sheet 205, 216, 218–9, 294
bank statement 205–6, 208–9, 214, 216, 219, 294
bar charts 162–3, 196, 199, 203
barcodes/barcode reader, 19–20, 22, 28, 273, 294
biometric devices 32–3
blocked letter style 129
block range 187, 191–2, 201–3, 294, 299
blogging 148, 262–3
Bluetooth® 17, 22, 24, 47, 253, 298
Blu-ray Discs 37, 40–1, 294, 300
Braille 21, 29– 31, 294
browser 48, 162–3, 253, 260, 294
business cards 113–4, 149–51, 161, 295
business documents/lettters/reports 82–3, 96, 114, 116, 140–1, 178, 183, 294
business names/trademarks/logos 282, 284, 294
business proposal, 171, 176–7, 185
bytes 34–5, 40–1, 294, 297

C

cabinets 267, 269–70, 275
cache memory 35–6, 40, 295
Canva® 149, 237
capital 62, 165, 205, 210, 219–20, 222, 295, 299, 301, 303
caps 80, 104, 121, 152, 156, 161, 203, 296
caps lock 62–5
cards 20, 36, 149, 151–2, 161–3, 184, 295, 299
cash balances 220, 295
cash deposit 209, 214
cash invoices 207
cash sales 218
cells 64–5, 143–6, 150, 186–91, 193, 201–2, 204, 212–3, 216, 218, 221, 224, 294–5, 301, 303
central processing unit 3, 11, 13, 295
chairperson's agenda 114, 122–6, 139, 294
characters, special 4, 20, 22, 26–7, 31, 56, 63, 79, 104, 298, 301–2
charts 5, 25, 187, 196, 199–202, 204, 237–38, 240, 243, 290–91, 293, 295
circular letter 117, 128–9, 136–42, 290, 295
cloud storage 40–2, 259–60, 295
column break 100–1, 155
column headings 144–6, 192, 196, 203
column range 187, 191–2, 201, 212, 294–5
columns 92, 100–1, 124, 143–6, 155–6, 186–8, 190–3, 195–6, 201–5, 208–10, 212–7, 222, 224, 234, 295–7, 301–3
composite key 224, 229, 234–5, 295
computerised devices 2, 17, 118
computerised environment, 2, 5, 34, 38–9, 44, 51–3, 55, 162–3, 252, 258, 264, 266, 295–6
continuation pages 135–6, 139–41, 295
contract of employment 165, 167–8, 185
contracts 113, 164, 167–9, 183–5, 204, 286, 294, 298, 302
conveyancing documents 164–15, 169–70, 183, 185, 295
copy and paste 63, 106–7, 150, 302
copyrights/copyright protection 110–1, 282–5, 295, 303
Creative Commons License (CCL) 282, 284, 295
creativity 10, 143, 162–3, 181, 282
credit 20, 35, 205, 209–10, 214, 216, 220, 295, 299, 301
creditor 205, 209, 214, 220, 295, 299
ctrl 56, 58, 106–7, 110–1, 253
current assets/liabilities 205, 218–20, 295–6, 299, 302
cursor 16–7, 22–3, 32–3, 47–8, 98–9, 105–7, 109, 143–4, 155–6, 189, 191, 196, 212–5, 244–45, 299–300
cyberbullying/crimes/security/threats 9–11, 250, 267, 270, 274, 295

D

data 4–6, 9–12, 14–5, 18–20, 34–42, 139–41, 144–6, 155, 161, 186–91, 193–4, 196–7, 201–4, 223–6, 230–6, 253, 269–74, 290–1, 295–7, 299–303
database management, 14, 223–4, 234, 296, 301
databases, 9–10, 13, 116–7, 194, 223–6, 229–34, 237, 272, 274, 293, 296–7, 301
data centres 37–40, 296
data collection 291
data entry 188, 190, 223, 233
data labels 200
Datasheet View 229, 232, 234, 236, 296
data tab 193–5
data types 187–9, 202, 212, 227–8, 232, 273
debit cards 20, 35
debtors 205, 220, 295–6
deleting/overtyping 105
Design View 227, 229, 233–4, 296
desktop computers 7, 12, 23, 36, 296, 299
devices 2, 12–8, 22–6, 29–33, 35, 47–8, 252, 259–60, 282, 284, 294–5, 297–302
devices and data 274, 295
digital cameras 18–9, 23
diodes 26, 31, 296
directories 45, 52–3, 57, 105, 107, 264, 266, 270, 274, 297–9, 301
domain names 253, 261, 282, 299

E

e-communication 45, 51, 252, 255–6, 259–61, 263, 296, 300
EHDDs (External hard disk drives), 36–7, 40, 297
electronic communication 45, 251–63, 289
electronic devices 2, 13, 51, 260, 295
electronic filing systems 264–5, 273, 275–6
emails 131, 133–4, 138–9, 147, 150, 174, 177, 252–4, 256–3, 267, 272, 295–6, 299
encryption 267–8, 274, 296
encryption keys 268, 275
endorsement 164–5, 167, 183, 185, 296
ergonomics, 39, 52–3, 296
esc/escape key 56
ethics 277–9, 281, 283–5, 289, 297
etiquette 279–80
event reports 178, 183, 297
Executive summary 176–7, 179
expenses 186, 188–9, 203, 205, 210–1, 217–8, 220, 222, 301, 303
external devices 8, 22, 269–70, 298
extranet 12, 37, 40, 252, 297, 299
eye-tracking cameras 21–2, 294, 297

F

field attributes 229, 234–5, 297
field name 227–9, 233, 236
fields 117, 150, 224–5, 227–8, 231–6, 250, 262, 293, 295–7, 301
file-extension types 273
file integrity and security 267, 271
File Integrity Management System (FIMS) 267
file management 274, 296
file-retention policy 272
filtering 186, 193, 224
financial data 255
financial documents 204–5, 211, 213, 221, 293
Finger placement/positioning 55, 58–60, 67–9, 71–2, 76–7
firewalls 38–41, 267, 270–1, 274, 295–7
flash drive 37, 41–2, 302
flash memory 37, 40, 297
flow charts 143, 157, 161–3, 293, 297
flyers 84, 89, 92, 143, 156–7, 161–3, 297
fn, 56, 297
fonts 49, 52–3, 86–9, 93–5, 99–100, 129, 151–2, 155, 175–6, 192, 292, 297–8, 302
footers 45, 83, 93, 96–8, 109–11, 129, 297–8
foreign key 224, 234–5, 297
forms 2, 19, 25, 112–4, 116–17, 146–7, 156, 161–3, 184, 201, 223–5, 230, 232–6, 250, 252, 273–4, 281–2, 284, 294–8, 300
formula bar 187–8, 191, 201, 212, 216, 297
formulas 145, 187–9, 201–2, 204, 212–16, 219–22, 294, 297, 301
function keys 55–6, 63–5, 105, 297
function library 212, 220–1, 297
functions 32–33, 41, 44, 56, 93–4, 216, 220–1, 233–4, 250, 259, 295, 297, 299

G

gesture-recognition devices 21–2, 294
gigabytes 34, 37, 40–1, 297, 302
globalisation 10
Global Positioning System (GPS) 30–3, 297, 299
GPU (graphics processing unit) 29, 31, 303
graphical data 238, 243–4
graphics card 25, 29, 31, 297, 303
graphics software, 4, 14, 237
graphic tablets, 17, 29, 31, 297
graphs, 99, 186–7, 196, 199–202, 204, 237–8, 243, 290, 293, 297
GUI (graphical user interface) 17, 48

H

hackers 264, 270
hard disk drive (HDD) 37, 41
hardware 3, 5, 12, 25, 203, 297, 300
headers 83, 93, 95–8, 109–11, 116, 129, 139, 144–5, 293, 297–9
headings 88, 91, 93–4, 110–1, 119, 122–3, 135–6, 140–1, 144, 152, 171, 175–6, 180–1, 192, 194–5, 199, 208–9, 211, 297
hierarchical structure 160–1, 184, 264, 275, 300
hire-purchase agreements 164–5, 169, 183, 185, 294
home keys 58–60, 62–3, 66, 79, 298
home row 58, 60–2, 64–9, 71–4, 79–80, 299, 303
home tab 49, 52–3, 85–90, 106–8, 151–3, 175, 189, 192–3, 239–40, 298
hotspotting 253,
hyperlink 101, 244
Hypertext Markup Language 254, 260, 298
HyperText Transfer Protocol 253, 260, 298

I

IHDDs (internal hard disk drive) 35–6, 40, 298
income 205, 216–7, 220, 222, 298–9, 301
income and expenditure 205, 220, 299, 301
indexing 264–5, 272, 274, 298
inkjet printers 27–8, 31, 298
innovation 8, 143, 184, 298
input data 9, 17, 22, 303
input devices 4, 15–9, 21–3, 29, 32–3, 47, 63, 263, 298–9, 302–3
insertion point 48, 52–3, 56, 63–5, 99, 101, 106, 188, 296, 298, 300
insert tab 99, 101, 129, 150, 156–57, 160, 196, 202, 243–6, 298
instant messaging 254, 261, 298
intellectual property, 9, 281, 284–5, 295, 298
intellectual-property rights, 281, 284, 298
internet 5, 9, 13, 18–9, 34–5, 39, 48, 252–3, 255–6, 260–1, 294, 298, 301
intranet 37, 40, 252, 298
inventory database 20
invitations 84, 89, 114, 124, 126, 149, 151–5, 161–3, 298, 300
invoices 114, 146, 205–7, 220, 298
I/O device 25–6, 28–31, 294, 297, 303
IoT 256
IP (Internet Protocol) 253–4, 261, 281–4, 298–9
italics 83, 88, 93, 176, 294, 298

J

job application forms 146
journals 98, 109, 161, 178, 288, 296–7
joysticks, 16, 22–3, 294
jpeg 273–4, 276, 297
jump drive 41, 302
justification 85, 110–1, 165, 179

K

keyboard 4, 7, 14–7, 21–4, 44–6, 51–3, 55–6, 58, 62–8, 73–4, 79–80, 105–6, 238, 297–8, 300–3
keyboard mastery 43–53
keyboard operator 44, 46, 52–4, 78
keys 16, 21–2, 43, 48, 51, 55–68, 70–1, 73, 76–80, 105–6, 143–4, 294–303

L

LAN (Local Area Network), 252–3, 271
laptops 7, 11–3, 17, 19, 24, 34, 39, 45, 47, 238, 298
laser printer 19, 27–8, 31, 298
lasers 31, 37, 40–1, 300–1
layout pane 237–8, 249, 298, 300
leaflets, 156, 161–3, 184, 298
legal documents 49, 88, 90, 114, 164–5, 184, 293, 298, 303
letterheads 97, 104, 112, 115–6, 128–9, 133, 136, 139–41, 149, 171, 299
letters
  blocked, 118, 129, 135, 140–1
  indented, 136, 140–1
  lowercase/uppercase 62–5, 73, 92, 94–5, 122
licence 282, 284, 295, 300
literary documents 164, 181, 184, 299
lower row/keys 71–4, 79–80, 299

M

machine learning 255
magnetic ink character recognition (MICR) reader, 20, 22, 299
magnetic strip reader 20, 22, 299
mail merge 116–7, 139–41, 293, 299
mainframe 3, 6, 11–2, 35, 299
malware 9–10, 265, 270, 274–5
manuscripts 57, 80, 86, 93, 96, 109–11, 114, 239, 241, 299–300
margins 83–4, 93–5, 109, 118–9, 121–2, 129, 133, 140–1, 152, 165, 175, 179, 299, 302
memorandum 119–21, 139, 170, 299
memory 3, 6–7, 12, 35, 37, 40–1, 59–60, 281, 297, 301–3
memory cards 18, 34, 37, 40–1, 296, 302
memory sticks 35, 40, 300
menus 49, 52–3, 82, 84, 88–9, 97, 143–4, 149, 151–4, 157, 161–3, 175, 245, 298–9, 302
metadata 267, 270, 274, 299
microcomputers 7, 11–2, 299
microphones 4, 7, 12, 14–5, 18, 22–3, 26, 203, 299, 302
minutes 46, 66, 80, 114, 116, 122–8, 139–41, 285–6, 293–4, 299

305

modifier keys 56, 62, 64–5, 105
motherboard 3–5, 12, 32–4, 36, 40, 298–300
mouse/mice 16, 24, 47, 51–3, 295
mouse techniques 47, 52–3, 288, 299

N

NAS (Network-attached storage) 37–40, 299
navigation/keys 56, 64–5, 237, 249, 300
netbooks 7
netiquette/internet-use policy 284, 279, 299
net loss 205, 217, 220, 301
net/network 12, 299
net profit 205, 218–20, 301
newsletters 28, 92, 116, 143, 156, 161–3, 184, 300
non-volatile 35–6, 40, 42, 296, 300
normal view 237, 249, 300
notations/special notations, 115, 129, 139–141, 300
notebooks 7, 13
number keys 75–6, 79, 300, 302
number pad 56, 63, 66, 300
numeric keypad/keys 16, 55–6, 63, 66, 78–80, 300

O

Open Educational Resources (OERs) 282, 284–85, 300
optical mark recognition (OMR) reader 19, 22, 300
operating systems 2, 4, 12, 35, 44, 48, 268–9, 300
optical character recognition (OCR) 19, 162–3
optical drive 40, 300
optical input devices 15, 18, 22, 300
organisation chart/flowchart 160–3, 184, 300
output device/peripheral, 25, 29, 31, 300
overwrite protection 267–8, 274, 295
owner's equity 219, 295

P

page numbering 96, 109–11, 300
page setup 49, 52–3, 83, 94, 116, 158, 250, 298
paper sizes 94, 112–4, 118–9, 129, 136, 140–1, 151–2, 156, 162–3, 165, 175
passwords 47, 234, 260, 267–8, 275
patents 267, 282–4, 300
paysheet 210–11, 215, 220, 292, 300, 303
peripherals 3, 5, 12, 15, 17–34, 38–40, 44, 46–7, 299–300, 303
phablet 8 11–4, 17, 32–3, 300
pie charts 162–3, 196, 198, 200, 202–3, 215, 291
plagiarism 283–5, 292, 300
podcast 254, 261–3, 300
Portable Document Format (PDF) 58, 64–5
portfolios 137, 287–88, 292–93
ports 4, 12, 15, 22, 29, 34, 36–40, 297–8, 300
presentation 14, 17, 147, 149, 196, 200–2, 204, 237–44, 246–50, 288, 291, 293–4, 296–8, 300–3

press release 180–1, 184, 301
primary key 224–5, 229, 234–6, 295, 297, 301
printers 7, 12, 25–9, 31–3, 48, 192, 196, 294, 296, 298, 300–2
professional behaviour 279–80, 285
profit 205, 210, 216–20, 295, 297, 301, 303
profit and loss account 205, 216–8, 220, 301
projectors 5, 12, 14, 25, 29, 31–3, 300–1
proofreading 70, 79, 81, 96–111, 129, 133, 164, 279, 299, 301
protocols 2, 12, 41, 252–3, 261, 301
punctuation keys, 79, 301

Q

QR code 20, 273
qualitative data 290–1
quantitative data 290
queries 133, 223–4, 230–6, 301
questionnaires open-ended, 146, 290
QWERTY keyboard 16, 55, 63–5, 301

R

radio 28, 180, 182, 253
(RAM) random-access memory (RAM) 35–6, 41, 301
receipts 113–14, 130–32, 205–7, 220, 261, 273, 300–301
relational database 223–25, 236
relocating/reshaping/resizing 245, 249, 301
reports 97–8, 100, 109, 125–6, 175, 178–9, 201–2, 223, 227, 230, 233–5, 296–7
resizing 200–1, 301
restart 48, 52–3
resume 148, 162–3, 178
retention, 264–5, 272, 274–5, 294, 301
retrieving 31, 51–3, 82, 139, 230, 234, 264, 266, 296, 301, 303
revenues and expenses 211
ribbon 44, 48–53, 57–8, 82, 84–9, 96, 99, 106, 108, 186, 196, 200–1, 231–2, 301–3
robotics 9–10, 256
rows 58, 92, 143–6, 184, 186–8, 190–3, 201–4, 208–13, 224, 228–9, 234, 288, 295, 301–2

S

safety practices 38–9
salutation 118, 128, 136, 138–41, 250, 301
SBA (School-based assessment) 116, 137, 140–1, 277, 287, 289, 291, 293
Scientific reports 178, 184, 301
scope of work 170, 174–5, 185, 278
server computer/servers 6, 12, 35, 37, 40, 253, 256–7, 296, 299, 302
shortcuts 16, 51, 56, 63, 83, 102–3, 105, 302
slides 4, 202, 237–8, 240–50, 293–4, 296, 298, 300, 302–3
smartphone/smartwatch 8, 12–3, 16–8, 29–31, 252, 256, 289–90, 299–300, 302
software 3–5, 7–8, 10, 12–3, 16–7, 19, 22, 29–30, 38–40, 44, 101, 253–4, 259–60, 294–5, 297, 302–3

sort 49, 144, 194, 202, 221–2, 226, 230, 232, 250, 252, 257
sound adaptor/cards 25, 28, 30–3, 294, 302
source documents, 86, 95, 100, 106–7, 178, 204, 206, 208, 221, 273–4, 276, 296
space bar 56, 58–60, 63–7, 69, 71–2, 76–7, 302
spaced caps 104, 119, 123
speakers 5, 12, 25–6, 28, 30–3, 139, 203, 294, 300, 302–3
special effects 83, 89, 94, 244, 249–50
SSDs (Solid state drives) 37, 40–1, 296, 302
storage capacity 5, 34–6, 38–42, 252, 263, 265, 270, 294, 296, 300–1
streaming platforms, 10, 254, 261–2, 302
sum and average 216
supercomputer 6, 12, 14, 32–3, 302
SWOT analyses 178
symbols/symbol keys 47, 66, 74, 76–80, 83, 96, 98–100, 105, 109–11, 231–2, 240, 243, 300, 302

T

table of contents 175–7, 292
tablet 8, 11–3, 16–7, 88, 252, 300, 302
technical documents/reports 98, 164, 170, 176, 178–9, 184–5, 302
templates 64–5, 146–7, 149, 152, 161–4, 175, 184, 281, 289, 302
terabytes 34–6, 41, 302
text effects 89, 94, 99, 129, 152, 161–3, 170, 177, 245, 249, 297
text-to-speech generator 29, 31, 302
thermal paper/printers 27–8, 31–3, 113, 302
thumbnails 237–8, 247, 249, 302
title page 176–77, 292
title slide 239, 249–50, 293, 303
toggle keys 56, 62, 64–5, 78
touchscreen 7–8, 12, 14, 17, 22–3, 26, 32–3, 48, 302–3
trading account 205, 216–7, 220, 301, 303
transitions 238, 246–7, 249–50, 303
trial balances 205, 209–10, 213, 216, 220, 303
turnaround documents 273–4, 276, 296, 303

U

unauthorised access 267
unique identifier, common 224
Universal Resource Locator See URL
uppercase 62–3, 66–71, 73–4, 89, 92, 94, 103–4, 119, 123, 165, 301, 303
URL (Universal Resource Locator) 74, 253–4, 261–2, 299
usability 17, 22, 267, 303
USB 5, 36, 40–1, 54, 270, 274, 297, 299
user interface 15, 22, 303
user manual 157

V

VAT (value added taxes) 207
video adaptor/card 25, 29, 31–33, 297, 303
videoconferences 9, 19, 24, 254
virtual keyboard 16, 22–3, 303
viruses 9–10, 38–9, 234, 265, 270, 287
voice-to-text generator 23
VOIP (Voice Over Internet Protocol) 254–5
volatile 35–6, 41, 301, 303

W

WAN (Wide Area Network) 253, 271
watermarks 83, 96, 99–100, 110–1, 303
web browsers 4, 253
website 128, 131–2, 134, 138, 147, 150, 156, 162–3, 177, 180–1, 249, 252–3, 262–3, 302
Wi-Fi® 22, 24, 48, 253, 298
will/testament 184, 303
wired ports 5
wireless 17, 47, 253
work standards and ethics 277–9, 281, 283, 285
workstations 7, 12–3, 39, 45, 47, 51, 92, 278–9, 295, 303
World Wide Web 5, 12, 252, 255, 303
worm 274, 299

Y

YouTube 35, 255, 281

Z

zip 74, 273
Zoom 254

Acknowledgements

The Publishers would like to thank the following for permission to reproduce copyright material:

Text acknowledgments

pp. 4, 253 Google™ search engine is a trademark of Google LLC; **pp. 4, 254-255, 286, 290** Google Docs™ is a trademark of Google LLC; **pp. 4, 38, 48-51, 53, 57-58, 63-64, 82-93, 96, 98, 100-105, 112 116-118, 129, 136, 140-145, 149-150, 152, 155, 157-158, 161-162, 164, 178, 186-250, 253-255, 270, 288, 291, 293-294, 296-299, 301** Used with permission from Microsoft; **pp. 5, 26** 2026 © All Rights Reserved. HDMI; **pp. 17, 22, 24, 47, 253, 298, 304** © 2026 BLUETOOTH SIG, INC. ALL RIGHTS RESERVED; **pp. 18, 156, 255, 288** © 2026 Meta; **pp. 22, 25, 26, 48, 253, 398** © 2025 Wi-Fi Alliance. All rights reserved; **pp. 33, 35, 255-7, 281, 307** YouTube is a trademark of Google LLC; **p. 38** Google Drive™ is a trademark of Google LLC; **pp. 38, 254** Google Workspace™ is a trademark of Google LLC; **pp. 40, 256** Gmail™ is a trademark of Google LLC; **p. 149** 2024 All rights reserved Placeit by envato; **pp. 149, 237, 304** © 2026 All Rights Reserved. Canva®; **pp. 181, 255, 281** © 2026 Meta; **pp. 181, 255, 281** © 2026 Meta; **pp. 181, 255, 289** © 2026 TikTok; **p. 186** Google Sheets™ is a trademark of Google LLC; **p. 186** Copyright © 2026 Apple Inc. All rights reserved; **p. 186** © 2026 Intuit Inc. All rights reserved; **p. 237** Google Slides™ is a trademark of Google LLC; **p. 237** © 2025 Prezi Inc; **p. 237; p. 237; p. 253** Chrome™ is a trademark of Google LLC; **p. 253** Firefox is a trademark of the Mozilla Foundation in the U.S. and other countries; **p. 254** Google Meet™ is a trademark of Google LLC; **p. 254; pp. 254, 307** Copyright ©2025 Zoom Communications, Inc. All rights reserved; **p. 255** Copyright © 2024 Atlassian; **p. 255** © 37signals LLC; **p. 255** © Copyright 2026 Sprout Social, Inc. All Rights Reserved; **p. 255** © 2005-2026 ProProfs; **p. 255; p. 270** © 2026 McAfee, LLC. All Rights Reserved; **p. 270** Copyright © 2025 Gen Digital Inc; **p. 270** Copyright © 1997-2025 Bitdefender; **p. 270** © 2025 Gen Digital Inc. All rights reserved; **p. 281** © 1997-2026 Netflix, Inc; **p. 281** © 1996-2026, Amazon.com, Inc; **p. 290** Copyright © 1999-2026 SurveyMonkey.

Photo acknowledgements

p. 3 *tl* © MainlightPhoto.com/stock.adobe.com; **p. 3** *tr* © Belish/stock.adobe.com; **p. 3** *bc* © stockphoto-graf/stock.adobe.com; **p. 5** *tl* © jipen/stock.adobe.com; **p. 6** *cr* © vladimircaribb/stock.adobe.com; **p. 6** *cr*, **p. 34** *bc* © Gorodenkoff/stock.adobe.com; **p. 6** *br* © tab62/stock.adobe.com; **p. 7** *tr* © Denis Rozhnovsky/stock.adobe.com; **p. 7** *cr* © maxoidos/stock.adobe.com; **p. 7** *cr* © BillionPhotos.com/stock.adobe.com; **p. 8** *tr* © frog/stock.adobe.com; **p. 8** *cr* © HelgaQ/stock.adobe.com; **p. 8** *cr* © Marcela Ruty Romero/stock.adobe.com; **p. 16** *cc*, **p. 55** *cc*, **p. 62** *tc*, *bc*, **p. 66** *bc*, **p. 78** *bc* © Gresei/stock.adobe.com; **p. 16** *bc* © azure/stock.adobe.com; **p. 16** *bc* © nikkytok/stock.adobe.com; **p. 16** *br* © Emre Akkoyun/stock.adobe.com; **p. 17** *bl* © Alina/stock.adobe.com; **p. 17** *br* © DragonImages/stock.adobe.com; **p. 18** *cl* © Ricardo/stock.adobe.com; **p. 18** *cr* © paffy/stock.adobe.com; **p. 19** *tr* © mehaniq41/stock.adobe.com; **p. 19** *cl* © Elles Rijsdijk/stock.adobe.com; **p. 19** *cr* © Song_about_summer/stock.adobe.com; **p. 19** *bc* © bonnontawat/stock.adobe.com; **p. 19** *br* © Swapan/stock.adobe.com; **p. 20** *tc* © vchalup/stock.adobe.com; **p. 20** *tr* © Yurik_1000/stock.adobe.com; **p. 20** *bc* © Farknot Architect/stock.adobe.com; **p. 21** *cc* © Chansom Pantip/stock.adobe.com; **p. 26** *cc* © Alla Chesnokova/stock.adobe.com; **p. 26** *bc* © kuremo/stock.adobe.com; **p. 26** *br* © MSTTANZILA/stock.adobe.com; **p. 27** *tr* © Destina/stock.adobe.com; **p. 27** *cc* © Wire_man/stock.adobe.com; **p. 27** *cr* © jannoon028/stock.adobe.com; **p. 27** *br* © PL.TH/stock.adobe.com; **p. 28** *tr* © nikshor/stock.adobe.com; **p. 28** *bc* © Adil/stock.adobe.com; **p. 29** *br* © Mihail/stock.adobe.com; **p. 30** *tl* © bonnontawat/stock.adobe.com; **p. 30** *tr* © Rawpixel.com/stock.adobe.com; **p. 36** *cr* © NilsZ/stock.adobe.com; **p. 36** *cr* © Gorodenkoff/stock.adobe.com; **p. 36** *br* © mbongo/stock.adobe.com; **p. 37** *cl* © Emoji Smileys People/stock.adobe.com; **p. 37** *cc* © ILYA AKINSHIN/stock.adobe.com; **p. 37** *cr* © ArtyArt/stock.adobe.com; **p. 46** *tr* © ChayTee/stock.adobe.com; **p. 47** *cr* © Sejal/stock.adobe.com; **p. 49** *cc*, **p. 49** *tr*, **p. 50** *cr*, *br* **p. 51** *tr*, **p. 54** *cl*, **p. 57** *cr*, **p. 84** *cr*, **p. 85** *cc*, **p. 86** *tc*, **p. 87** *tc*, *cc*, **p. 89** *bc*, **p. 90** *br*, **p. 91** *tr*, **p. 96** *br*, **p. 144** *cc*, **p. 158** *cc*, **p. 188** *cc*, **p. 189** *cc*, *bl*, *br*, **p. 190** *cc*, **p. 191** *bc*, **p. 192** *cc*, **p. 195** *cc*, *cc*, **p. 196** *tc*, *bc*, **p. 198** *cc*, **p. 199** *tc*, **p. 200** *cc*, **p. 212** *cc*, **p. 213** *tl*, **p. 226** *bc*, **p. 227** *cc*, **p. 229** *tc*, **p. 230** *tc*, **p. 233** *cc*, *bl*, **p. 239** *cc*, **p. 240** *cc*, **p. 241** *tc*, **p. 242** *tc*, **p. 244** *cc*, **p. 245** *br*, **p. 246** *tc*, *bc*, **p. 247** *bc*, **p. 248** *bc*, **p. 256** *br*, **p. 258** *cc*, **p. 269** *tc* Used with permission from Microsoft; **p. 122** *cc*, **p. 137** *cc*, **p. 156** *cl* © Creative Snapshots/stock.adobe.com; **p. 147** *tc*, **p. 150** *cc* © Markus Mainka/stock.adobe.com; **p. 149** *br* © fallesen/stock.adobe.com; **p. 151** *br* © KMNPhoto/stock.adobe.com; **p. 155** *cc* © exopixel/stock.adobe.com; **p. 156** *tr* © R Studio/stock.adobe.com; **p. 156** *tr* © Anastasia Lugovik/stock.adobe.com; **p. 156** *tr* © ake1150/stock.adobe.com; **p. 173** *cc* © mipan/stock.adobe.com; **p. 177** *cr* © anatoliycherkas/stock.adobe.com; **p. 177** *tr* © Who is Danny/stock.adobe.com; **p. 180** *cc* © AlenKadr/stock.adobe.com; **p. 205** *cl* © Kumeko/Shutterstock.com; **p. 267** *bc* © Irfan 85/stock.adobe.com; **p. 280** *tr* © Ivan/stock.adobe.com; **p. 281** *tc* © Sabrina/stock.adobe.com; **p. 282** *tl* https://creativecommons.org/mission/downloads/; **p. 282** *cl* OER Global Logo by Jonathas Mello is licensed under a Creative Commons Attribution 3.0 Unported license (CC BY 3.0), http://creativecommons.org/licenses/by/3.0/; **p. 283** *tc*, **p. 283** *tc*, *tc*, *tr* © 2026 Meta.

t = top, *b* = bottom, *l* = left, *r* = right, *c* = centre